BEETHOVEN IN AMERICA

Beethoven
IN AMERICA

MICHAEL BROYLES

INDIANA UNIVERSITY PRESS

Bloomington & Indianapolis

This book is a publication of

Indiana University Press
601 North Morton Street
Bloomington, Indiana 47404-3797 USA

iupress.indiana.edu

Telephone orders   800-842-6796
Fax orders   812-855-7931
Orders by e-mail   iuporder@indiana.edu

Manufactured in the United States of
America

Library of Congress
Cataloging-in-Publication Data

Broyles, Michael, [date]
    Beethoven in America / Michael Broyles.
        p. cm.
    Includes bibliographical references and
index.
    ISBN 978-0-253-35704-5 (cloth : alk.
paper) 1. Beethoven, Ludwig van, 1770–
1827—Criticism and interpretation.
2. Music—Social aspects—United States.
3. Popular culture—United States—History.
4. Composers—Austria—Biography. I.
Title.
    ML410.B4B869 2011
    780.92—dc23
                                2011018050

1 2 3 4 5 16 15 14 13 12 11

To Denise

CONTENTS

ACKNOWLEDGMENTS

Any large project depends on the help and goodwill of many people, and this book is no exception. I would first like to thank William Meredith, director of the Ira F. Brilliant Center for Beethoven Studies at San José State University, and Christopher Reynolds at the University of California, Davis. Both read the entire manuscript and offered many helpful suggestions. In addition, Bill was invaluable in suggesting material and sharing with me some of his own work. Patricia Stroh, curator at the Beethoven Center, was extremely helpful providing material, both during my visits there and by mail.

I owe a debt of gratitude to many people at other libraries and archives. Jenny Johnson at Stanford University went out of her way to locate and process material, and then Daniel Hartwig helped considerably after Jenny moved to a different position. John Powell at the Newberry Library did likewise when deadlines were approaching. Julia Ronge and Nicole Kämpken at the Beethoven-Haus were most accommodating in supplying material, and Julia further answered queries in detail about some of the Beethoven-Haus's experience with related issues in Germany. Craig Hanson at the Harvard Musical Association was quick to supply needed photographs, as was Janet Kerschner of the Theosophical Society of America. Gina Huntsinger of the Schulz Museum, Lara Davis of Peanuts Worldwide, LLC, and Diana Reeve of the Metropolitan Museum of Art were also most accommodating to my requests.

I want to thank many of the artists discussed here for providing images, material, and information related to their work: Sharon Selden Kozik, photographer of the image of Frank Kozik's bust; Fritz Hatton at Arietta Wineries; sculptor Kris Kuksi and his agent, Joshua Liner, at Joshua Liner Gallery; Adrienne Rich and her agent, Claire Reinertsen; Pavel Dubrosky, author, and Michaela Fisnar-Keggler, translator, of *Beethoven 'N' Pierrot*; Derek McLane, scene designer for Moises Kaufman's play *33 Variations;* and Shoko Kamara, who sent photographs of the sets from the New York Broadway production. Edward Dunne graciously allowed me to use his photograph of Symphony Hall in Boston. I would like to thank the artist John Jacobson, who generously improved some of my own photographic images, which needed help beyond my Photoshop skills.

I have many scholars to thank for sharing their own work, for responding to my inquiries, and for insightful and productive conversations. These include David Patterson, Scott Burnham, William Kinderman, Katherine Syer, Gayle Murchinson, Josephine Wright, Naomi Andre, Lawrence Schenbeck, Paul Luongo, Joseph Kerman, and Louis Lockwood. I must say that not all these scholars agree with many of my conclusions, but all were generous with their time and gracious in their responses to my inquiries.

This book has benefited in many ways from the work and stimulation of many graduate students. First I want to thank Christian Savage, Leah Harrison, and Shih-Ni Sun, who have worked at different times as graduate assistants at Florida State University. They certainly proved their mettle in locating hard-to-find bits of information. In addition, Christian, who worked with me as this project neared completion, proved to be an excellent copyeditor. Students in two graduate seminars also contributed significantly through their discussions, insights, and own research: Amy Dunning, Katherine Etheridge, Jason Hobratsch, Matt Henson, Sarah Kahre, John MacInnis, Heather Paudler, Christopher Phillpott, Jennifer Tally, Stephanie Thorne, and Elisa Weber. As in many seminars, the students taught me a lot.

Indiana University Press has been a delight to work with. That this is the second book I have published with the press says a lot in itself. Jane Behnken, sponsoring editor, was extremely helpful in the early days of laying out the project and then in working through the many issues and determinations of how the book would be handled. Her assistant, Sarah Wyatt Swanson, has done an excellent job of shepherding the project through different stages and has been highly responsive to my many concerns. Daniel Pyle, production coordinator, has been especially helpful in working with me and improving the many graphics in the book. Angela Burton, managing editor, skillfully oversaw the production. Finally, I owe a huge debt of gratitude to the copyeditor, Eric Schramm. He is one of the best copyeditors I have ever had, if not the best.

My final thanks go to my wife, Denise Von Glahn. Not only has she provided stimulating intellectual conversation, not only has she read the entire manuscript and offered many keen insights, but she has made my life richer in more ways than I could begin to enumerate. My life would be unimaginable without her. Thank you, Denise.

BEETHOVEN IN AMERICA

Introduction

In July 2009, a small group of scholars, performers, and Beethoven lovers arrived in California for the Third Bi-annual Convention of the American Beethoven Society, held at the Ira F. Brilliant Center for Beethoven Studies at San José State University. The conference had all the trapping of a scholarly meeting: learned papers, PowerPoint presentations, formal discussions in meetings and informal conversations during coffee breaks, and, as a highlight, two concerts on Beethoven-era instruments by the pianists Malcolm Bilson and Andrew Willis.

What made this conference different, however, were the attendees, both the presenters and the audience. This was not merely a gathering of specialists ready to argue over Beethoven's original genre intentions of op. 14, no. 1, although academics were amply represented. It was not a meeting notable for producing high-powered fireworks between Turks young and old bent on challenges, disputations, and revelations that would overturn established wisdom. Challenging ideas were very much in the room nevertheless, particularly from those approaching Beethoven from outside typical musicological perspectives. What distinguished the conference was its reach beyond disciplinary boundaries, and even beyond academia. Among the presenters were musicologists, music theorists, performers, psychiatrists, and at least two English literature specialists: one was president of the International Byron Society and another worked in cultural communications and music production in New York City.

The audience was even more varied. Many were there simply because of a love for and interest in Beethoven and his music. Some were musicians; some were not. But they were all eager to hear hard-nosed papers about motivic derivation from J. S. Bach's *Well-Tempered Clavier* in Beethoven's late quartets, psychological discussions of Beethoven's eminently analyzable personality, and the Romantic imagery of moonlight as found in the music of Beethoven's contemporaries.

One of the attendees, Lynn, lives in rural southwest Virginia, near Roanoke. She and her husband are involved in animal rescue. She heard the second movement of Beethoven's Seventh Symphony on National Public Radio a few years ago and found it a revelation: "It was like it released endorphins, it was transcending." She does not read music but in the last five years has become engrossed in learning about Beethoven, buying many CDs and reading all the relevant books she can get her hands on. She joined the American Beethoven Society and traveled across the country to attend the 2009 meeting. Even though, by her own admission, some of the more analytical papers are not fully intelligible to her, she relished the conference, hearing talks about Beethoven, listening to concerts, joining in the discussion, and meeting other people involved with Beethoven. That included many people like her who were there simply because Beethoven is important to their lives. Lynn has discovered that she likes all classical music, but there is something special about Beethoven: she joked that "he has even allowed me to get off of Prozac." More seriously, she has found that Beethoven allows her to get in touch with her spiritual being.

Lynn is not alone in her feelings for Beethoven. The Beethoven Center itself stands as a symbol of Beethoven's continued presence in America in the twenty-first century. Its inspiration and original support came from Ira S. Brilliant, a real estate developer in Arizona, for whom Beethoven held the same fascination as with Lynn. Brilliant became interested in Beethoven in 1978, when he was in the hospital recovering from hip surgery. On a bedside radio he heard Beethoven's *Eroica*. He was overwhelmed with the music and thought, "I must know the mind of the person who composed such beauty."[1] His business success enabled him to act on that imperative, and he began to acquire material related to Beethoven—letters, first edition scores, memorabilia. Soon he was on a first-name basis with many rare book and manuscript dealers throughout the world and was able to assemble an exceptional collection of Beethoven materials. Wanting his Beethoven materials to do more than sit on a shelf gathering dust, he met administrators at San José State University and, with Brilliant's collection as its core, the Beethoven Center was founded, the only such institution in America. As director and curator the center hired William Meredith and Patricia Stroh, respectively.

This book is for anyone who has attended a conference such as the one described above, or who might attend such a conference, or who just happens to be curious about Beethoven. For anyone interested in American society who might wonder how an unkempt German of Flemish descent who lived more that two hundred years ago still manages to be a universal symbol—of something—in a multicultural country that is fast replacing its original Western European heritage, this book is also directed. Most important, this work is addressed to anyone who wonders how this man reached the pinnacle of universal cultural recognition and what exactly it is that he represents. That last question has no simple answer but multiple answers, and in this book I hope to uncover many of them. For the past two hundred years Beethoven has meant different things to different people. He is indeed a morphing symbol, but he has proven an extremely resilient one. What he means to American culture at any point can at best be a snapshot that freezes a moment in time; like any moment it can never return, but its essence may resurface elsewhere. Thus a two-hundred-year look at Beethoven's impact on America, from his musical arrival in 1805 to the present day, can provide, if not a steady stream that coalesces into a coherent moving picture, at least a montage with patterns, similarities, and contrasts.

Why does Beethoven maintain such a powerful presence in a society with increasingly varied roots? The notion that Beethoven resides exclusively in a small but elite segment of American culture, among those supporting the European classical canon, is unsupportable, for Beethoven has become a symbol that transcends boundaries of aesthetic preference and ethnicity. Beethoven is a ubiquitous icon in virtually all corners of American society. How this came about and the place of Beethoven in contemporary American culture is the subject of this book.

The emotional power of Beethoven's music makes it seem personal, a genuine expression of his deepest self. Yet because of its abstractness Beethoven's image is protean: what his music stands for has never been fixed and has depended as much upon the position and the agenda of the interpreters as the content of the music itself. Thus interrogating how Beethoven has been portrayed, viewed, and appropriated by different social and ethnic groups provides another means of mapping prevailing cultural and social forces far beyond the world of music.

No study of Beethoven in America could ever be definitive, simply because the material is so vast: a single volume or even multiple volumes could never cover the topic. If all Beethoven sightings—performances, mentions, usages— were included, no book could be large enough to hold them. Thus what I present is inevitably a sampling of the different ways Beethoven and his music have appeared in American culture. I believe it is representative of the major tendencies and the principal manner in which he has been viewed. To scholars it should be considered an invitation to look further: there are many areas that would benefit from deeper probing. For instance, I have hardly touched upon Beethoven's presence in American literature. The spread of Beethoven's music throughout the many areas of the country awaits local or regional studies. It is safe to say that any chapter in this book could be expanded into a volume unto

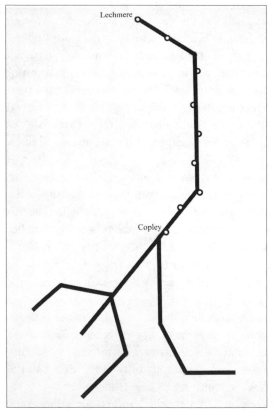

FIGURE INTRO.01

Boston MBTA Green Line

itself. For students, there are many dissertation topics here. After the flurry of sketch studies in the 1970s, Beethoven needs to be reexamined in terms of twenty-first-century culture.

The Beethoven trajectory I have found is analogous to the Green Line of the Boston T (the MBTA). If one boards at Lechmere, the northeastern end, all trains run on a single track until Copley. They then begin to branch eventually into four different routes, although all run roughly parallel through Back Bay. The organization of this book is the temporal equivalent of this spatial configuration. There is a single path or trunk line through the nineteenth century, as the Romantic, deified, transcendental Beethoven image is established. Thus the first part of the book, which traces the growth of Beethoven's iconic status, is chronological.

When his music first appeared in America in 1805, the notion of music as art was foreign to American thinking. What musical activity existed was considered either informal entertainments or participatory activities, in particular military bands or choral groups, which usually had only a loose connection if any to church choirs. The latter were first to perform Beethoven's music with any regularity. Thus, rather than his symphonies, string quartets, or piano sonatas, the oratorio *Christ on the Mount of Olives,* one of his less important pieces, first introduced the American public to Beethoven.

A significant change in Beethoven's status in America occurred around 1840, coincident with the founding of several orchestras in Boston and New York. Seeds for the iconic Beethoven were planted as his symphonies were heard regularly for the first time. The impetus came from Germany with the Romantic image that had coalesced around Beethoven even before his death.[2] When Romanticism and the accompanying practice of Beethoven veneration came to America, however, it assumed a special shape, through the influence of the Transcendentalists. John S. Dwight in particular, along with Margaret Fuller and Francis James Tuckerman, established the principal shape of the Beethoven image, which would morph but never be displaced, even in the twentieth century. To Dwight, Beethoven's music had a universal, moral, almost religious purpose, its worth directly proportional to its abstractness and its distance from any attempts at poetic association. Other commentators bought half of Dwight's argument: they glorified Beethoven but, like many Romantics, could not sever his music from programmatic associations, many of which involved elaborate flights of fantasy far beyond the kernels found in Beethoven's biography.

The Gilded Age expanded upon the transcendentalist vision and saw an even stronger Germanic tone imprinted on American musical culture. Although German musicians had influenced American life since the Revolutionary War, their impact became particularly apparent in the second half of the nineteenth century with the arrival of many immigrant musicians from German-speaking areas. Heated debates over the direction of American musical culture arose in part because of this influx, but Beethoven's music was by then too universally accepted to be seriously challenged. The Gilded Age also saw in Beethoven raw masculine power. It was a Beethoven highly appropriate for the age of iron and steel and the new city that characterized industrial America.

In the early twentieth century, the trunk line branches into several directions, necessitating a thematic approach as different interpretations of Beethoven run simultaneously. Just as the Green Line carries passengers who boarded at a trunk stop, however, so virtually all interpretations of Beethoven depend on images developed in the nineteenth century. Thus the second and longer part of this book traces various branches through the twentieth century, each with its own stops, destinations, and highlights.

Beethoven veneration continued into the early twentieth century. By this time Beethoven himself was all but deified and considered a moral being beyond mere mortals. Glorification reached a zenith in 1927, the centennial of Beethoven's death. This, of course, was not a purely American phenomenon, as virtual Beethoven worship can be found on both sides of the Atlantic.

Soon an inevitable reaction set in, and various agents, each with a different agenda, began to redefine Beethoven. In modernist circles, where anything Romantic was disdained, Beethoven's reputation plummeted. The emotional power that gained Beethoven's music its iconic status in the nineteenth century became an albatross threatening to relegate the composer to the position of canonic has-been. Yet Beethoven's appeal was too strong for even the modernists to ignore, and he underwent a transformation, from quintessential Romantic to supreme classicist. Poetic content was shunned as scholars sought to demonstrate the organic perfection of his compositions. This practice peaked in the 1970s, when scholars focused intensely on his sketches in order to explicate the nature of his long-range structural thinking. Underlying this development was an emphasis on science, which intensified in the United States after the Soviet launch of Sputnik in 1957. Fed by both the reaction against Romanticism and the prestige of science, the structuralist Beethoven became the prevailing Beethoven of the American classical musical world throughout much of the twentieth century.

Modernists were not alone in redefining Beethoven. Unlike the nineteenth century, which witnessed a single extended trajectory culminating in a uni-

versal conceptualization of Beethoven—Beethoven as Romantic godhead—
the twentieth century saw many different societal groups take that myth and
bend and shape it to their own ends. Beethoven became a commodity, albeit a
highly prized one, and he moved far beyond his classical music home and acquired meanings that would have astounded anyone who had been in the grips
of the earlier nineteenth-century vision.

Beethoven as a spiritual vessel of God became an important theme in some
unorthodox religious movements of the twentieth century, particularly Theosophy, which had a considerable impact on a number of musicians in the
1920s. The nine symphonies, for instance, were specifically tied to the "nine
spiritual mysteries."

The notion that Beethoven was black gained currency in the 1960s, as a
number of African Americans, promoting black pride, black power, and black
separatism, argued that Beethoven had African ancestors, which consequently
made him an important symbol within such movements. This assertion raises
issues regarding historical evidence about Beethoven's ethnicity and the nature of Afrocentrist assertions about Western culture. Beethoven's role as a
cultural signifier raises questions as to how and why black nationalists and
separatists specifically singled out a German musician who resides at the heart
of the classical canon to advance arguments designed to disassociate themselves from European culture.

Beethoven has retained a major presence in literature, film, and theater
throughout the twentieth century, both as a subject and through his music.
Beethoven has inspired or appeared in novels, poems, and plays. These works
vary from the Beethoven of musicological research (33 Variations) to a man
of terror ("The Ninth Symphony of Beethoven at Last Understood as a Sexual
Message") to a phantasmagorical psychoanalytic look inside the head of the
composer (Beethoven 'N' Pierrot). Three biographical films, The Life and Loves
of Beethoven, Immortal Beloved, and Copying Beethoven, have been produced,
in addition to many television documentaries, and his name has been adopted
in movies for dogs (Beethoven) as well as porn stars (The Opening of Misty Beethoven). Beethoven's music has been used in dozens of movies, sometimes diegetically (i.e., heard within the story by the characters themselves), sometimes
not. Hollywood, always sensitive to the box office and hence public taste, provides a vivid barometer of the Beethoven impact on America throughout the
twentieth century and into the twenty-first. It is also instrumental in shaping
public perceptions. I discuss several of these films in detail.

Portrayals of Beethoven in film differ dramatically from his portrayals on
the stage. Beethoven movies have been produced as mass-media entertain-

ment, whereas plays and poems that make use of Beethoven tend to be more avant-garde and experimental, aimed at a more intellectual, elite audience. The similarities and differences in how Beethoven is depicted in these different media allow one to gauge how consistent Beethoven's image is throughout different cultural and economic strata in this country. One finds a more nuanced presentation in the theater, but the main difference seems to be the extent that each medium does or does not cling to the more traditional view of the legendary Beethoven, the powerful, Romantic, defiant artist, the composer of his middle or heroic period.

Throughout the twentieth century Beethoven's music has been adapted to prevailing popular music genres. "It's Beethoven, but It Swings" appeared in the 1930s, Walter Murphy's "A Fifth of Beethoven" in the 1970s, "Beethoven Virus" and "Boogie Woogie and Beethoven" in the 1990s. In each case (and in many others) the inclusion of the name Beethoven in the title invites interrogation of the cultural meanings that the name carries for the intended audience. A crucial piece was Chuck Berry's "Roll Over Beethoven," which, ironically, did not use Beethoven's music. It brought the name Beethoven into the popular music world and, by essentially placing rock 'n' roll on an equal plane with classical music, it invited popular artists to incorporate Beethoven into their music.

Postmodernism brought at least two challenges to Western musical culture: to the special place of the classical canon in a hierarchy of musical values, and to a patriarchal orientation that characterized most of the history of Western music. Beethoven was at the center of both challenges, the former because his music has formed the very core of the canon, the second because feminist writers have seen his music as representative of a set of structures that embodied male patriarchy.

While both challenges are international, they have engendered a particularly acute reaction in the United States because of the strength of the youth movement, the presence of rock and some forms of jazz as alternatives to classical music, the perception that the classical canon does not reflect America's cultural heritage, and the importance of feminist criticism in the American academy. Beethoven's privileged position was challenged, but he retained most of his status in part due to his growing presence outside the canon.

It is not surprising that an icon as familiar as Beethoven would be incorporated into the world of commerce and advertising. A few of his better-known compositions have been used in numerous television commercials, and his name has been used to sell items from automobiles to watches. Marketing Beethoven busts, dolls, action figures, coffee mugs, T-shirts, or anything else that can bear an image has become a massive industry, and Beethoven branding may also be found in real estate ventures and wine labels. LVB is even a stock market symbol of a company that clearly wishes to trade on the letters' musical association.

Ironically, the nineteenth-century image turned out to be central to virtually all the twentieth-century permutations and uses. Beethoven entered popular culture as much on the strength of his reputation as on the strength of his music, and that reputation came from the myth of the deified, defiant, battling Promethean genius.

In one sense, this book addresses a most basic historical question: Who is Beethoven? In this case, who is the figure that inhabits the American cultural imagination? Beethoven as he exists in the memory and imagination of the American public cannot be separated from any understanding of the man himself. Furthermore, differing interpretations of Beethoven allow one to track changes in American culture, society, and indeed politics. Incongruous as it sounds, through Beethoven one can better understand how American society has evolved.

Whether the many visions of Beethoven that have been promulgated bear any relationship to the actual person scholars have defined is a secondary issue, although not necessarily a trivial one. This book is about Beethoven's many manifestations in the American consciousness, ultimately about what Beethoven means to twenty-first-century America. Meaning, of course, resides in many small acts, events, statements, and performances. Together one must search for similarities, changes, continuations, and disjunctions. There is no one-theory-fits-all approach, no single way to approach such a disparate collection of materials, except to sort through them and wait for the evidence to speak. That is what I have done. Only the reader can decide if I have listened carefully.

PART ONE

Arrival & Sacralization

1

Arrival in America

*T*HE STORY OF BEETHOVEN IN AMERICA begins in Charleston, South
Carolina, in 1805. It was a fitting location, for until the local economy
was decimated in the War of 1812, Charleston had a greater concentration of
wealth than any other city in the country. At the time of the American Revolution, Charleston was the fourth-largest city in North America, and although it
was only one-third the size of Philadelphia, its per capita wealth, measured by
estates, was six to eight times that of Philadelphia, New York, or Boston. Nine
of the ten wealthiest men in North America lived in Charleston or its immediate surroundings.[1]

Charleston is situated in a protected harbor where the Ashley and Cooper
rivers meet and flow into the Atlantic Ocean. In the lowlands surrounding
Charleston, rice farming flourished, planters prospered, and the rivers made
for easy transport to the port. Charleston had one other advantage for transatlantic trade. Its location, at that spot where the Gulf Stream suddenly veers
outward into the Atlantic heading toward Europe, was a boon for sailing ships.

Charleston prospered for reasons other than the rice trade, however. Since
its founding it had had close ties with the West Indies and thus became the
center of the slave trade in the colonies. Before the importation of slaves was
abolished in 1807, hundreds of thousands of slaves, as many as forty percent

of those brought to America, passed through the Charleston slave market. Rice farming especially created a heavy demand for slaves, for the work was hard and the conditions onerous. The heat and humidity, combined with the marshy fields that rice needed, not only created possibly the worst working environment that any slaves encountered, but were also ideally suited to the breeding of malaria. The death toll among rice field workers ensured a continuous demand for the arriving ships.

Conditions at the rice plantations also meant that any plantation owner who could afford to live elsewhere did so. Running the plantation was entrusted to overseers. The economic success of the rice trade thus allowed the rise of a class relatively close to the British aristocracy, a landed gentry who lived off the proceeds of the estate but who managed it from a distance. Freed from the grim reality of the plantation and its cost in human suffering, the gentlemen of Charleston and its environs emulated the British upper class in many ways; as Lord Adam Gordon observed when visiting in 1765, they stood apart from the inhabitants of other colonies in the degree to which they still considered England their true home. Almost all wealthy Charlestonians had visited England, and most sent their children there to be educated. Alexander Hewitt, visiting from England, commented on the social refinement of Charlestonians and of the "assemblies, balls, concerts and plays, which were attended by companies almost equally brilliant as those of any town in Europe of the same size."[2] In one sense, then, Beethoven arrived in America on the backs of African slaves.

To further their interest in music, the gentlemen of Charleston founded the St. Cecilia Society in 1766. Modeled directly on similar organizations in Europe, its function was to provide regular concerts for its members. Membership was carefully restricted to the male gentry, women being allowed to attend only as a guest of a member. Concerts were potpourris, featuring ensembles, soloists, and vocalists. At first many of the members participated in the concerts as amateurs, particularly in the orchestra, but as a critical mass of professional musicians arrived in Charleston, a greater differentiation between performer and audience ensued. By 1805 the performers were professionals. Until 1820 they offered fortnightly concerts followed by a ball during the social season, roughly November to May, although there were several years of interruptions during the Revolutionary War and the War of 1812. Restricted as it was for most of its existence, the St. Cecilia Society was the most important musical organization in Charleston and arguably in the United States during the early Federal era. It was an appropriate debut for Beethoven.

To celebrate Passion Week in Charleston in 1805, the German-born conductor Jacob Eckhard arranged a special oratorio concert on April 10 for the St. Cecilia Society. Eckhard opened the event with a "grand overture" by Ludwig van Beethoven. One year later, Eckhard programmed a similar concert for the same pre-Easter celebration, this time not only opening the program with an overture by Beethoven but closing it with a "finale" by the composer.

The content of the program needs translation, as words were used differently then. The term oratorio does not necessarily mean that an oratorio was performed. This was a generic word that referred to any concert of mostly sacred or mixed sacred and secular music. If the opening piece on a concert was orchestral, it was usually called an overture, whether it was or not. Beethoven had written only one overture by this time, to the ballet *The Creatures of Prometheus,* and it was not well known. The 1805 overture was probably the first movement of a symphony. It is even more likely that the overture and finale by Beethoven in 1806 referred to one of his symphonies, as a concert would often begin with the opening movement of a symphony and close with the last, in effect creating for the entire program a large symphonic sandwich. Nothing is known about which Beethoven symphony it was, although we can guess that it was the First. Only the first three had been composed by 1806, and it is unlikely to have been the Third, the *Eroica.* The outer movements were too big and too difficult for an oratorio program, and it is hard to imagine that it would have already been known in Charleston at this time. It had received only a private performance in Vienna before 1805 and was not published until 1806. The Second Symphony is also an unlikely candidate, as the long slow introduction to the first movement would hardly be appropriate for the purpose of opening a varied program.

A more puzzling question is how Beethoven managed to get to the shores of America in 1805. Specifically, where did Eckhard obtain the score of a Beethoven symphony? Clearly he did not bring it with him. Eckhard emigrated to America in 1776, when Beethoven was five years old. In 1786 Eckhard was offered a position as organist at St. John's Lutheran Church in Charleston, a post he held until 1809, when he moved to St. Michael's Episcopal Church because it had a much larger and better organ. He remained in Charleston until his death in 1833, and there is no record of him traveling to Europe before 1806. In the pre-steam years of sailing ships, a European journey was not a light undertaking. Someone else must have imported the piece and brought it to Eckhard's attention, but who we do not know.

Nevertheless, Eckhard almost certainly did perform at least part of a Beethoven symphony, and we may pinpoint Beethoven's official debut in America as having been in Charleston on April 10, 1805.

For a few years afterward the Beethoven trail becomes cold. For reasons that are not clear, the St. Cecilia Society attempted no more Beethoven symphonies prior to 1820. Nicholas Butler, in his study of musical patronage in Charleston, speculates that they may have been too heavy for the lighter, more hedonistic tastes of the Charleston aristocracy, or there may not have been the orchestral forces to perform them. The latter problem, however, did not deter musicians in other cities. Possibly Beethoven was too revolutionary, too close to emerging Romanticism, to sit well with the conservative Charleston elite. Members of the St. Cecilia Society were more aligned with an eighteenth-century gentry approach to music rather than Beethoven's more intense emotionalism. There is one record of a "Fantasie with variations" by Beethoven, a solo keyboard work, being performed on March 16, 1813. Otherwise, Charleston would have nothing to do with him.[3]

If there are any concert programs with Beethoven's name on them anywhere between 1805 and 1813, I have not been able to find them. Yet scraps of evidence, a hint of activity, and a casual comment suggest that he was not entirely ignored. A series of Amateur Subscription Concerts was given in Philadelphia from 1809 to 1812, although neither programs nor advertisements that list pieces exist, so the programming remains a mystery. Louis C. Madiera, however, reported that in the years prior to 1820, a group of amateurs, consisting of some of the best musicians in the city, along with invited guests met regularly to perform, among other works, the quartets of Beethoven. They also attempted to put together an orchestral ensemble, but as far as we know nothing came of that. Madiera's description fits almost perfectly the Amateur Subscription concerts, though the musicians may not have all been amateurs. This does not mean that even in Philadelphia in 1810 there were ringers among the performers as much as that the distinction between amateur and professional at the time was not always a hard-and-fast one.[4] After 1812, either Madiera's group continued to meet and play for themselves, without the formality of the Amateur Subscription concerts, or since the concerts had been only for members and invited guests, not for the public, the concerts could have occurred outside the historical glare of public documentation. It is not hard to deduce, however, which Beethoven quartets were played. The six quartets of op. 18, published in 1800, were by far the most accessible, both technically and musically. The other quartets of the 1800 decade, the three Razumovsky Quartets, op. 59, and the two single ones, op. 74 and op. 95, are possible, but even in Beethoven's time these lay outside Viennese audiences' understanding. Except possibly for op. 74, performance of these pieces by amateurs with little introduction to Beethoven would have been a daunting experience. The late quartets, the ultimate challenge for any string quartet throughout the nineteenth century, can of course be discounted: they would not be composed for another ten years.

Also lying outside the public record is activity in the home. It is impossible to gauge in how many homes Beethoven's music was a regular visitor, for unless something tragic or scandalous occurs, a young lady practicing a Beethoven piano sonata in the parlor is not the stuff of news. The growing interest in having a piano in the home, however, grew markedly in this period. In 1791 there were only twenty-seven pianos in Boston.[5] By 1810, according to Loesser, almost every house between the Delaware and the Schuylkill, the area around Philadelphia, had a piano or harpsichord.[6] This is not a geographical distinction. A few years later, in Boston, Lowell Mason observed that "among the wealthy every parlor must have a piano."[7] This imperative was soon to spread to the middle class, as piano manufacturing began in earnest in the United States around 1800 and pianos thus became more affordable. Prior to 1800 almost all pianos had to be imported from Europe.

Between 1813 and 1820, Beethoven's name begins to appear on public programs, with even a few symphonic performances. After the Charleston beginning, the next known Beethoven symphony performance occurred in the Moravian community in Nazareth, Pennsylvania. The Moravians, also known as the Unitas Fratrum, Unity of Brethren, were a Protestant denomination that first emerged in the fifteenth century in Moravia, today part of the Czech Republic. They were followers of Jan Hus, a theologian who was burned at the stake in 1415 for his heretical views. After considerable growth and even more persecution, including near annihilation in the Thirty Years War, they reemerged in Saxony under the patronage of Count Nicholas Ludwig von Zinzendorf, who encouraged them to expand geographically. They settled in Bethlehem and Nazareth, Pennsylvania, in 1741.

With a central European background, the Moravians brought with them a highly developed instrumental music culture. A small farming community attempting to tame a wilderness had little place for professional musicians, but many of the settlers were proficient on musical instruments, and the active musical life they had in Saxony continued. There was an orchestra, many chamber groups, and concerts. They brought a rich collection of scores from Europe, including many works of Haydn, Mozart, and other classical composers. Beethoven's First Symphony, perhaps in a chamber version, was performed by the Collegium Musicum of Nazareth on July 13, 1813. The Moravians had a full orchestra, but the only score of the symphony in their still-extant library is a nonet version published in Europe in 1808. Otto Albrecht, who examined the Moravian records, is reasonably certain that all four movements of the piece were performed.[8]

The Moravian performance, however, created no surge of interest or ripple effect for Beethoven in Federal America. It was held for a relatively isolated

German community lying in the foothills of the Pocono Mountains, and it is doubtful if anyone outside the Brethren heard the symphony. Some four years later, Beethoven's First Symphony received another performance in Lexington, Kentucky. Since Philadelphia, New York, and Boston had not yet touched a Beethoven symphony, how did one show up in Lexington? By 1817 Lexington was no longer on the western frontier, but was still relatively removed from the world along the eastern seaboard. For many years the principal barrier to westward expansion had been the Allegheny Mountains, and while Daniel Boone and others had forged the Cumberland Trail in 1775, travel to the west was still a challenge. In that context, one Anthony Heinrich arrived in Lexington in 1817. How Heinrich, a former wealthy Austrian merchant, ended up in Lexington, and how he came to direct a Beethoven symphony there is one of the strangest tales in the American Beethoven saga.

Oscar Sonneck, one of the pioneer historians of American music, called Heinrich "the oddest figure in American musical history."[9] Heinrich was born in Schönbüchel in northern Bohemia in 1781, and in 1800 he inherited an estate and a large international import and manufacturing business. This made him one of the wealthiest merchants in central Europe. Seeking to expand his business he came to America in 1805, and sometime between then and 1810 he married a young woman from Boston, whose name is unknown. By 1810 he was in Philadelphia directing the orchestra at the Southwark Theatre as an amateur. He had studied violin as a youth, and during his travels in Europe he obtained a valuable Cremona violin, maker unknown. Since Cremona was the home of the Amati, Guarneri, and Stradivari family, one can only guess.[10]

In 1811 disaster struck. Because of the Napoleonic wars, the financial markets in Austria and hence much of eastern Europe collapsed. Heinrich, along with the Austrian government, went bankrupt. Possibly to recoup what he could, Heinrich and his pregnant wife left for Europe in 1813, and after giving birth to a daughter at Heinrich's ancestral home, his wife, suffering terrible homesickness, became so ill that Heinrich decided they must return to America. Because of her own illness their daughter, Antonia, was left behind with relatives. Almost immediately upon their return to Boston his wife died.

Heinrich found himself in America broke and widowed and with his only child a continent away. He returned to Philadelphia to play in the theater orchestra again, but this time to earn a living. Soon he was invited to direct the music for the one theater in Pittsburgh, and Heinrich began the three-hundred-mile journey on foot. At this time it was a journey into the wilderness, over and through the Allegheny Mountains to a town of seven thousand. The theater itself, in the words of the actor Noah Ludlow, was "the poorest apology for one I had then ever seen."[11] Not surprisingly, almost as soon as Heinrich arrived the theater went bankrupt.

Heinrich now made a crucial decision. He was alone, isolated even from the East Coast, with no means of support, and still grieving over the loss of his wife and his inability to see his daughter. Rather than return east he decided to continue west, destination Lexington. He had been captivated by the vastness and splendor of nature that he had seen on his way to Pittsburgh, and he may have wanted to lose himself in the wilderness, but he also made a shrewd choice. Lexington was the largest city west of the Alleghenies, a cultural center, and home to the theatrical empire of Samuel Drake. By 1817 Drake had established regular performances in Lexington, Louisville, Frankfort, and Cincinnati. Spinoffs from his company went as far as Nashville and Fayetteville, Arkansas. Since Heinrich had experience in theater orchestras, it offered intriguing prospects, and there would not be the level of competition he would find in the large East Coast cities. Besides, he was already halfway there.

Heinrich's stay in Lexington turned out to be different from what even he thought. Soon he received an invitation to live on the estate of Judge John Spiegel, where he was a guest for two years. He spent the spring and summer of 1818 in a log cabin on the estate and began to compose. He had no training in composition, but by 1820 he had finished his Opus 1, a potpourri of piano, violin, and vocal pieces, which he called *The Dawning of Music in Kentucky*. An original, eccentric, dense, and complex collection of music, it created a stir in Boston, where it was published. John Rowe Parker, editor of the music magazine *The Euterpeiad*, immediately pronounced Heinrich the "Beethoven of America," and Heinrich for the rest of his life exploited the moniker "the Log Cabin Composer."

When he first arrived in Lexington, Heinrich quickly demonstrated his worth as a theater musician. An "Amateur" writing to the *Kentucky Reporter* "notices with pleasure, that the music at the theatre has been greatly improved by the acquisition to the band of one of the first Violin performers in America. On Monday evening last, we heard with exquisite delight the finest Solo ever performed on that instrument in our Orchestra." Heinrich is not named but the amateur observes that this soloist is a stranger newly arrived in Lexington, that he wants to remain there, and that he plans to give a concert in the next week.[12]

Exactly one week after the amateur's communication, Heinrich did precisely that. Like many musicians at the time who wished to announce their presence, he gave a benefit concert.[13] He had quickly ingratiated himself to the musicians in town, for the concert was lengthy and, according to the program,

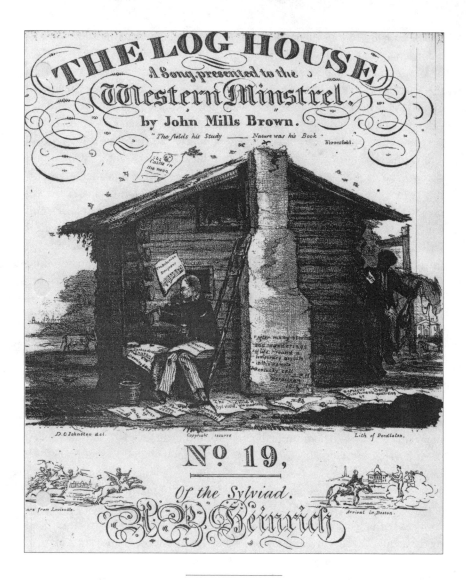

FIGURE 1.1

Cover of "The Log House," by Anthony Heinrich.
Heinrich is pictured composing the piece.

included a "Full Band." The word "band" at the time meant any instrumental ensemble from two or three players to what we would today call a symphony orchestra. A full band in this context could have any number of meanings. Even though Lexington at the time was a small town of 5,000 inhabitants, 1,500 of whom were slaves, Drake's theatrical activities meant the presence of musicians: every theater had to have an orchestra, and theaters were the only regular source of employment for most instrumental musicians in Federal America.

The first piece on the program was called a "Sinfonia con Minuetto," by Beethoven, which was almost certainly the First Symphony. The printed program does not answer two questions, however: What exactly was played, and who played it? Did it include all four movements? A more intriguing but equally unanswerable question regards the instrumentation. How much adaption needed to be done? Was there really a full complement of woodwinds, including oboes and bassoons? Could this have been the European nonet version used by the Moravians in 1813? Even if he had a full band, it might have been easier to spread the nine parts over whatever orchestral members there were rather than reduce the full score. Finally, where did the score come from? Did Heinrich bring it with him, or did someone already have it in Lexington? It is more likely that Heinrich had obtained it in Philadelphia, although had it already been in Lexington, Heinrich's may not have been its first performance. The presence of this program tantalizes more than satisfies, giving intriguing bits of evidence that naturally leads to more questions than can be answered. Whatever remains in the shadows of the past, however, this much seems clear: Heinrich directed a performance of at least part of a Beethoven symphony in Lexington, Kentucky, on November 12, 1817.

By 1820, Beethoven's music had begun to seep into American musical culture, here and there a single piece finding its way onto a program. Most of what we have seen was instrumental music, the genres that Beethoven is known for today: the symphonies, the sonatas, the string quartets. In Federal America, however, Beethoven's reputation rested more than any other on one other composition, his oratorio *Christ am Ölberg* (*Christ on the Mount of Olives*), which was also known as *The Mount of Olives*. The English, troubled by having Jesus appear on stage in what they considered an operatic setting, modified the libretto, and eventually a new version appeared titled *Engedi, or David in the Wilderness*. Because of the close cultural ties between England and America that remained long after the Revolution, this title is also found in the United States, although somewhat later than 1820.

Christ am Ölberg is not one of Beethoven's most inspired pieces. Federal Americans were attracted not to the oratorio as a whole but to the final chorus, "Welten singen Dank und Ehre," which was printed in 1818 as the Hallelujah Chorus. The popularity of this less-than-outstanding work had as much to do with the musical situation in Federal America as with the quality of the composition itself. Music in America was not considered art but entertainment. It was meant to be enjoyed much as one enjoyed a good barbecue, a pint of rum,[14] or a horse race. Thus if a rousing chorus, such as the finale of *Christ am Ölberg*, was appealing, that the work as a whole lacked artistic merit mattered little. Furthermore, musical developments in Colonial and Federal America favored choral works over other types; as a result, choral societies were by far the most popular type of musical organization in the eighteenth and early nineteenth centuries.

Various circumstances favored choral over instrumental music. There were only a handful of professional musicians in the country, mostly in the large cities where either a church or theater position could support them. Even the most successful had to supplement their income by other means, teaching, operating a music store or a publishing business, or being engaged in trades unrelated to music. William Billings, the most prolific American composer of the eighteenth century, was a tanner. The only instrumental musical organization found throughout America, especially outside the few large cities where theatrical orchestras existed, was the military band, which had developed during the Revolutionary War. With each city and town retaining its own militia, the accompanying band was a source of civic pride. For male amateurs, playing in the military band was an acceptable musical outlet. Women, whose rightful place was considered to be in the home, played the piano and sang. There was little gender mixing, at least in music. In 1800, Frances Mallet, Filipo Trajetta, and Gottlieb Graupner, three immigrant musicians of three different nationalities, joined to form a conservatory in Boston. Their advertising was gender specific: piano and voice lessons for girls and wind instrument study for boys.

Where the sexes could and indeed did mix was in the choral societies. These were a direct outgrowth of musical and religious issues in the eighteenth century, particularly in New England. Well into the eighteenth century, the Puritan church service was a daunting experience. Men and women sat separated on hard benches and listened to a sermon that often lasted more than three hours. The job of the minister was to terrify the congregation about the dangers and the torments of hell. The titles of the sermons of Jonathan Edwards, the best-known preacher in early eighteenth-century New England, hint at what those three hours must have been like: "The Eternity of Hell Torments," "The Torments of the Wiked [sic] in Hell, no occasion of grief to the Saints in Heaven," and "Sinners in the Hands of an Angry God." The historian Vernon Parrington referred to them as "notorious minatory sermons" that "sank deep into the memory of New England, and for which it has never forgiven him."[15] Puritanism was not for the weak.

After the sermon the congregation sang a Psalm, and here was the flaw in the service, from the clergy's point of view. Unaccompanied Psalm singing was the only music allowed in the Puritan service, and without an instrument to hold the congregation together each singer could go his own way (women were not allowed to sing), bellowing out lustily the Psalm, extending it, adding ornaments, or even inventing a whole new tune. The congregation took full advantage of this part of the service, singing vigorously, ignoring rhythm or even melody, and paying little attention to those around them. To the clergy, chaos reigned. Aesthetics aside, however, the clergy saw a more serious problem. The emotional release that the singing of the Psalm allowed wiped out the effect of the sermon itself. It was as if the congregation were purging themselves through song from the horrors that the minister had tried to impose upon them.

The clergy fought back. They decided to organize singing schools, to teach the members of the church to sing properly and decorously, from written notes rather than free improvisation. This would be a way to confine the flights of emotional frenzy. Soon the singing school became one of the most popular organizations in Colonial New England, but having won the battle, the clergy lost the war. The singing school usually met once a week for a period of six to fourteen weeks and was taught by a musician, often an itinerant from the outside, hired specifically for the occasion. At first the singing school was to meet in the church, but soon it moved elsewhere. By the late eighteenth century a tavern was a favorite meeting place, and after the lesson the tavern master or the singing school leader would frequently take a fiddle off the wall and lead a round of dancing, the participants all the while enjoying the offerings of the tavern. Not surprisingly, the singing school became an immense attraction to young people, who lived in a society in which there were few social outlets and even fewer opportunities for the sexes to intermingle. It served the participants, especially the youth, well, but was far from what the Puritan ministers had originally envisioned.

The singing school spread from New England throughout the country, and from the singing school more elaborate choral organizations or singing societies grew. The first seems to have been the Stoughton Music Society, founded in 1786, soon followed by the Independent Musical Society in Boston, the Hubbard Musical Society in Ipswich, New Hampshire, and the Franklin, the Salem, the Middlesex, the Massachusetts Musical, and the Norfolk Musical Societies. The names of several societies included Handel and Haydn, including those in Boston, New York, and Lexington.[16] The names reflect the importance of two pieces of music to the early societies, Handel's *Messiah* and Haydn's *Creation*. Most of these societies were founded for the purpose of improving music in the churches, which meant they performed at least some sacred music. As often as not, however, they had no direct connection with a church, and, like the singing school, most members joined for other reasons. The societies might provide music for civic or ceremonial occasions, or they might just put on occasional concerts. Whatever their stated purpose, and whatever their real purpose, they were very popular. Their appeal was both as a social group and a musical outlet, because they allowed participants to be involved in music without the training and practice an instrument required.

Within that context, Beethoven's oratorio *Christ am Ölberg* appeared. Since few programs or newspaper announcements of these societies have survived, it is impossible to tell how many times it was sung, but by 1820 it clearly was popular, especially the final chorus, later called "the first Beethoven piece to make an impression in this country."[17] In 1820 a person identified only as S. P. M. wrote a letter to the editor of the *Euterpeiad* in which he called the work "the pride of modern oratorios." He then placed it on a par with "the unrivalled productions of great Handel himself" and suggested its superiority to works of Haydn, whose *Creation* "must soon retire, notwithstanding its numerous excellencies, to a respectable station in the background."

Also reflecting the popularity of *Christ am Ölberg*, a new choral society in Portland, Maine, founded on January 16, 1819, called itself the Beethoven Society. This was three years after the Handel and Haydn Society of Boston was formed, and the choice of Beethoven over Handel or Haydn was not coincidental. It was a direct slap at the Boston organization: "And while a similar society in Boston has inscribed on their escutcheon the celebrated names of Handel and Haydn, the Beethoven society of Portland assumes the name of one, whose genius seems to anticipate a future age, and labors for the benefit of posterity."[18] Handel and Haydn were considered the past; Beethoven was the future. It was just prior to the formation of the Portland society that the final chorus of *Christ am Ölberg* was printed in America as the Hallelujah Chorus. According to Otto Albrecht, Beethoven's Hallelujah Chorus soon challenged

Handel's in popularity.[19] Since Beethoven's chorus was familiar in this country well before its American publication, and since publishers followed musical taste, the title is more an indication of how singers referred to it than an attempt by the publisher to sell more copies by sowing confusion with Handel.

Between 1815 and 1820, publishers began to cash in on Beethoven's new-found popularity. The publisher Allyn Bacon brought out his Piano Sonata for four hands, op. 6, in 1815, and in 1818 the collection "Twenty Four Sonatas for the Pianoforte . . . from Mozart, Haydn, Beethoven, Steibelt . . . and other esteemed authors," which included two pieces by Beethoven, neither of which were sonatas. In Charleston, where Beethoven had first landed in America, Charles Gilfert published Beethoven's Rondo in C, op. 51, no. 1, and Six Variations on a Theme in G in 1817. The real measure of Beethoven's popularity, however, lies with the many other pieces attributed to him. In this time of loose copyright, publishers found it lucrative to attach whatever name to a piece that they thought would encourage sales. Whether the piece was legitimate or even who actually wrote it was irrelevant. Thus we find four waltzes by Beethoven, even through Beethoven did not compose waltzes. Two are at least legitimate Ländler, German dances upon which the waltz was based, that Beethoven did write. The other two were given detailed and fanciful titles: "Prince Blucher's grand waltz" and "Bonuparte's [sic] waltz as performed in Vienna." The waltz craze was just catching on in America, and one can be certain that some other name, such as Mozart, would have been attached had the publisher not thought Beethoven's name would attract more buyers.

Tracking American publications of Beethoven's music is at best an indirect measure of his popularity. The existence of scores with American imprints tells us that there was some demand for Beethoven's music. The absence of such scores, particularly for the bigger pieces, such as sonatas or string quartets, tells us nothing, however, for most music at this time was imported from England. Sometimes it was imported commercially through music stores that existed in all large cities, sometimes privately through transatlantic travelers or correspondence with family members still in Europe. In 1799 William Tudor was in Paris. Tudor was the brother of Frederick Tudor, who later became known as the "ice king," having made a fortune cutting ice from the rivers and lakes of New England and importing it to the South. William wrote to his mother about music: he had purchased about eighty sonatas, fifteen overtures, a set of quartets, and a number of small pieces. Beethoven's name is not mentioned, and it is unlikely that much Beethoven music would have been available in 1799, but Tudor's purchase, about $400, was a huge sum for the time. Although few private imports would be that large, Tudor's activity indicates a conduit undoubtedly followed by many other Americans. Since most pianos and other instruments were imported from Europe before 1820, it is not surprising that most sheet music would also have been. Early newspapers regularly contained advertisements of music stores announcing the arrival of instruments and music, although they seldom catalogue the contents by individual composers.

One of the clearest measures of Beethoven's popularity was his mention in the *Euterpeiad,* a Boston musical magazine published from 1820 to 1823. It was the same magazine to which S. P. M. sent his letter about the *Mount of Olives.* The *Euterpeiad*'s importance lay in its uniqueness. It was the only musical magazine in Federal America that took music seriously and that had any staying power. Three-plus years may seem a short life for a magazine, but compared to others in the nineteenth century, it continued into venerable old age. Had John Rowe Parker, the founder, not been such a bumbling businessman, it probably would have lasted longer. Parker was a member of the merchant class in Boston and had inherited wealth, most of which he lost in bad business dealings. His activity did take him to Europe frequently, however, where he could observe a much more sophisticated musical culture. Although not a practicing musician—that would have been unacceptable for a Boston Brahmin at the time—Parker developed a keen interest in music and was one of the few people in Federal America to see the artistic value of secular music beyond entertainment. In 1817 he began writing a music column in the *Boston Intelligencer and Morning and Evening Advertiser,* one of the principal newspapers in Boston. By 1820 he decided to expand with his own magazine, giving it the same title as his earlier column.[20]

Beethoven was often praised in the magazine. Parker took some of the material from British magazines and other, unidentified sources, but he also wrote some material himself. One poem extolled a young pianist's performance of a Beethoven concerto:

> *On hearing Beethoven's difficult Concerto played with*
> *full Orchestra accompaniments by a young lady*
> *not twelve years old.*

> You that possess soft souls to feel,
> Who wrapt in Music's softest lays
> With extacies, your ears will fill,
> When fingers swiftly plays.

Although she least expects it here,
Fond tribute, demands my praise,
Her tones, will linger on the ear,
So early taught in youthful days.

She bears my mind, on grandeurs wings
To Musics loftiest fount,
To feast at Science's purest springs,
And endless joys recount.

This probably refers to Alexis Eustaphieve, the daughter of the Russian consul in Boston. According to Parker, by the age of twelve she was studying the
"master pieces of Kalkbrenner, Ries, and the gigantic Beethoven himself," and
she possessed "possibly the largest private collection of music in the United
States."[21] Yet there is no extant record of a public performance of a Beethoven
concerto with orchestra at this time. The poem seems to have been original;
above it is the heading "For the Euterpeiad." It is possible that this performance occurred elsewhere, even in Russia, or that the term "full orchestra" is
a euphemism. More likely the performance was a private one in Boston at the
Russian Consul's residence, accompanied by a few amateur and possibly professional musicians.

Two other lengthy articles in the *Euterpeiad* that discuss Beethoven were
copied directly from European magazines. This was not an unusual practice
for American journals, and the original source was normally acknowledged.
In a two-part article on "Modern Music," which originally appeared in the
British *Gentleman's Magazine,* Beethoven is described in laudatory and gendered terms: "This author, who is now the first master living, is bred up purely
in the new school, and possesses great and original powers. Though less perfect than Haydn, he disdains to imitate him; his genius loves to rove in the
darkest recesses of modulation, which impart to his compositions a peculiar
strength and rudeness; and the science which has been nursed in the lap of
Italy, is now masculizing in the regions of the earth."[22]

An article taken from the Scottish magazine the *Edinburgh Pamphlet* attempts to distinguish Beethoven's style from those of Haydn and Mozart. The
essence of the argument is that Beethoven's music is not as polished, proportional, or regular. But he is powerful and moving in a way that neither Haydn
nor Mozart are: "We think his subjects of a higher order, more original, more
deeply affecting, more general, more fervid, we had almost said more super-
human, than the strains of any other composers. They work more powerfully

upon our sympathies, we feel something like the sensations produced by an odour never smelt before. Such his melodies appear; his harmonies are equally peculiar." Beethoven is also discussed in gender terms here: He has "entered further than any other upon the rugged domain of dissonance," and "the works of the great master are less remarkable for purity and correctness, than for a certain brilliancy and masculine energy of style which are more easily to be felt than described." The power, the masculinity, and the ability to move the listener already point to a Romantic vision that, while clearly not unique to America, would become integral to Beethoven's American image later in the century.

Parker clearly wanted to indoctrinate his readers into the power of Beethoven's music, even though, with the exception of the Hallelujah Chorus of the *Mount of Olives,* not much Beethoven had been heard. There was a performance of Beethoven's Piano Sonata no. 12, op. 26, in 1819 by Sophie Hewitt, believed to be the first of a Beethoven piano sonata in America; the daughter of musician James Hewitt and later the wife of another musician, Louis Ostinelli, she would become one of the most established pianists and organists in Boston, a rare status for a woman at the time. Beethoven symphonies, meanwhile, were heard only occasionally and, except for Charleston, in out-of-the-way places. American references to Beethoven, such as S. P. M.'s, more often than not were to his vocal music. One such example was an advertisement placed by a Mr. Huntington in the *Euterpeiad* for his Grammatical Music School, in which he specified that he would teach young ladies "in the pure style of singing" and would use "fashionable songe duets, and choruses of Handel, Haydn, Mozart and Beethoven." Thus, at least to readers of the *Euterpeiad,* Beethoven's reputation preceded familiarity with the bulk of his music. He was a celebrity before most people had an opportunity to hear why.

Between 1820 and 1840, performances of Beethoven's music continued to be scattered and irregular. The Second Symphony was played by the Musical Fund Society, the most important musical organization in Philadelphia, at their inaugural concert in 1821. In two concerts in Boston in 1831, Charles Zeuner, newly arrived from Germany, performed on the piano "A Favorite Cotillion, with Variations for the Pianoforte, composed by Beethoven." Exactly what the piece is and what part of it Beethoven composed is not clear.[23]

On September 9, 1839, Edmund Simpson, manager of the Park Theatre in New York, presented a new opera company that had just arrived from England. They brought with them an opera never before heard in the United States, Beethoven's *Fidelio.* New Yorkers were used to opera as light fare, and if the critics' remarks are any guide, locals were perplexed, even bewildered, by the work.[24] The writer for the *Corsair,* probably Nathaniel Parker Willis, resorted to vague third-person rumor rather than comment directly on the merits of the opera itself: "Musicians tell us that [*Fidelio*] is a most masterly effort of genius, abounding in all the elements of a sublime, lyrical opera." In New York at the time, opera and "sublime" were seldom used in the same sentence. Willis then played it safe, praising the singers in the company. The writer for the *Knickerbocker* pursued a similar strategy; he focused on the instrumental parts, finding them "beautiful and touching."

Especially noteworthy regarding Beethoven's reception is this comment from the *American,* September 10, 1839, which exalted the composer even beyond Parker's tributes: "Oh! May you give your spirit up to him fearlessly! He will transport you to other worlds, and infuse a thousand strange and thrilling sensations—will cradle you in his arms until, in admiration of his strength, you forget how powerful you are, and when he has poured those notes into your ear, and you are filled with tremblings, of golden wires half conscious of their own thrilling—he leaves you petrified, enchanted—in a silent dream where even the echoes have subsided."[25]

This statement is something of a landmark in U.S. Beethoven attitudes. It is the first inkling of a reputation that would predominate by the end of the nineteenth century and would culminate in the composer's virtual deification by the early twentieth century. It was not *Fidelio,* however, that ushered in a new, widespread appreciation of Beethoven. While the opera did appear occasionally in the repertoire over the next several years, it was only when all the Beethoven symphonies began to appear frequently in the 1840s that the glorification of Beethoven began in earnest.

Beethoven was making other inroads. Out of the spotlight young pianists had begun to plunk away on the Beethoven sonatas, and occasionally their efforts found their way into the historical record. Thomas Wentworth Higginson, a cousin of Henry Lee Higginson, founder of the Boston Symphony Orchestra, refers to his sister as "one of the first in this region to play Beethoven," around 1830.[26] Samuel Jennison, recalling his time at Harvard in the 1830s, remembered a "graduate, a devoted amateur, rooming in Massachusetts," studying Beethoven sonatas, "then just beginning to become known."[27]

Thus as late as 1840 Beethoven was known and respected in America, but few were aware of his music. That changed dramatically in two of the largest cities in the 1840s, Boston and New York, and soon spread throughout the country. A conflux of factors came together to transform the American musical landscape and, with that, to establish both Beethoven's canonicity and popularity.

The first and probably most important factor, which had nothing to do with music directly, was the railroad. As tracks began to appear in the 1830s, distance and time were altered radically. Prior to the railroad most travelers were lucky to manage twenty to thirty miles a day. The trip from Baltimore to Philadelphia took three days, in coaches that were at best uncomfortable and on roads that were subject to delays, difficulties, and danger. Ship travel between ports was possible, but steamships were not yet common, and sailing ships were slow and uncertain. Other water routes, either rivers or canals, offered somewhat better travel, but these did not always connect the important population centers. The Erie Canal, linking the Hudson at Albany with Lake Erie at Buffalo, had been completed in 1825, and, while important as an opening to the West, it soon became obsolete as railroad tracks crawled westward. When Baltimore and Philadelphia were joined, that three-day trip was cut to five hours.

The railroad opened America to the traveling virtuoso. By the 1840s European virtuosi, well established on the continent and starting to feel the competition from their numbers, began to look across the Atlantic to what seemed a lucrative and virgin field ripe for picking. In the early 1840s they began to arrive and created a sensation. One of the first, the violinist Ole Bull, opened American's ears to what the violin could do. Fiddlers existed everywhere, and even those who had heard Anthony Heinrich had no idea of the level of virtuosic excitement the instrument was capable of in the hands of someone like Bull. Other instrumentalists followed suit, including the violinist Henri Vieuxtemps, the cellist Henry Knoop, and the pianist Harold Meyer.

No one, however, created quite the sensation that the soprano Jenny Lind did on her visit in 1850. P. T. Barnum, showman, shrewd businessman, and possibly the most successful promoter in American history, was keenly tuned to American tastes, or to what could be exploited. Something in both Lind and the rapidly developing American musical scene caught his eye. Thus began a strange, unlikely alliance between the demur, refined "Swedish nightingale" and America's huckster extraordinaire. Her visit and Barnum's shrewd tactics succeeded beyond anything the American public had seen, and can best be compared to the Beatles' invasion of 1964. Barnum auctioned off the first ticket for $225, equivalent to $6,380 in 2009 dollars.[28]

While neither Lind nor the other virtuosi featured Beethoven on their programs, they did much to further the notion of music as a powerful, moving experience. John S. Dwight, who was to become the leading spokesman in America for music as high art (see chapter 2), gave voice to that change in attitude when he first heard Ole Bull. Dwight later came to believe that virtuosic display such as Bull's and manipulation of public taste à la Barnum only demeaned the nature of the art, but that was not his first impression. On that occasion Dwight wrote to his friend, the poet Lydia Marie Child: "The most glorious sensation I ever had was to sit in one of his audiences, and to feel that all were elevated to the same pitch with myself, that the spirit in every breast had risen to the same level."[29] Dwight knew that something was changing in musical America, but he had not yet had time to reflect on what it meant.

The factor most directly related to Beethoven's impact was the development of orchestras in New York and Boston and their success with the American public. Prior to the 1840s, a number of musical societies existed on the East Coast: the St. Cecilia Society of Charleston, the Musical Fund Society of Philadelphia, the Philoharmonic Society of Boston, three Philharmonic Societies in New York. None of these, however, should be equated with modern orchestras, such as today's New York Philharmonic. Orchestral ensembles were one part of musical societies, whose concerts featured a wide-ranging potpourri of offerings. As in Charleston and Lexington, a typical concert would normally open and close with a piece by the "full band," which usually meant orchestra, and in between would be a variety of offerings, solo instrumental or small ensemble pieces, songs, glees, improvisations, by whatever and whoever was available. The concerts were like variety shows meant purely for entertainment and amusement. The orchestras themselves were pickup groups, consisting of members of the society, professional musicians hired for the occasion along with some amateurs. According to most reports, the performance level ranged from barely acceptable to abysmal.

New societies in which orchestral music was more than a stage curtain to open and close a program emerged in both Boston and New York in the 1840s. Even though each city took a strikingly different path to that point, each city arrived at the same place almost simultaneously. In Boston the path spun off from the main road of sacred vocal music that had dominated public musical activity since the founding of the Handel and Haydn Society in 1815. Lowell Mason, the most important figure in the effort to instill in Americans a more uplifting style of hymns and sacred music, had become president of the Handel and Haydn Society in 1827. By 1832 he was discouraged with the level of singing in churches and had come to the conclusion that the only way to improve church music was to found a new society devoted to that cause. The problem, it should be noted, was not the same as the one that so riled the earlier Puritan preachers. Mason believed in a decorous, proper type of music more aligned with the European tradition. To further that end he left the Handel and Haydn

Society to found the Boston Academy of Music. Article I of the Academy's constitution states that "its object shall be to promote knowledge, and correct taste in music, especially such as is adapted to moral and religious purposes."[30]

The society provided vocal instruction for both adults and "juveniles," sponsored lectures, formed choirs, and presented concerts. Buried in Point 8 of a long list of objectives specifying how the Academy would realize its goals was what may have been Mason's real motivation: "To introduce vocal music into the schools." Mason had come to the conclusion that the only hope for improving church music was to start when people were young, and the only way to make that happen was to get music instruction into the school curriculum.

For the first three years of the society Mason's plan worked. He was appointed "Professor," with one assistant, George J. Webb, and by the third year he and Webb were teaching music to some 2,200 pupils, in various locales, including some private schools. By 1835, the Academy had become a success and a major force in the musical community. Then it all began to change because of one person, Samuel Atkins Eliot.

In 1835 Eliot replaced Reverend Jacob Abbott as president of the Boston Academy of Music. How he came to be elected and why he even wanted the position is not known, but in retrospect his agenda was clear. Singlehandedly, he transformed the Academy from a religious-oriented, pedagogical organization into a secular concert-giving institution with an orchestra as its centerpiece. Primarily because of the Academy, Boston witnessed a seismic shift in the musical landscape from 1832 to 1840; symphony replaced Psalmody.

Eliot was an unlikely figure to instigate a musical revolution. As a member of one of the most important families in Boston, he was not expected to disturb the status quo, and he was not expected to be involved in music. At first he did not and was not. Like most wealthy young men from Boston, he graduated from Harvard College, in 1817. He went to Harvard Divinity School but decided not to pursue a ministerial career, although he remained active in his family's Unitarian church. He spent three years in Europe, from 1820 to 1823, gaining culture, and upon his return he married the daughter of another wealthy merchant, Mary Lyman. Financially he was set for life.

Throughout the 1820s Eliot gave no evidence of any interest in music, other than singing in his church's choir. During his three-year European sojourn he sent back many letters about the places he visited and the sights he saw, especially the museums and galleries. Eliot was clearly interested in the visual arts, but there is not a single mention of music.

What seemed to have changed Eliot's mind was the sudden death of his brother William in 1829. William was two years older and had displayed as

Samuel A. Eliot

FIGURE 1.2

The only known image of Samuel Atkins Eliot, mayor of
Boston and president of the Boston Academy of Music,
taken from *Mayors of Boston: An Illustrated Epitome of
Who the Mayors Have Been and What They Have Done*
(Boston: State Street Trust Company, 1914), 15.
The original of what appears to be a
daguerreotype is lost.

much interest in music as was possible under his class restrictions. It was almost as if the musical mantle had been passed to Samuel, and he felt obliged
to take it up. He never became a performer, but he devoted considerable time
after that both to musical organizations and to writing about music in various
literary journals. As an advocate for music in class-conscious Boston, he was
ideally placed; he was not only a member of the socioeconomic elite, but active
in politics. He was mayor of Boston from 1837 to 1839 and a member of Con-

gress in 1850 and 1851. Daniel Webster described him as "the impersonification of Boston; ever-intelligent, ever-patriotic, ever-glorious Boston."[31]

On assuming the presidency of the Boston Academy, Eliot immediately began to make changes, although he had to go slowly. He hired an instrumental professor and made an arrangement with an amateur society to form an orchestra. He also stated in the Third Annual Report (1835) that the academy was not devoted strictly to sacred music "as has been supposed." By 1837 he hinted at his agenda but felt it was not yet time to reveal it, observing only that "plans of more extensive usefulness, and wider fields of effort have presented themselves to our minds, and these not of a visionary nature; but we have been obliged to content ourselves with merely contemplating them as objects which we should be able to compass at some future time."[32]

It is not clear whether Lowell Mason's presence still loomed over the Academy, but by the next year he was for all practical purposes gone, having achieved his long-desired appointment as superintendent of music in the schools of Boston. For whatever reason, in 1838 Eliot brought his agenda into the open. He announced his intention to concentrate on an orchestra and to let the choirs atrophy through calculated neglect. When a member of the choir resigned, no effort was made to replace him. At first Eliot's efforts met resistance, but not from the sacred music community. Eliot tried to enlist all the instrumental professional musicians in Boston into one orchestra under the Academy's umbrella, but many were skeptical that it could succeed financially or were concerned about the Academy's oversight. Lacking was a strong instrumental leader who had the prestige to pull the musicians together. Eliot was also aware that the public itself was familiar only with theater orchestras, which were at best chaotic, haphazard, and undisciplined, whose main function was to bellow out popular tunes, often shouted from the audience, and which performed in an environment so rowdy most men would not bring their wives. The public would need to be persuaded that his orchestra was different.

Eliot proceeded cautiously, at first blending a few lighter orchestral pieces with glees and choruses, but by 1841 he thought they were ready for the final step. Eliot abandoned the chorus completely, used the entire finances of the Academy to secure twenty-five to thirty of the best players in Boston under the direction of Henry Schmidt, whom he had already hired, and announced that from then on the Academy would be devoted to orchestral concerts.

The plan worked. The 1841 season was a success far beyond what Eliot could have imagined. The Musical Cabinet referred to the concerts as "a new era in the history of music in Boston." John S. Dwight, writing many years later, looked back upon that time: "Many can remember how eagerly these concerts were sought, how frequently the audience was large, and what a theme of enthusiastic comment and congratulation these first fresh hearings of the great masters was."[33]

What made this crowd so enthusiastic, and why this reversal from attitudes prevalent only a few years earlier? As with any change there were a number of factors, but the most important can be summed up in one word: Beethoven. The repeated performances of Beethoven's symphonies had an emotional impact on Boston audiences like nothing before, not just in Boston but throughout America. When the only way to hear a symphony was through a live concert, repetition was important. From 1841 through 1847, when the rise of a competing orchestra forced the Academy to abandon its performances, the Academy gave between six and eight concerts a season. In those seven years, Beethoven's Fifth became the favorite and was performed at least twelve times, the Seventh at least nine, and both the Fourth and the Sixth four times. While other symphonies, such as those of Haydn, Mozart, and Mendelssohn, were presented, none were repeated as often as Beethoven's.

Dwight attributed the establishment of classical music in Boston to the repeated performances of Beethoven symphonies, particularly the Fifth, at the Academy of Music in the early 1840s. Recalling that time from the 1880s, Dwight observed that "the first great awakening of the musical instinct here was when the C-minor Symphony of Beethoven was played" by the Academy of Music. In 1844 he had noticed that the "performance and subsequent frequent repetition" of Beethoven's Fifth created a "living bond of union between audience and performers, an initiation into a deeper life."[34]

What happened in Boston closely paralleled events in New York, although the circumstances were quite different. Boston had been a relatively homogeneous city ethnically. In the early years, the Puritan theocracy was not inviting to many ethnic groups, and later colonial Bostonians were not especially welcoming, either. The one immigrant group that arrived in large numbers were the Irish, beginning in the 1830s. By 1855 Boston was thirty percent Irish, while Germans, who composed significant minorities in many cities after 1849, were only one percent.[35]

New York, by contrast, had been a polyglot city from its founding. New Netherland, the original Dutch colony, contained at least a dozen nationalities. Killiaen Van Rensselaer, who established a patroon, or plantation, on the upper Hudson River, recruited Norwegians, Danes, Germans, Scots, and Irish in addition to Dutch. According to the Jesuit priest and later martyr Father Isaac Jogues, eighteen different languages were spoken in the immediate area of Manhattan Island in 1644. In 1709, thousands of Germans from the German Palatine area settled in the Hudson Valley area, many moving to New York City. The Revolutionary War swelled the German population. England brought more than 29,000 German mercenaries, or Hessians, to America, and after the war at least 12,000 chose to remain. Even though they fought on the losing side, most had been forced into service and were only too glad not to have to return to Europe.[36] Many French, who fought on the American side, also chose to remain. Italians began to appear around 1820, most fleeing from revolts against Austria, which ruled much of the Italian peninsula at the time. Beginning around 1840 large numbers of Irish came, and starting around 1849 Germans began to arrive en masse, many as political refugees of the revolts of 1848.

New York thus became a city of ethnic neighborhoods, a trend that continued as immigration swelled through the First World War. Some Beethoven performances within these communities were attended strictly by members of the community. In 1841 George Templeton Strong, a wealthy supporter and staunch fan of music in New York, attended such a concert by the German Society at the Tabernacle, a large concert venue in the city. The performance closed with Beethoven's Fifth Symphony, probably the first performance of the work in America. The symphony puzzled Strong: "It was generally unintelligible to me, except the Andante," and he also noticed the audience: the hall was "jammed with Dutchmen like a barrel of Dutch herrings. I scarcely saw an Anglo-Saxon physiognomy in the whole gallery."[37] Beyond Strong's condescending description, it is clear that this was an event for the German community. Only a year and a half later, with the founding of the Philharmonic Society of New York (today's New York Philharmonic, the oldest symphony orchestra in America still in existence), did the Fifth Symphony become familiar to the mainstream concert audience in New York.

The 1842 orchestra was not the first New York Philharmonic, but rather the fourth. The first three were founded in 1799, 1816, and 1824, and each had its own demise. These were all primarily private social groups, consisting mostly of amateurs who met either weekly or bi-weekly, played music, and then enjoyed refreshments and socializing. They would give regular private concerts for the benefit of members of the society and their invited guests and usually presented at least one public concert each year, normally followed by a ball for which the orchestra provided the music. This pattern was typical for concerts in Federal America, and even in these early attempts the parallels between Boston and New York are striking. In Boston there were at least two other orchestras before the 1840s, the Philoharmonic Society, founded in the 1790s, and the Apollo Society, founded in 1824.

These societies of the 1790s were organized in both cities by European immigrant musicians who quickly established themselves as the leading instrumental musicians of their respective metropolises. In Boston, Gottlieb Graupner had emigrated from Germany and arrived in Boston with his wife, Charlotte Elizabeth Rowson, a member of a British theatrical troupe. In New York, James Hewitt emigrated from England in 1792. Both soon became leaders of theater orchestras, the one type of steady employment for an instrumental musician. Both had to supplement their income with other activities, and both opened music stores. Neither city at the time would be considered large by today's standards; in the 1790 census New York had a population of 33,131, Boston 18,320. New York was the largest city in the country, edging out Philadelphia (population 28,522), and Boston was third.

Because most of the activities of these societies were private, they left few records. We are able to trace more details about them only from when their activities became more public, mostly in the 1820s. Least visible of all are their demises, for silence in the public record does not mean they ceased to exist. The first New York Philharmonic Society probably collapsed when Hewitt, after a contract dispute with the Park Theater, left New York for Boston. The second Philharmonic, the most elusive of all, appeared in 1816, about the time Hewitt returned to New York. All that is known about it is one concert announced for December 7, 1816. That this was not the 1799 society was stressed in the announcement, which stated, possibly to ensure that no one mistook it for the older organization, that it was "the first effort of an infant institution." It was never heard from again.

Much more is known about the third Philharmonic, founded in 1824, which had no connection with Hewitt (he was no longer in New York). The constitution and bylaws have survived, indicating a growing interest in music by upper-class New Yorkers as well as a mounting tension between amateur and professional musicians. The constitution refers to promotion of the "science of music," a term that meant the cultivation of European classical practice, and it bars professional musicians from any governing authority. A board of wealthy New Yorkers would manage the institution. Membership was divided between subscribing members attending concerts and amateur performing members. Professional musicians could belong only as associates. Membership was also limited to men, a stricture common at the time, with the number of ladies each member could invite depending on the level of his membership.

The founding of this organization has parallels in Boston, where a group of nine prominent citizens attempted to found a strikingly similar organization in 1826. The Boston effort went no further than a detailed printed circular, however, which outlined the purpose, goals, and justification of the proposed society. In tone, explanation, and proposed governance the circular may well have been modeled on the 1824 New York Philharmonic. Boston, it appears, was not ready for this type of musical organization, or at least the elite were not ready to fund it.[38]

On December 17, 1824, Dennis Étienne, a French hornist from the Paris Conservatoire, conducted the first concert of the new New York Philharmonic. It included as the closing number, listed as a "finale," a movement of Beethoven's Second Symphony.[39] Interest was so high that four hundred extra tickets were put on sale for the extraordinary price of two dollars. Seldom did any concert ticket go for more than one dollar at the time, and many sold for less. Perhaps a Beethoven symphony was part of the first instance of ticket scalping in the United States.

With this auspicious beginning, the society's future seemed assured, and except for some grumbling from a self-styled critic, Musaeus, writing to the *New York American,* concerts for the next two years appeared to be successful. Some of Musaeus's complaints were probably legitimate, such as the lack of proper instrumentation—not enough violins and some wind instruments—but his tone undoubtedly was influenced by the society's refusal to grant him membership. Yet he provided more information about the society than exists for any of the previous ones.

Soon, however, the society made a fatal decision. In 1825 Manuel García arrived from Spain with a small troupe to present the first opera in the United States in the original Italian. English theatrical troupes had performed opera in America but had treated operas mostly as skeletons on which to hang an evening's entertainment. Not only were they translated into English, the libretto was often modified to be more attuned to current situations, and in many cases English ballads were substituted for the original arias. In one performance of Mozart's *Don Giovanni,* the lead role was played not by a singer but an actor, so they simply omitted all music from his part. García, however, promised the real thing.

Excitement ran high at first and newspaper reviews were ecstatic, but soon interest dwindled. The novelty wore off, and the troupe, with a limited repertoire, repeated the same operas again and again. After a few months the opera company was in serious financial difficulties, exacerbated by the impending loss of its star singer, María Felicia, García's eighteen-year-old daughter; she had married, much to her father's chagrin. In the fall of 1826 García and what was left of his troupe departed for Mexico.

The Philharmonic Society unfortunately intertwined its fate with the García company. Many of the musicians formed the orchestra for the opera performances, and on at least four occasions García singers appeared in Philharmonic concerts. Further compromising the Philharmonic, in May 1826, as financial difficulties began to mount for García, the Philharmonic board agreed to a guarantee of $1,500 to the troupe, equivalent in 2008 dollars to $1,140,861.[40] As a consequence, when the García Troupe departed in October of that year, the Philharmonic was in serious financial difficulties. Regular rehearsals were suspended because of the debt they incurred, and their final concert occurred on February 27, 1827. Gracchus, writing in the *New York American*, implored New Yorkers to attend to help save the society, but apparently it was not enough. Like its predecessors, the third New York Philharmonic Society was never heard from again.[41]

The fourth, final, and ultimately most important New York Philharmonic Society was founded in 1842 on very different principles from the 1824 model. It was created by musicians themselves, to be run by musicians. For several years prior a number of musicians in New York lamented the absence of a decent orchestra, and finally on Saturday, April 12, 1842, Ureli Corelli Hill called a meeting of professional musicians in New York with the idea of forming an orchestral society. Hill was an American violinist and conductor who in 1837 had returned from Europe after studying with Ludwig Spohr, considered one of the finest violinists as well as an outstanding composer in his time. Anthony Heinrich, then in New York, was selected to serve as chair of the meeting. In the next two weeks a constitution was adopted, and Hill was elected president and chosen as its conductor. The constitution stipulated that membership would be limited to seventy and only to professional musicians, although not all would necessarily be orchestral performing musicians. The society would present four concerts a year, and performing members would be paid $25 a year for their efforts. The society was a cooperative in that any profits at the end of the year would be divided among the members. Repertoire and conductor would be chosen by the members, and compositions by American composers were encouraged.[42]

The Society gave its first concert on December 7, 1842, with an orchestra numbering between fifty and sixty, a large ensemble for the time. In contrast, the Academy of Music Orchestra had thirty-one players. The program was lengthy, featuring chamber and vocal music, including two opera scenes, as well as orchestral music. It opened with Beethoven's Fifth Symphony and also featured a scene from Beethoven's *Fidelio*.[43] The sheer size of the orchestra as well as the performance level impressed the audience and critics. George Templeton Strong, who could make no sense of Beethoven's Fifth Symphony when he had heard it performed by the German Society, gave no indication whether it was more intelligible to him, but he did comment that it was "splendidly played" and that the instrumental part of the program was "glorious."

This was in comparison to the vocal performers, one of whom "sounded like a hand organ," and another whose voice cracked completely. Newspaper reviewers were also pleased with the overall level of performance and the very fact that virtually all the professional orchestral musicians in New York were on the stage at the same time, but they had quibbles with some aspects of the performance. Nevertheless, all judged the concert a success, and Beethoven was launched in New York.

Two more similar programs were held during the first season. Each of these concerts also opened with a complete Beethoven symphony, the Third and the Second Symphonies, respectively. The Philharmonic Society programmed more contemporary works and had a wider range of music than the Boston Academy, but Beethoven symphonies still formed the core of its repertoire. Through the 1840s the Second, Fourth, Sixth, Eighth, and Ninth Symphonies were each played once, the Seventh three times, the Third and the Fifth four times. The performances of the Fourth, Eighth, and Ninth were the first in America. Thus over the course of twenty-eight concerts, the New York audiences heard seventeen performances of a Beethoven symphony. This far outstripped presentations of any other composer.

In 1850 Samuel Jennison, a Bostonian, was asked to give the annual lecture to the Harvard Musical Association. For his topic he chose "Music in the Past Half-Century." He noted the changes that had occurred in Boston in only the past few years, including chamber concerts of the Harvard Musical Association and the orchestral concerts of the Academy of Music. Music occupied a very different place in 1850 than it did even in 1840. Not only were major instrumental ensembles thriving, but the entire notion of music as an art had begun to take hold. Even though Jennison's frame of reference was Boston, it could easily have pertained to New York. Dramatic changes had occurred in two of the largest cities in the country, and Beethoven's music had become lodged deep in the mind and heart of concertgoers in New York and Boston. The second half of the nineteenth century would see Beethoven's impact grow, as more of his repertoire became familiar, and as performances of his music spread from coast to coast, to large cities and small towns. Americans would also grapple with questions that had already begun to surface about the meaning of music, its role as art, and its place in society. Beethoven would turn out to be at the center of all of those questions.

2

Defining Beethoven

ON THURSDAY, DECEMBER 22, 1808, Beethoven's Fifth Symphony premiered in Vienna, and the public heard for the first time the most famous motive in all Western music, *da-da-da-dum*. The program was long by any standard, and would surely have taxed the attention span and derriere of any concertgoer today. It consisted of the Fifth and Sixth Symphonies, the Fourth Piano Concerto, the Choral Fantasy, parts of his Mass in C, an aria, as well as a section in which Beethoven improvised at the keyboard. The concert was not a rousing success, largely because of numerous performance problems, including a complete breakdown in the Choral Fantasy, which necessitated starting all over again.

A second performance of the Fifth in Leipzig some two weeks later went better and received favorable comment in the press. More important, however, the Leipzig firm of Breitkopf and Hartel published the score of the symphony in April 1809. The score soon came into the hands of E. T. A. Hoffmann, who in July wrote a seventeen-page review for the *Allgemeine Musikalische Zeitung*, the most important musical journal at the time. The review is a landmark in music criticism, situating Beethoven in nineteenth-century thought and establishing the Romantic credentials for music in general. Hoffmann considered abstract instrumental music the pinnacle of Romanticism, the genre that defined the Romantic urge of the nineteenth century: "Only instrumental music . . . can express with purity music's peculiar nature. It alone gives definition to the art. Music is the most romantic of all the arts; one might even say that it alone is purely romantic."[1]

In Hoffmann's view, Beethoven built on the work of Haydn and Mozart, but only he "penetrated into its [music's] innermost essence." While Haydn's and Mozart's music was imbued with the Romantic spirit, only Beethoven was a "purely romantic composer," and consequently a truly musical one. Hoffmann admitted from the start that the Fifth Symphony profoundly moved him, and as a result he found it necessary to go beyond the accepted manner of criticism "to capture in words the feelings this composition aroused deep within [my] heart."

Hoffmann's review, only six months after the premiere of the symphony, had a profound effect on both sides of the Atlantic. It set the tone for both the nineteenth century and for Romanticism. American writers on music, who if anything were even more enthusiastic about Beethoven than Hoffmann was, absorbed Romanticism within a framework of Transcendentalism, an idealistic movement centered in New England. How Hoffmann's Beethoven compares to the Transcendentalists' is essential to understanding the image of Beethoven that emerged on this side of the Atlantic. By the 1840s the Beethoven flag was firmly planted on U.S. soil, mainly in the larger eastern cities, and it soon spread throughout the country. What did this music, particularly the symphonies, mean to the many who were hearing Beethoven for the first time? As writers grappled with the profound impact that Beethoven's music had on nineteenth-century Americans, as Beethoven came to epitomize the Romantic composer and his music Romanticism itself, both Hoffmann's and the Transcendentalists' visions played an important part in establishing an image that affected not only Beethoven but classical music itself well into the twentieth century. Even today the image remains an important aspect of the American musical world.

From the Transcendental writers, several themes about Beethoven and his music emerged that eventually became part of the mainstream nineteenth-century view of the composer. His music came to be understood as having special spiritual and hence sacred qualities, something that was soon transferred to Beethoven himself. Margaret Fuller and John S. Dwight, both Transcendental writers, were pivotal in this development. He was also associated with nature, an area not only important to the Transcendentalists but fundamental to any understanding of America.

Because Transcendentalism, nature, and sacralization were closely related in the nineteenth century, any discussion of one often bleeds into the others. A fourth issue, however, stands somewhat apart. To a country reveling in Manifest Destiny and the virility of the Gilded Age, Beethoven's music was perceived as having special manly qualities. This placed it in contrast with the complex gender minuet of the nineteenth century, which usually consigned music to women's sphere. Many saw Beethoven's music as different.

In some respects Transcendentalism is similar to late twentieth-century postmodernism: it is difficult to define, impossible to pin down, and characterized by as many variants as individuals in the movement. For most, however, nature lies at its very core. If Transcendentalism had a guru, it would be Ralph Waldo Emerson, and if Transcendentalism had an ur-statement, it would be Emerson's 1836 essay "Nature." Emerson knew it was an important document: he gave the same title to the overall book in which the essay was published, and he reprinted the essay eight years later in another book, *Essays: Second Series.* As John Gatta points out, one measure of its importance was its ability to inspire other writers, Henry David Thoreau and other Transcendentalists in particular, but also the nature essayist John Burroughs, the environmentalist John Muir, and the novelist, poet, playwright, and feminist Mary Austin.[2]

Emerson's "Nature" is about more than nature. It is about man's place in the cosmos, about God, the soul, reason, language, beauty, and nationalism. It is a metaphysical, religious, and aesthetic statement. This was not quite the same perspective held by the Romantics in Europe. They indeed found solace, comfort, and an element of spirituality in nature. Nature for them, however, as Ernest Lee Tuveson explained, is panentheistic, meaning that God is manifest therein but nevertheless remains separate. The panentheist would find evidence of God in nature but would not find God himself. In contrast, the pantheist believes that God is actually present in nature, "that God is immanent in or identical with the universe," "that God is everything and everything is God."[3]

Emerson embraced pantheism, although "Nature" did not state this specifically. That itself distinguished him and, to an extent, American Transcendentalism from European Romanticism. Emerson does not speak of nature in the commonsense meaning. Ask people what nature means to them, and almost everyone would conjure images of the world unmodified by man, images of forests, rivers, and wilderness, as opposed to cultivated fields, cities, or roads. Emerson acknowledged that, but he made an important distinction: he noted that as he looked out on a "charming landscape" he saw several farms; various neighbors owned the farms, but none owned the landscape. More important, Emerson referred to nature in the philosophical sense, meaning "not me." In nature, one encounters the spiritual because God is all around, God is every-where, he is in everything. When in nature, the self dissolves, as Emerson stated in one of his most famous passages: "Standing on the bare ground,—my head bathed by the blithe air, and uplifted into infinite space,—all mean egotism vanishes. I become a transparent eye-ball; I am nothing; I see all; the currents of the Universal Being circulate through me; I am part or particle of God."

The transparent eyeball is perhaps Emerson's most memorable image, and though it was satirized even in his own time, it is the essence of his Transcen-dental thought. Within it is a reciprocal vision; the viewer sees, while at the same time the boundaries between the viewer and nature—God—disappears. The self no longer exists. This concept is common with many religions, in-cluding both Christianity, where Jesus urged his disciples to lose their lives in order to find them, and Eastern religions, such as Taoism and Zen Buddhism, where the individual identifies with the cosmos. In some ways it is antithetical to nineteenth-century Romanticism, which glorified the exploration and ex-pression of the individual self.

Emerson had little to say about music—he admitted that he had neither an ear for it nor interest in it—but he spoke deeply about art. For him art repre-sented nature: "A work of art is an abstract or epitome of the world. It is the re-sult or expression of nature, in miniature." Nature is a "sea of forms" that must be perceived as a whole, creating something akin to an all-encompassing or-ganicism. Beauty lies in the perfection and harmony of nature's forms. Lan-guage had metaphorical significance to Emerson, as did art, a point on which most modern linguists would agree. Emerson distinguishes between words that are spiritual and words that express facts, but whereas most people would assume that words used to express spiritual values are metaphorically derived from words that designate natural facts, Emerson reverses the order: "Every natural fact is a symbol of some spiritual fact." This is the essence of Emerson's Transcendentalism: spirit comes from nature.

By the early nineteenth century the Puritan view of nature, as a dark threat-ening force through which the pilgrim must travel to reach the celestial city, had been completely turned on its head. Many Americans did view nature as something to be conquered, but that was in the tangible sense of land to be occupied. Nature, using Emerson's distinction between the farm and the landscape, was something to behold. The farm may have been the wilderness tamed; the landscape was nature glorified.

The idealization of nature was a common Romantic theme on both sides of the Atlantic. Yet in America it took turns that distinguished it from its representation in Europe. Its very presence in America was significant. Much of America was still a wilderness, a grand, gigantic canvas whose splendor dwarfed anything that Europe had to offer. Europe indeed had the Alps, and only later in the century when American explorers discovered the Rocky Mountains could America compete in that arena. But even before that time, nature was omnipresent in America, remaining for much of the country close to its pristine state. An entire school of painting, the Hudson River School, emerged to capture this aspect of the American continent. That the Transcendentalists closely identified nature with God was only one of several manifestations of America's wonderment at the natural world in the early nineteenth century. According to Barbara Novak, the nature-is-God equation was also at the heart of the Hudson River School ethos.[4]

It is thus not surprising that Beethoven's Sixth Symphony, the *Pastoral*, rivaled the Fifth in popularity in the nineteenth century. During the seven years the Boston Academy of Music held concerts in the 1840s, the Fifth was heard twelve times and the Sixth nine times, far more than any other compositions. A similar pattern was later repeated in New York. During Theodore Thomas's years as conductor of the New York Philharmonic, 1877–1891, the Third Symphony, the *Eroica,* and the Sixth were each played five times, more than any other composition by any composer. The Fifth, along with Schubert's Ninth Symphony and Schumann's First and Second, was performed four times; only a few other pieces, including Beethoven's Ninth, received as many as three performances.[5]

The popularity of Beethoven's *Pastoral* Symphony comes as much in spite of as because of its championship by critics such as Margaret Fuller and John S. Dwight. Both felt that it evoked nature beautifully, and both spoke to that point at some length. Fuller viewed the symphony as a nature canvas, painting a bucolic image of "the enameled fields on a day of bluest blue sky," the peasant's dance, the storm, the birds, "all these glorious gifts nature makes to every man, each 'green and bowery summertime.'" Yet for Fuller it was too close to the surface, too picturesque; it was a "popular composition" that "does not require a depth in the life of the hearer, but only simplicity to feel its beauties."[6]

Dwight saw the painting less literally, closer to Beethoven's own admonition, "mehr ein Ausdruck der Empfindung als Malerlei" (more an expression of feeling than painting). True to his Transcendental heritage, he viewed the symphony as an expression of man's identification with nature rather than a description of nature. According to Dwight it reminds one of the sensation of experiencing nature, not nature itself: "They do not say; look at this or that . . . but they make you feel as you would if you were lying on a grassy slope in a summer's afternoon."[7] Yet Dwight acknowledged a fundamental factor, despite the emphasis on nature and its importance to Transcendentalism: the Sixth does not speak of abstract values in heavy religious tones which, as we will see, he found in other Beethoven compositions.

For American painters of the nineteenth century, particularly the Hudson River School, the giant landscape paintings were a direct, detailed, overt expression of the twin notions of the immanence of God and God in nature, which was at the heart of the Transcendental argument. The paintings were also a reminder of the awesomeness of nature, of nature sublime. Man appears in the canvases, but only to demonstrate his insignificance, as tiny figures dwarfed by the environment that surrounds him. If to the nineteenth century the Hudson River School canvases were visual representations of a pantheistic God, the Beethoven symphonies were his voice. They were the aural equivalents of the great nature paintings, and for some, at least, they served the same purpose.

Barbara Novak posits two types of nature painting in the nineteenth century, "grand opera" and the "still small voice." Grand opera describes the large canvases of the Hudson River School, of Thomas Cole, Frederick Edwin Church, and Albert Bierstadt. The still small voice refers to the much smaller paintings of the luminists, such as Martin Johnson Heade and Fitz Hugh Lane. To Novak, the real heroes of nineteenth-century American paintings are the luminists. The larger, grander paintings were too close to the European style, to the Claudian conventions, while the smaller work of the luminists, with its classic rather than Baroque style, more convincingly maintained the myth of pristine nature.[8]

There is little question where Beethoven's aural canvases lay within Novak's framework. Beethoven's symphonies are grand opera at its most spectacular. With the possible exception of the Sixth Symphony, they are, again to borrow from Novak, the operatic sublime. Even the Sixth, with its colorful depiction of a peasant dance and a storm, redounds in operatic imagery. Yet to follow Novak in her argument leads to a paradox: for her the transcendence of Emerson, the Swedish theologian and mystic Emanuel Swedenborg, and spiritualism is found in the work of the luminists, not in those of the operatically sublime. In contrast to the giant canvases that call attention to both painter and spectator, luminist painting abolishes the egos of both, bringing to mind Emerson's transparent eyeball.

Yet when the Transcendentalists identified with music, it was with Bee-thoven and particularly his symphonies. The works' strong roots in German culture matched the Transcendentalists' own, as did their perceived basis in the Kantian sublime.[9] Luminist paintings were private, aristocratic, and con-tained, a formula not designed to capture the public. Beethoven symphonies were powerful, expansive, and dynamic, meant to appeal to large segments of the population, as did the paintings of the Hudson River School. In spite of their grandeur, or possibly because of it, their emotional power upon Tran-scendental writers swept away the question of whether Beethoven could fit into the Transcendental aesthetic and transformed it into a question of how this can be done. Dwight's answer, that the sublimity in Beethoven's music is close to God himself, not only provided the most enduring definition of Bee-thoven for America, but added another dimension to the elusive concept of Transcendentalism itself.

Fuller and Dwight spoke of Beethoven more frequently and considered his impact more thoroughly than any other writers of the nineteenth century. Their statements began to appear in the early 1840s, coincident with two events in Boston: the regular performance of Beethoven symphonies, and the found-ing of two important Transcendentalist magazines, *The Dial* and *The Har-binger*. *The Dial* appeared from 1840 to 1844 and was succeeded by *The Har-binger*, which was published from 1845 to 1849. Fuller was the original editor of *The Dial*. Later, Dwight continued writing music criticism in his own journal, *Dwight's Journal of Music*, which had by far the longest run of any American music journal in the nineteenth century, from 1852 to 1881.

Fuller's and Dwight's comments about Beethoven were as different as their personalities, but they both saw in Beethoven a Romantic composer who epito-mized the Transcendentalist aesthetic. Dwight was a dreamer, a wispy person-ality floating through life as if on a cloud, cushioned from the realities of the world. His keen sense of morality shaped his vision of art and of Beethoven. Fuller was in every way rooted in the world. As passionate as she was brilliant, as charismatic as she was aloof, she was one of America's first true feminists. Whereas Dwight's attachment to Beethoven was always reserved, tempered by intellectualism, Fuller allowed herself to be fully intoxicated by him. For a time he was one of the great passions of her life.

Born into a society that expected women to marry, stay in the home, and raise a family, and that considered a proper woman's education to be finishing school with a dabbling of literature, art, and social graces, Fuller was deter-mined to strike a different path. Her father, Timothy Fuller, an attorney who

was later elected to Congress, insisted that she have a rigorous education from an early age. Although her father was loving in a stern New England way, and she was not abused as Beethoven himself had been as a child, she must have identified with him. She had to recite for her father each evening, and later wrote: "As he was subject to many interruptions, I was often kept up till very late; and as he was a severe teacher, both from his habits of mind and his ambition for me, my feelings were kept on the stretch till the recitations were over."[10] By three and a half she had learned to read and by seven she was translating Latin passages from Virgil. At eight she discovered Shakespeare, on her own. Later at fourteen she was sent to a typical girls school, that of the Misses Prescott, in Groton, Massachusetts. She endured it and left after two years. In her twenties she began publishing short articles and reviews and secured teaching positions, first at the Temple School founded by Bronson Alcott in Boston and then at the Greene Street School in Providence, Rhode Island.

In 1839 Fuller moved back to Massachusetts, and there began the work that would secure her reputation. While continuing to write she instituted "conversations," discussions for women that were designed to compensate for their lack of education, as well as probe the question of just what women's roles were. Although Fuller had long recognized "that I was not born to the common womanly lot," her feminist leanings began to emerge with these conversations.[11] They also contain her first mention of Beethoven.

Since these discussions were as she named them, conversations, where Fuller would first lecture on a topic and then lead discussion with the women present, no transcript of what was said survives. Thanks to a summary probably written by Elizabeth Peabody, at whose home the conversations occurred, at least Fuller's general thought was preserved.[12] In the eighth conversation, likely from early 1840 (the entire series of twenty conversations occurred between November 1839 and May 1840),[13] Fuller turned to music:

> Of music as a language Miss F. spoke with enthusiasm. Its power to excite thought—especially Beethoven's. She spoke of music as a mere expression of thought and feeling—Something consecrated from all lower ends than beauty—the singing voice *sacred*—the lyre and other instruments set apart for this high communion of Soul with Soul and the sense of awe that one worthy to touch this consecrated instrument would cherish.— (It was very beautiful but I cannot remember it).[14]

This, of course, raises a question: Just what did Fuller know about Beethoven at the time? She was not a trained musician, and the first Beethoven symphony would not be played in Boston until 1841. Her reference to Beethoven may have been prompted by two concerts that were given in late 1839. Sometime before January 4, 1840, the pianist Frederick Rakemann, who was touring the United States, teamed up with two local musicians, both German immigrants, the violinist Henry Schmidt and the cellist Theodore Hach, to perform two Beethoven's trios. During that same season the English singer Joseph Phillip Knight appeared and performed "Rosalie," a cantata that Charles Edward Horn had adapted from Beethoven's song "Adelaida." In a letter to Emerson dated November 4, 1839, she refers to verses on Beethoven that she had written, although she admits they "are very bad, but not without glimmers of my thoughts."[15] Something obviously inspired her to poetry, either Rakemann or Knight. Unfortunately, these poetic efforts are lost. In another letter to Emerson, dated July 5, 1840, Fuller commented, "I hear Rakemann play frequently," and regretted that Emerson did not live closer so she could take him with her to "two or three musical entertainments. Especially one eveg [sic] when Knight was here and sang Beethoven's Rosalie."[16] It seems unlikely that even Fuller could have dragged Emerson to a concert.

One of Boston's musical milestones occurred on April 3, 1841, when the Boston Academy Orchestra presented its first performance of Beethoven's Fifth Symphony. Fuller was profoundly moved. Two days later, still under the sway of the excitement the piece generated, she described her feelings in a letter to her friend, the Unitarian leader William Henry Channing:

> Oh William, what majesty what depth, what tearful sweetness of the human heart, what triumphs of the Angel mind! Into his hands he drew all the forces of sound, then poured them forth in tides such as ocean knows not, then the pause which said It is very good and the tender touch which woke again the springs of life. When I read his life I said I will never repine. When I heard this symphony I said I will triumph more and more above the deepenin[g] abysses.[17]

A year later Fuller again discussed the Fifth, this time in print. She had had time to step back from that first impression, but the force that overwhelmed her that night had not dissipated. Her description is part of a lengthy article in *The Dial* on the "Entertainments of the Past Winter." She discusses many pieces, musical and theatrical, but none with the passion embodied in her writing on the Fifth. To Fuller the symphony is a metaphysical piece that strips one to the very core of one's existence and that goes to the very heart of creation. No paraphrase can do justice to her rhetoric:

But in the Fifth Symphony we seem to have something offered us, not only more, but different, and not only different from another work of his, but different from anything we know in the clearness with which we are drawn to the creative soul, not of art or artist, but of universal life. Here with force, and ardent, yet deliberate approach, manifold spirits demand the crisis of their existence. Nor is the questioning heard in vain, but, in wide blaze of light and high heroic movement, more power flows forth than was hoped, than was asked. With bolder joy, with a sorrow more majestic, life again demands and meets a yet more gold-like reply. New swells of triumph precede powers still profounder, worthy to precede the birth of worlds. These are followed by still sublimer wave and crash of sound smiting upon the centre, then pouring its full tides along. Wide wings wave, and nothing is forgot, all lies revealed, expanded, but *below*. Human loves flow like silver threads amid the solemn mountains and fair vales, and a divine intelligence showers down the sun and shadow from an equal height.

Fuller finds in the symphony the demands of the Sibyls and Prophets of Michelangelo and the spirits of Dante's Heaven, but it is more than that: "The effect of the symphony on memory is an intimation of that love with its kindred energy, beyond faith as much as beyond sight, for all is present now, and the secret of creation is read. This, not Haydn's, is '*the* Creation.'"[18]

By this time Beethoven had become her support and inspiration, both his life and his music a confirmation to persist no matter the odds, to stand up to discouragement, doubt, and social forces that looked askance at her choices. She had long known that the ordinary fate of an upper-class woman in Boston was not for her. She felt trapped in her gender, but Beethoven became her liberator, and for a time even more. In another letter to Channing she referred to the composer as "my hero."[19] In a biographical sketch in *The Dial* she wrote, "Beethoven, towering far above our heads, still with colossal gesture, points above.... Beethoven seems to have chronicled all the sobs, the heart-heavings, and godlike Promethean thefts of the Earth-spirit."[20]

On November 25, 1843, she heard the Academy of Music play Beethoven's Seventh Symphony. On returning home, she wrote a letter to Beethoven, a private statement—it remained unpublished in her journal—in which she poured out her heart. The Fifth Symphony had moved her profoundly; the Seventh Symphony, which others have found orgiastic, aroused desires far beyond metaphysical considerations of the universe. The letter is addressed to "My only friend," and she refers to Beethoven as "Master." It is in many ways a passionate, intimate love letter. She laments her fate as a woman: "Thou didst borrow from those errors the inspiration of thy genius. Why is it not thus with me? Is it because, as a woman, I am bound by a physical law, which prevents the soul from manifesting itself?"

She pleads: "If thou wouldst take me wholly to thyself _____!" and sees herself as wife and mistress: "But thou, oh blessed master! Dost answer all my questions, and make it my privilege to be. Like a humble wife to the sage, or poet, it is my triumph that I can understand and cherish thee: like a mistress, I arm thee for the fight; like a young daughter, I tenderly bind thy wounds. Thou art to me beyond compare, for thou art all I want."

In *The Dial* Fuller had compared Beethoven to Michelangelo and Dante. In this letter he stands above them all: "The infinite Shakespeare, the stern Angelo, Dante,—bittersweet like thee,—are no longer seen in thy presence. And beside these names, there are none that could vibrate in thy crystal sphere. Thou hast all of them, and that ample surge of life besides, that great winged being which they only dreamed of. There is none greater than Shakspeare [*sic*]; he, too, is a god; but his creations are successive; thy *fiat* comprehends them all." The letter closes: "Master, I have this summer envied the oriole which had even a swinging nest in the high bough. I have envied the east flower that came to seed, though that seed were strown to the wind. But I envy none when I am with thee."[21] Thus while despairing of her gendered role in a confining society, her passion, which approaches the erotic in this letter, is nonetheless expressed in the language of a traditional female role of her time.

By 1844 Fuller was exhausted from her many literary activities in Boston. She had already relinquished editorship of *The Dial* to Emerson, and soon moved to New York to work for Horace Greeley's *New York Tribune,* mainly writing reviews. She became its first female editor in 1846. In more than 250 columns she not only reviewed literary works but used her position as a platform to speak out for causes, especially women's rights, an issue in which she was already engaged. In her many books and articles, she advocated that men and women be treated equally. She believed that education was the key to women's advancement and that women should not be confined to the home and traditional professional roles, such as teaching: "If you ask me what office women should fill, I reply—any . . . let them be sea captains if you will."[22] She felt that marriage as constituted in nineteenth-century America trapped women in a straitjacket, and argued for many causes where rampant injustice was apparent, such as prison reform, abolition, and the treatment of Native Americans.

Fuller went to England in 1846 as the *Tribune's* first female foreign correspondent. There she met a young Italian, Giovanni Angelo Ossoli, a supporter
of the Italian revolutionary Giuseppe Mazzini. They soon moved to Italy together to fight for the establishment of a unified Italian republic. Italy at that
time consisted of a patchwork of small principalities, some of which were controlled by foreign states, including France and the Austrian Empire. Soon they
had a child—the records are unclear as to whether they ever married—and
then, whether as a result of her activities in Italy or her relationship with Ossoli, her view of Beethoven seems to have changed. In a letter written from
Rome on April 10, 1846, to her friends Marcus and Rebecca Spring, she admitted, "I have never loved any human being so well as the music of Beethoven yet at present I am indifferent to it."[23] Being so invested in Italian politics,
she would have been keenly aware of the control the Austrian Empire had on
parts of Italy. Her love of Beethoven may have been tempered by his Teutonic
music and his personal identification with Vienna. More likely, having found
a true, flesh-and-blood revolutionary in Ossoli, she no longer had need for the
real but metaphysical personage.

After Mazzini's cause was lost, Ossoli and Fuller were forced to leave; returning to England they boarded the ship *Elizabeth* for a five-week journey
back to the United States. Fuller had premonitions about the voyage, about
something: "I am absurdly fearful and various omens have combined to give
me a dark feeling. . . . It seems to me that my future upon earth will soon
close. . . . I have a vague expectation of some crisis—I know not what."[24] Her
premonitions proved correct. On board a smallpox outbreak occurred, which
took the life of the captain. As the ship neared New York, with an inexperi-
enced first mate at the helm, the ship ran aground off Fire Island. Many leapt
overboard and swam to shore. What happened to Fuller and her family is not
clear, except that they did not survive; of the three only her son's body was
found. Thus after a voyage of five weeks, within a few miles of the port of New
York and less than a hundred yards from Long Island, Fuller perished in a
shipwreck.

In contrast to the dynamic Fuller, John S. Dwight drifted through a conventional youth and education. Born into a middle-class Boston family—his
father was a physician—Dwight showed an interest in literature, music, and
not much else. Beginning in his teen years he studied piano and flute and acquired modest skills on both. He then attended Harvard College, graduating
in 1832. There he was a member of the Pierian Sodality, the undergraduate
musical organization that met once a week to play mostly lighter music infor-

mally. There was no opportunity to study music at Harvard, as it was not considered a subject worthy of a college curriculum, a point reaffirmed by the college faculty when in 1832 they rejected a student petition to have music courses introduced.

Upon matriculation, Dwight enrolled in Harvard Divinity School to prepare for a career as a Unitarian minister. He graduated in 1836 and after more than three years of substituting in various churches found a position as minister at the Unitarian Church in Northampton, Massachusetts, in 1840. He resigned after one year. Too unworldly, too ethereal to serve as pastor, he was not happy in the position, and he was also having doubts about his faith, even though Unitarianism was the most liberal religion in America. While at Harvard and afterward he had been pursuing his two main interests, German literature and music. His Divinity school dissertation, "On the Proper Character of Poetry and Music for Public Worship," was published in part in *American Monthly Magazine*. He also published several translations of German poems during the 1830s, culminating in 1839 in a book, *Select Minor Poems of Goethe and Schiller*.

Dwight's work with German poetry had important consequences. It established his scholarly reputation and opened doors for him throughout his life. The first was to the Transcendentalist club. Transcendental thought owed a profound debt to German writings, and many of the Transcendentalists were well versed in German literature. Dwight was invited to attend the "Symposia" at Emerson's house in 1836, and later he was the only musician invited to join the Saturday Club. In the Saturday Club intellect and power met. Formed to promote the exchange of ideas, it boasted some of the most powerful and wealthy men in Boston as well as most of its important literary figures, including Emerson, Henry W. Longfellow, and Nathaniel Hawthorne. Dwight was there not for his musical interests but for his reputation as a literary scholar. Bostonians came to love music, especially Beethoven, but to many of the elite it still did not have the intellectual prestige of the other arts.

After his ministerial fiasco Dwight was uncertain where to turn, when an unusual opportunity opened up. In 1841 George and Sophie Ripley decided to apply Transcendental thought to a bold experiment by creating a utopian community based on the ideas of the French socialist Charles Fourier. With about fifteen other Transcendentalists they established Brook Farm, a farming commune where labors would be shared and where principles of individual freedom and harmonious relationships would prevail. Dwight decided to join.

At first the experiment worked, and Dwight was put in charge of the farm's musical life and taught in its school. Although the members were expected to

labor eight to ten hours with farming tasks each day, they were more interested in artistic activities and entertainment than the condition of their fields.
Intellectually the commune was a rousing success, but in another sense that
doomed it from the beginning. Most of the members were urban intellectuals,
more at home with books than farm implements, more used to philosophical
discourse than practical land management, more interested in Shakespeare
than corn. By 1848 it was clear that the farm could no longer be sustained, and
the experiment ended.

While at Brook Farm, Dwight continued to write about music, mostly in
The Harbinger, for Brook Farm was close enough to Boston that Dwight was
able to attend many concerts. In fact, he often led outings so members of the
farm could attend, as if he were some sort of super camp counselor to the artistically starved intellectuals at the commune. As a consequence, Dwight published many reviews and a few other articles in *The Harbinger.* Dwight's review
of Beethoven's Seventh Symphony provides a vivid contrast between his and
Fuller's approach.

Whereas Fuller, on hearing Beethoven's Seventh symphony, sat down and
wrote a passionate, personal letter to Beethoven, Dwight chose to analyze the
work, discussing the continuity of the principal tonality of A and the economy
of rhythmic motives that provide unity. One must keep in mind the venues,
however: Fuller wrote in a private journal for herself, Dwight for publication.
Nevertheless, Dwight was clearly affected by the piece, and although he may
have tried to mask that emotion with technical language, what emerges from
the review is a profound sense of the mystery and depth of the composition.
There is no "fate knocks at the door" to guide the listener as in the Fifth Symphony, and consequently "to solve it one must have lived deeper and longer
than most of us." A New York program had suggested that the symphony
was about the fated lovers Orpheus and Eurydice, upon which Dwight hesitantly sought to amplify, not being entirely convinced himself. His conclusion,
while programmatic, is more ethereal, more symbolic, more Transcendental.
He compared the Seventh to the Fifth, which Dwight saw as "the great life-
struggle": the Seventh is more about victory, but of a special type, "a consecra-
tion of the faculties, and a production of such august beauty as not the yearn-
ing for, that he living in a higher sphere, alone could give. . . . The striving for
the infinite still marks Beethoven, but it is with calmer, clearer wisdom."

When confronted with Beethoven, Dwight could be as effusive as Fuller.
Dwight saw his reaction, however, not as personal but rather as representative
of Beethoven's effect upon the entire cosmos. In one essay Dwight explains
how music, especially Beethoven's, lifts people above themselves and creates

"one electric thrill [that] runs from heart to heart," finding the "one spirit in us all" that unites us.[25] In his discussion of the Seventh Symphony he goes even further, viewing Beethoven as prophet for a coming millennium:

> The music of Beethoven, we have said it more than once, is a presentiment of coming social harmony, a great hearts' confession of its faith, one of the nearest and clearest echoes of the approaching footsteps of the good genius of Humanity. He is the seventh note in the scale, the note which cries for the completion of the octave, the note whose correspondence is the passion of the soul for Order, the purified ambition, which no longer inverted and seeking only self-aggrandizement, contemplates a glorious hierarchy of all humanity, in which each, feeling his true place, and filling it, and led in it, may in one act help to complete and enjoy the universal accord, and this, in the only conceivable manner, satisfy the craving of each single soul to embrace the infinite at once.[26]

This is typical Dwight rhetoric, the assumption that however moved he is, however he reacts to music, he is speaking not for himself but for all mankind. In some respects Dwight knew that this was not true; he was aware of the popularity of a Henry Russell or a minstrel show, both of which he disparaged, and later he had a hard time admitting some modern music such as that of Wagner. Yet when it came to the classical masters Dwight heard in them something universal, and simply assumed that what he heard was universally shared. Dwight thus set himself up as everyman, although in reality he was a dreamy Transcendentalist, living in a rarefied world of aesthetic idealism far removed from the dynamic, industrial, Manifest Destiny–expanding, mercantile, Bible-thumping, slavery-torn country that characterized mid-nineteenth-century America.

Dwight was certain of a connection between Beethoven's reception and Transcendentalism. In 1881 Justin Winsor put together a *Memorial History of Boston,* a four-volume work that dealt with all aspects of the city, and he asked Dwight to write a chapter on music. Not surprisingly, Dwight discussed the importance of the Academy's performance of the Beethoven symphonies. He asked: Who was moved by these performances? Those with a musical background, he answered, those "trusting in authority," formed part of this privileged group. Most important, however, were those who belonged to what he called a "peculiar element then stirring in the intellectual and social life of this community, to minds in sympathy with what was idly called the 'Transcendental' movement." Dwight then noted that Beethoven and Emerson "came in, it may be said, together."[27]

In 1841 Dwight was asked to address the Harvard Musical Association, an organization that he had helped found in 1837.[28] There he articulated his beliefs about the nature of music. Dwight stated that music itself was sacred. He was careful, however, to distinguish music that he approved from music that he did not. Music whose purpose was mere entertainment—that is, most music that Americans would hear—was not true music but indulgence, belonging "to the ornamental, not the indispensable." Being an amusement, "it cannot enrich, ennoble, purify and perfect the powers and sensibilities of man"; it is "trivial and gay." True music, that is sacred music, was "elevating, purifying, love and faith-inspiring." The most sacred of all music was absolute instrumental music, and nowhere was God's vision more apparent than in Beethoven's symphonies. Are not some of the adagio movements of Beethoven's instrumental music "almost the very essence of prayer?—not formal prayer, I grant, but earnest, deep, unspeakable aspiration. Is not his music pervaded by such prayer?"[29]

Eight years later Dwight went even further with his idealistic view of music. Whereas Emerson saw God everywhere in his pantheist vision, Dwight saw him mainly in music. To Dwight, not only was all music sacred, not only was music religion, but it was the very voice of God: "It [music] is God's alphabet, and not man's." "It is the inbreathing of God, who is love." Music had the capacity to unite all mankind "at the heart of all things." Beethoven's music in particular is singled out: "Perhaps no music ever stirred profounder depths in the hearer's religious consciousness, than some great orchestral symphonies, say those of Beethoven." Dwight was apparently so moved by his sentiments regarding music and Beethoven especially that he closed this article on one grand, metaphor-crunching burst of excitement uncharacteristic of his typical ethereal, hovering prose: "His symphonies are like great conflagrations of some grand piles of architecture, in which the material substance seems consumed, while the spirit soars in the graceful but impatient crackling shapes of the devouring element, and is swiftly lost in upper air." Although this flash of rhetoric seems almost contradictory to his more sustained view of music as the voice of God, nevertheless Dwight by mid-century had elevated the music of Beethoven to a new level and established a vision of the composer that, in spite of many permutations, challenges, and much questioning, has lodged itself in the American psyche, where it may still be found today. More than any other person, Dwight defined Beethoven to Americans for at least the next 150 years.[30]

Dwight's view of Beethoven changed little after that—it is hard to conceive how he could have taken this line of thinking much further—but his influence had begun to spread in the 1840s and then increased considerably in the 1850s. In 1845 Albert Brisbain, proponent of Fourierism, the social theory upon which Brook Farm was built, invited Dwight to give a series of lectures on music in New York City, "on the genius and science of music." Brisbain, aware of the uncertain position that music held in his city, hoped that that would "give a deeper insight into the subject than is now possessed."[31] The *New York Tribune* publicized the lectures heavily, possibly because its editor, Horace Greeley, was sympathetic to the ideas of Fourierism. Dwight received a ten-inch column in Greeley's paper announcing the second lecture, and a glowing review of the series as a whole: "Mr. Dwight's lectures mark an epoch in the musical history of New York; for, although we have had the opportunity of hearing so much fine music, it is perhaps the first time that we have had a clear and wise assertion of the dignity and compass of the art."[32] The *Courier* and the *Inquirer,* however, not invested in them as the *Tribune* apparently was, panned them. At the least Dwight's appearance in New York and the press coverage he received expanded his reputation beyond Boston and introduced to New Yorkers a view of music that may not have been all too prevalent.

In 1851 Dwight conceived an ambitious project, a musical magazine that would "insist much on the claims of classical music and point out its beauties and meanings, not with a pedantic partiality, but because the *enduring* needs always to be held up in contrast to the ephemeral." Its tone would be "impartial, independent, catholic, conciliatory, aloof from musical clique and controversy." With financial support from the Harvard Musical Association, of which Dwight was president, and personal friends, *Dwight's Journal of Music* was launched on April 10, 1852. There had been at least two attempts at such a magazine before: the aforementioned *Euterpeiad,* from 1820 to 1823, and Theodore Hach's *Musical Magazine,* the real predecessor of Dwight's journal, from 1839 to 1841. Most musical magazines that existed in the nineteenth century were either collections of easy music for the dilettante or house organs of a music publisher, designed to advertise their wares.

The circulation of Dwight's journal and how extensive was its reach into musical America remain a mystery, but it was at least unique in its longevity. The fortunate musical magazines lasted perhaps two or three years; most folded in less than that. Dwight's survived for twenty-nine years, publishing altogether 1,051 issues. It received a major boost in 1858 when Oliver Ditson, one of the more prestigious publishing houses in America, agreed to publish it.

Throughout the tenure of the journal, Dwight continued to campaign for the classical masters, especially for Beethoven, a stance that did Beethoven much good but that did not serve Dwight well. In 1879 Dwight and Ditson had a serious disagreement about the direction of the journal; Ditson wanted

Dwight to be more sympathetic to modern music. After all, he reasoned, this was what Ditson was in the business of selling. Dwight, guided by his ideals, was immovable; he held his ground and as a consequence he and Ditson parted ways. Dwight was able to find another publisher, but the die was cast. After two more years, with flagging subscriptions and Dwight's own exhaustion, the last issue appeared on September 3, 1881. Encomiums, which often appear for the deceased, poured in, and at minimum they suggest that Dwight's journal was no local Boston affair. In addition to Boston newspapers, *Harper's Weekly*, the *New York Tribune*, the Cincinnati *Church's Musical Visitor*, the *London Figaro*, and the *London Musical Times* all lamented its loss. Whatever many may have felt about Dwight's views, geographically the journal had a long reach.

As Dwight's influence was on the wane, Beethoven found another champion in Theodore Thomas. Although Thomas had no connection with Transcendentalism, his feelings for Beethoven were as strong as Dwight's or Fuller's. They were important, because by the last decades of the nineteenth century Thomas had become the most powerful musician in America. Born in Essens, East Friesland, in 1835 (before Germany was a unified nation), Thomas immigrated to the United States in 1845 when his father, a town musician, felt a better life awaited in America. By this time Thomas had become an excellent violinist and already performed professional gigs. In order to help support his family Thomas was soon playing in theater orchestras in New York, and at age thirteen he enlisted in a navy band with his father. After one year he gained a discharge from the navy and began, on his own, a concert tour of the South. Now a young man of fourteen, Thomas acted as manager, entrepreneur, and performer: he would arrive in a town, secure a hall (usually the dining hall of a restaurant), put up posters announcing a concert by "Master T.T.," and collect money at the door before walking to the front of the room and performing. A surviving daguerreotype of Thomas at this time shows a young man of considerable poise and self-assurance, an almost cocky demeanor, one clearly certain of his abilities.

In 1850 Thomas returned to New York and began to play in various orchestras, quickly rising to concertmaster in Louis Eckert's ensemble. He joined the fledgling New York Philharmonic in 1854 and in 1857 began a series of chamber music concerts with the pianist William Mason and a few other musicians. They were billed as the "Mason and Thomas" concerts and are considered an important landmark in American musical history. At this time Thomas was twenty-two years old. In 1862 he formed his own orchestra and until 1888 toured extensively throughout the country with it, appearing in both large

FIGURE 2.2

Theodore Thomas at fifteen. Thomas became the most influential art-music conductor in the United States in the nineteenth century. His self-assured, almost cocky presence is apparent in this daguerreotype. Photo courtesy of The Newberry Library, Chicago. MMS Thomas Box 3, Folder 200A.

cities and small towns. The pace was hectic, and the list of places Thomas visited is staggering: between September 29 and November 18, 1874, Thomas's orchestra gave forty-eight concerts in cities ranging from Albany, New York, to Zanesville, Ohio. This tour included large cities such as Baltimore and Chicago, which he circled back to several times as he was blanketing the Midwest, and smaller towns such as Jacksonville, Illinois, and Fitchburg, Massachusetts. In the spring of 1884 he accomplished his most ambitious touring project, starting in New York, proceeding to San Francisco, then returning to Chicago, giving altogether sixty-five concerts. This became known as Thomas's "March to the Sea."[33]

Post–Civil War America saw many virtuosos undertake extensive tours throughout America, as the railroad finally stretched from coast to coast. For most, the pace was hectic and the schedule grueling. In spite of the prevalence of the railroad, it was an ordeal—trains did not move at twentieth-century speed, allowing little time for the artist to rest in any one place, and accommodations were often sketchy, even primitive in some towns. Often the only sleep possible was on a train itself. It was bad enough for a single virtuoso. That Thomas managed to do this with a forty-piece orchestra is nothing short of astounding. He refused to compromise on the road, insisting that he appear always with his full orchestra. One can only imagine the stir caused by forty-plus classical musicians, many of whom were German, arriving with their instruments in a small town such as Keokuk or Fort Dodge, Iowa.

In spite of this touring schedule, Thomas also managed to serve at the same time as music director of the New York Philharmonic, the American Opera Company, the Brooklyn Philharmonic Society, and the May Festival in Cincinnati, and for one year as director of the Cincinnati College of Music, in addition to other independent conducting jobs. He created enough stir that in 1869 P. T. Barnum attempted to sign him to become part of his "menagerie." Thomas was flattered that Barnum was willing to place him "advantageously before the public, beside the fat woman and the elephants," but he graciously declined the offer.[34]

In 1889 Thomas Norman Fay, a Chicago merchant, asked Thomas if he would be willing to come to Chicago if the city could guarantee him a permanent orchestra. Thomas is reported to have replied, "I would go to hell if they gave me a permanent orchestra." Soon a group of wealthy citizens, led by Fay, formed the Chicago Orchestral Association, the forerunner of today's Chicago Symphony Orchestra, and Thomas became its first musical director. In spite of some early difficulties, Thomas and the orchestra succeeded and he remained there until a stroke suddenly took his life in 1905.

When it came to programming, Thomas was uncompromising.[35] Among the moderns he became an important champion of Wagner, but Beethoven held a special place for him. Beethoven was, according to the conductor's friend of many years, George Putnam Upton, his favorite composer. He felt Beethoven reached everyone, rich or poor. In an interview Thomas commented: "Take Beethoven's music, it is something more than mere pleasure; it is education, thought, emotion, love, and hope. I do not doubt that when my orchestra plays one of his symphonies, every soul in the audience is stirred in a different way and by a different suggestion. I care not from what station in life come the thousands who sit back of me. Beethoven will touch each according to his needs."[36]

Thomas discovered to his surprise that residents in many of the smaller towns in mid-America wanted to hear serious repertoire, not light fare. In 1883 residents of St. Joseph, Missouri, and Burlington, Iowa, telegraphed Thomas asking him to substitute Beethoven symphonies for some of the more popular pieces scheduled. According to Charles Locke, who helped arrange the tour, "The musical culture showed throughout the West by the enthusiastic reception of the best classical music was a surprise to Mr. Thomas and the whole company. It was a discriminating interest that was shown, and not an interest worked up because it is 'the thing' to admire classical music."[37]

When speaking of Beethoven and instrumental music, Thomas could sound almost Transcendental: "The man who does not know Shakespeare is to be pitied; and the man who does not understand Beethoven and has not been under his spell has not half lived his life. The master works of instrumental music are the language of the soul and express more than those of any other art."[38] This statement bears echoes of Dwight, who, writing in full Transcendentalist mode for *The Harbinger,* had commented, "When you have heard Beethoven, you are a changed man."[39]

Even though Thomas was hardly the quiet contemplative Transcendental type—he could be brash, blunt, and bullying—like the Transcendentalists, nature satisfied a special need for him. He had a home, Felsengarten, in the New Hampshire mountains where he would spend his summers and where, he acknowledged, he got his inspiration: "Nature is all music, and whatever she whispers to us is the heart of melody and the soul of rhythm. Some of us are lucky enough to catch a few of her disjointed words, and are allowed to tell them to our brothers. That is called inspiration."[40]

For some symphony orchestras Beethoven was a presence that loomed over them and the audience literally. A photograph of the Boston Symphony Orchestra, taken in 1891 when Arthur Nikisch was conductor, shows a full sym-

FIGURE 2.3 ABOVE

Boston Symphony Orchestra in Boston Music Hall, 1891, with the statue of Beethoven looming over the orchestra. The hall was the home of the BSO until 1900.

FIGURE 2.4 BELOW

Boston Symphony Hall, the home of the BSO since 1900. The medallion above the proscenium bears Beethoven's name. Photo courtesy of Edward Dunne.

phony orchestra by modern standards, dominated by a statue of Beethoven behind the players. That is what the audience would see as they watched a performance, no matter what the composition.[41] When the new Boston Symphony Hall, the current home of the Boston Symphony Orchestra, was built in 1900, the statue came down, probably in order to make room for a pipe organ, but Beethoven's presence remained. A large, elaborate gold medallion above the proscenium has engraved in the middle of it one word, Beethoven.[42]

Part of Beethoven's appeal in the nineteenth century was the way in which he broke gender barriers. Throughout the century, writer after writer commented on how masculine Beethoven's music was. As early as 1820 John Rowe Parker reprinted two articles from British magazines, a common practice at this time. The first, titled "Modern Music," referred to Beethoven's "strength and rudeness," how he has entered "the darkest recesses of modulation," and observed how, thanks to Beethoven, music was "now masculizing in the regions of the earth." The second speaks of how Beethoven has entered "upon the rugged domain of dissonance," and how they are remarkable for "a certain brilliancy and masculine energy of style." Even though these comments originated in Europe, Parker's choice to reprint them indicates that he believed they resonated for the new country. Curiously, in the early twentieth century, when the composer Charles Ives was attempting to rescue music from the "pansies," he believed it was through dissonance and clashing harmony that music could be made masculine. Beethoven and Parker apparently got there some eighty years earlier.[43]

In 1842, William W. Story delivered the annual address to the Harvard Musical Association. Much of it consisted of a poetic description of Beethoven's Fifth Symphony, which he called "the work of his complete manhood." He then described the symphony as a struggle, with Beethoven eventually triumphing over fate. It was in many ways the Horatio Alger metaphor for the nineteenth-century man. About the same time, John Knowles Paine, the first music professor at Harvard University, spoke of Beethoven's "manly character and elevated ideas."[44] This entire line of thinking, however, did not reach its apex until the twentieth century when W. J. Henderson, in reference to the Fifth, claimed that Beethoven celebrated "not a man, but manhood," and saw the work as "the expression of the superman."[45] Even though Henderson wrote this to celebrate the centennial of Beethoven's death in 1927, his thinking is a product of the Gilded Age. He was born in 1855, began writing for newspapers when he was fifteen, and held the position of music critic for the *New York Times* from 1887 to 1902.

This particular framing of Beethoven contradicted prevailing nineteenth-century thought that held that certain spheres of activity belonged to men and others to women. At the broadest level, the world of work and business, and by extension the public sphere, was for men. The home, the raising of children and the guardianship of morals, was the province of women. Music belonged to women's sphere. The essayist Park Benjamin explained that music and painting "depend most upon qualities which are rather attributes of the female character than of the sterner and less sensitive."[46] A few years later a Mrs. Child commented in the same magazine, "Music is the soprano, the feminine principle, the heart of the universe."[47]

An important component of the gender distinction was between the active and passive. A man was meant to act; he was to be found in public securing the necessary means to support a family. It was a rough, difficult, and not always morally upright environment he had to negotiate, but not to do so was possibly the worst blotch a man could have on his character. Breadwinner in the family was not only the most important role he played, but that which defined his manliness and, indeed, his entire person.

Women were to be passive and reflective, softer, sensitive, and delicate. They were expected to guard the home from the corrupting influence of the outside world, and to maintain propriety at all times. Instilling virtue in children was critical, not only for girls but for boys as well, for whom success later in life depended heavily on character. The historian Robert Wiebe observed that if the perfect mother didn't exist, "if mother actually drank and cursed and broke up the furniture, she had to be replaced (figuratively) or invented."[48] The ideal woman was the ideal mother, and her domain was the home.

A man who indulged himself in the arts, who engaged in pursuing a career in music, was looked upon askance, as if lacking the proper manhood. A fictional character, Aunt Tabitha, gave "fireside chats" in the journal *Godey's Lady's Book*. In one she advised her nephew to give up his habit of writing poetry while in college: "According to my way of thinkin', when a young man gets into a notion of making varses, singin' songs, and fiddlin' and dancin', he's a poor critter; and, if I was a gal, I wouldn't have him for husband a bit sooner than I'd cut one of my fingers off."[49] As a boy in the 1880s, Charles Ives faced acute embarrassment when he had to stay in and practice the piano when other boys were out playing. He developed a strong veneer of masculinity to cover his musical talent: when someone heard about it and asked him what he played, he would answer, "Shortstop." Later, he constantly railed against "sissies" and the emasculation of music, and he chose specifically not to pursue a musical career because it clashed with his strong sense of responsibility to provide for his family. Knowing that his music was too harsh to be readily accepted by much of the public, he commented, "If he [a musician] has a nice wife and some nice children, how can he let the children starve on his dissonances." Ives was acting on core nineteenth-century notions of gender.

This, of course, does not mean that men did not pursue musical careers. One of the ironies of the separate-sphere doctrine was that women should not appear in public even though they may have had immense musical talent. The concert stage was overwhelmingly male. Much of the gender tension was removed, however, because most of the professional musicians in the nineteenth century were foreign. After the unrest in Germany in 1848, large numbers of German musicians flooded into the United States, and they soon came to dominate the world of classical music. That was not a problem in their adopted homeland, however; they were not Americans and consequently the gender strictures seemed not to apply.

American men did participate in music, sometimes as players, as long as it was on the right instruments and more often as concert attendees. Concert attendance was perfectly acceptable in part because women needed an escort. A respectable woman simply did not attend a concert alone. For some men it was a duty that they accepted as inevitable. For others it was a pleasure, and the need to escort wives, daughters, or women friends gave them a cover—they did not compromise their masculinity. For young men courting, it was an important gesture, all part of the delicate mating game that is universally played out under both expressed and understood rules. For the up-and-coming young man of the Gilded Age who was not born into his situation, advice books flooded the market, explaining carefully and in great detail his expected behavior.

Gendered behavior extended to the choice of instruments. For men, particularly in smaller towns, the most common role was wind instrumentalist. Winds were closely associated with military bands, usually with a local militia. Since virtually every town had a militia, performance in the band was considered acceptable. The many military bands of the Civil War era gave further impetus to this trend. Outside the band, however, the flute was considered the proper instrument for gentlemen, and the upper classes looked down upon string instruments, as they were associated mostly with dance music. The German Francis Grund, who lived in the United States from 1827 to 1836, observed that he did not hear a single amateur play the violin during his entire stay; gentlemen confined themselves to the flute. Samuel Jennison reported that during his four years at Harvard, from 1835 to 1839, he knew of only two string players, one violinist and one cellist. Members of the Pierian Sodality, an amateur music club at Harvard, persuaded the violinist to set his instrument aside and take up the flute. He was lucky; at least he got in. Earlier, in 1830, the Arionic Sodality, another undergraduate musical organization, "voted that a nondescript freshman . . . heard scraping a fiddle be neglected," that is, turned down.[50] In his 1826 "Address on Church Music," Lowell Mason advocated the use of instruments in church. In the absence of an organ, the instrument he considered the most desirable, Mason favored the violoncello. He admitted that he wanted to favor the violin, but he could not because of its too many "irrelevant associations." To Mason irrelevant meant secular, profane, or vulgar.[51]

String instruments came more into favor later in the century, possibly because of the immigration of German musicians who demonstrated what strings could do, but they remained masculine instruments. Ladies were not expected to play them, although many did, as witnessed by the orchestras of many women's clubs. A proper woman had three musical possibilities open to her: piano was the most important, since by the Gilded Age a piano was a customary piece of furniture in the parlor of any middle- or upper-class home. Here the lady of the house presided, proper music being an important component of setting the proper moral atmosphere for the home. Girls were taught to play, not only for their own adult lives when they established a home, but as an important part of their contribution to the mating ritual. The study of voice was also acceptable, and a third route was the guitar. Throughout much of the nineteenth century the guitar was considered a female instrument.

For both sexes, however, performance was not to be taken too seriously. A young woman could develop extensive talent, but marriage often meant an end to serious practice. In any event, public appearances were out of the question. A man could engage in music as long as it remained strictly an avocation, and as long as it did not take up too much of his time. For a man to make it his career was a different matter.

Although Margaret Fuller was too discreet to ever refer explicitly to the masculine nature of Beethoven's music, it is hard not to read her thoughts, especially in the private letter to Beethoven, as anything but a reaction to the masculine power and force of Beethoven symphonies. In a more public forum, she referred to the "colossal gesture" that characterizes Beethoven's music.[52] Her terminology was appropriate; Beethoven as a colossus and an Übermensch align perfectly with the virile dynamism that underlay the Gilded Age.

3

Deification and Spiritualization

*T*HANKS ESPECIALLY TO JOHN S. DWIGHT, a Beethoven performance in nineteenth-century America became more than a musical event, but a sacralized, uplifting experience, a moment not only of transcendence but of communion with the Almighty himself. Beyond sacralization the only step left for Beethoven was deification, and by the early twentieth century Beethoven was viewed in both Europe and America as, if not a god, at least a pure, moral being somewhere above the world that normal men inhabit. In 1925 Eugen D'Albert echoed the American image of Beethoven when he eulogized the composer in advance of the centennial of his death: "Unassailable, spotless, immeasurably strong in the depths of his spirit, he stands alone. In his unfathomableness and sublimity he is like the ocean. See it well forth from its deepest depths, breaking into foam and calling with a voice of thunder; then, soft and gay as a little child, smoothing itself out before our delighted eyes. Such was Beethoven's elemental nature, such his pure and beautiful soul."[1]

In Germany, sculptor Max Klinger draped Beethoven in a Roman toga and created a Beethoven-as-Zeus sitting majestically on a throne. In France, José de Charmoy designed a Beethoven monument that portrayed the composer with a bare, muscular torso and an idealized head that resembled more a Greek god than a nineteenth-century musician, looking down at humanity from atop a giant pedestal. Such images in general might not sit well in a democratic

American society, but would they be unacceptable as a statement about Beethoven?

The French sculptor Émile-Antoine Bourdelle cast several large bronze heads of Beethoven that similarly glorified him, one of which the Metropolitan Museum of Art in New York acquired in 1927. In their bulletin the curators proudly described their purchase: Beethoven was a great man "suffering, silent, grim, determined," the head, "majestically, broodingly embryonic . . . there is in this head something of the abbozzo, of the ideal unattained, of incompletion confronted with human frailty." At the base of the sculpture Bourdelle had inscribed, "Moi je suis Bacchus qui pressure pour les hommes le nectar delicieux" (I am Bacchus who presses for men the delicious nectar). There is little question what the museum thought of this depiction: they placed the sculpture at the top of the main stairway of the museum.

It is no coincidence that the piece was acquired and exhibited in 1927, for this was the centennial of Beethoven's death, accompanied by commemorative events throughout the Western world. In the United States, Columbia Records spearheaded the efforts, recruiting a committee chaired by George Eastman that included, as the label bragged, "twenty-two college Presidents and educators." The committee was in close contact with and undoubtedly took ideas from the Beethoven Committee of Vienna, which had been assembled to for the same purpose.

The American committee made elaborate plans to celebrate Beethoven throughout the week of March 20–26 (Beethoven died on March 26) in 500 cities in the United States. In Boston, Serge Koussevitzky served up a seven-concert feast that included all nine symphonies, the *Missa Solemnis,* as well as assorted string quartets, piano sonatas, and other chamber music. Walter Damrosch, conductor of the New York Symphony Orchestra, appeared as pianist with the violinist Harold Baur to premiere a piano-violin arrangement of the *Grosse Fuge.* Damrosch also conducted two performances of the Ninth Symphony.

For record companies, the Beethoven celebration was a public relations bonanza. The whirlwind of activity that followed the development of electronic recording techniques in the mid-1920s created a highly competitive situation for the big three, Columbia, RCA, and Decca. Columbia distributed Beethoven's complete symphonies and most of his string quartets, trios, sonatas, overtures, and concertos to radio stations throughout the country, urging them to devote Beethoven week to those recordings.

The American commemorative committee had other initiatives as well. Plans called for a sermon on "the religious aspects of Beethoven's music" and an "address on the civic influence of music," to be distributed to religious and civic

MOI JE SUIS
BACCHUS QUI
PRESSURE POUR
LES HOMMES LE
NECTAR DELICIEUX

leaders, including mayors. Commemorative exercises, lectures, and tributes were to be given in schools, churches, and community organizations. As part of Koussevitzky's Boston celebration, one evening featured testimonials and an address by the British Beethoven scholar Ernest Newman. In New York, Bishop Manning held a mass at the Cathedral of St. John the Divine "entirely devoted to Beethoven." Damrosch gave two lectures, one on Beethoven's Fifth Symphony, another on the Ninth. In over 350 cities, thousands of church services honored Beethoven with such sermons titles as "Beethoven's Claim to Immortality," "Music and Religion; in Honor of the Beethoven Centenary," and "The Life and Work of Beethoven."[2] At the Hotel Ambassador in New York, letters from seven governors eulogizing Beethoven were read.[3]

Olin Downes, music critic for the *New York Times*, attempted to put Beethoven in historical perspective, only to succeed in placing him beyond history. Acknowledging the different schools of composition that existed in 1927, the classic, the Romantic, and the "vaguely term[ed] 'moderns' or 'ultra-moderns,'" Downes found Beethoven outside them all: "He stands alone, four-square to the universe, beyond either time or classification." Downes saw in Beethoven what D'Albert did: he stood beyond time "because the soul was so great and because the man succeeded so marvelously in writing music direct, unadorned, from the very bottom of that soul. Beethoven is Beethoven, brooding, gigantic." Beethoven's music is "as confounding as the daily yet miraculous phenomena of nature."[4]

Writing in *The Musical Quarterly* one month later, Edward J. Dent was even more direct: "Beethoven has become a religion." He also indicated that this attitude was not confined to America: "It is a matter of historical fact that Beethoven, more than any other musician, brought about that religious attitude towards music in general which has been prevalent for half a century or more in Teutonic and Anglo-Saxon countries."[5]

The commemorative committee also commissioned a centennial essay by the composer and music critic Daniel Gregory Mason to be distributed free to mayors, religious leaders, other officials, and schools throughout the country.

FIGURE 3.1

Émile-Antoine Bourdelle, *Head of Beethoven*, acquired by the New York Metropolitan Museum of Art in 1927. The French inscription translates as "I am Bacchus who presses for men the delicious nectar." Image copyright © The Metropolitan Museum of Art / Art Resource, New York.

Mason's essay, designed to set the tone for the celebrations, was curiously of another stripe. Mason was notorious for his anti-modernist views but is here the modernist. He is cool, distant, and analytical in his approach to Beethoven. Above all, he is the erudite professor lecturing his students about the stuff of music history. He is restrained, ever intellectual, and slightly condescending as he categorizes genres, historical influences, structures, and biography. His language smacks of academia. He divides Beethoven's instrumental music not into four types, not into four genres (much too sophisticated a term), but rather into four departments: solo piano, chamber, orchestral, and solo with orchestra. Possibly Mason, already a professor at Columbia, had his eye on the MacDowell chair he was soon to inherit, and he was already thinking how to reorganize its Department of Music.

Mason also acts the Ivy League elitist, disdaining the popular and giving thanks that Beethoven never descended to such a level. Yet to Mason, Beethoven is neither highbrow nor lowbrow; his music is "for all sincere and intelligent men and women." The closest Mason comes to unearthing spiritual values in Beethoven is his admission that in Beethoven is the sublime. He finds it not in the music, however, but in Beethoven's ability to overcome his deafness and to continue, with patience and by force of will and discipline, to turn out great music. Unfortunately, Mason quickly drops that point as he digresses into one of his many rants about the poverty of the moderns who have all the technology but are unable to equal what Beethoven did.

Seven years before, Mason had written another commemoration essay on Beethoven, this for the 150th year of his birth. Here is a Romantic Mason, interested in expression and with a vocabulary to match. He speaks of Beethoven's "long-maintained breathless pianissimo, sudden violent contrasts," and describes his music as heroic, romantic, tragic, pastoral, corybantic, bacchanalian, deeply humane, and religious. Mason fully buys into the Romantic image of the great artist succeeding in spite of, and because of, great suffering: "To every perceiving heart he becomes a symbol of our tragic humanity, which has to traverse pain to find happiness, and to which beauty is revealed only after far journeyings." The change in Mason from 1920 to 1927 mirrors the change in Beethoven's stock among the moderns, the one group that did not espouse the spiritual or the Romantic Beethoven. More than anything, the moderns wanted to distance themselves from the excessive emotionalism of Romanticism with which Beethoven was too identified, although, as we will see, they could never quite give him up.

Amidst the eulogies, celebrations, and deifications of 1927, one small book by a British writer ultimately had a greater impact on Beethoven thought on both sides of the Atlantic than possibly any other written at that time. In *Beethoven, His Spiritual Development*, J. W. N. Sullivan did not create the notion that Beethoven's music is spiritual, but he defined the spiritual in Beethoven for the twentieth century.

Sullivan was an unlikely candidate to write a book probing Beethoven's spiritual life. He was neither a musician nor a music scholar, and he had nothing to do with religion, either mystical or mainstream. He was known as a writer on science, an autodidact who had little formal training in mathematics or physics, but was precocious enough to be one of the few people in England to understand the intricate equations and reasoning behind Einstein's general theory of relativity when it first appeared. His ability to translate relativity into language that the educated layman could understand secured his reputation as a science writer and gave birth to the belief that he was a physicist. As a consequence, Sullivan gained entrée into the highest intellectual circles in England, in particular becoming a close friend of Aldous Huxley.[6]

Sullivan claimed to be Irish, brought up in Maynooth, Ireland, and educated by Jesuits for the priesthood. The Jesuits schooled him on Thomas Aquinas until they became convinced that with his superior intellect he would soon become a skeptic, which turned out to be prescient. As a consequence he was dismissed and eventually made his way to England. But this autobiographical sketch, which Huxley as well as Sullivan's second wife believed, is a complete fabrication: Sullivan was born and grew up in East London, the son of a former seaman who became an official in a Protestant mission. Sullivan's father did not learn to read or write until he was eighteen, and Sullivan himself left school when he was fourteen. In class-conscious England, Sullivan probably did not want his lowly origins known.

Sullivan claims to have been interested in music from a very young age, but the extent of his training is unknown. He described his young years: "As a boy I lived in a sort of perpetual day-dream. My great preoccupations were mathematics and music. I was taught music from a very early age—six or seven, I believe. Mathematics I discovered for myself."[7] Sullivan does not elaborate on his musical training—not that he is to be believed.

Sullivan had Beethoven on his mind some years before his book appeared in 1927. In a letter to his friend Middleton Murray in 1922, he referred to a book about Beethoven that he was writing, and in the same year he wrote a lengthy review of H. E. Krehbiel's English translation of Alexander Wheelock Thayer's biography, *The Life of Ludwig van Beethoven*, which had just appeared the year before. It is ironic that Thayer's study, still considered the gold standard of Beethoven biography, was written in German by an American in the nineteenth century but did not come out in English until Krehbiel's 1921 translation. At the conclusion of Sullivan's review he adumbrates what would become some of the central themes of his own Beethoven study:

> The unearthly serenity that we find in [Beethoven's] late music is the crown of a struggle that faced everything, avoided nothing, and which overcame. We see just what he meant when he reproached Goethe for being moved to tears by music. He jumped up and spoke scornfully. "Artists are fiery; they do not weep," said Beethoven. It was the fire, and not the tears, which enabled Beethoven to be triumphant. It is the history of this process which would be the real Life of Beethoven.[8]

Sullivan drew upon his experience with science to justify his investigation of the spiritual world of Beethoven, arguing that recent scientific developments—relativity theory, in particular—if nothing else reveal the limitations of science, proving how little we actually know about reality. Thus Sullivan the scientist can legitimately consider Beethoven's spiritual realm.

Sullivan assumed that Beethoven's life and character and music were intricately bound together: "I believe that in his greatest music Beethoven was primarily concerned to express his personal vision of life." Sullivan sought to explore how Beethoven's vision developed, particularly how the unfolding of his life affected and ultimately determined what he wrote. Sullivan was not interested in correlating events and compositions; as he states, "the life-work of a great artist is not some kind of sumptuous diary." Rather, he examined Beethoven's inner life, his "spiritual development," and used events only as they affected and shaped Beethoven's person and character.[9]

Sullivan distinguishes three different types of music: pure, spiritual, and programmatic. Pure music is music with no referent, in which the listener simply takes delight in the combination of sounds being heard. Program music has a specific referent, although that does not mean it describes something. Such music "communicates musical experiences analogous to extra-musical experiences that may be associated with some definite external situation." In other words, it communicates the composer's reaction to the object or event; it does not depict the event. Spiritual music occupies the highest rung in Sullivan's ordering of musical values, communicating "valuable spiritual states" or "spiritual experiences." The line between the spiritual, the pure, and the programmatic is not always clear and depends upon the composer's own spiritual growth. In fact, Sullivan admits that "all the greatest music in the world, and some of the worst, does suggest a spiritual context." Thus spirituality in music does not equate with greatness in music, but to Sullivan life and music inexorably mix.[10]

Beethoven's suffering is the key to his spirituality. As Beethoven's life unfolded and his suffering increased, with his deafness, his loneliness, and his gradual retreat from society, Beethoven's music deepened in spiritual content. Important milestones along the way were the *Eroica*, the Razumovsky Quartets, the *Hammerklavier* Sonata, the Ninth Symphony, and the late string quartets.

Sullivan dismissed the Napoleonic connection with the *Eroica* and saw in the symphony instead a reflection of the Heiligenstadt Testament, the lengthy letter Beethoven wrote to his brothers in which he confesses his growing deafness and his determination to continue as an artist. To Sullivan, no matter how much Beethoven contemplated Napoleon as hero, the profound understanding of the heroic that the *Eroica* exemplifies could only have come from personal experience. The *Eroica* is Beethoven's musical statement of his despair and the subsequent defiance of his fate by turning to creation as Beethoven promised in the Heiligenstadt Testament. The symphony captures Beethoven's spiritual state at the time and represents a gigantic step in his spiritual growth. Like many other writers, Sullivan also believes that musically the piece was a turning point, although for different reasons than most: "The whole work is a most close-knit psychological unit. Never before in music has so important, manifold, and completely coherent an experience been communicated."[11]

Beethoven, however, had not yet reached that point where he could express his inner state directly. Napoleon served as an important deflection, and Beethoven's use of stock musical types such as the funeral march in the second movement suggests a public ceremony rather than any introspective expression. This same issue pervades the Fifth Symphony as well, which up to Sullivan's time was considered Beethoven's most powerful emotional statement until the Ninth. In reference to Beethoven's alleged comment about the opening notes of the Fifth, "Thus fate knocks at the door," Sullivan argues that the Fifth Symphony is not about experience but about a concept, fate, "that conditions experience." Throughout the heroic decade, the years roughly 1802–1812, Beethoven was therefore coming to terms with his spiritual self but was not yet capable of the direct, unembellished expression of it.

Sullivan believed that Beethoven's firm belief in the "morality of power" during the heroic decade limited his spiritual development. Beethoven had written, in a letter to Nikolaus Zmeskall, that "power is the morality of men who loom above the others, and it is also mine."[12] Although not a misanthrope, Beethoven did hold many men in contempt, an attitude that served him well in a time of revolution, as he was able to challenge the aristocratic restraints under which Haydn was willing to remain, and from which Mozart never successfully broke. He saw himself as a superior being, deserving the respect and adulation that comes with genius. Yet ultimately Beethoven achieved his fame not because of his ability to convert the morality of power into compositions of great strength and expressiveness, but, according to Sullivan, because "a greater destiny was reserved for him."

Before that could be attained, however, Beethoven had to work out the conflict of his deafness and the loneliness that ensued, his desire to succeed and the necessity of finding a different path than the virtuoso composer-performer and his conception of the heroic, which remained Promethean. To Sullivan the search for that path occurred primarily in the string quartets, a much more intimate, introspective medium than the symphonies, which present the hero publically before the entire world. The search began in the three Razumovsky Quartets, particularly in their slow movements. By the third of the quartets Beethoven is drawing on the deepest recesses of his being to uncover something almost atavistic: "It is as if some racial memory had stirred in him, referring to some forgotten and alien despair. There is here a remote and frozen anguish, wailing over some implacable destiny. This is hardly human suffering; it is more like a memory from some ancient and starless night of the soul."[13]

By 1812 the spiritual struggle, if not resolved, was "taken for granted and ignored."[14] Sullivan finds the Seventh and Eighth Symphonies, written in 1812, remarkable in their absence of suffering. This moment was not to last long, however, as events that followed presented Beethoven entirely new challenges. First was the situation with the "Immortal Beloved," the appellation Beethoven gave to an unnamed woman in a passionate love letter that indicated Beethoven thought he had found a deep, reciprocal love. It turned out not to be so, and to this day scholars are uncertain of her identity. Then came the death of his brother Kasper Carl, and the fight between Beethoven and Carl's wife, Johanna, over custody of Beethoven's nephew Karl. This conflict resulted in years of litigation, and Beethoven's tempestuous relationships with both Karl and Johanna were to occupy him the rest of his life. (Anyone who has seen the movie *Immortal Beloved,* however, should know that while the identification of the Immortal Beloved is still in dispute, we can say unequivocally that she was *not* Johanna.)

Beethoven had reached a spiritual nadir by 1817. The years 1812–1817 had been remarkably unproductive by Beethoven's standards, but amidst the relatively barren compositional landscape of the teens, the *Hammerklavier* Sonata appeared in 1817.[15] To Sullivan it stands alone, in neither Beethoven's second nor third period. It is testimony to a man without hope, a statement of a man who has drained his resources, whose world has come to an end. It is the work of a man in transition, one who has come to "the end of a process, an end that contains within itself no new beginning," but who must go through the depths of suffering before he can reach the higher level of consciousness manifested in the late quartets.[16]

Beethoven was never a regular churchgoer, except as a youth when his job as organist necessitated his presence, but in the last decade of his life religious music was much on his mind. He studied the medieval church modes and based at least one quartet movement on them; he sought in vain to obtain a copy of Bach's B-minor Mass; and, most important, he completed his own *Missa Solemnis*, one of his largest and most important compositions. It stands with the Ninth Symphony as the two gigantic works from the first half of the 1820s. Yet for Sullivan these pieces reveal a public Beethoven, one who continues "to address his fellow men as one of them."[17] With the late quartets, Sullivan believes Beethoven enters a new phase in which he is beyond human suffering, living in an isolated world apart from ordinary human life, alone with his thoughts and his inner sounds. The late quartets are a manifestation of the final step in a spiritual journey, whereupon Beethoven has arrived at a state of almost mystical consciousness. The journey can be seen in even the chronological ordering of the quartets. The first of this series, op. 132, is that of a man who still feels human suffering. With op. 130 and op. 131 Beethoven arrives at transcendence. (Opus numbers, listing order of publication, do not always conform to order of composition.) Sullivan believes that even the *Grosse Fuge* of op. 133, gnawing, grating, teeming with a sense of terror, is of a man who has come to accept his own condition. In it, "Beethoven had come to realize that his creative energy, which he at one time opposed to his destiny, in reality owed its very life to that destiny." Like many writers, Sullivan finds the C-sharp minor quartet, op. 131, to be Beethoven's most spiritual outpouring, where Beethoven's mystic vision reaches its pinnacle. That leaves only the last quartet, op. 135, a lighter, more transparent composition, one of a man who has come to terms with his existence, "fundamentally at peace."[18]

The spirituality that Sullivan ascribes to Beethoven is not religious in the Western sense but reminiscent of spiritual journeys of many Eastern religions, although Sullivan does not overtly say so. Beethoven's quest, similar to a Buddhist's search for enlightenment, could come about only through suffering, until finally a state is reached where pride, ego, and worldly existence are left behind. It is a vision at odds with the Romantic conception of Beethoven, which owes more to the heroic personage, the author of the Heiligenstadt Testament. The Romantics depicted a Promethean Beethoven, a composer defying his fate, even on his deathbed, where he is found suddenly opening his eyes and shaking his fist at a thunderstorm before falling back, dead. Sullivan's Beethoven is not Klinger's giant sitting on a throne, or Bourdelle's head looming above the main stairway of the Metropolitan Museum of Art. He is closer to the transcendental figure that John S. Dwight depicts, a composer whose music, by its very abstractness, connects with a pantheistic God, but without the transcendental emphasis on God.

In one sense, Sullivan's concept of spirituality through suffering connects to a tradition that predates Romanticism, the eighteenth-century notion of the sublime. Edmund Burke and Immanuel Kant had distinguished between the sublime and the beautiful. To oversimplify a complex and nuanced argument, the beautiful was pleasant but the sublime was profound. While the beautiful elicits feelings of pleasure, the sublime embodies a sense of awe and terror. Sublime emotions, however, produce a deeper reaction to artistic works and ultimately a sense of the noble. These terms were also gendered: the beautiful was associated more with the female, the sublime more than the male. This aspect is discussed further in chapter 6.[19]

In another sense, Sullivan's depiction is little more than Romantic cliché: the artist must suffer to create. Unlike the nineteenth-century Bohemians who inhabited the garrets of Paris or the small islands in the Mediterranean, however, suffering for Beethoven involved more than an unencumbered poverty. It was a struggle against the body itself, against the debilitation of those very physical qualities that musicians pride most. Yet the extent of Beethoven's physical infirmities, of which deafness was only one, as well as his mental instability, his rages, his paranoia, only enhance his Romantic image. Beethoven's suffering was more than sufficient to grant him an honored place in the Romantic pantheon.

While musicians and writers did not always mention Sullivan throughout the rest of the twentieth century, his presence loomed over it like a giant ethereal force, seeping into this crack and that crack, shaping performances, interpretations, and perceptions of Beethoven, or simply giving legitimacy to a view that seemed at odds with the prevailing hard-edged modernism that had come to dominate American musical thought. Many writers, trained to acknowledge intellectual debts, did refer specifically to Sullivan. Daniel Gregory Mason considered Sullivan "clairvoyant of Beethoven's mental processes." Robert

Haven Schauffler's popular biography, *Beethoven: The Man Who Freed Music,*
which appeared ten years after Sullivan's book, has the imprint of Sullivan all
over it. He cites Sullivan's discussion of several pieces, such as the *Hammerklavier* Sonata, the String Quartet op. 131, and at times he quotes Sullivan at
length. Beyond the specific references, his book attempts to do much what Sullivan did, to probe the deeper meaning of Beethoven's life and works. In doing
so he draws on many of Sullivan's ideas, such as the greater depth, intelligence,
and capacity for synthesis that Beethoven possessed, his emphasis on Beethoven's deafness and suffering, and the spiritual synthesis found in the late quartets as well as the singular importance of the *Hammerklavier* Sonata. Even in
the twenty-first century, scholars who have little truck with spiritual issues
have found Sullivan's discussions about specific pieces insightful.[20] And while
many writers have found Sullivan convincing, even many who have not have
found they could not ignore him.

Ralph Wood dismissed Sullivan as irrelevant mainly because he was writing for dilettantes and did not discuss music in technical terms. Wood's argument was that since Beethoven was a musician, the only meaning that matters is musical meaning for musicians. Much later, Robert Hatten dismissed
Sullivan's interpretations as "musings." Hatten, who advocated a semiotic approach to Beethoven, wanted interpretations with a strong theoretical basis.
Writing about the same time as Hatten, Kevin Korsyn looked more favorably
upon Sullivan, as scholars were returning to a discussion of musical meaning.
Like Hatten, however, he wanted a more logical, verifiable process, and advocated the use of literary models, which are "vulnerable to deconstruction."[21]

Most musicians did not reference Sullivan directly, but the presence of a
spiritual element in Beethoven's music was perceived as at least evocative in
their performances. Arturo Toscanini, arguably the best-known conductor of
the early and mid-twentieth century, believed that his job was to subjugate his
own musical instincts to those of Beethoven, to interpret the score literally, in
effect to channel Beethoven. According to one writer, in a 1927 performance
he succeeded: "He was no longer Toscanini, but Ludwig van Beethoven—the
Beethoven of the surging First and the grandiose Ninth Symphonies. . . .
Beethoven was in his eyes, his fingertips, his baton."[22]

Leonard Bernstein, if anything, went even beyond Sullivan. In an imagined
scene he called "Bull Session in the Rockies," Bernstein suggested that Beethoven was merely a cipher, writing down what was conceived in heaven and
passed to earth through him. Rightness characterizes his music. The dialogue
here is between Bernstein (LB) and "Lyric Poet" (LP); Bernstein concluded:

LB: Our boy has the real goods, the stuff from Heaven, the power to make you feel at the finish: *Something is right in the world. There is something that checks throughout, that follows its own law consistently: something we can trust, that will never let us down.*
LP (*Quietly*): But that is almost a definition of God.
LB: I meant it to be.[23]

Later in the century, writers applied another word to Beethoven's music, particularly his symphonies: ethical. Of all terms we have encountered, this is the most perplexing. None of the writers who use it—Joseph Kerman, Alan Tyson, and Scott Burnham—define it. Kerman and Tyson, who together wrote the Beethoven entry for the *New Grove Dictionary of Music and Musicians,* use it in relation to the symphonic ideal to distinguish the symphonies of Beethoven from those of his predecessors, specifically Haydn and Mozart. They associate it with the dynamic quality of Beethoven's music and a suggested or overt programmatic content, which together give his music "an unmistakable ethical aura." They also connect it with Donald Francis Tovey's categorization of Beethoven's music as "edifying," and with Sullivan's emphasis on Beethoven's spiritual development.[24]

Some fifteen years later, Burnham also used the word ethical to contrast Beethoven's music with Haydn's: "Beethoven's music is thus heard to reach us primarily at an ethical level, Haydn's primarily at an aesthetic level."[25] Burnham arrived at this statement when nuancing James Webster's argument that many of the traits that we value in Beethoven's music can also be found in Haydn's. According to Burnham, although some precedents can be found, important fundamental qualities of Beethoven's music are unique: music of great (sonic) weight—think of Beethoven's symphonic sound—and a forward drive "coursing forth ineluctably, moving the listener along as does the earth itself."

Kerman, Tyson, and Burnham clearly perceive Beethoven's music as one of great force, weight, and power, and in Kerman's and Tyson's case, one freighted with extramusical meaning. Yet what makes it ethical? It is hard to reconcile a piece of music with the philosophical concept of ethics. One can connect to the general Romantic notion, Platonic in origin, that listening to Beethoven's music will make you a better person. I don't believe for a minute, however, that Kerman, Tyson, and Burnham are being that vague, or, for the late twentieth century, that anachronistic. There must be another reason for their use of the term ethical.

When queried, Burnham and Kerman were both kind enough to provide an explanation. Burnham: "As best I can reconstruct what I was thinking with my use of the word 'ethical,' I would say that it is closer to Sullivan's 'spiritual' than to some strict sense of the study of ethics. I wanted a word that would sound as an opposite to 'aesthetic,' that would resonate with 'ethos' and that would thus be heard to resonate with values and virtues traditionally (and consequentially) associated with heroic Beethoven, such as 'overcoming.'" Kerman has admitted that he is not sure what he meant by a word he used almost thirty years ago, but that "Sullivan was an important book for me and my generation."[26]

Thus Sullivan influenced all three writers, and at least by implication the term ethical is associated with spiritual in some sense. Burnham also makes clear that the traditional Promethean view of Beethoven, the hero struggling and persisting against odds, is part of the mix. The term ethos is likewise important: it refers to the inner spirit or character of a person, or those traits that shapes a person's essence.

There may be one more reason for the use of the term ethical. All were writing in the late twentieth century, when the intellectualization of music prevailed, and meaning beyond the structural or tensive combination of tones was discouraged. Open expression of subjective feeling or flights of extramusical fancy were discouraged. Kerman had tested that boundary in his book on the Beethoven quartets, which looked beyond much analytical detail to describe Beethoven's aesthetic and in one sense his spiritual growth, although the term spiritual (specifically spiritualization) enters only in discussion of the late works, and there only in passing.[27] Burnham's book, which appeared in 1995, was a landmark in the revival of the consideration of meaning in discussions of classical masterworks, or, to use the technical term, hermeneutics. Within the structuralist framework in which Burnham and Kerman were writing, however, and equally important within late twentieth-century culture in general, terms such as spiritual or sacred, which Dwight had used to describe Beethoven's music, were too invocative of a moral or religious tone. Something more secular and a bit more intellectual was needed. "Ethical" satisfied those demands.

In the final analysis, it is difficult to be precise about what spiritual or ethical means in this context, and in the final analysis it may not matter. What Sullivan, Kerman, Tyson, Burnham, Downes, and many other writers have in common is an awareness that Beethoven's music is powerful and moving, that it hits the listener in the gut in a way that goes beyond intellectual appreciation and is difficult to articulate in language normally used to explicate more cerebral aspects of the art. Awe in the presence of a powerful force can elicit many responses, ranging from the secular sublime to religious certainty, and for many, both lay listeners and sophisticated musicians, Beethoven's music can at the least overwhelm the listener with its sonic force and teleological sweep. To convert such impressions to specific or, even worse, scientific language is difficult at best. These writers, some of the most gifted when it comes to musical description, have managed to go beyond traditional musicological terminology to convey what they sense as the essence of Beethoven's music, certainly the essence of his continuing presence and historical success. Possibly the best one can say is that Beethoven's music affects the listener in ways that few other composers do.

Hoffmann in Germany had invoked the sublime and helped usher in Romanticism; Dwight in America had invoked the sacred and placed Beethoven at the center of transcendentalism, a move that led to the sacralization of his music throughout the nineteenth century. While many mainstream twentieth-century writers grappled with Beethoven within the context of the spiritual and ethical, others found in Beethoven a particularly strong religious current. One group of writers, however, elevated him above even the demi-god role that some in the twentieth century, such as Bernstein, had projected. This very special role for Beethoven happened mostly in nontraditional religious movements, but in ones that closely connect to the arts in the twentieth century. With these writers Beethoven was not always a god, but he was God's servant, and his music was attributed, directly, unequivocally, and specifically, to God.

By far the most important religious movement in regard to both Beethoven and its impact on the arts was Theosophy, which originated in the nineteenth century and which found a sympathetic audience with artists and intellectuals in the United States after World War I. Theosophy was co-founded by an unlikely pair, the American journalist Henry Steel Olcott and the Russian immigrant Helena Petrovna Blavatsky. Its origins lie in the spiritualist movement, which attained great popularity in the nineteenth century. Spiritualism is the belief that human spirits exist beyond the grave and that they can communicate with living persons, most often through mediums.

In 1847 two sisters, Margaret and Katherine Fox, moved into a farmhouse in Hydesville, New York. Soon they heard strange rapping noises in the house, which they believed came from under their kitchen table. They became convinced that the sounds were made by spirits trying to get in touch with them and that they could even decipher the rappings. Perhaps they were influenced by Samuel Morse's telegraph, which had begun to operate only three years before. In any case, news of their claims spread and curiosity seekers descended upon the house in droves.

Soon the Fox sisters moved to New York and began holding séances, which became something of a rage. Horace Greeley, founder of the *New York Tribune,* was interested and sent a reporter, Henry Olcott, to investigate. Olcott became convinced and wrote several articles and later books on the subject. By the 1850s many intellectuals became involved in the spiritualist movement; they included Harriet Beecher Stowe, William Lloyd Garrison, George Ripley, Lydia Maria Child, William Cullen Bryant, and James Fenimore Cooper, as well as early feminists Susan B. Anthony, Frances Willard, and Elizabeth Cady Stanton.

Spiritualism was further popularized, or exploited, by P. T. Barnum, who took the Fox sisters on tour. Soon séances could be found everywhere, on the crudest kitchen table as well as in the most elegant, velvet-draped, chandeliered drawing room. Its greatest appeal, however, was to the working classes as an alternative religion, for it needed no church intercession, no clergy, no priests, no external authorities to tell the parishioner how to think, act, or believe. An unlettered laborer was on the same footing as a learned minister. Like many movements of the nineteenth century, it was a democratizing force.

Olcott, however, was ambivalent about this development. He had by then achieved success beyond his original position as a reporter and was accepted into the metropolitan elite, but he remained in many ways a social reformer. His belief in spiritualism never flagged, but he was concerned about its populist spread. At that point he met Helena Petrovna Blavatsky.

Blavatsky was a Russian immigrant from the Ukraine. Her father had been an army officer and her husband a provincial governor of the czar. Soon after she married, she left her husband and found her way to Turkey. The next twenty-five years of her life, however, are a mystery that Blavatsky did her best to shield. Dozens of biographers have attempted to penetrate the shroud that surrounds those years but to no avail. We know that she traveled widely, apparently conducted séances, and in July 1872 arrived in New York. It was there that she read some of Olcott's writings and contacted him. In spite of the vast differences in their backgrounds and lifestyles—he the proper upper-class social-reforming New Yorker, she the bohemian-aristocratic Russian—their common interests led them to launch a reform of spiritualism, to wrest it from the throes of "whiskey-drinking and immoral men and women," as Olcott called them, that is, the common people. In addition to their writings, they began to hold meetings with other spiritualists, and it was at such a meeting in 1875 that Olcott proposed a new organization, the Theosophical Society. The original purpose of the society was more rational than mystical, however: it was to be devoted

FIGURE 3.2

Madame Helena Petrovna Blavatsky and Colonel Henry Steel Olcott,
founders of Theosophy. Courtesy of Theosophical
Society in America Archives.

"not to the comparative study of Asian religious traditions but to the scientific
investigation of spiritual phenomena."

When most of the population believed that the soul was real and eternal,
when many mysteries still remained for science to unravel, spiritualism did
not seem an unreasonable phenomenon, and understanding how the deceased
communicated appeared to be a lofty goal. Further, both Olcott and Blavatsky
believed that Christianity had no lock on truth, and they sought through the
texts of other religions, especially Asian ones, a universal wisdom and harmony. Harmony did not last long, however, between Olcott and Blavatsky. Olcott saw the society as a way to reform spiritualism, which had not only become intertwined with a segment of the population he considered morally
suspect, but which had in too many cases become the province of frauds and

exploiters. Once purged of undesirable elements and practices, he saw it as open to all.

Blavatsky focused more on the esoteric, the mystical. Blavatsky believed that by going back to ancient texts, ancient wisdom that had been lost could be recovered, and that this would be of great benefit to modern humanity. She claimed, however, that only a part of ancient wisdom could be revealed because some of it would not be understood today, and it could be dangerous for the profane mind to have it. She recognized a semi-divine group of people, called the Masters of Wisdom, sometimes referred to as the adepts, who retained at least some of the ancient wisdom. She never identified exactly who these masters were.

Blavatsky scoured ancient texts, Hebrew, Greek, Sanskrit, Hindu, Egyptian, and many others. Her timing was not entirely coincidental; she lived just as many ancient texts were appearing in modern translations, thus making it possible to read, compare, and cherry-pick what served her best. She sought to reveal the "original meaning of myths and doctrines," and to demonstrate that all religions have an identical source.[28]

Blavatsky's approach was eminently reasonable and her motives commendable, although scholars have cringed at some of her interpretations. These texts, however, which are real, verifiable, historical documents, were insufficient for her purposes or beliefs. To go further required a research methodology beyond that of earthly textual exegesis and comparison. From the masters she learned of a cosmic memory bank, the "Akasha Records," which could be accessed through clairvoyant techniques. The texts she found there were in an otherwise unknown language, "Senzar." Even the alphabet was supposedly unique. Two of her books contain extracts of these texts, mainly the "stanzas of Dyzan," translated from these sources.[29]

With the cosmic memory bank, Blavatsky's writing crossed a line, common in many religions. It was no longer her account but a divine revelation not subject to verification or interrogation. For the disciples, it must be accepted as truth. Blavatsky also arrived at this point by doing precisely what spiritualism did best, or at least claimed to: communicating with the spirit world and receiving messages from them. She took it to an entirely different level, however. Rather than a few greetings from deceased relatives, she tapped into an entire universe of wisdom that had been lost to the world.

Because of her beliefs, Blavatsky saw the society as a small group of the chosen, the adepts, the masters. Her own aristocratic background in Russia contributed to her sense of the shape of the society. It was to be hierarchical, not democratic; there were ascended and unascended masters. Finally, she and Olcott reached a compromise: Olcott remained the head of the society and Blavatsky formed a special Esoteric Section, thus creating a division that lasted well beyond the deaths of both founders.

By the 1920s a group of ultramodern composers had emerged in the United States; they had organized several societies and begun to have a significant impact on musical thought. Charles Ives, who preceded them, was virtually spent as a composer, but new figures such as Henry Cowell, Edgard Varèse, Carl Ruggles, Aaron Copland, Dane Rudhyar, and Ruth Crawford Seeger created music in a new, challenging avant-garde style that built upon the foundation Ives and others had laid. While most wanted to celebrate the new modern age, with its emphasis on science, experimentation, and exploration of new sonic possibilities, and all wanted to excise Romanticism, many were drawn to seeking some sort of spiritual dimension to their lives. More than any other movement or religion, Theosophy filled that purpose.

For a time Cowell lived at Halcyon, a community of Theosophists in California, where he met Rudhyar. Later Cowell was to introduce Seeger to Theosophy. Rudhyar was so involved in Theosophy and other spiritual movements that he later gave up composition to become one of the foremost writers on astrology and other esoterica. Rudhyar also saw dissonance as spirituality manifest in sound, thus providing a spiritual imprint on the ultramodern movement itself. If anything united these various composers and set them apart from the established musical world, it was their unstinting use of dissonance.

What did these musicians find in Theosophy that drew them to the movement? For the most part it was the Olcott, not the Blavatsky wing, that appealed to them. After Blavatsky's death in 1891, Olcott defined the objectives of the Theosophical Society: to form a nucleus of the universal brotherhood of humanity, without distinction of race, creed, sex, caste, or color; to encourage the comparative study of religion, philosophy, and science; and to investigate unexplained laws of nature and the powers latent in humanity.[30] The scientific bent of Theosophy, which Olcott stressed, and the interest in world religions, particularly those of Asia, which was at the heart of both Olcott's and Blavatsky's views, appealed immensely to these composers. Except for Rudhyar, the mystical stream of Theosophy was less important, although a strong belief in intuition as compositional inspiration and as giver of music—in effect reducing the composer to little more than a vessel through which sounds pour—runs through the otherwise cerebral, experimental creative life of the avant-garde.

With Theosophy, several streams of thought about music were thus in place, which had only expanded by the second half of the twentieth century. From spiritual to spiritualism to spiritual mysteries to God to the cosmic memory bank to universal brotherhood, it is easy to slip from the considered idealism of Sullivan into the circle of the occult, and by the late twentieth century Beethoven was thoroughly ensconced there. Sullivan had for many legitimized the consideration of Beethoven compositions, especially symphonies and quartets, as spiritual journeys. The 1920s avant-garde had brought Theosophy into the mainstream of musical thought, and in so doing opened the door to any number of esoteric and mystical interpretations of his music.

Two American books of the late twentieth century discuss Beethoven within the framework of the occult: *Beethoven's Nine Symphonies Correlated with the Nine Spiritual Mysteries,* by Corrine Heline, and *Beethoven and the Spiritual Path,* by David Tame. Each book has an undeniable mystical quality, each uses the word esoteric frequently, and in each astrology is an important component. Although Tame's book never refers specifically to Theosophy, it was published by the Theosophical Publishing House. That Theosophy was open to many differing points of view was stressed by the publisher itself. Each of its books contains the following explanation of Theosophy: "A world organization dedicated to the promotion of the unity of humanity and the encouragement of the study of religion, philosophy, and science, to the end that we may better understand ourselves and our place in the university. The Society stands for complete freedom of individual search and belief."[31]

Tame argues that Beethoven's music is capable of "revolutionizing our consciousness." "Part III of this book is therefore intended to be a piece-by-piece guide to understanding and using the music of Beethoven toward the goal of self-transformation." He sees Beethoven as a world conqueror, a conqueror of hearts. Tame then explains how this happens: Beethoven's music uplifts our spiritual centers, our chakras, and "even, to some extent, lastingly transform[s] who we are." In the music of Beethoven exists the consciousness of God, which the listener absorbs.[32]

For Tame, as for many writers, Beethoven's deafness was critical to his personal and musical evolution, but he gives a different reason from most. While Beethoven's deafness cut him off from attending to sound, which Tame refers to as the *ahata* of Sanskrit, it allowed Beethoven to hear the *anahata,* the "unstruck Cosmic Sound."[33] Thus the sounds of Beethoven's music are the sounds of the universe.

Tame also struggles with the paradox that has perplexed many biographers of Beethoven, namely, how a man of such lofty, sublime music could also be such an explosive, violent, temperamental, and disagreeable person. Tame has a ready answer for that, which to my knowledge no other biographer has proposed: Beethoven was a Sagittarian. Without getting into a debate regarding the nature of Sagittarians, let it be noted that Tame spends an entire chapter on this issue, although he recognizes that without our knowing the exact time of Beethoven's birth it is impossible to go beyond discernment of his Zodiac sign.

After sketching Beethoven's life in some detail, Tame then gets to his principal argument, in a chapter titled "Beethoven and the Spiritual Path." The imprint of Sullivan is all over this chapter. Tame distills two characteristics from Sullivan that summarize Beethoven's life: life as suffering, and heroism as achievement. He then equates Beethoven's life with that of the Buddha.[34]

Yet Beethoven struggled. He was not pure and he could not shed his self until the *Eroica*. For Tame, the *Eroica* is the turning point in Beethoven's life and creativity; indeed, the first part of the book is called "Before the *Eroica*." With the *Eroica* Beethoven succeeded because he gave himself to God, "to serve selflessly, at a higher level of purity, devotion and determination,"[35] and because he did this he "received"—not composed, not was able to compose, not had the musical maturity or even spiritual depth to compose—the *Eroica*. That was the deal, the tradeoff, writes Tame. Beethoven became pure and devout and came through a period of trials, and for his efforts received the *Eroica;* later, after coming through another period of trials, the rewards multiplied: the *Hammerklavier,* the *Missa Solemnis,* the Ninth Symphony, and the late quartets. This is a theme common in esoteric literature, that the creator is a vessel through which cosmic wisdom reaches the world. It is at the heart of one strain of Theosophy; Blavatsky received the "Akasha records" in the unknown language of Senzar. It is also significant that the pieces Tame mentions are precisely those that Sullivan stresses.

For Tame, as for Sullivan, the late string quartets are the capstone of Beethoven's spiritual evolution, and he quotes at the top of the chapter on these works Sullivan's remarks about how they represent a spiritual synthesis. Tame, however, adds a layer of esoterica not even hinted at in Sullivan: five secret rays. Many mystical religions, going back to at least the sixth century BCE, embrace the concept of seven rays, which are often associated with light. To cite only two of many examples in early Christian iconography, seven rays of light emanate from the dove representing the Holy Sprit or from the head of the Madonna. The Hindu and Vedic deity Agni is represented with seven rays of light emanating from his body. The seven rays is an important part of Theosophy, where each ray is ascribed a specific meaning or quality.

Beyond those seven, Tame claims that there are five secret rays, or "creative emanations." This conveniently adds to twelve, an important number in the occult, and even in music, which according to Tame is represented in "the seven major and five minor keys of the diatonic scale." The seven rays represent "outer, tangible phenomena," the five "inner, less overt phenomena." Although the seven rays are derived from the five, the final stage in the perfection of the soul comes from the five, which take over where the seven leave off.[36]

The seven rays are represented by the symphonies. Although there is something of a numerological problem here, which Tame doesn't explain, one can surmise that Tame would dismiss the first two symphonies, as for him Beethoven's spiritual journey begins with the *Eroica*. The late string quartets represent the five secret rays. Thus, "the symphonies are for the triumph of the outer person; the late string quartets for the perfection of the inner person."[37]

Each quartet symbolizes some metaphysical concept, which Tame gives in a chart (see Figure 3.3). He also relates them to the five fingers of the hand, using "the esoteric Law of Correspondence." The thumb, being the most solid appendage, is associated with the most solid of the quartets, op. 127, which he calls the "thumb quartet." The forefinger "points the way," which op. 132 does stylistically, as it points toward the later works. The middle finger, being the strongest, is associated with op. 130. The ring finger, representing "divine union and love," is assigned to op. 131, "the most mystical of the quartets." Finally, the little finger, "the most delicate and refined," is associated with the "neoclassical" op. 135. Almost as an afterthought, Tame observes that the heart meridian in acupuncture ends at the tip of this finger.

Heline's book on Beethoven belongs to a different tradition than Tame's, namely, Rosicrucianism, although the variant of Rosicrucianism she espoused had a heavy overlay of Theosophy. Heline was a follower of Max Heindel, who founded the Rosicrucian Fellowship, a mystical Christian group in 1908. The origins of Rosicrucianism, which are usually traced back to the early 1600s, are at best murky. Tradition holds that a Brotherhood of the Rose Cross (thus the name Rosicrucian) was founded then, and that it draws heavily upon ancient, esoteric wisdom, although unlike Theosophy it was a specifically Christian order. Some followers trace its origins back to Moses, Solomon, ancient Egypt, or even to Adam. Some branches of Rosicrucianism were closely aligned with Freemasonry, not only in their organization, rituals, and teaching but in their founding. In some orders only Masons were admitted into the Rosicrucian Brotherhood.

Heindel's Rosicrucian Fellowship was unusual in its close connection with Theosophy. Heindel, whose real name was Carl Louis von Grasshof, was a German immigrant who came to the United States in 1895. By 1903 he had become active in Theosophy, as an officer of a lodge in Los Angeles and as a lecturer. On a visit to Europe in 1907, he claims he was visited by an elder

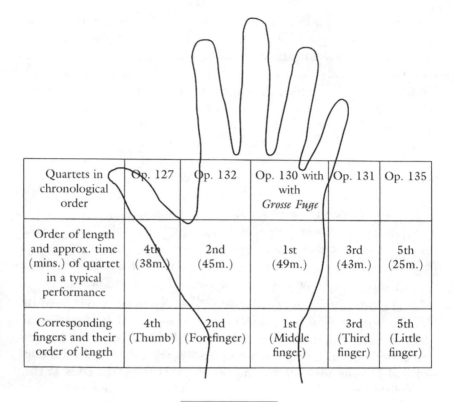

Quartets in chronological order	Op. 127	Op. 132	Op. 130 with with *Grosse Fuge*	Op. 131	Op. 135
Order of length and approx. time (mins.) of quartet in a typical performance	4th (38m.)	2nd (45m.)	1st (49m.)	3rd (43m.)	5th (25m.)
Corresponding fingers and their order of length	4th (Thumb)	2nd (Forefinger)	1st (Middle finger)	3rd (Third finger)	5th (Little finger)

FIGURE 3.3

David Tame's chart that uses the hand to relate metaphysical concepts, including "five secret rays," to Beethoven's late string quartets.

brother of the Rosicrucian Order, tested and then spirited off to their temple, somewhere near the border between Germany and Bohemia. For a month he was instructed in ancient wisdom, which he explained in his book *Rosicrucian Cosmo-Conception*. Ellwood describes the order he founded on his return to California as essentially Theosophical in belief, with an all-Western atmosphere and considerable emphasis on astrology and initiatory symbolism.[38] Heline applies the latter especially to Beethoven.

Heline, who was born into a wealthy family in Alabama in 1882, moved to California in her late teens, where she spent five years as a disciple of Heindel. It is not clear what the relationship was between the German nobleman and the aristocratic southern lady, but he encouraged her and soon she began writing and lecturing about the occult. She also met Theodore Heline, a Shakespearean actor, lecturer, and teacher of Rosicrucianism, and later editor of several Rosicrucian and New Age publications. They married in 1938.

Like Heindel, like Blavatsky, Heline had her own mystical experience. She was transported to the Lord's Supper, not to the main room where Jesus dined with his disciples, but to a second room where Mary presided and was busy handing out assignments. There, Mary instructed her to write an interpretation of the Bible, which became her magnum opus, the seven-volume *New Age Bible Interpretation*. Altogether she wrote twenty-eight books, including five on music: *Beethoven's Nine Symphonies, The Esoteric Music of Richard Wagner, Color: Music in the New Age, The Cosmic Harp,* and *Music: Keynote to Human Evolution*.[39]

To Heline, Beethoven's music is not the creation of a human mind, but rather music from "outer space," "celestial music—music which Beethoven brought down to earth and translated for human hearing." Beethoven was placed on earth for this purpose, and on this Heline is unequivocal: "The definite mission of Beethoven was to serve as a messenger of cosmic music." Unlike Sullivan, Tame, Kerman, or even Stephen J. Rivele and Christopher Wilkinson, who wrote the screenplay for the 2006 film *Copying Beethoven,* Heline believes that Beethoven's most spiritual utterances do not lie in the late quartets but in the nine symphonies. These are the pieces in which Beethoven realized his mission most fully.

Important in Heline's thinking are the Nine Spiritual Mysteries, initiatory steps through which each aspirant must pass in his quest for wisdom. With the Ninth the aspirant has completed his journey and has become an adept. Each Beethoven symphony corresponds to one of the spiritual mysteries, and Heline discusses each in its symbolic detail, in an idiosyncratic blend of basic musicological fact and mystical rumination. Each is assigned a spiritual keynote: One—Power, Two—Love, Three—Strength, Four—Beauty, Five—Freedom, Six—Unity, Seven—Exaltation, Eight—Harmony, Nine—Consummation. These terms are derived by various means, often through extensive discussion about the nature of the work, some of which is taken from standard writing on Beethoven, such as that by Alexander Wheelock Thayer, Marion Scott, James Burk, Hector Berlioz, Vincent D'Indy, and Romain Rolland.

In addition to the spiritual keynotes, Heline connects each symphony with its place in the astral world and the "ladder of spiritual ascent" (see Figure 3.4). For example, the Second Symphony corresponds to the "second earth sheath called the Fluidic Layer," the Sixth Symphony to the "sixth layer of the earth," "the fiery stratum," and the Eighth to the "eighth earth sheath known as the

Atomistic Layer." She then elaborates the meaning of each of the layers in occult thought. The Second reflects "the harmonious, pulsating forces of the
etheric realm. The world of the Mystery has much to do with the secret of the
ethers, including the beings who inhabit this realm."[40]

Both astrology and numerology mix heavily in her interpretations of the
symphonies. Each symphony falls under a specific astrological sign, a point
that Tame also makes, although Heline's and Tame's do not always agree:

Symphony	Heline	Tame
1	Pisces	Capricorn
2	Aquarius	Aquarius
3	Capricorn	Pisces
4	Sagittarius	Aries
5	Scorpio	Taurus
6	Libra	Gemini
7	Virgo	Cancer
8	Leo	Leo
9	Cancer	Virgo

Numerology appears occasionally, as in her discussion of the First Symphony.
To cite three examples from the First Symphony, Beethoven consciously set
the introduction of the first movement into twelve bars, to correspond to the
twelve Zodiac signs, and in the finale "Beethoven . . . outlines cosmic principles or gives a blueprint of the universe as taught in musical Schools of Initiation." She states that the number of measures in the allegro, 288, gives "the
numerical value of nine which is the number of man and of Initiation." Similarly, the second movement consists of 250 measures, "the numerical value of
which is seven, a number fundamental in human evolution."[41] Although she
does not explain how the numbers nine and seven are derived from 288 and
250, she appears to have adopted a method common in Kabbalah, a mystical
Jewish discipline: add all the digits together and keep reducing until you have
a single digit. In this case, 288 = 2+8+8 = 18 = 1+8 = 9.[42]

Taken together, the symphonies symbolize a "Mystic Marriage," corre-
sponding to the nine initiations into the Nine Spiritual Mysteries. The marriage is possible because of the gendered nature of the symphonies: one, three,
five, and seven are masculine, focusing on the intellect, two, four, six, and
eight are feminine, focusing on the heart and intuition. Classifying the symphonies this way is almost as old as the compositions themselves—Robert
Schumann's characterized the Fourth as "that slender Greek maiden between

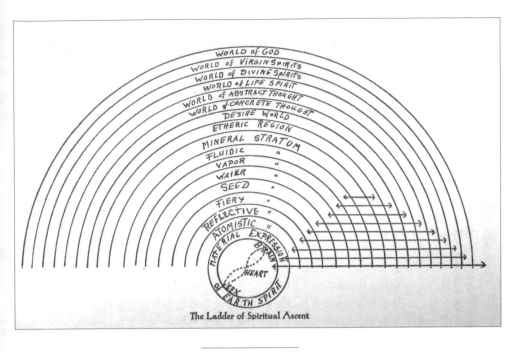

The Ladder of Spiritual Ascent

FIGURE 3.4

Corrine Heline's "ladder of spiritual ascent." Heline, a Rosecrucian, assigns
Beethoven's nine symphonies to various places on the ladder.

the two Norse giants"—although within this framework one, two, and, for
some, eight might present problems. This does not even engage the question of
the validity and especially the desirability of going down this gender road in
the first place.[43]

The Ninth Symphony stands alone, as the pinnacle toward which the ini-
tiate strives. By going through the first eight "Initiations" the aspirant has
learned to balance head and heart, and with the Ninth "he attains to the highest phase of mastership. He becomes an Adept."[44] Thus the spiritual keynote of
the Ninth Symphony, Consummation.

Tame and Heline both speak to the search for spiritual meaning that has
characterized American culture from the Pilgrims' landing at Plymouth Rock.
By the late eighteenth century the iron grip of Puritanism began to relax in
New England, and as the Western settlers confronted new experiences and
new spiritual needs, as America faced both the wild sublimity and the harsh

reality of nature, European solutions were not always compelling. Americans began searching for new spiritual models and new ways of confronting the mysterious universe. They did what Americans did best: they experimented. Hundreds of religious and spiritual groups emerged, some building on traditional Christianity, some looking elsewhere. A few became mainstream, or at least widespread, such as Unitarianism and Mormonism. Most had failed by the twentieth century.

Theosophy and Rosicrucianism came out of that milieu late compared to many other movements, and they were still in their development in the early twentieth century. Theosophy in particular spoke to the artists and intellectuals involved in early twentieth-century modernism. Its mystical nature, its amalgamation of many ancient traditions, its tolerance, its search for scientific underpinnings, and the belief in individual agency found a ready acceptance with the moderns. Theosophy was also receptive to the mysterious emotional power that seemed to emanate from Beethoven's music.

Thus what Sullivan saw and tried to explain in thoroughly nonreligious language, Tame and Heline also saw and translated into their belief structure. One can safely say that Tame and Heline go far beyond most readers when emotionally reacting to and understanding the music of Beethoven. While their interpretations embrace many esoteric phenomena that much mainstream America does not, their sense of Beethoven is consistent with that of many others. They draw upon their beliefs to explain what many have found inexplicable, the spiritual power of Beethoven's music. Yet the myriad of other writers who have addressed the spiritual dimension of Beethoven's music have confirmed that one does not have to be an occultist or a Christian or a Jew to sense that. Even confirmed atheists feel it.[45] The problem, however, is not feeling it; it is trying to explain it. This is a dialogue that shows no signs of abating. How a writer approaches the task and how successful she is depends not on Beethoven, but on the culture in which the writer belongs and the beliefs she holds.

PART TWO

Science, Scholars, & Critics

4

Beethoven, Modernism, and Science

For much of the twentieth century, Beethoven's public image remained largely unchanged. He was still the colossus who strode above the symphonic world hurling his thunderbolts in mighty crashes of triads and seventh chords. He was still the composer who stripped emotion to its barest, most primitive utterance, who wrestled with his contrapuntal demons until they relented, all the while fighting under the handicap of his own deafness. This view of Beethoven prevailed for much of the populace and could be seen in the press, in concert promotions, on FM radio, and in the popular media. This is the Beethoven of miniature action figures, of multiple internet sites, of commercials advertising everything from vintage wine to automobiles. This Beethoven will be encountered again and again in subsequent chapters.

Yet another Beethoven began to appear in the twentieth century, at first quietly among musicians and critics, then more prominently as performers took up this new view and through their own interpretations brought it to the general public. A new, less Romantic figure was the true twentieth-century Beethoven, a composer more attuned to the modern, urban, scientifically oriented technical world that characterized a new time and spirit. Not even the most ardent musical revolutionaries who wished to distance themselves from most of what had occurred in the previous century wanted to abandon Beethoven. He was simply remade, much the way successful popular figures from Frankenstein to King Kong fared on the Hollywood screen. As Romanticism finally waned and then was rejected, Beethoven the Romantic became Beethoven the classicist. How this happened and what it meant is a story of how several threads, involving science, the avant-garde, new technology, and, in the second half of the century, the growth of academia, weave together to create new ways of hearing and understanding Beethoven. This chapter considers the impact of modernism, the post–World War I climate, and the early-music movement on Beethoven. The next chapter assesses the impact of academic positivism, the rise of rock 'n' roll, and the Cold War on how Beethoven was viewed. Curiously, all these threads weave together to create a tapestry of varied patterns but still an overall consistent design.

Like other cultural movements, twentieth-century modernism was complex, making it almost impossible to define precisely. Scholars often disagree on what it encompasses, who fits into the rubric, or what its most salient features are. Without attempting to resolve the dispute, I note two characteristics found in American musical modernism that on the surface seem diametrically opposed. One stresses intuition and spiritualism, the other science and innovation. These two elements coexisted for much of the century, at times within the same person, and together defined separate tracks that represented Beethoven's music. Chapter 3 has already considered the former; this chapter examines the latter.

American modernism arose first in the art world early in the twentieth century. It centered around Alfred Stieglitz and his gallery at 291 Fifth Avenue in Manhattan, which opened in 1905. Stieglitz himself, a pioneering photographer, wished to abandon the prevailing painterly school of photography in which photographers attempted to imitate the ethos of nineteenth-century paintings. His goal was to record the world of steel and concrete, the urban reality of the new century, with all its contradictions, social stress, and dynamism. He aligned himself with other artists who pursued post-impressionist abstraction.

While Stieglitz's work and his gallery flourished, American modernism remained a local movement, known mainly to an adventurous circle in New York, particularly the artistically oriented of what was then the principal bastion of Bohemianism, Greenwich Village. That all changed with one event in 1913, the International Exhibition of Modern Art held at the Sixty-ninth Regiment Armory in New York City, better known as the Armory Show. For the first time, the general public saw some of the most radical works of art from the United States and especially Europe. The show created a sensation. Newspapers carried accounts of it, including photographs of some of the more radical works and conversations about them. The following conversation, allegedly heard by a reporter, appeared verbatim in the *New York Times:*

"Have you been to see the Cubists and the Futurists? Yes? Well, could you make anything out of it?"

The answer usually was:

"Why, I don't know much about art, but it looked to me like a mess of nonsense."

The same reporter who recorded that comment then went to Kenyon Cox, considered one of the more prominent artists of the time, for his reaction. Cox minced no words: "The thing is pathological! It's hideous! . . . These men have seized upon the modern engine of publicity and are making insanity pay."[1]

After its New York run the exhibition moved to Chicago and then Boston; altogether an estimated 300,000 people saw it. Whatever the reaction, modernism was no longer a hidden affair, known only to a few sympathetic aficionados. It became entrenched in American culture.

Musical modernism, it seemed, lagged far behind its artistic cousin. Through the 1910s music heard at most concerts was little changed from what appeared in the 1880s. Yet musical radicalism was present, only hidden away, out of public view, in such places as Redding, Connecticut. There Charles Ives continued his foray into modernism that he had begun in New Haven in the 1890s. Ives knew he was creating new and controversial music, in style and complexity far beyond what the public would accept. As a consequence, he decided not to enter the music profession formally, but instead maintained an extremely successful career in the insurance business. At night and on weekends he composed. He was much aware of what was happening in Europe but made little attempt to connect directly with the European moderns or even to get his music performed. Scores piled up, only to be discovered later. Ives was clear about his choice: he didn't want his family to "starve on his dissonances."

Somewhat later than Ives was Leo Ornstein. A Jewish immigrant who came to the United States in 1906, Ornstein suddenly discovered his own modernist style in 1913. He was more public about it, because he was his own performer. A talented concert pianist, Ornstein created a stir wherever he went with his ultramodern works, such as *Danse Sauvage* and *Suicide in an Airplane.* His appeal was due in part to the outrageous novelty of his music, and the audience's privilege of witnessing a small, wiry man beating a piano into submission.

FIGURE 4.1 A–B

Cartoons from 1917 about pianist and composer Leo Ornstein,
depicting him as a radical futurist.

Many saw Ornstein as a solitary phenomenon, a lone futurist voice in the wilderness. While it is true that few others played his music during the 1910s, he was fully plugged into the Stieglitz circle and through his connections with artists and writers brought music into the modernist movement. He also gathered around him a coterie of young people who became leading figures in the ultramodern movement when it achieved full public recognition in the 1920s.[2]

Another important musical development occurred in 1923, when Edgar Varèse formed the International Composers Guild (ICG) in New York; with its founding, musical modernism began to attract attention much as the Armory Show did in 1913, although the audiences were much smaller. Varèse had arrived in the United States in 1915 and was immediately appalled with the apparent lack of innovation that he found on the American musical scene. He called the musical organizations that he found "Bourbons," "mausoleums—mortuaries for musical reminiscences," and only after several failed efforts did he succeed in altering the American musical landscape with the formation of the ICG.[3]

The ICG, the League of Composers that soon followed, and other similar organizations began sponsoring concerts and publishing journals. Ives by this time was no longer actively composing, and Ornstein was on his way to disappearing into a self-imposed obscurity, but new composers emerged, encouraged by the success of these organizations. Varèse, Aaron Copland, Henry Cowell, Carl Ruggles, and Ruth Crawford Seeger are some of the better known. All wanted to exorcise the ghost of Romanticism and create new types of music that they felt were more in touch with the world as it then existed.

How did they react to Beethoven, the arch-icon of nineteenth-century Romanticism? Writers associated with these groups or critics reviewing them assumed that they wanted nothing to do with him. In reference to an early concert of the ICG, critic W. J. Henderson commented, "It seems that these international composers are pretty much all of a mind. Bach and Beethoven, and worst of all, Mozart, the overgrown baby of the tone art, are all dead and ought to be buried."[4] Paul Rosenfeld noted, "All attempts to continue in the exalted and ecstatic style begun by Beethoven, developed by Wagner and perhaps abused by Strauss, Mahler, Scriabine, and the twentieth century romanticists, are condemned by it as bad."[5] Yet this was not the case of many modernist musicians. Some, such as Ornstein, merely distinguished their compositional process from Beethoven's: " I do not conceive of music in the way Beethoven did—as a mosaic of themes and motives."[6]

Ornstein's attitude was less anti-Beethoven than a recognition that he lived in twentieth-century America. "We must realize that we live in a different age, our customs, our manner of living, we ourselves are not at all like the people of Bach's time—or Beethoven's, or Haydn's."[7] Later in the century Harry Partch echoed the same sentiment: "If you mean that Beethoven should become our one musical standard, I think it's also a pity. . . . This isn't Germany, and this isn't the eighteenth century."[8] Implicit in these comments was the assumption that Beethoven's music represented a specific time and place, and that the early twentieth century represented something radical in comparison. While the romantic image held his music to be timeless, transcendent, and universal, modernist composers directly challenged the romantic assumptions about Beethoven's privileged position. They could, however, call upon a romantic doctrine that, ironically, remained central to modernism: progress. This concept provided an important justification for their own work, yet the specter of Beethoven still loomed large.

Except for the urge to distance themselves, there was little backlash or negative feeling about Beethoven among composers themselves. For some, Beethoven was simply part of the classical monolith, part of the "great styles of the past," as Charles Seeger dubbed it when he grouped together Beethoven, Bach, and Palestrina, or what Ruth Crawford Seeger called "the great tradition of Bach, Beethoven, Brahms." Carlos Chávez criticized professional musicians for "their mistaken believe that music *is* Bach and Beethoven."[9] Others mostly ignored him.

Yet many modernist composers retained a healthy respect for Beethoven. Ives made that clear in his *Concord* Sonata, when he essentially equated Emerson with Beethoven and quoted the famous opening motive of the Fifth Symphony. This was an extreme compliment, as Ives revered Emerson. Ives saw Emerson on a mountaintop and represented his solid nature with Beethoven's "sturdy Fifth Symphony motive." The Beethoven quotation is not without ambiguity, however, for when it appears later in the sonata, it is difficult to tell if Ives is quoting Beethoven or Frederick Charles Zeuner's hymn tune "Missionary Chant." The distinction may be without a difference, however, as Zeuner himself probably drew his hymn from the opening motive of Beethoven's Fifth. Raiding classical instrumental music for melodies was common among the advocates of a more scientific (their term) type of hymnody in the early nineteenth century. On a broader programmatic level, Ives's use of the Fifth's opening motive may also be appropriate, as Ives sought to capture the spirit of Concord, Massachusetts, in 1840, when the literary intellectuals who constitute the sonata's programmatic movements were in the throes of transcendentalism. As we know, Beethoven's symphonies were being heard in Boston for the first time then, and they held an almost hypnotic grasp on many of the transcendentalists.

Some modernists found in Beethoven inspiration for their own innovations or continued to turn to him for models. Varèse's biographer and friend
Ferdinand Oullette claimed he was Varèse's favorite composer, and reported
that the Scherzo from Beethoven's Seventh Symphony gave Varèse his first
sense of a "projection in space," a compositional feature that would become
central to his later aesthetic. When interviewed by the *Sante Fe New Mexican*
in 1936, Varèse referred to Beethoven's Ninth Symphony repeatedly and called
it "the greatest choral work." Georges Antheil, shortly after completing his
most infamous piece, *Ballet Mécanique,* embarked on a large-scale *Symphony
in Fa,* which according to Linda Whitesitt was created out of a love for his latest musical hero, Beethoven.[10]

The modernists' Beethoven, however, was not that of the Romantics. Gone
are the elaborate imaginary programs. Gone are the laudatory poems. Gone
are the concerns about masculinity. Gone are the quiverings of those who
stand within the powerful sounds of his symphonies. Instead we have an organic Beethoven, a Beethoven whose structure breathes an unqualified mastery of overall design, whose every note relates to the grand scheme that underlies each of his pieces.

He is no longer revered, his music no longer sacrosanct. Paul Rosenfeld
speculated that Beethoven's sonatas might somehow be "treated" by Henry
Cowell's tone clusters, and as a consequence made more effective. While a Cowell tone cluster is a long way from a Beethoven triad, Rosenfeld's suggestion
of tampering is not unique to the twentieth century. In the nineteenth century
Richard Wagner and Felix Weingartner, among others, modified the orchestration of Beethoven symphonies. Whatever the outcome, however, they did
not want to change Beethoven but rather to retain his original sense, and to
adjust Beethoven's sounds to that of the modern orchestra, which was larger
in size and included many instruments that had been improved since Beethoven's time. Theirs was essentially the original instrument argument in reverse: they wanted to retain the orchestral balance that they believed instrumental advancements threatened. Rosenfeld, on the other hand, felt a need to
adopt Beethoven not just to the twentieth century but to the ultramodern concept of harmonic imperative and evolution. If Rosenfeld's suggestion were im-
plemented, a level of dissonance unimagined by the composer himself would
overlay Beethoven's entire harmonic structure.

The principal tactic that musicians, critics, and historians of the early twentieth century adopted to make Beethoven respectable was to strip him of the
Romantic aura by redefining him as a classicist. The transition proved remarkably easy, and if not universally accepted by the public, who continued
to revel in the powerful image that the nineteenth century bequeathed, and if

resisted by some holdouts among writers and performers, the classical Beethoven came to dominate both musical and scholarly thought for much of the century. The change only began in the 1920s, roughly the same time musical modernism began to coalesce around the new societies, although the societies themselves had little direct effect on this. The League of Composers' magazine, *Modern Music,* for instance, said little about Beethoven specifically, even though they discussed other early composers, such as Gesualdo, Monteverdi, and J. S. Bach. Beethoven's name occurs frequently but usually as one of several composers, such as Haydn, Mozart, and Brahms, who represent the classical tradition, especially the Viennese school.

The makeover began with a few comments buried here and there in critical writings, and like so many interpretations of Beethoven was not strictly an American phenomenon. Olin Downes, who at first did not come out and say Beethoven was a classicist, sounded one of the principal lines of argument in favor of Beethoven's classical status in 1927. As the centennial year of Beethoven's death, newspapers and magazines were flooded with articles about Beethoven, most eulogizing him in extravagant, hagiographic prose. Downes stressed Beethoven's devotion to musical structure, particularly organic form, and compared Beethoven's creative process to that of an organism growing "before our eyes."[11] The concept of organicism emerged in the late eighteenth century, originally in botany, and was soon applied to music. It threaded its way through nineteenth-century thought where it gained great currency and became a sine qua non argument for later twentieth-century modernist writers who wished to place Beethoven firmly within the classical framework.

In 1930 Daniel Gregory Mason stressed the values of organicism in Beethoven's music, emphasizing his tight structure and economy of means. Speaking of the Second Symphony, Mason observed how "all the strings are tightened, and flabbiness, diffuseness, meaningless ornament, and filling are swept away." Beethoven was "forcible, concise and logical," his music admitted of no superfluities, no distractions, making it "compact, close, rigorously thematic." In a *Musical Quarterly* article of the same year, replete with both male chauvinism and German ethnocentricity, Colin McAlpin not only stressed the classical in Beethoven but related it directly to form: "For in both these composers (Bach and Beethoven) the idea of law and order—of obedience to the formative intellect and regulative reason—greatly prevailed. They relied supremely on the masculine powers of formulation; . . . Theirs was essentially the Germanic genius for the organization and control of ideas. Hence the superiority of Germany in the matter of symphonic structure and classic form."[12]

Yet even before Mason's and McAlpin's comments, Beethoven as classicist was articulated clearly and directly. One year after Downes's discussion of Beethoven's organicism, Guido Adler and Theodore Baker stated unequivocally, "Beethoven, despite all the sublime flights in the works of his latest period, was grounded throughout in classicism. He never shook the formal foundations and principles of classical music, or broke them down." They then derided "superfluous attempts . . . to prove that Beethoven's last period belongs wholly to romanticism." By 1937 Downes himself recognized Beethoven as specifically within the school of Viennese classicism: "Beethoven, with all his energy, spirituality and humanitarian impulse, remains in music a descendant of the eighteenth century and one whose line as a composer is to be traced directly to the masters of the Viennese school."[13]

With modernism came a different performance ethos, a more restrained, more deliberately-faithful-to-the-score approach to the Beethoven corpus. Arturo Toscanini became its most famous advocate, feeling that the performer should not interject himself but should attempt to reproduce what Beethoven wanted. This did not mean, of course, that there was no interpretation, nor that Toscanini did not have his own ideas of how Beethoven should sound. Toscanini's Beethoven in many ways was anti-Romantic: the tempos are quick, the attacks crisp, the texture transparent. Some critics, however, read even into Toscanini's performances an unabashed Romanticism. As an indication that the image of Beethoven as demi-god continued unabated in some circles, Lawrence Gilman penned the following about a Toscanini performance of the *Eroica:*

> The vast pattern of the score still moves gigantically across the tonal skies: we hear the cyclopean tread of Beethoven's mighty music, with its appalling immensity of grief and terror, and its climax on that unexampled page in which the implacably reiterated octaves of the brass cut menacingly through the orchestral gloom, as if Beethoven had for a moment opened some Seventh Seal of an ancestral revelation, and the trumpets of the Apocalypse had begun to sound, and the sun and stars had fallen into the abyss.[14]

Beethoven worship was not to die on the ascetic vine of performance restraint.

Even before Toscanini's interpretation of Beethoven symphonies became famous, the change toward a modernist aesthetic can be seen in Fritz Kreisler's 1926 recording of the Beethoven Violin Concerto. The 1920s had witnessed the new electronic recording technology replacing the older acoustical approach, the result being not only a much better sound but also the ability to capture a greater range of sound. Large-scale compositions could be recorded in their entirety, and suddenly the possibility of the entire classical canon on recordings was a reality. Recording companies scrambled to commit to disc as much of the repertoire as possible. This of course included Beethoven. Kreisler, considered the preeminent violinist of his time, was a logical choice for the violin literature. He recorded the Beethoven Violin Concerto for Victor on December 14–16, 1926. In this recording emotion is restrained. The playing is technically beautiful, and there is little Romantic schmaltz; glides, portamentos, are minimized, articulation and rhythm are precise, phrasing shows no exaggerated gestures. His colleagues recognized the significance of Kreisler's interpretations: Joseph Szigeti stated that if Kreisler's playing were prose, it would be the antithesis of purple prose, and Carl Flesch wrote that Kreisler "was the first who most nearly *divined in advance* and satisfied the specific type of emotional expression demanded by our age." Kreisler's performance of Beethoven's Violin Concerto is all about Beethoven, not about Kreisler.[15]

Just how much Kreisler's approach differed from the Romantics is illustrated in reports of performances of the same Beethoven concerto by Eugene Ysaÿe in the late 1880s or 1890s. Carl Flesch commented that "in his hands the Beethoven concerto suffered an imaginative remodeling of the original into a personal experience, which did not leave much of the unadulterated Beethoven spirit." Lest this comment be challenged on the grounds that Flesch was writing later under the sway of a modernist aesthetic, the critic of the *World* directly contemporaneous with Ysaÿe observed, "Who can think of Beethoven, or even of music, whilst Ysaÿe is titanically emphasizing himself and his stupendous accomplishment, elbowing aside the conductor, eclipsing the little handful of an orchestra which he thinks sufficient for a concert in St. James's Hall, and all but showing Beethoven the door."[16]

The modernists' Beethoven was inextricably tied to possibly the most powerful cultural force of the twentieth century: science. Without going so far as to reduce a century to a single overriding theme, à la the old German notion of Zeitgeist (the spirit of the times), one would nevertheless be hard pressed not to mention science and technology as a dominant aspect of the twentieth-century world. The scientific revolution that began with the Enlightenment came to full fruition in the twentieth century, paradoxically even as many values of the Enlightenment itself were overturned.

For 250 years the world had belonged to Newton. He had defined its principles, which formed the basis of Enlightenment science and the many inventions that it spawned, and gave it the momentum to take it through the Industrial Revolution. Napoleon had said, "There can be only one Newton, for there was only one universe to discover." In the early twentieth century, however, scientists began to discover entire new universes—relativity, quantum mechanics, the genome—and the Newtonian world began to look a bit tattered, if not completely shredded.[17]

Each decade seemed to bring new discoveries, new theories, and breakthrough inventions. Max Planck deduced the quantum in 1900, Einstein's special theory of relativity was published in 1905, and sound recording and film, present in the 1890s, came into their own in the century's first decade. In the 1910s the structure of the atom was discerned, Henry Ford introduced the assembly line, soon to be followed by the first red, yellow, and green traffic light, and Einstein's general theory of relativity advanced the mind-bending idea that light itself, the one constant in the universe, bends. The 1920s saw commercial radio become a reality, electronic phonograph recording replace the acoustical process, and the appearance of sound motion pictures. Scientists in the 1930s succeeded in splitting the atom, the Empire State Building was completed in fourteen months, air conditioning was invented, and commercial aviation, including the first transatlantic route, became viable. The 1940s witnessed the atom bomb, the formulation of the big bang theory, man breaking the sound barrier, commercial television, and two devices that would revolutionize the music industry, the LP and the tape recorder.

By mid-century it seemed that science had transformed American life. News could be witnessed as events unfolded, and space shrank as faster automobiles, better roads, and air travel redefined distance. As electronic media and high-fidelity sound reproduction spread music to the farthest corners of the country, Beethoven was everywhere. His works for the first time could be heard in the home of the most musically illiterate person with a sound quality that approached that in the concert hall, and with the capacity to hear an entire movement, sometimes an entire piece, with no need to change between three-minute scratchy recordings. FM radio and television completed the technological assault on barriers to experiencing music. FM allowed what in the twenty-first century would be called continuous streaming of music, where even the longest opera could be heard as one would hear it in performance.

Television soon took care of the visual dimension. It allowed one to see as well as hear a concert, although with inferior sound. Even that limitation could be overcome with simulcast, where the live sound of a televised concert was broadcast over a related FM station. In the face of this sort of competition some classical musicians, Glenn Gould especially, believed that the traditional concert, a product mostly of the nineteenth century, had outlived its usefulness and would soon be buried in the avalanche of new technology. Gould's view was that of an aurally oriented fanatic to whom the music itself, and only the music, mattered. It did not take into account the pleasure taken in the visual aspect of the performance and architectural surroundings that enhanced the concert experience, the excitement and tension of witnessing live music making, and not least the importance of the concert as a social as well as a musical event.

The classical music train was not derailed during World War II, but it slowed and in some cases encountered unexpected stops. Many musicians found themselves in the armed forces, and war rationing, especially gasoline, severely curtailed travel for both musicians and audiences. Recordings suffered because of a lack of shellac, an essentially ingredient in 78 RPM records, which were still the only commercial source of recorded music. Except for refugees from central Europe and other musicians wishing to flee the European theater, the transatlantic passage so critical to American music culture was all but closed. A perusal of the pages of *Musical America,* the standard weekly about classical music activity in the United States, reveals a society continuing to embrace classical activity, but affected in many ways by the war effort (see Figure 4.2). In 1943 the Philadelphia Orchestra had to cancel a scheduled tour because of travel restrictions. String quartet members found themselves wearing army uniforms. Cartoons from *Musical America* summarize the problems musicians and the musical public faced (see Figure 4.3). Composers prominent in the 1930s, such as Aaron Copland, Roy Harris, and Samuel Barber, continued to premiere new works, but only as the war came to an end did a new generation of composers, with new and radical ideas, began to make themselves heard.

The war had so completely disrupted Europe and so thoroughly mobilized American society that there was a sense of starting fresh after the war. Much of Europe was in ruins, and composers there wished to turn their backs on a past they cared not to remember. America was exhausted but exhilarant. It had won two wars, in Europe and in the Pacific, and emerged as the dominant world power. With that came both cultural and economic clout as well as greater participation on the world stage, a situation that brought American and European musicians closer. The exodus from Nazi-dominated Europe had already resulted in many European musicians fleeing to the United States; now with the end of the war and greater ease of transportation, the Atlantic became a two-way highway. Unlike the transatlantic travels of the nineteenth and early twentieth centuries, where young American musicians went to Europe to learn, the road was filled with mature musicians from both sides of the Atlantic whose schedules crisscrossed the ocean.

FIGURE 4.2

"They Shall Have Music, in War as in Peace, A String Quartet at Fort Dix:
Privates Ira Baker, Irving Nussbaum, Jascha Bernstein, and Jules Baker."
Musical America, February 10, 1943.

The mood of exhaustion that hung over the entire world took unusual turns
in music. At its core was a search for anonymity. Composers on both sides of
the Atlantic voiced a desire for a non-emotional, non-personal abstract style
that would do little more than probe the possibilities of new sound and structural combinations. It is hard to find two composers whose work is more disparate than Pierre Boulez and John Cage. Yet in the 1940s and 1950s their
trajectories were strikingly similar, as was for a time their close personal relationship. Boulez, coming of age in post–World War II France, saw nothing but
remnants of a dead past around him and wished to bury it all, every scrap of it.
Boulez repudiated his father (because he was bourgeois), the church, and even
his compositional heritage, including his mentor, Rene Leibowitz. He was out-
spoken about his rebellion: "It is not enough to deface the Mona Lisa because
that does not kill the Mona Lisa. All the art of the past must be destroyed"; "In
art one must kill one's father."[18]

FIGURE 4.3

World War II cartoons from *Musical America*.

Cage was anything but an angry young man, but shortly after World War II he also moved to a new compositional approach that in many ways was an even greater break with the Western tradition. From roughly 1952 onward, Cage's music was predominantly based on chance, allowing aleatoric operations, ranging from dice to the Chinese book of changes, *I-Ching*, to random computer-generated numbers, to determine the content of the composition. Silence and the sounds of the environment became as important as notes chosen by the performer. In addition, those notes did not need to be played on a musical instrument or, if they were, to be played in the instrument's traditional fashion. A Cage composition might contain the sound of the performer drinking a glass of water with a contact microphone on his throat, or slapping the case of a grand piano as he walked around it.

Cage's aleatoric approach was derived from Zen Buddhist concepts of the individual in relation to the world. Boulez's method, called total serialism, was essentially eighteenth-century Deism in tones. Deism believed that God was the great clock-winder who created the universe, set it in motion, and then let it run. Total serialist composers derived a set of rows or patterns of succession for virtually all parameters of music—pitch, rhythm, dynamics, and, where appropriate, timbre—and allowed the application and manipulation of the rows to govern the composition. The composer had choice in ways that the row was manipulated, and some permutations could be quite complex, but nevertheless the piece was, if not preordained, at least limited by the mathematical potential of the original rows. Total serialism was an intricate, highly mathematical, cerebral, and scientific approach to musical composition. It fit the times perfectly.

Not all composers, even those who adopted serialism, were angry young men. In the United States Milton Babbitt developed many of the principles of serialism independent of Boulez, probably even before Boulez.[19] For those seeking primacy, a concern important to the twentieth-century world, a strong case could be made for Babbitt as the originator of total serialism. He certainly became both one of its prime exponents and one of its most articulate spokesmen. Babbitt, who had studied composition before World War II, was also a mathematician, and he approached serialism from that perspective. Whatever the musical verdict on serialism, it was a mathematician's delight.

What total or integral serialism and chance both did was lessen if not eliminate personal expression. If musical choices were left to outside agencies, the opportunity for the composer to interject his personal feeling was diminished. At best the composer could become anonymous. For a brief period after World War II this was the goal in music, literature, art, and drama. Wiley

Sypher, writing about literature during this time, entitled his book *Loss of the Self in Modern Literature and Art*. Boulez stated, "If it were necessary to find a profound motive for the work I have described, it would be a search for . . . anonymity." Essential to Cage's aesthetic was to renounce control over sounds, to eliminate the will of the composer. Earle Brown, who worked closely with Cage and developed his own aleatoric approach, spoke of "the underlying acceptance of a kind of autonomy and a bypassing of subjective control." Lukas Foss, who experimented with "improvisation workshops," called the results "anonymous workshops" and claimed, "We were the first people, I think, in the trend for anonymity which is built current into musical expression."[20] The composer Stephen Hartke summarized the post–World War II style as "sleek, glossy and anonymous."[21]

In such an environment there would seem to be little place for Beethoven, who for 150 years embodied personal expression. The serialists and chance composers mostly ignored him, but even though they represented the new, the experimental, the avant-garde, their place in the musical mainstream was severely circumscribed. They occasionally made headlines and were frequently discussed in academic circles, but their music was not heard often, and, when it was, audience reaction guaranteed that it would not be frequently repeated. The most serious chasm between composer and audience since the advent of public concerts occurred at this time, even though conductors and performers tried to convince the public that they should listen to the new music. The old Puritan argument, that one has a responsibility to these musicians and to oneself to understand this music, whether one enjoys it or not, simply did not work. It never convinced the public, but this argument had later consequences for how Beethoven was to be perceived in the second half of the century.

In the meantime, the public continued to embrace Beethoven. Nearly twelve percent of all pieces programmed by ten major orchestras from 1945 to 1950 were by Beethoven, more than any other composer. Only Brahms was close behind (nearly eleven percent), and after that were Tchaikovsky and Mozart (five percent each). Beethoven performances at the New York Philharmonic represented eighteen percent of the orchestra's work during that time. While this percentage is far less than the twenty-eight percent that the Philharmonic programmed of Beethoven's music between 1842 and 1850, the total repertoire for orchestral music had expanded exponentially in the century between the orchestra's founding and the end of World War II. In other words, Beethoven had a lot more competition but still bested them.[22]

Another study of the repertoire of twenty-seven major American orchestras found similar results. Between 1940 and 1970, ten to twelve percent of all orchestral pieces performed were by Beethoven. There was a slight dip in 1940 when his percentage went just below ten percent, and Brahms performances peaked to edge out Beethoven for that year. Otherwise his dominance is clear, rising steadily to nearly thirteen percent in 1970, the last year of the survey— also the year of the Beethoven bicentennial.

Sales of Beethoven recordings tell the same story. The arrival of the LP record and the manufacture of high fidelity and then stereo equipment that was affordable for the average consumer created an entirely new demand for recordings, and Beethoven's music led the way. By 1952 there were already 329 LP sides of Beethoven's music available. In 1952 alone, another 400 sides were issued. That list included the complete piano sonatas by Wilhelm Kempff, the complete string quartets by the Pascal Quartet, and two sets of complete symphonies, conducted by Bruno Walter and Felix Weingartner. In addition, Toscanini's famous recordings of the Beethoven symphonies, though not released in a single set, had been issued separately. The many other individual recordings of Beethoven symphonies included no fewer than eighteen versions of the *Eroica*.[23] Comparative statistics with other composers are not available, but clearly there was a thirst for Beethoven's compositions among the American public.

By the 1950s the classical Beethoven was firmly in place. Two of the most prominent writers on music of the post–World War II era stated firmly and unequivocally that Beethoven belonged to the classic and not the Romantic era. William S. Newman, in his monumental book *The Sonata in the Classic Era,* discussed Beethoven within that framework. Later, when he followed with another volume, *The Sonata since Beethoven,* he explained his choice: "Clementi and Beethoven were still writing sonatas in the early 1820s; yet in spite of increasing signs of those Romantic style innovations in their later music, they remained largely oriented toward Classic sonatas styles."[24] Charles Rosen discussed Beethoven at length in his book *The Classical Style.* Beyond his inclusion of Beethoven in a book with such a title, Rosen left no doubt about his position: "Beethoven, indeed, here enlarged the limits of the classical style beyond all previous conceptions, but he never changed its essential structure or abandoned it."[25]

Another non-Romantic view of Beethoven entered the classical music mainstream in the 1980s when practitioners of the early-music movement began to push beyond the generally accepted temporal wall of the mid-eighteenth century, usually identified as the year in which J. S. Bach died (1750). The movement, which had its beginnings in turn-of-the-century England, gained force and attention throughout the Western world after World War II.[26] At first its rallying cry was authenticity, which, as musicologist Richard Taruskin pointed out, made some sense when performing a repertoire that was mostly unknown with a performance tradition that had not survived. Early practitioners had little choice but to seek, through contemporary documents, what clues there were about how the music should sound. From this effort, however, a performance style began to congeal, creating a twentieth-century tradition for older music. As long as performers stayed within a repertoire unfamiliar to the public, using large arrays of instruments whose exoticism created its own visual feast, there were only arcane debates within the early-music fraternity itself about what should happen.

Around 1980, early-music performers began to look covetously at more recent repertoires, first the later eighteenth century, much of which yielded to their approaches, and then the nineteenth century, specifically Beethoven. The first efforts, toward the piano sonatas, fit easily within the early-music framework, as Beethoven's pianos were different from the modern concert grand. Performance on the eighteenth-century fortepiano was controversial only when adherents claimed that Beethoven should be performed on it exclusively, and most never made such a statement. The performer could exercise the same degree of flexibility in interpretation as any artist, the only limitation being what the instrument itself could produce. To adherents it created a type of emotional freedom unavailable on a nine-foot concert grand where a sonata had to be adapted, however unconsciously, to the larger instrument with different characteristics of timbre and sustaining ability. Audiences found it a refreshing exercise to hear performances at least close to the sound that Beethoven had in mind.

When early-music conductors, notably Roger Norrington and John Eliot Gardiner, began to perform the Beethoven symphonies, the question of their intentions not only became more controversial but spilled out into broader issues about what the early-music movement itself represented. Norrington was the most successful early-music conductor interpreting Beethoven, if success is equated with renown. He solidified his position in London in 1987, when he organized a "Beethoven Experience," a term curiously reminiscent of both John Cage and Jimi Hendrix. This event featured book exhibits, lectures, lecture-demonstrations, various recitals, including a dance recital, and Beethoven symphony performances on original instruments, all conducted by Norrington. For the festival, Norrington conducted excerpts of the First through the Seventh Symphonies as part of lecture-demonstrations, and gave complete performances of the Eighth and Ninth Symphonies. It was not the first time he had performed Beethoven—he was in the process of recording all nine symphonies for EMI—but the concentrated emphasis on Beethoven as an early-music subject caught the public's imagination.

John Rockwell, music critic for the *New York Times,* found the event liberating, enlightening, and invigorating. While his original dispatch was mostly descriptive, he did not hide his own reaction, pronouncing the experience fascinating, intellectually convincing, and eminently successful. He accepted fully the validity of the approach, calling it "the most thoroughgoing examination yet of what Beethoven's symphonies sounded like at the time of their premieres."[27]

Two weeks later Rockwell amplified on his original report with an article titled, "Old Instruments May Herald the Future." He remained taken with the notion that original instruments, early-music techniques, and adherence to Beethoven's tempi were to redefine the concert world as we know it: "The early music movement as a whole can now be called the most exciting innovation in the performance of the standard repertory. It is difficult to believe that the comfortable, conservative world of the modern symphony orchestra and opera house—classical music's most prestigious, glamorous performing institutions—can ever be quite the same again." And once again, Beethoven led the attack, bringing the early-music movement out of the shadows and into the mainstream. Rockwell reaffirms that the Beethoven he heard at the Beethoven Experience was indeed the true, original Beethoven: the performance "seems the way music actually was at the time of the Napoleonic wars, and it helps us relive Beethoven's own revolutionary genius."[28]

Had Rockwell actually looked at what was happening in the esoteric byways of the early-music movement, however, he would have known that when he wrote these lines the notion of authenticity had already come under sharp attack and was, if still breathing, on life support.

The most sustained critique occurred in the journal *Early Music* in 1984. In separate articles, Richard Taruskin and Nicholas Temperley called into question the very premises underlying the notion of an authentic approach. Taruskin brought this out into the open in 1990 with a lengthy article in the *New York Times,* whose title, "The Spin Doctors of Early Music," clearly revealed his view. Temperley in 1984 was particularly harsh on the movement, calling it more about novelty than authenticity, finding the advocates arrogant in their claims, and dismissing the notion that we could ever recreate a performance as it was done in Bach's or Beethoven's time. To him the early-music movement was a fad "that will melt away as surely as the snow."[29]

Like Temperley, Taruskin, who at one time had been active as a performer of early music in New York, saw it for what it was, a specifically twentieth-century approach to music making, with a twentieth-century, not an eighteenth-century, or Renaissance, or medieval aesthetic. Taruskin's critique was not all that different from Temperley's, but he went considerably further in explaining its twentieth-century roots. Authenticity had robbed music of its personality. To be authentic meant to adhere strictly to what we know or believe we know about the original performance situation of the music under consideration. Further additions robbed the piece of its authenticity. Thus, "the first thing that must go in a critical edition, as in the kind of 'authentic' performance I am describing, is any sense of the editor's or performer's own presence; any sentiment, as Rousseau would have said, of his being."[30]

Even Norrington, universally considered one of the most perceptive and talented musicians of the early-music movement, came under criticism in this context for his Beethoven performances. He chose Beethoven's tempi all right, but once chosen he adhered strictly to them, in spite of indirect evidence that Beethoven himself wanted no such thing: he expected the performer to be flexible once Beethoven had indicated the starting point.

Thus limiting possibilities of interpretation to the available evidence from the composer's time resulted in a musical performance that was, if not true to the past, much in tune with the present. It was a modernist approach closely linked to post–World War II positivism. It had already been adumbrated by Toscanini, whose fame expanded even further after the war. It celebrated "the autonomous work of art," a concept found in literary studies and then in music in the form of theory and analysis. "This profoundly modernist viewpoint decrees that the work of art is not to be described or valued for its effects (e.g. on the audience) or its human interest (e.g. with respect to its creator), but strictly on its own formal, quasi-mechanistic or quasi-organic terms." Taruskin then quotes E. D. Hirsch: "The spirit killeth, but the letter giveth life," and summarizes the authenticity movement as "a positivistic purgatory, literalistic and dehumanizing, a thing of taboos and contingences instead of the liberating expansion of horizons and opportunities it could be and was meant to be."[31]

As depressing as this sounds today, it fit the postwar mood. Taruskin may have been overzealous in his rhetoric, but what he found in the authenticity movement was not different from what Boulez, Cage, Babbitt, Foss, and other composers desired: anonymity, removal of personal expression, in sum depersonalization. That desire could be fulfilled by positivism in scholarship, by integral serialism or indeterminacy in composition, and by authenticity in performance. All were consistent with a tone that characterized the arts in the years after the Second World War.

5

"The Warm Tropical Summer
of Sketch Research"

Beethoven and the Cold War

WHEN BEETHOVEN DIED IN 1827, he left behind some 5,000 pages in manuscript. These included not only autograph scores and letters, as expected from any composer, but also items that made Beethoven's legacy unique. There were the conversation books, which Beethoven maintained so that people could communicate with him after he became totally deaf. No other composer has provided posterity with such an intimate record of his daily interactions, although, because Beethoven usually responded orally, we read only one side of a conversation. Beethoven's other legacy was approximately 4,000 pages of sketches, reflecting a lifelong habit. While nearly all composers sketch their musical ideas on paper, none have done so as constantly and obsessively as Beethoven, and none preserved the quantity that Beethoven did. Unlike Mozart, who worked out much of his composition in his head, Beethoven seems to have written down virtually every thought, no matter how trivial or unformed. The smallest motive, the most fragmentary idea, Beethoven committed to paper. He had large sketchbooks to work from at his desk; he had smaller ones that would fit in his pocket so that he would never be without one during his many extensive walks. Beethoven was always, always sketching.

Beethoven moved his lodgings frequently; unhappy with one place he would not hesitate to move to another. In his thirty-five years in Vienna he lived in at least twenty-six residences, not counting more than forty country rooms that he rented during the summer.[1] Yet in spite of this peripatetic life, he clung to his sketches, even as he piled up stacks and stacks of them. It is remarkable that he never threw them away. Works long since completed or projects abandoned years before, he guarded his sketches as his most precious private possession. The sketchbooks *were* Beethoven.

After his death the sketches were at first treated casually. When Beethoven's estate was sold in auction, the music firm Artaria and Co. purchased most of his manuscripts; considering the sketchbooks of little monetary value, the publisher gave out individual pages as souvenirs, much like people send Christmas cards. For over one hundred years only a handful of scholars paid attention to the sketches, and even those who did questioned their value. The first scholar to systematically examine the sketches in the nineteenth century, Gustav Nottebohm, felt that they revealed little about the compositions themselves, and that their use would be confined mainly to biography. A few other writers attempted to generate interest in the sketches, notably Paul Mies and Karl Lothar Mikulicz, but for most Beethoven scholars the sketches held only minimal interest.

Part of the problem lay in gaining access to or in some cases even locating the sketches. Thanks to Artaria's generosity to his friends and customers, many of the sketchbooks were in pieces, scattered throughout Europe, often in private hands and with parts missing. Although most remained in Germany, the political upheavals there, starting with World War I, the inflation and economic chaos of the 1920s, the Nazi takeover in the 1930s, and finally World War II, created significant barriers to any scholar wanting to examine them. Compounding the problem was the destruction and disruption caused by the Allied bombing during World War II, and the division of the Berlin Library between East and West Germany at the beginning of the Cold War. For a time

---

FIGURE 5.1 FACING

Peter Johann Nepomuk Geiger,
Beethoven Sitting in the Woods.
Courtesy of Beethoven-Haus Bonn.

it was not clear to scholars whether specific material was held in either the East or West German library.

In spite of these many complications, scholars were able to concentrate on the sketches shortly after the war. With most of Beethoven's compositions published, the Beethoven-Haus in Bonn, the semi-official guardian of all things Beethoven, began to publish the sketchbooks. Their method was straightforward: each page would be transcribed exactly as Beethoven wrote it, without scholarly emendation. Anyone who has looked at a Beethoven sketch knows that this is not as simple as it sounds. Common wisdom holds that, as Lewis Lockwood expressed it, Beethoven's sketches "range from difficult to indecipherable."[2] In their joint work on the subject, Douglas Johnson, Alan Tyson, and Robert Winter compared their task to "taming the beast of illegibility."[3] Beethoven's sketches are messy and often have important information, such as clefs, left out (see Figure 5.2). The Beethoven-Haus employed a type of transcription known as "diplomatic," a philological term that technically means an exact rendering, but in this case it means that the transcriber made his best guess at what Beethoven intended.

And there the situation remained until around 1970 when American scholars, with unprecedented zeal and enthusiasm, suddenly became interested in the sketches. Why the unexpected focus on sketches after they had lain dormant for so many decades? What motivated Americans to plunge fully into the world of Beethoven sketches, to the extent that for a brief period any Beethoven scholar who did not deal with them was looked upon askance by the American Beethoven fraternity? No matter the issue or problem involving Beethoven, I can personally attest that the first question that musicologists of the time would invariably ask was *Are you working with the sketches?*"

Sketch scholarship can be among the most technical and arcane of academic activities, encompassing not only the problem of transcription, but of dating and even assigning sketches to their intended pieces. Beethoven's first ideas for a composition might be a small snippet of a motive inserted among other pieces, sometimes so removed from its final configuration that his intentions are not clear at all. Beethoven also had the habit of jumping forward and backward and jotting down ideas for more than one piece in a short span of pages, so that pagination has little to do with temporal continuity or even compositional identification. Even before Beethoven's scribbling can be examined, however, there is the problem of reassembling, ordering, and dating the pages, which involves specialized techniques such as determining when and where the paper was manufactured; extensive knowledge of watermarks, translucent symbols embedded in paper that manufacturers used as branding;

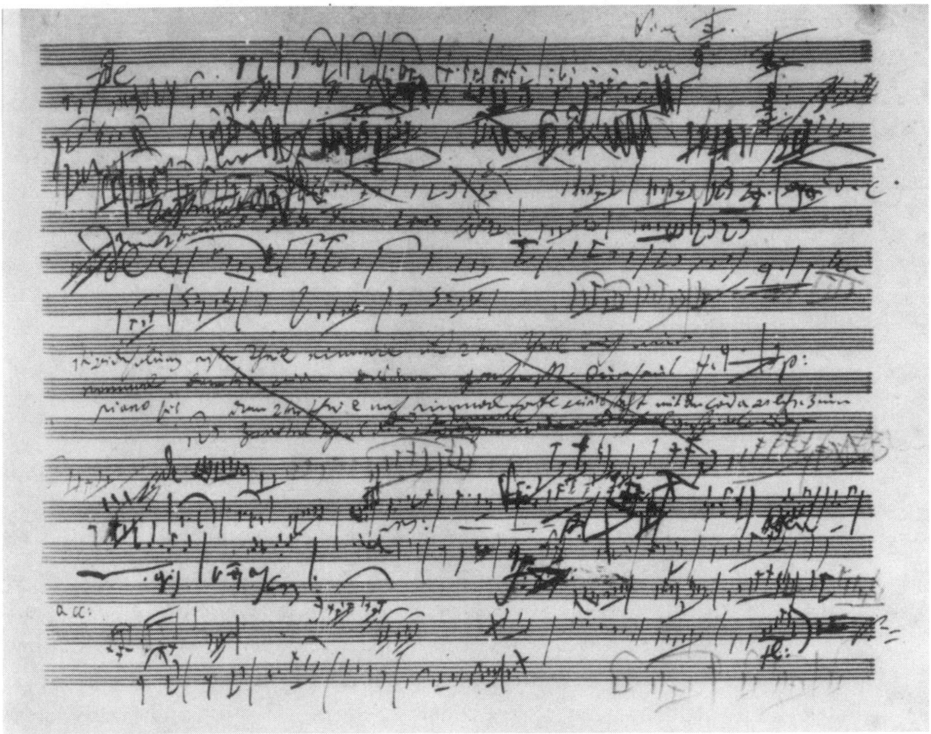

FIGURE 5.2

A page of Beethoven's sketches for the Eighth Symphony,
in what is now known as the Peter Sketchbook, c. 1812.

and even how larger folios were cut, folded, or assembled to create a notebook.
Further requirements are a thorough familiarity with German and nineteenth-
century German script, sufficient familiarity with the entire Beethoven corpus to allow identification of fragments—Beethoven seldom tells you what the
sketch was for, and many fragments never became part of a finished composition—and a temperament suited to slow, painstaking, detailed work.

When asked why they engaged in sketch research, most scholars would cite
purely disciplinary reasons. For some it was the sheer fascination with such a
large body of material. For others it was a mentor who brought the approach
from Germany. Internal developments within the world of musicology and
humanistic research also contributed to the ascendancy of sketch research, as

some scholars found themselves boxed in, with older approaches seemingly having run their course and only a murky horizon in view for new ones. Production of modern editions of important European music of the past, musicology's former primary focus, had for the most part been accomplished. Guido Adler, one of the pioneers in musicology, identified a descriptive style analysis as one of the field's principal goals, but that was one hundred years ago. Disciplinary evolution demanded new worlds to conquer, and sketch research seemed to fit the bill.

There were also practical reasons for the proliferation of sketch studies in the 1970s. The number of graduate students entering musicology in American universities increased dramatically between 1960 and 1970. With many students searching for dissertations, the 4,000 pages of sketches seemed a gold mine, something that had all the requisites of a satisfactory dissertation: as a large body of primary sources that required considerable knowledge and skill as well as infinite patience to decipher, sketches held out the promise of insights gained in no other way, and the entire corpus could be easily divided into manageable chunks, either through the study of specific sketch books or individual compositions. The focus on a musical score as well as the sheer bulk of material was reminiscent of the many Renaissance dissertations that had dominated musical scholarship in its earlier days, when the prime rite of passage for an aspiring musicologist consisted of transcription and discussion of older manuscripts involving considerable puzzles, not the least of which was deciphering an arcane and obsolete notation. It is no coincidence that many Beethoven scholars of an earlier generation, including Elliot Forbes, Joseph Kerman, and Lewis Lockwood, did their dissertations on Renaissance topics.

Yet the most important reasons scholars so embraced the world of sketch studies are to be found outside the ivory tower, although few musicologists have acknowledged this. The sudden rise and intense focus on sketch studies reflected the cultural moment. International alignments following World War II, cultural nationalism, incipient questions regarding the Western classical music canon, and particularly the Cold War are all mirrored in the work and the motivations behind sketch activity in the 1970s. While the musical results of sketch studies have been thoroughly discussed, how they touched on these broader issues and how that placed Beethoven in American culture remains a little-told story.

Cultural connections can be understood, however, only with some knowledge of work before 1970 that led up to the expanding interest in sketch studies. Some of the early attempts to incorporate sketches were far outside traditional musical scholarship. In 1936 the psychologist Paul C. Squires published

"Beethoven's Concept of the Whole" in the *American Journal of Psychology*, in which he used Nottebohm's sketches for the *Eroica*, Beethoven's "workshop records," to study the "mental processes involved in musical production." Squires demonstrated considerable familiarity with the literature on Beethoven and advanced some controversial claims. One was that the *Gestaltung*, that is, the overall form, is better in Beethoven's fast movements than his slow movements. According to Squires, the fast movements have a "higher degree of goodness" due to "the well-known psychological fact that, up to a critical region, depending upon the operation of a complex of conditions, increase of pulsation rate effects a heightening of the 'goodness' of tonal structure."[4] Squires never defines what the "goodness of tonal structure" means, but irrespective of the soundness or datedness of his argument, its most significant aspect is its appearance not in a musical but in a psychological journal.

An article by Oswald Jonas in 1940 anticipates the sketch approaches of the 1970s. Jonas was originally motivated to write about a sketch found in the New York Public Library for Beethoven's *Clärchen Lieder*, a group of songs that Beethoven included in the incidental music for Goethe's play *Egmont*. He was motivated to do so because Georg Kinsky had not listed it in his *Handbook of Beethoven's Egmont Music*. Jonas felt the sketch to be worth discussing beyond this oversight because it shed light on the origin of the two such songs. Of interest here is Jonas's methodology: he surveyed other sketches and situated his in relation to them, and then determined what inferences are possible regarding how Beethoven came to the final product, the songs themselves. This approach foreshadows later scholars' methods, although most activity did not begin in earnest for another thirty years.[5]

Before work could proceed beyond the occasional examination of a single sketch or sketchbook, scholars needed some sense of the order, magnitude, and provenance of the sketches. How many existed, what was available, and where was it? In 1953 Jonas himself estimated that over 4,000 Beethoven sketches lay unpublished, and the Beethoven-Haus in Bonn, which had emerged as the center of Beethoven activity, began to take the lead in inventorying and making them available. American scholars, however, frustrated by both the methodology and the rate of progress at the Beethoven-Haus, soon advanced an alternative approach.

In 1964 Joseph Kerman issued a call for a new American musicology, in which he suggested that American musicologists find their own voice separate from the Germanic tradition, which dominated most American universities principally because of the large exodus of scholars from Nazi Germany. Kerman's solution was "criticism," and while sketch studies was not foremost in his mind, at least in the paper he read before the American Musicological Society and the subsequent article based on it, his philosophy suggested a difference: sketch studies should be less about literal transcription and more about interpretation. Sketches could be used to provide insight into pieces, into the compositional process, and even more broadly into Beethoven's aesthetic premises.

The firestorm that Kerman's paper created only reinforced a growing restlessness among young American scholars. But if criticism was the thing, why emphasize sketch studies? The two hardly seem congruent.

Kerman began to answer that question two years later in an article on sketchbooks housed in the British Museum in London. He noted first that, with minor exceptions, little had been done with the sketches, but he ventured no reason why. After a detailed examination of the sketches to the Andante of Beethoven's Sixth Symphony, in which he stressed issues regarding the larger plan for the movement as opposed to melodic or rhythmic details, Kerman concluded by briefly arguing the value of such study: specifically, the compositional process. The sketches provided a way to get inside the composer's head and trace his thoughts from the earliest rough hints of a piece through the myriad problems of working it out until it emerged, complete, bearing the full imprint of Beethoven. After first noting the difficulty and the necessity of coordinating all the sketches for a piece and then establishing a chronology, Kerman addressed the importance of this approach: "Studies of this sort allow us to come closer to an understanding of the compositional process than any other branches of musical scholarship that come easily to mind. And while an understanding of the compositional process is not equivalent to insight into the work of art as such, it is, once again, a closer route to such insight than is provided by most of our other scholarly activities."[6]

While at the British Museum, Kerman began to investigate another group of sketches that interested him even more than those on the Sixth Symphony, a group of loose leaves known as the Kafka Miscellany that date back to Beethoven's Bonn days and extended through much of the 1790s. He first published a lengthy article on them and then a complete edition, including a facsimile and transcription of the original sketches. The edition proved to be an important event, a turning point in the history of Beethoven sketch scholarship.[7]

Kerman envisioned that his work would indeed launch a new interest in sketch studies. In the introduction to his study, he observed the discrepancy between how well known the sketchbooks were and how little serious scholars have engaged them, and he pointed to his own efforts as a heuristic wake-up call: "Yet the present editor is persuaded that the Beethoven sketches in general . . . constitute a source for the study of great potential that has remained largely untapped. Considering the celebrity of this material, it is remarkable how few sketchbooks have been published in usable editions, and how little serious work has been done with them, whether from the historical, analytical, critical, or psychological points of view."[8]

Kerman's edition of the Kafka Miscellany, published in 1970, stands in stark contrast to his own study of the string quartets of Beethoven, published only three years earlier, where his analysis rested ultimately upon his own intuition, something he stated forthrightly. This surfaces most clearly when he grappled with the problem: What happens when fact and intuition clash?

> Three obvious moves are possible in dealing with the problem. The first follows the instinctive tendency of the analyst, which is to instruct himself (and others) to experience aesthetic fact that begins merely as observed fact. This tries to bring intuition around. The opposite move is to call the observed data into question on grounds of error, irrelevance, taking out of context, and so on. This tries to bring observation around. Only if these do not meet the situation should an aesthetic breach be conceded between ends and means within the work of art itself.[9]

Kerman brought to this study not only a highly developed aesthetic sense, but a sophisticated set of analytical tools, and possibly an unsurpassed ability to express musical insights in language. In spite of the success of his book— still one of the most perceptive studies of the quartets—I also believe that it could not have been written after the 1960s. It is both typical of its time and yet somewhat foreign to its time. It is too personal to be a representative study in the positivistic, speculative-phobic world of postwar, Teutonic-dominated musicological scholarship. Yet it is perfectly congruent with the descriptive, humanistic, non-theoretic, pre-postmodern, pre-deconstructionist world of the humanities in the 1950s and early 1960s. Kerman's study is in the same mold as Charles Rosen's *The Classical Style*, which was published in 1971. Together they mark, in Beethoven scholarship, the last throes of descriptive, quasi-analytical studies of classical music that assume organicism as its primary endpoint, that approach pieces as *sui generis* art objects, that rely principally upon the author's musical instincts as a determinant of aesthetic values, and that subordinate context and reception to issues of stylistic change and evolution. This may be one reason for the interest in sketch studies in the 1970s.

The descriptive-stylistic approach seemed to offer little future, and American scholars were restless under the positivistic curtain. Postmodernism, still in its infancy, was well beyond the horizon of musicological scholarship.

Aided and abetted by Kerman himself with his 1966 article on the Sixth Symphony, the tide had already begun to turn away from descriptive-stylistic approaches by the time Kerman's quartet book came out. Yet there was only a trickle of sketch activity. As typical of academic publishing, the quartet study, or at least most of the work on it, undoubtedly predated the publication of the Sixth Symphony article. Most striking about the quartet book is the sheer absence of any discussion of Beethoven sketches. There are only occasional references to them, and they play virtually no role in Kerman's central analyses.

Other studies from the 1960s confirm the relative absence of the sketches in Beethoven scholarship. In 1964 Ernest Sanders wrote a detailed study titled "Form and Content in the Finale of Beethoven's Ninth Symphony," and in the same year Karl Geiringer did a similar analysis of the *Diabelli Variations*. Neither of these studies used sketches at all. It is unlikely that any similar analytical discussion that ignored the sketches would have even found publication ten years later, in the heyday of sketch studies.[10]

There were, to be sure, some Beethoven sketch studies in the 1960s. In 1966 Alexander Ringer examined sketches for an uncompleted *Erlking* in the Gesellschaft fur Musikfreunde in Vienna.[11] But by 1970 what had been a small stream of activity widened into a deluge. At a conference on nineteenth-century music in Saint-Germainen-Laye, discussion of the topic "Problems of Musical Creation in the Nineteenth Century" generated extraordinary interest. Of special note was Lewis Lockwood's paper, later published, which gave a theoretical framework and justification to the use of sketches.[12] Since the year 1970 coincided with the bicentennial of Beethoven's birth, the entire classical musical world was focused on Beethoven. It was an ideal time to introduce new directions. Numerous articles appeared that used sketches extensively, and the question of compositional process, the most promising area of investigation that centered on sketches, became a dominant theme. Younger scholars in particular, searching for dissertation topics, took up the challenge of sketch investigation.

In 1973, three of the most prominent senior scholars in the field, Joseph Kerman, Lewis Lockwood, and Alan Tyson, established a new journal, *Beethoven Studies,* which, according to Kerman, "invites mostly (if not exclusively) contributions dealing with sketch problems." In reality *Beethoven Studies* published many non-sketch articles, particularly on topics of Beethoven biography, but the bias was clear: sketch research was the favored domain. Kerman, in a retrospective article published in 1982, acknowledged that sketch studies had not flourished until the 1960s, and that it was mostly an American phenomenon. Even though Alan Tyson, the editor of *Beethoven Studies*, was British, Kerman defended his national orientation by noting that "his [Tyson's] musicological orientation is really less native than American."[13]

In the introduction to volume 1, Tyson argued that Beethoven studies was still in the nineteenth century. He pointed out the three principal accomplishments of nineteenth-century Beethoven scholarship: a major biography (A. W. Thayer's *Life of Beethoven*), publication of the complete edition of the composer's works, and Nottebohm's pioneering sketch studies. Tyson then argued that nothing followed of "the same comprehensiveness and acuity." He suggested that the very magnitude of these accomplishments may have inhibited further scholars from following in the footsteps of their esteemed predecessors. In fact, most of what happened since then maintained a nineteenth-century tinge to it.

So what did Tyson have in mind for scholars? They should pursue new texts (of music, letters, sketches) with commentary, not just transcriptions with minimal annotational apparatus. He wrote of "opportunities missed," such as of reassembling within a single publication sketches that were originally together but became scattered. Second, with regard to interpretation, including the historical, analytical, and critical, "there has been little work that is penetrating and original." And third, Tyson regarded manuscript studies as both important and newly possible, for sources had become more accessible, more easily circulated with microfilm, and enhanced by investigations such as papers types.[14]

Underlying Tyson's specific arguments is a powerful modernist agenda. Tyson wanted to wrest Beethoven scholarship from the nineteenth century and associate it with twentieth-century modernism, as discussed in the previous chapter. While he outlined an agenda that incorporates virtually all areas of Beethoven study, in reality he was most interested in source studies, careful and critical examination of the many types of sources, letters, autographs, and especially sketches. This is hard-nosed, scholarly work at its most scientific. The volume itself reflects Tyson's leanings. Virtually every contribution is in one way or another a source study. Most involve detailed examination of sketches, with conclusions that are not only appropriate for the material but for Tyson's purpose. These particular studies were by scholars who would tend to dominate Beethoven scholarship for the next twenty years: Joseph Kerman, Lewis Lockwood, and Richard Kramer. Curiously, the one interpretative chapter that is not fundamentally a sketch study is not by a musicologist but a composer, Andrew Imbrie. The other three contributions in this volume, by Douglas Johnson and two by Alan Tyson, are positivistic studies, involving solving problems with sources themselves by using newly developed methods, or simply presenting newly discovered sources.

Yet by the late 1970s doubts about the value of sketch studies were creeping into Beethoven scholarship. In 1978 Douglas Johnson, who had written a dissertation under Kerman on a set of Beethoven sketches and who with Alan Tyson and his student colleague at Berkeley, Robert Winter, would publish an extensive inventory and reconstruction of all known sketchbooks, raised serious questions about the value of sketch research. Johnson, drawing a hard-and-fast separation between biography and musical analysis, a point that harkened back to Nottebohm in the nineteenth century, argued that sketches may have some utility in biography, but virtually none for analysis. He was even skeptical of the payoff for biography, "since the obvious difficulties they pose may seem out of proportion with the nature of the results they yield." The problem in analysis lay in the relationship of the sketch to the piece itself: If it is close to the final version, then of what interest is it? Why not study the piece instead? If it differs significantly from the final version, then it represents only what Beethoven rejected, and of what value is that in examining the piece?[15]

As might be expected, Johnson's essay created no small reaction from the Beethoven sketch fraternity. Scholars questioned the hard division between biography and analysis that Johnson postulated, and noted that his own concept of analysis, focusing on Schenkerian methods, was narrow. They also challenged the very notion that sketches could not yield important analytical information, by taking the argument to Johnson's own turf, citing how even Schenker used sketches to support and strengthen what might be tenuous connections in Beethoven's compositions. Finally, scholars noted that biography itself, particularly when applied to how compositions relate, can be an important dimension in understanding Beethoven's music.[16]

Johnson was not alone in questioning the continuing viability of sketch studies. Prompted by the discussion elicited by Johnson's critique, which was originally presented at the 1977 Congress of the International Musicological Society in Berkeley, Sieghard Brandenburg, director of the Beethoven-Haus, delivered what might be called a eulogy for sketch work. Referring to the Congress as the watershed meeting in relation to sketch studies, he called the time between 1970 and 1977 "the warm tropical summer of sketch research," with its "occasional exotic blooms," and expressed concern that the field, "more than a hundred years old, lapses once again into its prior comatose condition." He lamented that the "brief renaissance" of sketch studies is "now forever and gone," and predicted that sketch research in the future will "be confronted once again by apathy and neglect on the part of the vast majority of musicologists."[17]

It should be stressed that Brandenburg did not oppose sketch research; in fact he was involved in it himself. He was concerned with its fate, and in that he was overly pessimistic. His predictions of its demise were grossly exaggerated, although that brief exultant flurry of activity that characterized the 1970s would never be equaled. Many scholars who had begun sketch research at that time continued, some producing their best work in the 1980s and later. Others continue to the present. Even the major monograph *Beethoven Sketchbooks,* which Johnson coauthored with Tyson and Winter, did not appear until 1985. The two time lags between conception and completion of a scholarly project and between completion and publication explain part of the mid-1980s date. Yet the work, which for the first time provided scholars bibliographic control and a relatively complete inventory and provenance of all sketchbooks, did not elicit the upsurge in activity that one might expect. Sketch studies would continue, but they would no longer dominate the Beethoven scholarly landscape. When Joseph Kerman was asked, in 2007, about the fate of sketch research after the 1970s, he remarked that he did not think it disappeared; it just went underground.[18]

The 1990s brought signs of change in the Beethoven world. In 1992 a group of scholars attempted to pick up where *Beethoven Studies* and the German journal *Beethoven Jahrbuch* had left off. The last issue of these two journals appeared in 1982 and 1983, respectively. The editor of the new *Beethoven Journal,* Christopher Reynolds, in an introductory essay, observed that the field of Beethoven research has "changed considerably." Reynolds acknowledged that more traditional methods, specifically sketch studies, was still alive, but he stressed new, fresh approaches, such as a revival of interest in literary associations and other extramusical issues in Beethoven's music, and a greater emphasis on the context in which Beethoven's music was created. Sketch studies might still be around, but to many they had become middle-aged and stodgy.

The rise and for a time virtual obsession with sketch studies reflected in particular two trends in American culture, both of which can be traced to specific and unrelated events of the 1950s. In 1956 Chuck Berry released his hit record "Roll Over Beethoven." The following year, on October 4, 1957, the Soviet Union launched the first orbiting satellite, Sputnik. Berry's song was a challenge to the status quo, of both the popular and the classical musical world, and a reminder that the hierarchical divisions of the nineteenth century were no longer to be assumed. Sputnik was simultaneously a shock, a wake-up call

and an announcement that a new era, the space age, had begun. Although neither had an immediate impact on how Americans perceived Beethoven, the effects of both on scholars' activities would be readily apparent by the 1970s.

With Berry's mega-hit, rumblings of a backlash against the classical canon,
which had been present in segments of the art-music world since the early
twentieth century, came fully into the open. Yet in 1957 there was little danger
that the position of classical music would be dethroned. The LP, high fidelity,
and then stereo recordings had created a heightened interest in classical music,
as the repertoire became available as never before. According to some statistics, by 1960 there were twice as many symphony orchestras and seven times
as many opera companies in the United States as there had been in 1940. Only
with the solidification of youth culture in the 1960s did the classical canon
seem in danger. "Roll Over Beethoven" reached an even broader audience when
covered by the Beatles in 1964, and then by many other artists, such as Tom
Jones, Jerry Lee Lewis, and Gerry & the Pacemakers. Berry's song, discussed
further in chapter 11, was less anticlassical than an assertion that rock 'n' roll
was more than the latest popular fad, but a new, viable, enduring style. It fit
right into the 1960s, with its youth emphasis and mantras such as Abby Hoffman's maxim "Don't trust anyone over thirty" and Bob Dylan's song "The Times
They Are a-Changing." The youth of the 1960s seemed to challenge all aspects
of inherited Western culture, not just classical music. Academicians began to
take notice of the products of 1960s pop culture, but most of the interest occurred outside of music, particularly in American Studies departments, where
the lyrics of song writers such as Dylan were studied as poetry, and in history
departments, where songs connected to the civil rights movement and later
Vietnam War protests were at least acknowledged. Musicology was still bound
to the Western fine arts tradition, and the new field of ethnomusicology was
more interested in music of exotic and far-off places.

Beethoven scholars held a special place in the world of musical scholarship, only challenged by scholars of J. S. Bach, as their composers represented
the highest embodiment of the classical canon. In Beethoven's case, scholars
stressed the complexity of his thought, symbolized by sketch scholars with the
phrase "compositional process," and they implied that Beethoven occupied an
entirely different realm in the compositional universe than the less sophisticated purveyors of rock 'n' roll. That many sketches were what Joshua Rifkin
termed "continuity drafts," where Beethoven blocked out the entire movement
in order to see the shape and the overall plan, reinforced the perception that
Beethoven was preoccupied with large-scale structure and design. As sketch
research demonstrated, Beethoven's music was larger, deeper, more coherent,

and on a level that neither Chuck Berry nor the many popular musicians of the 1960s could hope to approach. Not even the Beatles, touted by classical musicians for their innovation and sophistication, could compare with Beethoven. No matter what Berry or Dylan said, Beethoven's music, and by extension the classical canon, stood apart.

I do not believe that sketch scholars set out overtly to defend the canon—one can safely say Chuck Berry is hardly in their writings. Yet their tone was important in the defense of the canon. The frontline of the battle, however, was waged more in journalism than in scholarly writing. In 1981 critic Donal Henahan attempted to distinguish classical from pop in what was intended as a tongue-in-cheek *New York Times* article, "Do You Speak Classical or Pop?" Although he sought to represent both sides, his bias toward classical music is clear throughout the article. Yet he does provide a succinct summary of how each side thought at the beginning of the 1980s: "The Classicist finds it incomprehensible that most Pop music is expressively crude and formally slipshod. To Pop musicians and their fans, music is simply cathartic self-expression, so for them the Classical tradition's stress on form and endless shades of expression must look like little more than emotional constipation."[19] Although the distinction between the two types of music today seems less clear and less important, it did not appear that way in the 1970s. The cerebral as opposed to the emotional was stressed in classical music, whether by composers, in which a mathematical, atonal style held sway; performers, who favored speed and structural outlines over expression of feelings; or scholars, who spoke of overall design and complexity rather than poetic content. Beethoven, who had been seen as the Romantic composer par excellence by the nineteenth century, was made into a classicist, someone whose principal concern was formal structure.

The changes in post–World War II academia were important to the defense of the canon. If Beethoven's music was to be defended as special and different, it was important that it be done on scientific, that is, on positivistic grounds. The principal apologists for Beethoven were in academia, where in musicology positivism still reigned. As noted above, the older form of positivism, imported primarily from Germany, stressed an approach that disdained questions of value in favor of demonstrable, objective results. Yet the challenge that popular music posed was ultimately one of value. Sketch studies allowed value to be introduced within the cover of a rigorous scientific approach. Compositional process encompassed a wide range of possibilities, and engendered within the musicological fraternity considerable debate about exactly what it demonstrated that could not be gleaned from the piece itself, but at the very least it suggested a composer concerned with bringing to fruition works of un-precedented size, scope, and originality. Beethoven's struggles in one sense vindicated his compositions.

To even compare rock with the classical canon on its own turf, that of structure, however, would be to misunderstand the nature of rock itself, and to miss those qualities that made it such a threat to the classical world. Rock in the 1960s was more than entertainment: rock concerts were a shared experi-ence for those who attended and knew the code; rock also became a way of life, and as society seemed to split into multiple sub-cultures, especially among the young, lifestyle was often defined by the rock event. Even more impor-tant, rock embodied many elements of religion: the rock critic Albert Gold-man characterized rock as "spilt religion." In 1968 Benjamin DeMott, in an article entitled "Rock as Salvation," spoke of rock as a "religious force."[20] Rock concerts, including the daddy of them all, Woodstock, took on the character-istics of a religious revival, a large communal ritual in which the participants attained a mood of ecstatic release, transported by the pounding rhythms, the unrestrained emotionalism of the performers, and the sheer volume, all of which is designed for sensual overload. Drugs, it should be noted, cannot be ignored as part of the total experience. David Graham, in his 1984 film *Rock My Religion,* compared the rock event with a Shaker religious meeting and the tent revivals of the Second Great Awakening in the early nineteenth century, in which participants would become possessed, speak in tongues, roll on the ground, and be consumed with uncontrollable body shakes and jerks. A rock concert may have been secular, narcissistic, and built on the pleasures of the moment, and its intensity may have been enhanced by drugs, but for many youth it represented a set of values and manners far beyond the role of any tra-ditional event.

Goldman saw rock not only as a type of religion, but connected it directly with Romanticism, in its hyper-emotionalism and drive to ecstasy. The sac-ralization of Beethoven's music and later Beethoven himself had also come out of the Romantic response to the overwhelming emotional power listeners felt in his music. Thus by 1970 rock could not only lay a similar claim to the idea of sacralization as Beethoven, but could also trace it to the same roots. That the nature of the two types of music differed as much as the type of religion each represented could not negate the assertion of rock proponents, that rock was akin to religion.

Thus on several levels Berry's exhortation to Beethoven to "Dig these rhythm and blues" raises the question of the validity of the canon. Specifically, is there one canon or are there multiple canons? If the latter were true, then the pyramid of aesthetic values, so popular in the nineteenth century, would collapse, and the world of classical music that Beethoven epitomized would be just another choice of the consumer and would have no special privileged position. This question could also be framed in terms of sacralization: Is American musical culture monotheistic or polytheistic?

While the work of sketch scholars provided only an indirect response to Berry's and 1960s youth's challenge to the canon, their alignment with science was more clear-cut. The musical-mathematical association can be traced back to at least Pythagoras, but it received new life following World War II when many American composers gravitated to twelve-tone music. The most influential person in this movement was Milton Babbitt at Princeton University. Trained as a mathematician, he not only composed serial music that expanded on the ideas of Arnold Schoenberg, but he also gave theoretical voice to the movement itself. Babbitt specifically and overtly aligned himself with science. In his best-known article, "The Composer as Specialist," which *High Fidelity* magazine, much to Babbitt's chagrin, headlined "Who Cares if You Listen," he viewed the work of the composer as akin to that of the scientist and pleaded that it be considered as such.[21] Babbitt's own compositions, while extremely influential within the academy and among serial composers, had only a minor impact on the classical concert world, as did serialism in general. Musicology, though taking note of the new developments in compositional activity, continued much as it had, scouring records and documents, guided more by the German historian Leopold Ranke's charge to write about the past *wie es eigentlich gewessen*, "as it really happened," more than out of any concern about science per se. In hindsight, the alignment of music and science seems prescient and consequently has been much discussed, but at the time it was only one corner of one segment of the American musical world.

Sputnik changed all that. On October 4, 1957, the Soviet Union launched the first artificial satellite. It surprised even scientists who had long known that both countries were racing to put an object into orbit, not because the Soviets succeeded but because of its size, 184 pounds. American scientists had hoped to be able to put a 21-pound satellite into space by the following spring, but the Russians had demonstrated that they had rocketry capable of a far bigger payload than the Americans. A near panic ensued—if the Russians could put that large a satellite into orbit, what else could their rockets carry? While President Eisenhower sought to play down the military significance of Sputnik, Senate Majority Leader Lyndon Johnson is reputed to have wondered if those satellites could drop bombs on the United States like apples falling off a tree. Senator Henry Jackson, known as a defense expert, called Sputnik a "devastating blow to the United States' scientific, industrial and technical prestige in the world."

For many, it was less a question of military threat than the realization that a new age had begun. Jonathan Eberhart ran out to look at the night sky when he heard the news, "not because I thought I'd seen anything different . . . but because the sky suddenly *felt* different." A tenth-grader at the time, Eberhart went on to become a science writer, and years later he vividly remembered that on that October evening the sky "had certainly changed, and it would never be the same again."[22]

Americans rushed to catch up. Senator Mike Mansfield called for a new Manhattan Project; Eisenhower appointed the first presidential science advisor. Education in particular was targeted: the country decided it must do more for science education. Looking back twenty years later, Carol Schulz Slobodin observed, "The Soviet launch of Sputnik initiated a rekindling of the fervor (of the means and the ends of the natural sciences) that marked the earlier period of domination by the natural sciences."[23]

One of the immediate and important responses to Sputnik was the National Defense Education Act, which became law on September 2, 1958, less than one year after Sputnik. The bill was divided into ten provisions, all aimed toward "the fullest development of the mental resources and technical skills of its young men and women." While specifically targeting science and technology, it also affected many other areas of higher education. According to Secretary of Health, Education, and Welfare Arthur Flemming, its purpose was to motivate young men and women toward "those intellectual pursuits that will enrich personal life, strengthen resistance to totalitarianism, and enhance the quality of American leadership on the international scene."[24] Foreign language study was targeted specifically in the bill, which opened the door for research in many music-related areas such as folklore. In 1961, for instance, Catherine Stevens was awarded a grant to "make high fidelity recordings of Chinese popular entertainments including chanted poetry, Shantung music, comic dialogues, Honan opera, folktales, Peking opera, and Ming drama." Musicology was not targeted, but by encouraging foreign study and enhancing higher education in general, with large sums flowing into schools and to talented students, universities were on a stronger overall footing financially. They also gained in prestige in the community; according to Flemming, the NDEA specifically "recognizes that education is a national unifying force, and it regards an educated citizenry as the country's most precious resource."[25]

The closer musicology could appear to science, the stronger its position within the academy, and the better it could argue its case for both internal funding and recognition. Composers and theorists had already discovered that point, and in musicology German positivism made that an apparently easy adjustment. In 1975 the philosopher Peter Kivy described the nature of musicology in a communication to the most venerable of musicological journals, the *Journal of the American Musicological Society:* "The musicologist hopes to reach 'scientific' conclusions: 'scientific' merely in the sense of objective, open to verification and universal assent. Premises concerning the aesthetic character of music, being hopelessly subjective, and hence unscientific, are as unwelcome as the starfish to the clam." Kivy also observed that "such aesthetic premises are harder to avoid than one might think."[26]

Kerman's call for criticism, inherently interpretive and hence wrapped in questions of value, seemed to fly in the face of a rigid scientific bent. Were American scholars going to remain within the Germanic world that Kerman wished them to break from? Sketch studies, however, suggested a solution, a way to eat one's aesthetic cake and have it too. The Beethoven sketches provided a large body of evidence that promised hard answers to hard questions. Those thousands of pages gave the musicologist the equivalent of his own laboratory, and she could thus meet the scientist on his own terms; even though the material was different, the bulk of evidence gave it a cachet that no aesthetic-philosophical or analytical argument could even attain. To the academic world, where this issue mattered most, the American musicologist engaged in sketch research seemed what the Germans had termed him from the start, a *Musikwissenschafter* (music scientist).

Interpretation, however, could still reside in sketch research, but with a distinct twentieth-century orientation. Sketch scholars are essentially modernists, less because of the positivistic orientation of their research—even Lewis Lockwood pointed out how much interpretation lay in seemingly literal transcription, but only because the very *raison d'être* of the activity lay in the organicist assumption. Organicism, a concept borrowed from biology, stressed that a work of art such as a composition was a unified whole, and any small change would disturb the unity. Deciphering the sketches was justified as an attempt to understand how Beethoven arrived at the piece itself. Beethoven's groping for a solution, it was assumed, was a search for an abstract ideal, that which worked best, for Beethoven's realization of the fundamental vision of the composition. Beethoven himself described his methods to Louis Schössler: "Then [after hearing a theme] the working-out in breadth, length, height and depth begins in my head, and since I am conscious of what I want, the basic idea never leaves me. It rises, grows upward, and I hear and see the picture as a whole take shape."[27] The vision itself was organic, and the sketches were compared and discussed on essentially structural values: how well they fit into the overall scheme. Take away the existence of an overall scheme, and there is little reason to pour over Beethoven's hieroglyphics. Further, the assumption of sketch research, that there is a solution to be found, puts the sketch scholar that much closer to the work of the scientist. Beethoven's own working methods thus parallel those of scientists who seek to solve a problem or to unlock a mystery, which is accomplished by trial and error or by experimentation.

Of course, no scientist does random trial and error; experiments are guided by hypotheses and an overriding intellectual construct or vision. Take out the word "experiments" in the previous sentence and substitute Beethoven's sketching, and with some minor grammatical adjustment we have the fundamental assumption upon which sketch scholarship rests. Beethoven works as the modern scientist, and sketch scholars, in their reconstruction of Beethoven's twists and turns, align themselves fully with the historical side of science: evolutionary biology, archeology, and (in approach) geology. They dig, reconstruct, and hypothesize until they have uncovered the aesthetic key that explains the piece.

While the consequences of Sputnik had a direct bearing on higher education in general, echoes of the framework in which Sputnik resided, the Cold War, appear in musicological writings about Beethoven. Many sketch scholars adopted military terminology to describe what Beethoven did. Philip Gossett, in discussing the Sixth Symphony, a decidedly unmilitaristic work, refers to Beethoven being in "treacherous territory," but that "it must be entered."[28] Richard Kramer describes "a radical revision [of an unfinished concertante], attacking the first harmonic shape of the passage." Robert Winter, referring to the beginning of the third movement of the String Quartet op. 131, states that "any remaining illusions are shattered by the characteristic Beethovenian explosion which follows." Retreat seems a favorite tactic of Beethoven: Alan Tyson refers to a change Beethoven made in *Fidelio* as a "partial retreat" and describes how Beethoven, in composing his Piano Trio op. 70, no. 1, was at one time "forced to retreat to his sketchbooks." According to Amanda Glouert, "The end of the [second] movement [of op. 131] makes a retreat toward insubstantiality."[29] Terms such as advance and deployment are also found.

In what was to be the last volume of *Beethoven Studies*, Lockwood's examination of the first movement of the *Eroica* was titled "Eroica Perspectives: Strategy and Design in the First Movement." Twice in the article Lockwood refers to Beethoven's "long-range planning and compositional strategy." Lockwood recognized the militaristic cultural implications of the piece: In describing its history he refers to "vast battles [that] were waged over the programmatic interpretation of the Eroica, not without overtones of Franco-German rivalries in the post-Napoleonic and post-Beethovenian era."[30] Lockwood used similar terminology, of long-range planning and strategy, to describe the String Quartet op. 59, no. 1.

While the phrases in the examples above are of military origin, they are admittedly open to other interpretations, and I do not want to claim that each author used them to consciously advance a militaristic view of Beethoven. Collectively, however, they reflect a time in which war was part of everyday life. Sputnik, the Cold War, the fear of nuclear annihilation, and the ongoing Vietnam War were inescapable in 1970s American culture, and it would be surprising if some vestige of this were not found in writings of the time. Beethoven's life, music, and compositional process all suggest personal struggle, whether with tones or with the world around him, and it was only a small step for scholars who lived in a world in which armed conflict or the threat of war was omnipresent to portray Beethoven from that standpoint.

Groundwork for such imagery had been laid even in Beethoven's lifetime. Beethoven lived during the Napoleonic years when all of Europe was at war; he saw from a distance his own Elector at Bonn displaced, and later he personally suffered through the shelling of Vienna and the subsequent French occupation. Beethoven is alleged to have shaken a fist and yelled at a French officer, "If I knew as much about strategy as I do counterpoint, I would show you a thing or two." The history of the *Eroica,* a paradigmatic composition from Beethoven's heroic period, is tied overtly to Napoleon, as all evidence indicates that Beethoven intended to dedicate it to him and then at some point changed his mind. It may be no coincidence that the history of sketch research is framed by work on the *Eroica* sketchbook. Nottebohm's most important published work was his discussion of that very sketchbook, published in 1880, and in our time Lewis Lockwood, the most important present-day sketch scholar along with Joseph Kerman, has written a major study on it and, as of this writing, is soon to publish a complete edition.[31]

Beethoven's music was directly connected with other military struggles. His most popular composition during his lifetime, *Wellingtons Sieg* (Wellington's Victory), celebrated the victory of the British over Napoleon at Waterloo by reenacting the battle sonically, including the drumbeat cadences of the marching armies, their field tunes, and the percussive sounds of bullets. The opening motive of the Fifth Symphony became a symbol of victory for the Allies during World War II, as it spelled out "V" in Morse Code. The many programmatic interpretations attached to the Fifth Symphony have always had at their core some notion of struggle and eventual triumph.

Yet regardless of whether the language of sketch scholars was intentional or whether it was simply an attempt to echo Beethoven's own milieu and way of thinking, it fit too well within the prevailing temper of a society in which science garnered a special prestige because it was the nation's best hope for salvation in a time of war. Sketch scholars presented a compelling Cold War image, a picture of Beethoven as a commanding strategist, plotting and marshaling all his compositional forces to carve out masterworks. When issues such as expression and feeling were barely whispered in the musicological world, the sketch scholars presented us not a Romantic hero struggling to express deeply felt emotions, but rather Generalissimus Beethoven.

Generalissimus Beethoven is no mere fantasy construction. In writing to the publisher S. A. Steiner, Beethoven referred to himself as "Generalissimus," Steiner as "Lieutenant-General," and his partner, Tobias Haslinger, as "Adjutant-General." Sketch scholars were thus on firm ground as compositional process became compositional strategy, and Beethoven could be presented as one keenly attuned to a time of international strife and tension. In 1970 the entire country lived under the cloud of the Cold War, the specter of complete annihilation seemed a real threat to many, and the Vietnam War divided American society like no other event of the twentieth century.

Sketch scholars succeeded during the 1970s because they not only presented a Beethoven who resonated with the tone of post–World War II America and the Cold War tensions of the day, and not only because their work had all the requirements of solid, scientific scholarship, but also because their studies made for a good detective story.[32] They applied imagination, insight, and dogged determination to sort out the complexities that more than a century of careless handling had brought to the state of Beethoven sketches. At the same time, based on hard, even daunting empirical evidence, they separated Beethoven and, by extension, the entire classical canon from the popular musical genre of the day on grounds of aesthetic value. They were of their time.

6

Reactions to Modernism

Musical Meaning and the Classical Canon

*I*N 1972, AS THE CELEBRATORY SOUNDS of the Beethoven bicentennial lingered, and as sketch scholarship with its promise of scientific certainty was reaching its zenith, another voice commented on Beethoven with a very different message. Adrienne Rich's long journey from poet, Radcliffe graduate, wife, and mother had led her to a better understanding of herself and her place in a patriarchal culture that she could no longer endure. The daughter of well-to-do parents in Baltimore who was pushed by a somewhat tyrannical father, she had shown a precocious poetic ability as a child; after graduating from college in 1951, she married and settled down to have three children and write poetry. Unable to sustain the domestic role that the 1950s and early 1960s demanded, a divorce and a discovery of her own sexual orientation followed; her 1973 book *Diving into the Wreck, Poems of 1971 and 1972*, chronicled much of her journey.[1]

The title poem of *Diving into the Wreck* narrates the metaphorical adventure of exploring a sunken vessel under the sea. The diver-narrator is androgynous, "I am she: I am he," and the poem is more about the exploration of the wreck than the wreck itself, that is, those myths that bind men and women to traditional roles in society. Deeply stylized yet bluntly autobiographical, it is

Rich's own exploration of herself and her relationship to the world in which she lived. It is a powerful statement of one woman's embrace of all that the feminist movement of the 1960s and 1970s had awakened in her, and it represented an exploration with which many women could identify.

Buried deep in that volume was another poem, about Beethoven's Ninth Symphony. Possibly because of the impact of the title poem and others about personal gender relationships, "The Ninth Symphony of Beethoven Understood at Last as a Sexual Message" did not receive the notice that it might have, although some fifteen years later other events would bring it to the fore. The poem is short, here in its entirety:

A man in terror of impotence
or infertility, not knowing the difference
a man trying to tell something
howling from the climacteric
music of the entirely
isolated soul
yelling at Joy from the tunnel of the ego
music without the ghost
of another person in it, music
trying to tell something the man
does not want out, would keep if he could
gagged and bound and flogged with chords of Joy
where everything is silence and the
beating of a bloody fist upon
a splintered table[2]

Far from the sacralized view of the Ninth Symphony with its spiritual message, which was still prevalent in 1972, Rich sees in Beethoven a man frustrated by both his deafness and his powerlessness. Yet are they the same? For Rich, Beethoven is a man consumed by anger, screaming but not wanting to scream, tortured by the sounds of joy, driven by his own impotence and unable to control his rage. The gerunds pile up: "not knowing," "trying," "howling," "yelling," "trying," "beating." He is isolated, surrounded by silence, "gagged and bound and flogged with chords of joy." The music exists apart, a force that Beethoven cannot prevent and struggles to control. Whence comes the message? Is it Beethoven or the music? Is the music Beethoven's message, or does the music control Beethoven?

Rich, whose metaphors can be both general and specific, leaves no question what the Ninth Symphony is about. It is, according to the title, "a sexual message." Rich further implies that such content existed from its first performance but had lain unrecognized for 148 years; it is now "understood at last." Rich does not indicate any specific passages or movements where the message resides; she only hints at joy, at Beethoven howling and yelling at joy. She is apparently neither moved by nor comfortable with the intense, fortissimo reiterations of joy, for they seem to reference a crude patriarchal society governed by male anger and frustration. Beethoven's sexual outbursts are ones of terror. Here Beethoven is the hyper-macho man, a symbol of masculinity run amok, hiding under the cloak ("chords") of joy. Not coincidentally, the poem that follows this one is titled "The Rape."

Yet the poem is sympathetic to Beethoven, who is also the victim of his situation. His terror is his own silent world, his only sounds the ones that exist in his head. He injures only himself as he beats "a bloody fist upon a table." Beethoven is to be pitied as much as feared, as one who lives on the edge of his own sanity and is desperately trying to keep the despair in check. The music itself, however, what Beethoven cannot deny, assails the listener with the pent-up feelings of dread and horror. Therein lies the terror the listener feels.

Rich's poem was written within one year of the appearance of Stanley Kubrick's film *A Clockwork Orange,* in which Beethoven's Ninth Symphony is used as part of a tortuous Orwellian conditioning technique, which of course raises the question of influence. Rich claims that she had not read the source novel but did see the film, which she thoroughly disliked. According to Rich, "Whether a residual echo from the film's soundtrack had anything to do with the writing of the poem, I can't say." Her description of the situation from which the poem grew, however, suggests that the poem arose from the sounds of the symphony itself: "The night of writing the poem, as I recall, I had been listening to the Ninth on the radio, and it struck me again as it had before that the vehemence of the 'Freude, Freude' chorus had in it less of joy than a kind of desperation. I knew Beethoven was deaf by the time the Ninth was written. But the poem addresses a certain kind of male anguish and emotional isolation which as a listener I heard in the music. . . . It was not meant as a commentary on Beethoven himself."[3]

While celebrated in feminist literature and among poetry aficionados, Rich's poem lay unknown to most of the music world for some fifteen years. In 1997, however, Susan McClary quoted it in her critique of the Ninth Symphony and the entire terrain of the patriarchal-macho Western tonal structure. McClary's analysis, which originally appeared in the *Minnesota Theory Review* and later in modified form in her book *Feminine Endings,* stands today as possibly the most quoted, misquoted, and infamous comments on Beethoven's Ninth Symphony. The heart of McClary's infamous passage lay in one particular sentence in the original published essay, which refers to the moment of recapitulation of the first movement: "The carefully prepared cadence is frustrated, damming up energy which finally explodes in the throttling, murderous rage of a rapist incapable of attaining release."[4]

Even among those who have never read McClary, the "Beethoven as rapist" interpretation of the Ninth Symphony has become notorious. Yet is this a justified reading either of Beethoven or McClary? If not, what is McClary saying? Clearly this passage and the argument surrounding it need to be nuanced, and several scholars have discussed it at length.[5]

Robert Fink observes correctly that the oft-quoted McClary passage does not appear in *Feminine Endings,* even though some scholars have implied that it does. McClary removed it entirely from her book. Yet it is there, in print, and as Omar Khayyam in the *Rubaiyat* knows, "The moving finger writes; and having writ, Moves on: / nor all thy piety and wit / Shall lure it back to cancel half a line / Nor all they tears wash out a word of it."[6] There is no evidence that McClary has attempted to undo that sentence, much less shed any tears over it, so it stands.

To what extent it is a reasonable reading of Beethoven and to what extent it is part of McClary's own agenda is another matter. When she wrote "Getting Down Off the Beanstalk," postmodernism was just beginning to be felt in the world of musicology. McClary explicitly aligned with the movement, seeing it as a way "to clear a space in which a woman's voice can at last be heard *as a woman's voice.*"[7] The essay is not principally about Beethoven; she analyzes in some detail *Genesis II,* by Janika Vandervelde, and uses Vandervelde's approach to composition to contrast it with the patriarchal stamp that the Western tonal system has imposed upon five hundred years of musical composition.

For McClary, Western music is infused with eroticism: "Music after the Renaissance most frequently appeals to libidinal appetites: during the historical period in which the legitimation of culture moved from the sacred to the secular real, the 'truth' that authorized musical culture became expressly tied to models of sexuality." Furthermore, she argues, incumbent in tonality is male sexual desire, with its inherent erotic quality composed in its push to the climax. Even a cadence is a sexual event: McClary speaks of how Western listeners "*desire* violent annihilation through the tonal cadence."[8] An important aspect of desire is its own frustration, intensifying the experience by delaying release. Western musical structures, particularly sonata form, the principal pattern of most instrumental compositions of the late eighteenth and early nineteenth centuries, were based on the notion of frustration of desire. Even before McClary, the modernist theorist Leonard Meyer made "a musical impulse having tendencies toward a more or less definite goal" and "the temporary resistance or inhibition of these tendencies" the fundamental means of distinguishing high art from popular music.[9]

In this context, Beethoven's Ninth Symphony becomes the quintessential example of encoded male sexuality, and, according to McClary's reading, is deserving of its place as the most emblematic piece at the heart of the Western canon. Yet if desire is frustrated too much and release cannot be achieved, the ordinary violence of the cadence, a means of heightening emotion, assumes an entirely different quality. Pleasure gives way to rage, and any element of the erotic is subsumed in the overwhelming terror that the violence invokes. This is McClary's understanding of the recapitulation of the first movement of the Ninth Symphony.

The parallelism between Rich's and McClary's imagery is clear and overt, which McClary acknowledges. McClary, however, can point to specific measures in one movement to illustrate her point, while Rich refers to the work as a whole. McClary's specificity is important because many other writers have searched for metaphors to explain what Beethoven has created for this same passage.

For both Rich and McClary, the Ninth elicits terror. Terror had of course been an important dimension of aesthetics since the eighteenth century, when Burke and Kant distinguished between the beautiful and the sublime. Terror was closely related to awe, and both were associated with the sublime, which through the nineteenth century was considered the highest form of artistic expression. The sublime was associated with masculine empowerment, with pain and the annihilation of the self in the face of an overwhelming sense of power, whether it be Old Testament rhetoric, a Hudson River School landscape of vast mountain scenery within which people are mere dots on the giant canvass, or a grandiose symphony with a large orchestra, a massive sound in the days before electronic amplification.[10]

Anne K. Mellor, who described the above as "the masculine sublime," also found in Romanticism two types of female sublime. The first, prevalent in Gothic novels, "accepts the identification of the sublime with the experience of masculine empowerment." Empowerment is located in the home, in the form of a tyrannical father or priest, who perpetrates violence against women, including torture and incest. The novels thus bring the sublime into the domestic sphere, and through the societal institution of patriarchy destroy "the very bonds of affection and responsibility that constitute the bourgeois family." The second type of female sublime is more benign. It occurs in female writers, principally of the mountain and lake regions of the British Isles, who see nature not as terror or awe-inspiring, but as a "female friend, a sister, with whom they share their most intimate experiences and with whom they cooperate in the daily business of life, to the mutual advantage of each."[11]

For Second Wave feminism in the twentieth century the first tradition prevails, and both interpretations are an indictment of the patriarchal society dominant in the Western world, which Beethoven represents. He is, as Paula Higgins said, specifically referring to McClary's view, "the ultimate 'butch' composer, the testosterone Man, if you will, of nineteenth-century music."[12]

While Rich and McClary see the violence of the Ninth Symphony in the context of feminism, they were not the first to notice its violent character. The earliest metaphoric description of the recapitulation is in Robert Griepenkerl's 1838 novel *Music Festival, or the Beethovenians.* Here the characters Vicarius and Pfeiffer viewed the recapitulation as "the battle between the Old and New, the crucial gigantic and titanic battles of our times." After a dramatic technical description of the passage, of the open fifths, the intransigent F-sharp, and the motion of the violins—surprising details for a novel—Vicarius exclaims, "This is no street brawl; they are tearing off the granite tops of mountain ranges and throwing them at each other, they're scourging the boiling sea into the bridal bed of the earth. And suns and moons are their shields, fiery bolts of lightning their spears; out of their battle the dust of stars whirls heavenward."[13]

Somewhat later, the nineteenth-century theorist A. B. Marx, as Fink observed, "breathlessly describes the entire passage in one sweeping sentence." After referring to several musical details Marx adds his own metaphor: "Now the sovereignty of this idea is fully established . . . for twelve long measures (immovable like a terrifying specter, like the gloomily flaming Earth-Spirit that stood before Faust, which he conjured up but could not with stand)."[14]

To Romain Rolland the violence is meteorological: "This is the paroxysm of the tempest—the three apparitions of God on Sinai . . . totally surrounded by lightning and thunder. . . . We are at the heart of the hurricane. Masses of sound collide violently. The winds set themselves up in contrapuntal opposition to the strings; and the lightning bolts intertwine, both from the heights and depths."[15]

Donald Francis Tovey expands the natural phenomena to the universe: "Hitherto we have known the opening as pianissimo, and only the subtlety of

Beethoven's feeling for tone has enabled us to feel that it was vast in sound as well as in spaciousness. Now we are brought into the midst of it, and instead of a distant nebula we see the heavens on fire. There is something terrible about this major tonic, and it is almost a relief when it turns into the minor as the orchestra crashes into the main theme, no longer in unison, but with a bass rising in answer to the fall of the melody."[16]

The metaphors employed by Griepenkerl, Marx, Rolland, and Tovey, all men, are clearly about awe, terror, and violence. Each invokes a horrific scene, involving a person or a natural or astronomical event. They fit easily with Burke's and Kant's concepts of the sublime, which embraced terror and awe, and which, according to Mellor, dealt with male empowerment. They are all, however, about external events, none reflect the inner feelings of the observer, and none are overtly sexual. To state that McClary's and Rich's images are sexual would be to understate the obvious. For many men in Western culture, power and sex are often an assumed pairing, with sex in essence a byproduct of power; since more often than not men act from a privileged physical position and have the cultural stance of being the initiator, sex and terror often seem unrelated. For many women, however, the relationship has been and remains different. Yet sex and power cannot be separated, whether regarding the female who uses her wiles to gain advantage or who suffers as victim in an unequal power relationship. Women need be on guard, and terror constantly lurks as a potential threat, especially when encountering an enraged male who is out of control—such as Beethoven. The female sublime that Beethoven invoked for both Rich and McClary was Mellor's Gothic, a situation that can lead to horrific violations of the body as well as a reminder of male patriarchy that bordered on tyranny.

Needless to say, McClary's interpretation of Beethoven and of the entire Western tonal structure aroused no small amount of controversy. Whether her specific views are accepted or not, McClary interjected a female perspective that had been virtually nonexistent in Beethoven literature. She also heralded a larger shift in intellectual orientation regarding the consideration of Beethoven and the entire classical canon. Beethoven discussion was no longer dominated by modernist approaches. In the 1980s and 1990s a significant percentage of music scholars embraced postmodernism, which had a different agenda from what had prevailed throughout much of the twentieth century. For a time there was an internecine war between the "Old Musicology" and the "New Musicology," as scholars aligned with either modernism or postmodernism. In retrospect the controversy seems exaggerated, but was probably necessary because of the rapid hardening of positions. The old order had all but calcified. Postmodernists appeared as arrogant revolutionaries who wished to overthrow all vestiges of the principles upon which musicology had been based, while modernists, or positivists as they were called, appeared as struthious troglodytes who refused to realize that the principles upon which their discipline was founded badly needed revision. As the battle waned, a Hegelian synthesis emerged that incorporated elements of both viewpoints. Just as a few aging 1960s hippies can still be found, however, a few holdouts on both sides remain active.

Several tenets of postmodernism had a direct effect on how Beethoven was perceived: there was greater emphasis on the other, those people or groups who had been marginalized by the predominant society; the distinction between what was considered art music and what wasn't became more and more slippery until it all but collapsed; and important consideration of poetic meaning once again became acceptable.

The latter fundamentally changed the dialogue on Beethoven. Ever since Schenker published his major study on the Ninth Symphony, modernist comments on the finale grappled with the elusive question, "What is the form?" Even though it did not appear to fit classical models, many modernist writers felt compelled to shoehorn it into a structure derived from classical practice. As might be expected, results varied dramatically, with no consensus arising. It was considered a sonata form, a bar form (AAB), a set of variations, and a four-movement symphonic pattern reduced to a single movement.[17] Content was never completely ignored, partly because the piece had words, but that was not where modernist writers' principal interest lay.

As the influence of modernism declined, what many modernist scholars had derided as "speculation" once again became acceptable and as a consequence discussion of poetic meaning once again flourished. Some involved imaginative but learned flights of fantasy. Lawrence Kramer, a high postmodernist, focused on the Turkish March in the finale of the Ninth Symphony. This section had always been problematic, both a dissonant note amidst the idealist message of universal brotherhood and a musical incongruity in the inspiring symphonic-hymn-choral treatment of Schiller's "Ode to Joy." Turkish marches or Janissary bands were in vogue in Vienna in Beethoven's time, but music based on them, such as Haydn used in his Symphony no. 102 (the *Military*), or Mozart in the finale of his Piano Sonata in A minor, K. 311, or Beethoven in his Piano Variations op. 76, carried a tone of caricature comparable to that in nineteenth-century American minstrel shows. Turks were a detested ethnic group in Austria, not least because of the recent Austro-Turkish War

(1787–1791) or the devastating siege of Vienna in 1683, when the city nearly fell to the Ottoman Empire.

Kramer's essay "The Harem Threshold: Turkish Music and Greek Love in Beethoven's 'Ode to Joy'"[18] ranges from Hegel's concept of "universal history" as found in Herder and the Goethe-Schiller circle to the Hellenic dimension that embodies Dorian homoerotic love in military Sparta to the dwarfs Byron describes in *Don Juan*. These dwarfs, hideous creatures, "mis-shapen pigmies, deaf and dumb—Monsters,"[19] are there to guard the entrance to the Turkish harem, the "Harem Threshold," and to open the doors for those allowed to enter. Kramer then introduces the Turkish warrior-dervishes from Kotzebue's play *The Ruins of Athens*, for which Beethoven wrote an overture that contains a Janissary section derived from the dervishes. Kramer argues that while the dwarfs of Byron's plays "are at one level the very antithesis of these militant dervishes," they are "at another level their heirs." Kramer thus views the Turkish March through a lens of masculinity that is part Dorian self-sacrifice, as lovers in the army often desired to perish next to each other in battle, and part Turkish, as represented by the dwarfs at the harem threshold "that represent masculine danger at its most concentrated."[20]

Kramer never mentions whether Beethoven might have read Byron's poem. One assumes he considers that irrelevant, in contrast to a modernist historian who would probably focus on that question almost immediately.[21] Important to Kramer is the extent this narrative conforms to the symphony. Kramer is specific and detailed: he associates the beginning of the Turkish march section of the symphony, a sound "half guttural, half visceral, a travesty of the body as a source of vocalization,"[22] specifically with the "wondrous hideousness" of the dwarfs. Kramer's emphasis upon the dwarfs and the homosexual activity of the Dorians, the feminine fighters, are also both consistent with that dimension of postmodernism that focuses on the other.

Yet Kramer's work, although emblematic of postmodernist thought, also has deep ties to the past. It is reminiscent of the programmatic imagining in which even ultramodernist critics engaged, before mainstream twentieth-century modernism stripped away any such efforts under the guise of the superiority of a pure abstract art favored by many nineteenth-century writers from E. T. A. Hoffmann to John S. Dwight. For instance, Paul Rosenfeld, champion of Varèse, Ornstein, and other modernists, confessed to his listening habits: *Tristan und Isolde* on a phonograph conjured up for him "the perception of a dark, deep-lying regions of earth, the hearth of somber flames"; the entr'acte from Moussorgsky's *Khovanschina*, "the colossal tonage of mountains, the globe's entire weight, and with it the entire world's tragedy: continuous funeral marches endless as the mountains' lines; the vital progress from darkness into gray and into darkness again; the overwhelming sum of human pain and human defeat."[23] Kramer and Rosenfeld both may have been thoroughly modern (not modernist) in their outlooks, but they allow programmatic imagining not all that different from Romanticism. The principal difference is that by the late twentieth century such interpretation needed to be grounded in a deep and erudite reading of theoretical, literary, and other relevant sources.

Post-positivist approaches were also rebranded; poetic interpretation was no longer programmatic imaginings or literary allusioning, but rather hermeneutics. The term hermeneutics goes back to antiquity, where Greek writers as well as Old Testament and later New Testament scholars used it to describe reading divinely inspired texts to discern their meaning for those in contemporary society. That usage is similar to exegesis. Gradually the term hermeneutics broadened to include not just religious or even just written texts, but various forms of communication, including nonverbal. It can be applied to music in a variety of ways, but it usually means an understanding of the poetic content or meaning of a composition, often but not always in relation to the composer's intent.

Hermeneutics was practiced in music criticism and discussion throughout the nineteenth century, but never under that name. It was only in 1902 that Herman Kretzschmar applied the word to music.[24] It continued to be applied in the early twentieth century until positivism rendered any discussion of musical meaning, in the sense of attaching an affective or poetic interpretation to the composition, as inappropriate speculation.

Hermeneutics did not disappear during the reign of positivism, but anyone engaged in it fought an uphill battle. The most famous example came from Germany, where Arnold Schering closely associated many Beethoven compositions with literary and even biblical texts. He attempted to penetrate Beethoven's thinking using clues from either the manuscripts or the composer's external comments, and then he sought texts whose rhythm matched the rhythm of the piece.[25] The result was a textual underlay that for most scholars strained credulity. It should be noted that Schering's ideas were not entirely new; Joseph Momigny had done the same thing with a Mozart quartet and a Haydn symphony in 1806.[26]

American Beethoven scholars fared better than Schering, mainly because they were more cautious. Joseph Kerman had advocated criticism as a way out of what he saw as a sterile, value-avoidance analysis, which he had attacked in a famous essay, "How We Got into Analysis, and How to Get Out." He demonstrated the possibilities of a critical approach in his study of the Beethoven string quartets. In one sense Kerman remained within the province of descriptive style and structural analysis, but he was not afraid to assess value and to deal empathetically with affective issues. Rey Longyear, who connected several of Beethoven's works with what he called "romantic irony," drew heavily upon German literary sources to fashion an argument that necessitated discussion of mood. Frank Kirby addressed the question of the poetic idea in Beethoven, but he dealt with the Sixth Symphony, the instrumental piece for which Beethoven provided his most detailed program, and he did it within the framework of the eighteenth-century concept of the *Sinfonia caracteristica,* a symphony composed to represent a specific mood or character.[27]

Postmodernism made hermeneutical discussion fashionable once again, although it was not reserved for postmodernists only but soon became part of the general musicological dialogue. An important turning point in this regard came with Scott Burnham's study of the heroic element in Beethoven's music, *Beethoven Hero,* which appeared in 1995.[28] Other authors had addressed the question of the heroic dimension in Beethoven's music, but usually within a nineteenth-century framework of stylistic evolution or periodization.[29]

Burnham's book is broader. Its historical significance lies in his ability to synthesize various currents and tendencies in Beethoven scholarship into one narrative whole. Burnham limits his discussion to only a few pieces, specifically those that posterity has identified as representing the heroic Beethoven. In examining them Burnham acts primarily as historian. He grounds his musical discussions deeply in the pieces' overall reception and historiographic past, which include theoretical and analytical writings about them. He also adjusts his focus according to received perception of the individual piece. Thus when discussing the *Eroica,* the principal emphasis is on the many programmatic associations that have grown around it. He demonstrates that they encompass far more than Napoleon, but he makes no attempt to either reconcile the different interpretations or choose among them. This allows him to make an even more important point: "We must not for a moment think that the symphony is about these narratives, for it is precisely the other way around: the narratives are about the symphony."[30]

Later in a chapter titled "Institutional Values," Burnham examines the work of four theorists whose work has been particularly influential on Beethoven understanding: A. B. Marx, Hugo Riemann, Heinrich Schenker, and Rudolf Reti. He finds certain continuities in their work and notes that the musical values they have articulated are those that have underlain the values of Western music for the past two centuries: "thematic/motivic development, end-orientation and unequivocal closure, form as process, and the inexorable presence of line."[31] In other words, the musical characteristics of Beethoven's heroic style have established the standard whereby music of the past two centuries has been judged.

Burnham recognizes, however, that the work of these four theorists and others represents no monolithic or concordant approach. Each writer "projects onto Beethoven a somewhat different aesthetic concern," as each provides an insight into the principal concerns of his age. What makes Beethoven discussion unique is that the different values each theorist chose to emphasize, which Burnham summarizes as "spiritual import, subjective expressivity ultimately grounded in classical rationality, dramatic impulse, coherent integrity, dialectical process, and the possibility of transcendent heroism," have persisted.[32] While they represent in one sense two hundred years of German idealistic thought, they have transcended both time and place, to remain values through which both Europeans and Americans continue to hear Beethoven.

In his final chapter Burnham is able to bring together even more recent strands of Beethoven interpretation, to demonstrate one fundament that underlies many discussions of Beethoven as well as providing an important key to his persisting viability. For Burnham the word is presence, which he discerns as the "fundamental metaphor applied to Beethoven's heroic style." In Beethoven's music one senses the voice of a narrator, which one identifies with the self. Consequently the listener projects the self into the music. Simultaneously Beethoven's music manifests the sublime; essential to his most heroic works is an element of awe and overwhelming power. Yet the self and the sublime are not in combat for the soul of the composition or of the listener; the ego is not dissolved by the force of the sublime. The sublime empowers the self, and "the listener experiences an *aristeia*, a crowning moment of triumph and exaltation. One becomes literally enthused, flushed with the interiorized presence of the sublime." The sublime in a Beethoven composition is not an external other, a power to be feared; it is internalized, becoming a triumphant magnification of the self.[33]

What Burnham never addresses is the gender aspect of this interpretation. As Mellor states and McClary and Rich demonstrate, the sense of empowerment that the presence of terror leading to the sublime brings is specifically a masculine response. For most women terror is terror, and the self is neither annihilated nor exalted. The connection of the self to the overwhelming power many listeners feel when listening to Beethoven, in one sense a type of self-aggrandizement, is not a typical female response. A woman may be moved by Beethoven's most heroic music, as Margaret Fuller was, but the response, whether bordering on the erotic as in the case of Fuller or simply one of recoil and discomfort, or somewhere in between, is not something Burnham considered.

With the voice of the narrator, essential to Burnham's concept of presence, the many threads of Beethoven reception and interpretation come together, from the Romantic views of Hoffmann and the nineteenth-century theorist Wilhelm von Lenz through the twentieth-century analysis of Tovey and Schenker to the hermeneutical approaches of postmodern writers. Each is about a narrative, be it programmatic or abstract, be it about Napoleon, Fate, or the fundamental line that undergirds a piece. Burnham thus presents a universal view that admits many divergent and seemingly irreconcilable positions without dismissing or disparaging any. Burnham's book appeared at a crucial time in Beethoven scholarship, when doubt about Beethoven's continuing viability and the classical canon itself was rampant, and when scholars were either unsure about their future direction or certain of one and only one path. In that sense Burnham's study reflects its time, paralleling his own observations about the many studies that he examined. Burnham's principal achievement may have been his ability to see value in many lines of inquiry at a time when cultural wars about new approaches in musical scholarship were rife and a considerable degree of polarization within the musicological community existed. However one accepts Burnham's specific points, his work acknowledged the validity of disparate interpretations of Beethoven, not only of the past, but by implication of the future.

Any person of Beethoven's fame would be a natural attractor for biographers, and for generations and in many languages they have responded. Since 1977 four major biographies have appeared in the United States, all written by Americans—Maynard Solomon, William Kinderman, Edmund Morris, and Lewis Lockwood—and all have enjoyed considerable circulation and success.[34] This does not include two other English-language works, by the British writers Barry Cooper and David Wyn-Jones. Yet even though the four American biographies share many features, each is unique in its approach and emphasis. One might ask, since the basic facts about Beethoven are known and not likely to change much, why should another biography be written? Lockwood's answer was that each writer has his own perspective and may see many facts or issues, both biographical and musical, differently from his predecessors. As a consequence, comparison of these four works can be of particular value; together they summarize the place of Beethoven in America at the end of the twentieth and the beginning of the twenty-first centuries, and the ways that he appeals to various constituencies and cultural groups.

Biography by nature is a complex genre, and the biographer is faced with innumerable questions from the start. How does one tell an entire person's life in one volume? The first problem is what to include: How much detail does the reader want? Since even famous people have many mundane moments, how much day-to-day living really needs to be presented? Nineteenth-century biographers, intent on sacralizing Beethoven, might not probe too deeply into some of the more unsavory aspects of his life, or, if they were unavoidable, they might try to explain them as if defending the subject in a court of law. Biography can thus easily become hagiography. On the other hand, a biographer can select the more troublesome and even salacious aspects of a subject's life and create a biography as exposé.

Any good biographer will attempt to understand the motivations and character of the subject, but which methodology and approach to take will significantly affect the way the material is presented. Another question is the structure and organization of the book. Most biographies are chronological, for obvious reasons. Yet a biography can also break off into thematic chapters. Microhistory, in vogue a few years ago, suggested another type of organization. Microhistory arose as part of the attempt to escape the grand narrative, the story of movers and shakers, empire builders or destroyers, which in the musical world meant the canonical treatment of canonical composers. A microhistory study selects one particular event or situation and uses it as a pivot point around which all else turns. For Beethoven, his deafness could be an obvious choice. Psycho-biography, a part of psycho-history, also enjoyed considerable popularity in the 1960s and 1970s. Beethoven, the tortured soul that he was, seemed ripe for that, too.

Whatever strategy the biographer uses to get the story out, musical biography presents further problems, specifically that of how to integrate life and music. At the core of this issue is one's philosophy of art music: Is it autobiographical even at a subconscious level? Does it reflect the world around it? Or does it exist as an independent transcendental force? Regardless of the writer's stance, how does one integrate life and music into a readable whole? Are chapters on each juxtaposed? Are they treated separately or in a single narrative line? How important is discussion of the music, and to what extent should it be discussed? The notion of a pure, absolute instrumental music existing somewhere beyond life's realities, which has been so strong in Western music, has made the problem of integration, if not superfluous, at least vexing. It is important to remember that as each author answers these questions, the finished product tells almost as much about the author as the subject.

Maynard Solomon's biography, originally published in 1977 and reissued in new editions in 1998 and 2002, remains today the most popular Beethoven biography of the late twentieth century. The new editions contain only minor revisions. Solomon's study is an attempt at psychobiography. His interpretation is Freudian, based in particular on the concept of the family romance, in which the child comes to believe that his father is not his real father and replaces him with another, often someone of higher accomplishment or station. Beethoven believed that he was of noble birth, possibly the illegitimate son of a Prussian king. This "nobility pretense" (Solomon's term) colored the rest of his life, and even when confronted with seemingly incontrovertible evidence Beethoven refused to abandon it. For instance, he insisted that his birth certificate actually belonged to that of his older brother, also named Ludwig, who died in infancy. Only after a court of law, as part of the lengthy legal battles involving Beethoven's nephew Karl and the boy's mother Johanna, firmly rejected Beethoven's nobility argument did Beethoven attempt to come to terms with his situation.

What makes Solomon's biography provocative, the use of Freudian analysis to interpret Beethoven, is also what dates an otherwise significant study. To put it bluntly, Freud is no longer in. Few of Freud's theories are still held in repute, and Solomon himself is not a psychoanalyst, although at one time he was associate editor of *American Imago,* a psychoanalytic journal founded by Freud himself. What problematizes Solomon's biography is the extent that Solomon applies Freudian theory, such as his interpretation of *Fidelio*. In the opera, Leonore, hoping to rescue her husband Florestan, who was being held as a political prisoner, disguised herself as a young man named Fidelio in order to obtain a job as a guard in the prison. In the second act, she descends to the deepest part of the prison with the jailor Rocco, on orders to execute and bury Florestan. Eventually she succeeds in rescuing him. The descent itself takes on Freudian significance to Solomon, even though the libretto is not by Beethoven and even though Beethoven was not the first composer to set it:

A psychoanalyst would not fail to note that the descent into the bowels of the prison, where Florestan lies in a dark cistern—'a ruined well'—carries resonances of birth and rebirth. Viewed on this level, Leonore/Fidelio has gone in search of her/his own mysterious origins; and the freeing of

Florestan and his fellow prisoners becomes not only a liberation of the father/husband and brothers but a cleansing repetition of the birth process, a penetration of the ultimate creative mystery.[35]

Although this interpretation is not without merit, one must ask, when is a good melodrama just a good melodrama?

There is no question, however, that Beethoven's life begs for psychological interpretation. His quarrels with his brothers, his stormy relationships with nobility, his insistence on pursuing women who were unavailable either because of their marriage or social status or both, and most of all his obsessive, pathetic, and destructive relationship with his nephew Karl and sister-in-law Johanna all indicate the obvious, that Beethoven was a disturbed and unstable person. As psychology enters its post-Freudian age, one can only speculate the shape a psychological study of Beethoven today would take.

Reviewers used the word "bold" to describe Solomon's biography, and Solomon himself is known for his bold, provocative assertions, which border on but never quite cross over into the zone of recklessness. If one considers Solomon's study representative of a time in which Freudian-based biography was in vogue, and if one overlooks psychiatrists' testifying that Solomon's understanding of Freud is questionable, then his use of Freudianism still serves a purpose: it provides a structure that holds the entire book together.

This speaks to Solomon's greatest strengths: the thoroughness of his research and his ability to weave the Beethoven story into a coherent narrative that contains many insights. Solomon is most famous for his persuasive solution to the riddle of the Immortal Beloved, the identity of the woman to whom Beethoven wrote a passionate love letter. While not everyone accepts his solution, it has so far been the most convincing of many that have been proposed. Through a minute examination of contemporary records, Solomon was able to deduce that she was Antonie Brentano, who had probably been overlooked or rejected before because she was married with children and Beethoven was a friend of both her and her husband. The book's provocativeness, combined with the author's mastery of detail and ability to frame a story, have kept it in print through three editions and many changes in the American Beethoven landscape.

Solomon's musicological, especially biographical, studies of classical music figures have been a second career for him. He began as a record producer, founding Vanguard Records in 1950 with his brother Seymour. Specializing in folk music, Vanguard signed some of the most important singers before and during the folk music boom of the early 1960s, including the Weavers, Joan

Baez, Odetta, and music performed at the Newport Folk Festival. Only later did he turn to biography, and *Beethoven* was his first major book-length study. Since then he has published prolifically on Beethoven, Mozart, Schubert, and Ives. Kinderman and Lockwood, on the other hand, are long-established figures in American academia: Kinderman is a professor of musicology at the University of Illinois and Lockwood a professor emeritus at Harvard University. Both were highly trained musicians and musicologists from the start. Kinderman has also been active as a concert pianist, and Lockwood, while not pursuing a concert career, has played cello in several orchestras and continues to do so as a chamber musician. Each received their doctorates from institutions known for their Beethoven research: Lockwood from Princeton and Kinderman from the University of California, Berkeley. There are both at the heart of Beethoven academia. Even though they are separated by more than a generation, and even though their subsequent careers diverged, their academic background and emphasis suggest the desirability of discussing their Beethoven biographies together.

On the surface, Lockwood's and Kinderman's books share several similarities, but in their approaches and in the nature of their discussions they are radically different. Both sought to write a comprehensive one-volume study of Beethoven's life and music, and both emphasize the music. Lockwood choice is apparent in his title, *Beethoven: The Music and the Life,* as opposed to the more common ploy of musical biography in which the life precedes the music. Both integrate the biographical and musical portions into a single narrative rather than separating them as Solomon did. Similarities of these two studies extend even to the cover design, where the same portrait of Beethoven dominates.

Differences between these two studies encompass writing style, analytical approach, contextualization, compositions discussed, and intended audience. Lockwood's book might have been subtitled *The End of an Era.* It is the latest, possibly the last of the descriptive-adjectival modernist approaches—a straightforward tone with enough value-based musical description to push it beyond the realm of the positivistic. Lockwood deploys precisely what Joseph Kerman termed criticism. Lockwood is not quite of Kerman's generation, having matriculated at Princeton University in 1960, ten years after Kerman.

Lockwood, however, is no imitator of Kerman. He does not have Kerman's rhetorical flair, in part because he chose not to adopt his polemical tone. His is a clean, straightforward, no-nonsense approach. Lockwood may be considered the principal archaeologist of American Beethoven scholarship. He digs into a piece with great care, using both his keen intellect and his tenacity with sketches, until he has burrowed down and unearthed its very essence. It is safe to say that virtually no one has mined the sketches for as many insights as Lockwood has. His essences, however, are primarily structural; his approach remains modernist. He is interested in Beethoven's vision of the width and breadth of the piece and what the first inklings in Beethoven's mind were, then how it grows and eventually all fits together.

When he backs off from the excavation site, however, we see a different Lockwood. This particular book was written for the general public, and it presents an accurate, balanced discussion of Beethoven, particularly his life, which can be read in full confidence that all facts are correct and the latest research is incorporated. Yet there is a tension in this study, especially the musical portion. One feels the strong hand of an editor who is holding him to the surface, insisting that he not probe too deeply into the many compositions that he discusses, that he skim the surface rather than plow beneath the ground. At the same time, Lockwood refuses to be superficial. He is the academic traditionalist through and through and seems to want to provide more than might be suitable for the general public. At those times he provides his best insights. Two examples of the tension may suffice.

In discussing Beethoven's Piano Trio in C minor, op. 1, no. 3, one of the more important of Beethoven's early pieces, Lockwood mostly provides affective adjectives. He refers to it as a "tumultuous" work, dominated by "turbulence" in the outer movements. The first movement contains a "whirlwind of emotions." "The finale is even more decisive and emphatic in the rhythmic shape of its opening motifs, moving from its passionate *fortissimo* outburst to another C-minor murmuring first theme."[36] These adjectives provide a vivid sense of the mood of the piece, but they do not examine it in any depth.

When discussing Beethoven's *Grosse Fuge,*[37] originally the finale of the String Quartet op. 130 and later published as a separate piece, op. 133, he focuses more on the overall structure and the historical attempts to categorize it. This discussion is more satisfying in part because Lockwood has more space to amplify his thoughts, but also within his affective description he provides significant insights, as in the following paragraph:

> Decoding the larger form of the *Grand Fugue* presents as many problems as does studying the finale of the Ninth Symphony, and for many similar reasons. It is not a fugue in Bach's sense—the relentless working out of the combinatorial possibilities inherent in a single subject, or even at times two subjects. It is, rather, a poetic discourse of enormous size, a behemoth in which the fugal principle plays a leading role but is comple-

mented by other textures. Also, a dialectic is worked out from start to finish that can be read into many formal templates without quite satisfying the basic requirements of any of them.[38]

Lockwood is not only interested in working out the structures of individual movements, for which there are a number of charts, but of the unity of an entire work and how it can be placed within the classical tradition. The String Quartet in C-sharp minor, op. 131, has more movements (seven) than any Beethoven sonata-structure piece. Lockwood considers several ways that the piece can be viewed: as a "peculiar five-movement work," if the third and sixth movements are considered a transition and introduction, respectively. Another variant would be to consider the work in four large units: movements one and two together, with movement three a transition; the second unit consisting of movement four, an andante; the third unit, movement five, a scherzo; and the fourth unit the sixth and seventh movements, the sixth acting as an introduction to the seventh. What emerges, then, is the standard four-movement classical pattern, fast-slow-dance-fast. Lockwood suggests at least one other pattern.

Lockwood, however, is not content just to speculate that such is possible. By examining the sketches he finds that Beethoven had at least five different movement plans in mind, some of three, some of four, and some of five movements. All, however, had certain consistencies: an opening fugue, the andante variations in the middle, and a closing movement in E-flat major.[39] Lockwood offers no final suggestion on how the quartet should be heard, allowing the listener to make up her own mind, but he does provide historical support for a variety of possibilities.

The success of Lockwood's book speaks to the viability of the concert-going audience in the early twenty-first century. It is the book for season-ticket holders of the New York Philharmonic, active participants of the concert season in Boston, Philadelphia, or Houston, those sophisticates who want to know more about Beethoven and who understand enough musical terminology to follow discussions of the diminished-seventh chord and the Lydian mode. Lockwood thus serves as clear evidence that the image of Beethoven and the "competent listener," to use Leonard Meyer's term, still exists in the twenty-first century.

Kinderman's book, containing long score examples and involved musical descriptions, is written for musicians. While addressing both biographical and musical issues, Kinderman's emphasis is clearly on the musical. Biography appears primarily as a backdrop to explain specific works or Beethoven's musical development.

Like Lockwood, Kinderman is a traditionalist, but his work, much more so than Lockwood's, is grounded in German philosophical idealism. This is not surprising because Kinderman splits his time between Urbana, Illinois, and Berlin, Germany. He has thoroughly absorbed German culture, particularly the German intellectual tradition. Kinderman believes in universals, as in his opening statement: "No composer occupies a more central position in musical life than Beethoven." Kinderman does not indicate whose musical life here, a point not without significance in the multicultural contemporary world. He continues: "The last half century has increasingly demonstrated the universal scope of his legacy. His restless open vision of the work of art reflects a modern and essentially cosmopolitan attitude."[40] Kinderman thus presents the reader both the notion of Beethoven as a universal composer and the existence of a universal art.

Kinderman's view of Beethoven is primarily as a formalist, although he does move, somewhat hesitantly, toward programmatic interpretation. His intellectual heritage includes Schenker and, more important, the early twentieth-century English writer Donald Francis Tovey. Both Tovey and Kinderman were active concert pianists and sensitive musicians. Both stressed the narrative element in Beethoven's music, although Tovey couched it within the metaphor of the drama, whereas Kinderman is explicit about narrative. Each describes similar procedures in similar ways, however. Both rely upon descriptive analysis that stresses an essentially abstract, purely musical narrative/dramatic process. And each was a universalist, finding in Beethoven an element of sublimity that transcends the obvious. Even when Kinderman does discuss programmatic elements, such as with the Second and Third Symphonies (the Second in regard to Prometheus, the Third in regard more to a general concept of heroism than to Napoleon), the musical takes precedence over the programmatic.

Kinderman finds Beethoven's music rooted in the philosophical idealism of the late eighteenth and early nineteenth centuries: Kant and Hegel to an extent, but particularly Schlegel. He takes as his point of departure the concept that Beethoven explicated in a letter to Archduke Rudolph in 1819, that of the *Kunstvereinigung,* or "artistic unification": "In light of the struggle of the Jena circle to transcend the limits of Kantian and Schillerian aesthetics that we may best view the artistic enterprise that Beethoven himself provocatively dubbed *Kunstvereinigung.*" For Kinderman, "Beethoven's entire career may be viewed as embodying just such a progressive unification of artistic means."[41] This is essentially the formalist stance, although Kinderman is too subtle a thinker to be placed strictly within such limits.

But he himself is reluctant to break it. In his discussion of the *Galitzen* Quartets (op. 127, 130, 132), for example, Kinderman seems somewhat a traditionalist in search of the new. He strains to move beyond formalism, looking toward hermeneutics and narrative meaning, but he steps cautiously, testing the waters, never quite ready to plunge. In his discussion of the slow movement of op. 127 Kinderman focuses mostly on musical parallels between it and other works: the slow movement of op. 59, no. 2, op. 106, the Ninth Symphony, and the *Missa Solemnis*.[42] Most of these references have to do with symbolic meanings, and most cite others' opinions. Kinderman himself astutely discusses melodic similarities between the quartet, the symphony, and the *Missa Solemnis*. Yet he never quite draws an interpretative conclusion. We are left with a lot of tantalizing possibilities.

Kinderman's hesitancy surfaces when he raises the issue, at least obliquely, of the question of the abstract versus the programmatic. Very much in keeping with the interpretation of Beethoven that prevailed in the early twentieth century, Beethoven is presented here as the formalist, in contrast with the idea of Beethoven the *Tondichter* (tone poet). There has been much discussion, supported by considerable evidence, about the presence of programmatic content in Beethoven's music. This has opened the door to a variety of readings of Beethoven pieces, although such interpretation is not limited to the new musicology. But Kinderman, I believe, distorts what may be evidence for a programmatic basis for many Beethoven pieces in his attempt to push Beethoven's music in the formalist direction. He quotes a comment that Beethoven allegedly made to the English musician Charles Neate: "I have always a picture in my mind when I am composing and work up to it." Kinderman connects that with Beethoven's comment to Treitschke: "For my custom when I am composing even instrumental music is always to keep the whole in view." Kinderman associates this with "Beethoven's movement plans for works in progress [which] reflect his attempt to envisage the whole even before the motif's aims and individual sections have been." Possibly, but does Neate's reference to "picture" equate to Treitschke's whole? And what about comments by Beethoven's associates Ferdinand Ries, Carl Czerny, and Anton Schindler as well as evidence from completed pieces and sketches?[43]

Kinderman sees a narrative quality in Beethoven, but it is strictly and explicitly a musical narrative. So far this is consistent with narrative theory as applied by musicologists, but he goes further: value judgments hinge on the presence or absence of programmatic narrative or association. He compares the second movement of Beethoven's Fourth Piano Concerto—about which Schumann's description of Orpheus slaying the Furies still resonates—with

Gluck's setting of the Orpheus and Furies passage in *Orfeo*, and he finds Beethoven's effort superior, precisely because it is more abstract: "For Beethoven's *Andante* is far too subtle to allow a smooth fit between the stages in Orpheus's passage and the musical process we have described. Comparison with the famous setting of Orpheus and the Furies in Gluck's *Orfeo* reminds us of the greater musical integrity of Beethoven's movement."[44]

Kinderman takes a firm stance between music that is art and music that is less than art. Here is the Kantian distinction between the beautiful (music that allows easy assimilation, such as Strauss waltzes) and the sublime (music that goes beyond itself and in which the artist and interpreter become one). This can lead inflexibly to negative valuations where pieces do not evince the sublime, such as works that display Beethoven's humor and which could be quite rough. Kinderman gets around this problem by citing Jean Paul Richter's idea of comedy as "the sublime in reverse." Thus Kinderman can admit that the finale of the Second Symphony is comedy, but the "comedy of the sublime."[45]

Lockwood also deals with the question of comedy in Beethoven's music, particularly in his contrasts of Beethoven's two last quartets, op. 131 and op. 135. Lockwood grounds his talk in European sources, but not the heavy continental philosophy that Kinderman does. Rather, Lockwood finds connections with Shakespeare's exploration of both tragedy and comedy and the Czech novelist Milan Kundera's *The Unbearable Lightness of Being*. With these two literary references Lockwood discusses the difference between op. 131 as tragedy and op. 135 as a type of comedy that is "not a lesser form than tragedy but is its true counterpart, the celebration of the human in all things."

Following German thought, in particular that of Hermann Broch, Kinderman discusses kitsch in relation to Beethoven's *Wellington's Victory* and *Glorious Moment,* and he does not try to excuse Beethoven for either piece. Neither does he attempt to rationalize those moments in other works that to Kinderman overstep the bounds of the abstract. For Kinderman the abstract and the ethical are closely tied. He has little patience for Beethoven when he is most specifically descriptive, as in *Wellington's Victory* or in the *Pastoral* Symphony, particularly the storm. Like most scholars, Kinderman dismisses *Wellington's Victory* as unabashed kitsch, an unfortunate mar on Beethoven's compositional record. The *Pastoral* Symphony can be justified by Beethoven's own explanation, *mehr Ausdruck der Empfindung als Malerei,* but for Kinderman the storm cannot. He calls it "egregious tone-painting."[46]

While Kinderman and Lockwood differ in many of their views on Beethoven, both believe in the transcendent qualities of his music. Kinderman's philosophical leanings and relative freedom from concern about the intended audience allow him to be more overt on this point. Both writers advance an image of Beethoven firmly rooted in a hierarchy of musical and ethical values. Kinderman especially stresses the ethical. Lockwood is the American pragmatist and scientist who also feels Beethoven's music deeply and seeks to convey that feeling with a Yankee directness and plenty of evidentiary support. Kinderman presents to American audiences an essentially Teutonic orientation. He unabashedly promulgates an idealistic, abstract view of art and of Beethoven, a stance closely connected with German philosophical idealism. Yet Kinderman's views have roots in American thoughts: they go back to the nineteenth century, to the Romanticism of the American transcendentalists. Their continuing viability today is apparent not only in Kinderman's book, but in the impact that Kinderman had upon the American stage, as discussed in chapter 9.

Just how alive the Romantic image of Beethoven remains is seen in Edmund Morris's biography. The title itself, *Beethoven: The Universal Composer,* is telling. Solomon and Lockwood had presented the canonized Beethoven, Kinderman the transcendental idealist. Morris presents an unabashed Romanticist. Morris's book also has a different purpose than the others; it does not aspire to be a penetrating psychological study or a thorough summary of the composer's life and works. It is a short biography meant to be a lively read of a troubled genius.

Morris is neither a musician on the concert stage nor a musicologist in academia. He has a background that encompasses three continents: he was born and received his early education in Kenya, attended Rhodes University in South Africa, worked in London as an advertising copywriter, then immigrated to the United States in 1968, where he has lived since. He is best known as a biographer of American presidents, having published a three-volume history of Theodore Roosevelt, the first of which, *The Rise of Theodore Roosevelt,* won the Pulitzer Prize, and an authorized biography of Ronald Reagan, *Dutch,* which stirred considerable controversy. He wrote it half as history and half as novel, and included a character, his alter ego, who did not exist in Reagan's life. All this raises the question of why someone whose writing interests had been about politics at the highest level would want to add another book to the already bulging Beethoven biography shelf.

Morris answers this in part by stating that he is a pianist who has been studying Beethoven for a half-century. Even so, Beethoven would be an attractive subject to any biographer: a well-known name, a major figure in the history of Western music, and a story as dramatic and thunderous as it is poignant. Beyond vague expression of interest, Morris never revealed why he wished to turn from political to cultural biography, but perhaps he sensed a lacuna: in spite of all the Beethoven biographies in recent years, there was no short, quick, lively read. Morris supplied that.

Morris's discussion of Beethoven's music is unique among biographers. Because he is neither professional musician nor theorist, he does not attempt to analyze pieces for their internal nuances nor discuss their structure in detail, although he clearly understands theoretical terminology and doesn't shy away from it when needed. Yet his more general approach ultimately turns out to be one of the strong points of the book. Unconstrained by academic discourse, he launches into a series of vivid metaphors and descriptions that take the listener directly into the emotional heart of the piece. In essence, he focuses on the effect of the music, an approach much closer to how the general listener encounters Beethoven. Other writers have engaged this dimension, of course, but few in the twentieth or twenty-first century have done so with Morris's panache, and few have been able to blend the historical and the affective so effectively. His description of the beginning of the *Eroica* announces dramatically and succinctly what scholars have argued about for decades: the two opening E-flat chords "were the cannon shots of a new symphonic language." And in reference to his friend and pupil Ferdinand Ries's surprise at the French horn's anticipation of the tonic at the end of the development section against the dominant seventh chord of the strings, Morris writes: "What he had just heard—the anticipation of a resolution—went against every tenet of Classical procedure. A dominant seventh's desire to resolve onto the tonic is the most powerful force in Western music: to prevent it doing so amounts to coitus interruptus."[47]

Morris has clearly done his homework and covered much of the voluminous Beethoven literature. He derives considerable material from Solomon, including the assertion that a friend of Beethoven, Karl Peters, once offered his wife to Beethoven for the night. Unlike Solomon, however, who discusses this incident in some detail contiguous to Beethoven's correspondence with Nikolaus Zmeskall, where "fortresses" is used as a code word for "prostitutes," Morris doesn't give name or place to the story, only referring obliquely to the event to suggest the extent that enablers fawned over Beethoven. The implication is clear, however, and in one sense he goes beyond even Bernard Rose in his film *Immortal Beloved,* which depicts Beethoven as a lover who only had to wait for women to fling themselves at him. In Morris's view, men were even willing to give their wives to Beethoven. Buttressed by Zmeskall's question, "Would you like to sleep with my wife?" Morris's implication is clear: this was a pcrk of Beethoven's fame.

There is real question, however, whether the Peters incident occurred as Solomon describes it. The page from the conversation book itself is difficult to decipher and part of it is obliterated. More important, at the beginning of the conversation Peters wrote to Beethoven, "Around 5 o'clock I have to go to Gumpendorf with my wife," a sentence that Solomon omits, and that clearly implies that both of them were leaving. Peters also observed that it was bitterly cold that day, and apparently he offered Beethoven the use of their apartment, which was well heated. The German is "*Wollen Sie bey meiner Frau schlafen? Es ist so kalt.*" "Bey meiner Frau" could be a sexual reference, or it could mean "at my wife's place." To buttress his argument, Solomon states that Frau Peters had been described as "very promiscuous." The term used was *sehr leicht-sinnig*, which more accurately translates as "light-minded." In other words, Frau Peters may have been considered an airhead, but that's not the same thing as "very promiscuous." There is some evidence, controversial in itself, that Beethoven had affairs and that he may have visited prostitutes, hardly surprising for early nineteenth-century Vienna, but whether wives were sent his way in honor of his fame is another matter.

There are curiosities and idiosyncrasies in Morris's book. Why, of all Beethoven's compositions, did he devote the most space to a relatively obscure cantata, the *Joseph* Cantata, WoO 87, that Beethoven composed while still in Bonn and was never performed in his lifetime? In other cases, his interpretations range from somewhat naïve to extremely clever in their wordplay. He refers to Beethoven's quintet *in* strings, presumably the Quintet for Strings op. 29, and regarding the *Moonlight* Sonata he claims that "not now, or ever, could he [Beethoven] be called a Romantic," because the first movement "was cast in regular sonata form." On the other hand, his discussion of the Heiligenstadt Testament is memorable. It was in this remarkable document that Beethoven wrote to his brothers about his deafness and his determination to continue in spite of it, at one point describing the humiliation he felt when he was unable to hear a flute and a shepherd's song that someone with him had reported hearing. To Beethoven such incidents became a symbol of his plight. In his telling, Morris attributes to the flute "pantheistic overtones." How is this to be taken? The words are rich in verbal play and ambiguity. First, we can dismiss what many musicians would assume, that he refers to the flute's acoustic overtones; in fact, those overtones are no different from any other instrument's other than in relative intensity. Thus, "overtone" here merely denotes implication or suggestion. Yet what about "pantheistic," which normally suggests religious matters? The flute and the pastoral have gone together for centuries, but that still leaves a gap between the flute and the gods. Or does it?

Pantheism and the flute may not be that separate. The flute was the instrument of Pan (another of Morris's play on words), and it was the instrument of Henry David Thoreau and John S. Dwight, two Transcendental writers. Transcendentalism itself had a strong pantheistic element. Whether or not all this was on Morris's mind when he coined a simple phrase, it does illustrate, as with any writer who relies heavily on metaphor, the richness and depth of his prose.

Joseph Kerman described the String Quartet in F minor, op. 95, what Beethoven called *quartetto serioso,* as "not a pretty piece, but it is terribly strong—and rather terrible. . . . The piece stands aloof, preoccupied with its radical private war on every fibre of rhetoric and feeling that Beethoven knew or could invent."[48] Morris captured that same mood even more succinctly: the quartet was "as dense, black and bitter as a pickled walnut."[49]

History, affect, and musical details interlock in Morris's description of the opening of the Ninth Symphony, a work that calls upon any author to rise to the occasion:

> It was his downbeat, therefore, that produced the most revolutionary sound in symphony history: a long, hovering, almost inaudible bare fifth on A, seemingly static yet full of storm. High over this cloud layer, like reflections of distant lightning, a series of broken fifths dropped pianissimo and very slowly. This was not a symphony, but an epic. Now the broken fifths began to proliferate wildly, the drone swelled to a roar and a huge theme built of all the elements crashed down fortissimo. Beethoven's Ninth was under way, and for the rest of the century, symphony composers would struggle in vain to write anything that sounded bigger.[50]

This is not modernist writing; a modernist academic would have been pilloried for such rhetoric. It is, rather, Romanticism in full bloom. Yet by the time Morris wrote his biography and for the audience he addresses, one cannot say it matters. Past and present in Beethoven discourse have fused. Romantic, modern, postmodern stances seem to have collapsed with the new millennium. All is on the table, and Morris demonstrates that in spite of science, new emphases, and focus on "a unified, closed totality," another thread that began in the nineteenth century and continued through many views of Beethoven, adumbrated in Kerman's criticism and Burnham's poetic explorations, remains alive: Beethoven is the Romantic *Tonkunst,* capable of arousing deep personal feelings and powerful dramatic imagery.

PART THREE

Beethoven & the Dramatic Arts

7

Beethoven on the Silver Screen

*B*EETHOVEN AND A FRIEND STEP OUT into the street at night. The composer looks up and observes a beautiful full moon pulsing above. As they walk along Beethoven stops because he hears someone playing his Sonata in F (otherwise unidentified). He is moved by the performance: "Here is feeling—genius—understanding." He overhears a young woman inside lament to her brother that she cannot do the piece justice and wishes she could hear Beethoven's next concert. "Ah, my sister, why create regrets, when we can scarcely pay the rent." Deeply touched, Beethoven announces to his friend, "I will play for her." To their surprise he enters and discovers that the young lady is blind. "Snuff the candles and I will improvise for her in the moonlight." As the scene fades Beethoven sits down at the piano with a soft, ethereal glow filtering through the window and begins to improvise. Being a silent film we hear no music, but the final card leaves little doubt as to the piece: "Thus Beethoven's immortal sonata."

This three-minute silent film, titled *Beethoven's Moonlight Sonata*, is the first of many American films about Beethoven. Shot around 1920 by James A. Fitzpatrick, creator of numerous travelogues, it was part of the Master Musician Series distributed by Bell and Howell. As of this writing it is still available for viewing on the web.[1]

Since then, feature films about Beethoven have appeared in the 1930s, 1970s, 1980s, 1990s, and the first decade of the twenty-first century. This does not count several documentaries and the dozens of films that have used Beethoven's music. No other composer has had so much celluloid devoted to him. Chopin, Liszt, and Tchaikovsky were each depicted in films, as were many popular musicians such as George Gershwin, Glenn Miller, Benny Goodman, Jerry Lee Lewis, Loretta Lynn, and Ray Charles. Because *Amadeus* became such a hit, Mozart has only seemed to exert a longer shadow than this one well-known entry would suggest. Beethoven, however, has remained a subject of fascination for decades, and for obvious reasons. Beethoven's story has proved irresistible to Hollywood: a universally recognized name, a deaf composer, a defiant, volcanic personality, a tragic love life, and, finally, music of great power and emotion.

Hollywood, always sensitive to the box office and public taste, provides a vivid barometer of the Beethoven image in America throughout the twentieth century and into the twenty-first. Working loosely within the Beethoven story but never hesitant to enhance or invent entire situations for dramatic purposes, some aspects of Beethoven have remained constant, but others have morphed over almost a century. The Beethoven of the silver screen is not the only Beethoven of twentieth-century America but it is one of the most prominent and recognized ones. This chapter considers films about Beethoven; the next chapter examines how Beethoven's music has been used in film. Here the focus is on how Beethoven is portrayed rather than the merits of the films themselves.

Of the many films about Beethoven, three in particular stand out. Each attempted to depict in detail Beethoven the man, and each reached a broad mainstream audience: *Un Grand Amour de Beethoven* (1936), *Immortal Beloved* (1993), and *Copying Beethoven* (2006). *Un Grand Amour* and *Immortal Beloved* both center upon the same question: the mysterious woman whom Beethoven, in a passionate love letter, called his "unsterbliche Geliebte," the "immortal beloved," and whose identity is still disputed today. Beyond the topic of the immortal beloved, these two films bear little similarity. *Copying Beethoven* deals with a completely different issue, events leading to a performance of Beethoven's Ninth Symphony and the composition of the late string quartets, and shows only the Beethoven of his later years.

All three films may be considered detailed studies of Beethoven's character, sharing some traits and many differences. The Beethoven of *Un Grand Amour* is wise, thoughtful, and long-suffering. In *Immortal Beloved* he is temperamental, angry, and amorous. In *Copying Beethoven* he is intimidating, mercu-

A

B

C

rial, and at times scatological. Woven into all three films are lengthy discussions about the nature of art and what it means to be an artist. In all, Beethoven embodies the Romantic artist par excellence, one whose music transcends and compensates for his own personal shortcomings. Yet each film stands as representative of its decade and of the potential and limits of how an artist is presented.

Un Grand Amour de Beethoven, by the well-known French director Abel Gance, was the first full-length feature about Beethoven to have an impact in the United States, where it was called *The Life and Loves of Beethoven.* Gance had established a reputation as one of the great directors of the silent-film era with *J'accuse,* a three-hour documentary epic about the horrors of World War I. He followed that with his masterpiece, *Napoleon,* a six-hour epic. Gance had less success with talkies, but *Beethoven,* along with a sound version of *Napoleon,* are considered his two most important contributions in the sound era.

Gance tells the story of Beethoven's life from 1801 until his death. The film revolves around a love triangle among Beethoven, Juliette [Giulietta] Guicciardi,[2] and Thérèse de Brunswick, who are cousins in a well-to-do family. Beethoven has fallen in love with Juliette and intends to marry her, a possibility that disturbs her father. Thérèse loves Beethoven deeply and suffers as she sees her cousin succeed where she doesn't. Juliette, however, falls for the young, handsome, arrogant Count Gallenberg, who fancies himself a ballet composer but who lacks any musical talent. In his generosity Beethoven surreptitiously assists him by providing him music that he can shape as his own.

When Juliette announces to Beethoven that she plans to marry Gallenberg and move to Italy, Beethoven magnanimously accepts her decision, improvising the *Moonlight* Sonata as she speaks. Heartbroken, he decides to live in an abandoned mill where in dramatic fashion he discovers his deafness. He later proposes to Thérèse, who accepts, but Juliette, realizing that it is Beethoven she really loves, returns surreptitiously to see him. Beethoven rejects her, but as years pass he cannot bring himself to marry Thérèse. He finally tells her that he must live alone and suggests she join a convent, which she does.

The film quickly moves to Beethoven's last years. He is old and impoverished, none of his compositions sell, and by now he is taking care of his nephew Karl, who is portrayed as a self-centered, obnoxious, thieving ne'er-do-well. In the final scene Beethoven, who by this time lives in an abandoned monastery, learns that his *Eroica* and Ninth Symphonies are successes, but he mutters that "it is too late" and dies. The final image of the film shows Beethoven's face with the background blacked out, while the last movement of the Ninth is played. The image is clearly modeled on the plaster life mask that the sculptor Franz

Klein made of Beethoven in 1812. It has sometimes been confused with a death mask that Joseph Danhauser made after Beethoven died, and Gance may well have believed that Klein's cast was the death mask.

Visually, Harry Baur makes a hopelessly improbable Beethoven, and many of the other characters are one-dimensional, such as the obese violinist, ostensibly Ignace Schuppanzigh, who in real life Beethoven referred to as "Milord Falstaff." The film itself abounds in Romantic cliché but nevertheless has considerable dramatic power. The acting is excellent, especially Baur, despite his physical inadequacy for the role. Gance, true to his silent-film success, proves that he knows how to communicate the emotional content of a scene from visual images and facial expressions.

Gance paints Beethoven as a much more understanding, mature, and less selfish hero than in later films. Here he is generous and thoughtful, almost philosophical—this is a French film, after all—and the few occasional flashes of his famous temperament quickly dissipate. In this film Beethoven is a Job-like figure, suffering at the hands of fate and love, impoverished, and afflicted with his deafness, but he remains steady and forgiving. Gance, in presenting the sacralized, idealized Beethoven of the nineteenth century, demonstrates that this image still had considerable force in the first half of the twentieth.

Gance was famous for having pioneered the technique of many short rapid scenes in film, something he continues here. The opening scene is reminiscent of the 1920s film *Moonlight Sonata,* and serves the same purpose: to establish Beethoven's character and empathy. It is "Vienne, 1801," and Beethoven, walking down a street in his neighborhood, hears a woman inside a house distraught over her dying daughter. Beethoven enters, sits down at the piano, and plays the slow movement of the *Pathetique* Sonata, which the viewer hears in full orchestral transcription. As the camera pans between the face of the woman and the still form of the daughter, we see the mother become enraptured, visibly calmed and moved. Beethoven, without speaking, slowly leaves and continues his walk. The power of Beethoven's music as well as Beethoven's gentle nature are confirmed.

Interspersed throughout the film are scenes of almost childlike mirth. Here Beethoven has a pleasant, jocular household, with all the characters, including Beethoven, prone to dancing and laughing. Even egg throwing becomes a source of amusement. This, of course, is a far cry from the image that most biographers have drawn. In an early scene when Beethoven discovers that a plate of eggs his housekeeper has left for him are not fresh, he calls her in and, as she opens the door, he heaves one at her. Knowing Beethoven's impetuosity, she closes the door before it lands. He calls her again but this time Schuppanzigh

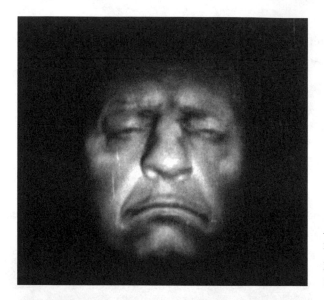

unsuspectingly comes in, receiving the rotten egg full in his face. All three, Beethoven, the violinist, and the housekeeper, then dissolve into uncontrollable laughter. Schuppanzigh, historically a fine violinist and leader of a string quartet that premiered many of Beethoven's chamber works, serves primarily as comic relief throughout the movie.

Yet comedy has a purpose in this film. Gance uses the merriment and laughter of the jovial household as a foil, pitting it against the pain that Beethoven suffers. At times the two are placed against each other in the same scene, a kind of cinematic counterpoint that parallels Beethoven's own contrapuntal tendencies. This is most apparent in the critical moment in the movie, often referred to as the "Immortal Beloved" scene. It is the longest in the film and one of only three sustained scenes, the others being when Beethoven discovers his deafness and resolves to continue his work, and the final scene that flashes between Beethoven on his deathbed and the premiere performance of the Ninth Symphony, which is chronologically inaccurate.

The Immortal Beloved scene moves between two rooms in Beethoven's house, each with its own prevailing mood. In one room Beethoven is working on the somber slow movement of the *Appassionata* Sonata, in another Schuppanzigh's string quartet and the housekeeper prepare a party to celebrate Beethoven's recently announced engagement to Thérèse de Brunswick. As Beethoven plays, Juliette quietly comes in a back door, having just arrived from Italy. She tells him that she loves only him, and pleads for the two of them to run away. When Beethoven hesitates, torn between desire and duty, she responds, "There is no happiness without cruelty, Ludwig." Meanwhile, the revelry continues in the next room. Believing Beethoven has assented, Juliette leaves to make preparations for their departure, and Beethoven, who has said nothing throughout their encounter, sits down at a desk and writes the Immortal Beloved letter. The quartet and housekeeper enter and begin to play, on toy instruments, Beethoven's Variations for Piano op. 76, sometimes known as the Turkish March. Beethoven, caught up in the buoyant music, joins in on a kazoo and they dance into the other room where the celebration feast is waiting.

Thérèse, coming into the first room through the same door that Juliette exited, spots the letter on his desk and begins to read. As Beethoven reenters, the opening motive of the Fifth Symphony punctuates the startled and distraught expression on his face when he sees Thérèse with the letter. To the inevitable question, "Is it for me?" Beethoven assures her that the letter is his engagement gift to her. Thérèse has forebodings, but she is convinced.

Once again the revelers fetch Beethoven with the Turkish March, and he leaves the letter on the desk. As Thérèse, who has stayed behind, gathers her

FIGURES 7.4 – 7.5

Un Grand Amour, two contrasting images from the same scene.
Beethoven reveling to his Turkish March, and Beethoven, when
he sees Thérèse reading the Immortal Beloved letter.

things, Juliette returns and Thérèse excitedly shows the letter to her. Thérèse's joy and the laughter from the next room create an ironic counterpoint to Juliette's stricken countenance and her sense that the letter is really for her. Before making a full martyred exit she gives Thérèse a note for Beethoven: "I am returning to Rome forever." The scene closes as Beethoven, having read her words and realizing what has occurred, sits at the piano and sings the Beethoven arietta, "In questa tomba obscura" (In this tomb, forgotten). Melancholy has invaded the engagement celebration.

The scene in which Beethoven discovers his deafness is cinematically the most celebrated and powerful in the movie. Frank S. Nugent, film critic for the *New York Times,* called it "one heartbreaking, tragic, gloriously exultant sequence."[3] Gance makes dramatic use of what was still a relatively new medium in the 1930s: sound. At the beginning of the scene Gance underlines its importance with a card stating, "Vint le matin le plus tragique de la vie de Beethoven" (The most tragic morning of Beethoven's life arrived). Beethoven is in the mill at Heiligenstadt. He hears a roaring noise and asks Pierro, a young man who is acting as his helper, "What it is?" Pierro does not hear it. Suddenly it stops. As Beethoven plays several chords on the piano the camera pans between Beethoven and Pierro. Each time it is on Pierro we hear the chords; when it is on Beethoven we hear nothing. Distraught, Beethoven wanders aimlessly through the countryside. As he does, cards flash on the screen:

> The voice of the beloved.
> The song of birds.
> Nevermore.

He does not hear a country fiddler, the sound of the mill, water, church bells, women washing and beating clothes. All is silence. As he looks in the water at his reflection, the opening phrase of the *Pastoral* Symphony comes to him. He returns to the mill, and to the strains of the second movement of the Fifth Symphony he writes the Heiligenstadt Testament. A violent thunderstorm occurs as he is writing, and Beethoven plays furiously the storm movement of the *Pastoral* Symphony on the piano. The storm passes and Beethoven glides into the final movement, the Rondo.

Fantastical as the film appears, the Gance story is not without some basis in the historical literature, including several of the minor scenes, such as the egg throwing—in reality Beethoven did not hit Schuppanzigh, and in reality the housekeeper was not in the least amused. Beethoven did teach Juliette Guicciardi when he was thirty and she was eighteen. In a letter written in 1801 to his friend Wegeler, Beethoven alludes to his encroaching deafness and a young woman that he loves: "My bad hearing haunted me everywhere like a ghost and I fled—from mankind. I seemed like a misanthrope, and yet am far from being one. This change has been wrought by a dear fascinating girl who loves me and whom I love. There have been a few blessed moments within the last two years, and it is the first time that I feel that—marriage might bring me happiness. Unfortunately she is not of my station—and now—it would be impossible for me to marry." Beethoven then announces that he will dedicate himself to his work, for that is all that is left for him. In some ways the letter is a prelude to the Heiligenstadt Testament.[4]

The closeness of Juliette and Thérèse in the film has basis in historical fact as well. Juliette's mother was born Susanne de Brunswick, and was the sister of Anna Elizabeth de Brunswick, making Juliette the first cousin of Josephine and Thérèse. Count Gallenberg was a composer of ballets and light music, he did marry Guicciardi, and they moved to Italy. They returned several years later when Gallenberg was given an administrative position at the Royal Imperial Opera. Beethoven sent Anton Schindler to call upon Gallenberg with a message about *Fidelio*, and when Schindler returned Beethoven asked him if he had seen Gallenberg's wife. Then Beethoven confided: "She loved me greatly, much more than her husband. . . . She was his wife before her journey to Italy. Arriving in Vienna, she sought me out weeping, but I spurned her."[5]

While Schindler's accounts can never be trusted—as we now know, he falsified many incidents—this conversation is verifiable, as it is preserved in one of Beethoven's conversation books. Yet even here Schindler is not honest. The words "arriving in Vienna" were added later, significantly changing the meaning of the passage. Without them, the timing of the meeting is ambiguous; it may very well have taken place before she left for Italy. It should also be stated that Schindler originally believed the Immortal Beloved letter was written to Guicciardi, and that it was written around 1803, although subsequent research has shown that not to be the case.

The Schindler narrative was dispelled by Alexander Wheelock Thayer in 1872, but until then it had considerable currency in the United States as well as in Europe. In 1860 *Dwight's Journal of Music* reprinted an excerpt from an essay by Anne M. H. Brewster, in which she repeats the story and connects the Immortal Beloved letter and the *Moonlight* Sonata directly with these events. The *Moonlight* Sonata was dedicated to Giulietta Guicciardi, so there is further external suggestion for this inference, although what Gance did with it is purely the product of his imagination. Yet the Guicciardi affair may have been even more emotionally wrought had Gance followed what most scholars now believe: Beethoven loved Giulietta to the extent that he kept a picture of her the rest of his life, but for Giulietta Beethoven's attention was probably a transient youthful infatuation. Such would not have made a good cinematic ending.

Even though *Un Grand Amour* is a French film, it reached a wide audience in the United States. It premiered in New York at the 55th St. Playhouse on November 22, 1937, and was popular enough to remain there until January 1938. Then in February it opened at three other New York theaters, the Yorktown, Plaza, and Eighth Street Playhouse. On April 22 the Trans-Lux Theatre began showing it.

The American reception of *Un Grand Amour* was such that Warner Bros. soon attempted to produce its own Beethoven film. In 1938 the studio announced a new project, to be titled *The Life of Beethoven*, for which Arturo Toscanini would conduct the orchestral sound track. The film was to be based on Hermann Heinz Ortner's play *Beethoven: Fünf Akte*, written in 1936, the same year *Un Grand Amour* appeared. In the 1930s and 1940s, Ortner was the most performed playwright on the Austrian stage. The celebrated actor Paul Muni, who had been born in eastern Europe and still traveled there, was to play the part of Beethoven in the film, and his likely familiarity with Ortner's plays may partly explain his interest in the project. A complex set of events prevented the film from coming to fruition, but the efforts that Warner Bros. made on its behalf speak to the impact of Gance's *Beethoven*.

Warner Bros. expected *The Life of Beethoven* to be their leading film for the 1939–40 season. Under the *New York Times* headline "Warners to Make 48 Feature Films" ran the subheading, "'Life of Beethoven,' with Muni, Heads Production Program for Season of 1939–40." Other stars were cast, specifically Lya Lys, a German-French actress who had appeared in a number of avantgarde films in France, most notably *L'Âge d'Or* (The Golden Age), a 1930 surrealist film directed by Luis Buñuel and written by Buñuel and Salvador Dalí. Filled with what were considered pornographic scenes and religious blasphemy, the film was eventually banned in France; its Paris premiere led to riots. Shortly afterward Lys moved to Hollywood and starred in several American films in the 1930s and 1940s.

Filming on the Beethoven project, however, did not begin, and in July Warner Bros. explained: "Rather than attempt to crowd 'The Life of Beethoven' into Paul Muni's schedule following completion of 'We are Not Alone,' the Warners have removed the film from this year's schedule and will make it in the Spring. During his leave of absence Muni will appear in Manhattan in 'Key Largo.'" This was not unusual for Muni, who played frequently on the Broadway stage.

At the end of March 1940, the project was still alive: "The studio has placed 'The Life of Beethoven' on its spring schedule for Paul Muni." But by July the entire project suddenly foundered as Muni and Warner Bros. clashed over another film. Warners had assigned Muni the role of the gangster John Dillinger in *High Sierra* in addition to the title role in *The Life of Beethoven*. Muni let it be known that he preferred to play Beethoven, but if he were to play Dillinger he wanted the script revised "to eliminate the gunplay." Muni had a reputation for making demands about scripts, which were usually met, but this time the studio found his request unreasonable. This was, after all, to be a 1940 gangster film, and, according to a Warners spokesman, had they acceded, the film would have been "about as attractive at the box-office as 'Juarez' or 'We Are Not Alone,' Muni's last two not very successful pictures."

Warners substituted Humphrey Bogart for Muni's role in *High Sierra* but allowed Muni to continue with Beethoven. Here the situation gets murky. Through his manager Muni announced that he "felt that Warners' efforts to find him vehicles, though well-intentioned, had not been successful." Even though Muni's contract called for him to make another seven pictures at $125,000 each, a large sum in 1940, Muni and Warners agreed to part ways and dissolve the contract. William Dieterle, who had directed several of Muni's films, went with him. With this dispute *The Life of Beethoven* died.

Immortal Beloved, like *Un Grand Amour*, attempts to cover much of Beethoven's life. Rummaging through Beethoven's belongings just after his death, Beethoven's secretary and factotum Anton Schindler discovers the Immortal Beloved letter and a new will giving his entire estate to her. The letter details an assignation that was to have taken place between Beethoven and the unnamed woman. Schindler then sets out on a quest to discover who this mysterious woman is. Visiting the hotel in Karlsbad where Beethoven's tryst was to have taken place, he secures her signature from the rolls but discovers that the name is illegible. Schindler then visits two women whom he believed might be the Immortal Beloved. Through long conversations with them and a series of flashbacks, Beethoven's life gradually unfolds. He is seen as the young lion conquering Viennese society with his virtuoso pianism; his deafness is revealed in two dramatic incidents; and Beethoven's rocky relations with his brothers and the long tragic story of his relationship with his nephew are chronicled. There are even brief scenes of Beethoven's childhood, which portray him suffering his drunken, physically abusive father. The film ends with Beethoven on his deathbed, the point at which it began.

Cinematically, the most powerful scene in the movie is the beginning. Following the last words of Beethoven's funeral service, the gates outside the church burst open as Beethoven's funeral procession begins. We suddenly hear the wildly cheering crowd of thousands who push around the casket and procession, to the sound track of Beethoven's *Missa Solemnis*. Finally, at the grave, Schindler delivers a moving oration that sets the tone for the film. Beethoven is eulogized as a man of mythic proportions, a tragic figure whose music is transporting and transcending:

> He was an artist and who will stand beside him. He was an artist and what he was he was only through music.
> The thorns of life had wounded him deeply, so he held fast to his art, even when the gate through which he had entered was shut. Music spoke through a deafened ear to he who could no longer hear it. He carried the music in his heart. . . .
> He withdrew from his fellow man after he had given them everything and received nothing in return. He lived alone because he found no second self. Thus he was, thus he died. Thus he will live for all time.

This particular eulogy was written by the Austrian poet Franz Grillparzer and was actually read at Beethoven's funeral by the tragedian Heinrich Anschütz. Clearly the Romantic image of Beethoven had overtaken him even before he was interred in the ground. That this image would remain in the popular mind as late as 1994, far beyond the postmodern rattling of academia, suggests just how deeply ensconced it was, even in the United States. By the time of Beethoven's death the idea of the composer as artist, as *Tonkünstler* (tone poet) rather than Componist (the eighteenth-century notion of a composer as artisan), was firmly a part of Austrian culture. It would take another decade and a half for that change to occur in American culture, but once there, it remained equally strong.

Further dialogue throughout the film reinforces this image of Beethoven. Countess Giulietta Guicciardi, one of Beethoven's loves, describes her first encounter with Beethoven's music: "His music affected me like nothing I had ever heard before," a sentiment echoed by other characters throughout the film. This passion also had sexual overtones. In anticipation of hearing Beethoven for the first time, Guicciardi observed, "I heard that Beethoven's music aroused such passion as to be dangerous. Some thought it obscene and unsuitable for the young." She soon discovers that her cousins Theresa and Josephine von Brunsvick had succumbed to Beethoven as well as to his music. As she narrates we see Beethoven playing the introduction to the first movement of the *Pathetique* Sonata in a formal palace setting, with the von Brunsvick sisters sitting in the front row. When the allegro begins the scene switches to a palace garden where, with Beethoven in hot pursuit, Theresa runs into a covered path, peeling off clothes with every step. Beethoven, of course, catches up with her and they dissolve into a passionate embrace, all to the strains of the first movement of the *Pathetique.*

Some reviewers criticized the sexuality of the film, particularly the portrayal of Beethoven as a musical Don Juan, but director Bernard Rose was clear about his purpose: "I wanted to show there was more sex and violence in Beethoven than in the Sex Pistols." This comparison was not random. Gary Oldman, who played Beethoven, had recently starred in the film *Sid and Nancy* as punk rocker Sid Vicious of the Sex Pistols. Oldman was known for his portrayal of dark, disturbing characters, such as Dracula in *Bram Stoker's Dracula,* Lee Harvey Oswald in *JFK,* and a sadistic hit-man in *The Professional* (also called *Léon*). In the latter movie Oldman was given the line, in reference to an impending shootout, "The calm before the storm reminds me of Beethoven." Since *The Professional* was released in November 1994 and *Immortal Beloved* the following month, both by Columbia Pictures, Oldman's line is probably no coincidence.

Oldman's experience, particularly with Sid Vicious, has many echoes in *Immortal Beloved,* and it limits the film. Even here Oldman makes a better rock star than a mature, untamed German composer. As film critic Mary Kunz observed, "Gary Oldman, who always gets to look brooding and wasted, plays—you guessed it—a brooding, wasted Beethoven."[6] The first time we see Beethoven, he rushes into a plush hotel room expecting to find his Immortal Beloved, only to discover that she had already left. He then trashes the room, smashing furniture and finally hurling a chair out the window. Are we watching Beethoven or Sid Vicious? Or are Rose and Oldman trying to make the point for 1990s audiences that Beethoven was the Sid Vicious of the Napoleonic era?

Oldman feigned total disinterest in Beethoven: "You come in, you make the marks, you say the lines. That's it. Whether I've discovered anything about Beethoven—I don't even know if I really care. He's not in my life. I won't bullshit you. Beethoven is just a bloke who wrote a few nice tunes and had an interesting life that Bernard wrote about." The interviewer did note a large biography of Beethoven sitting on his table, however, and Oldman himself was a pianist who had a keyboard in his dressing room so he could practice Beethoven passages to make sure his fingering at least looked authentic on the screen. He was even coached by Sir Georg Solti to play parts of the *Emperor* Concerto.

FIGURE 7.6

Immortal Beloved, which portrayed Beethoven as a
Don Juan figure. Here Theresa von Brunswick
entices Beethoven.

Oldman's comment thus has all the flippancy of a rock star—maybe Sid Vicious had not worn off. This attitude, however, was noted by one blogger: "You have a clueless Gary Oldman (Sid Vicious from the film 'Sid and Nancy') portraying Beethoven as some hapless Romeo from a bad soap opera script."[7]

The differences in critics' reactions to the film were in direct proportion to how well versed they were in Beethoven's life and works. Music critics generally panned it, as noted below; movie critics were more enthusiastic. How the music itself figures into the story was also an important part of its reception. For instance, Mick LaSalle, film critic for the *San Francisco Chronicle,* considered the music an important element of the drama: "Music floods the sound track, and not in random selections from the maestro's greatest hits. The pieces are chosen with taste and present Beethoven's point of view—either in counterpoint or highlighting the action on screen." Janet Maslin of the *New York Times* was even more emphatic and closer to Rose's intent: "Think of this as an extremely ambitious classical music video, with visual ideas that merely echo the moods of the music. The music tells its own story, and the music is glorious." Not coincidentally, perhaps, MTV was then at the height of its popularity.[8]

Rose not only worked from LaSalle's and Maslin's premises but went further than other films in making Beethoven's music the central focus of *Immortal Beloved*. In any film about Beethoven, music will be crucial, not simply because he wrote it but because the emotions within are so personal. Beethoven's music is Beethoven expressing his own feelings. Rose, an accomplished pianist, confirmed this to the *San Francisco Chronicle:* "In a certain sense you have to regard this as a musical, inasmuch as the film was written to the music and a lot of the scenes directly fit with certain pieces of music."[9] Setting aside the diegetic scenes, the sound track fits closely and precisely with the film. Indeed, the music choreographed the action: many scenes were shot while the music designated for it was being played. Thus in a real way the music came first and the action is a gloss on it, an inversion of normal film procedure.

Rose's choice of music is imaginative and unexpected. In one early scene, which has Beethoven giving a piano lesson to Giulietta Guicciardi, she is clumsily thumping her way through a Beethoven sonata while Beethoven sits, apparently lost in thought. Noticing that, Guicciardi purposely crashes down on the keyboard, an act that gains Beethoven's attention. He then tells her:

> You think because I did not stop you, that I am not listening.
>   A mistake is nothing. But the fact that you thump out the notes
> without the least sensitivity to their meaning is unforgiveable.
>   And your lack of passion is unforgiveable.
>   I shall have to beat you.

Both startled and intrigued by what she takes to be an erotic suggestion, Giulietta coquettishly holds up a limp wrist for the symbolic punishment, and is surprised when the slap is more than a tease. Coinciding precisely with the blow is the first staccato chord of the beginning of the *Eroica* Symphony. Immediately we see Beethoven and Giulietta walking through a garden as Beethoven describes his new symphony, about Napoleon, at the same time pushing through a group of aristocrats and yelling at them that their days are over. The scene then cuts to an open carriage, where Beethoven and Giulietta ride down a country road, their passionate embraces met with disapproving looks from others whom they pass. Throughout this section the first movement of the *Eroica* continues. Thus even the *Eroica* is imbued with erotic content, and sex and revolution are somehow conflated.

FIGURE 7.7

Immortal Beloved. Beethoven shoving aside aristocrats.

Another of Rose's imaginative musical choices occurs in the scene where Beethoven has determined to end his brother Casper's relationship with Johanna. He obtains a police order to have her arrested on a vague prostitution charge. We see Beethoven leading four policemen galloping on horseback through the countryside to Johanna's place. They break down a heavy fortress-like gate, run up a set of outdoor steps, and burst into a room where Casper and Johanna are together in bed. Yanking off the sheet, Beethoven screams, "Arrest that whore," only to find that Casper had married Johanna the day before. The entire scene is accompanied by the first movement of Beethoven's Violin Concerto. Considered one of Beethoven's more lyrical pieces, it seems an incongruous choice. Rose, however, uses those portions that feature the motive of five sharp staccato notes, originally played by the timpani to open the piece. They create both a sense of action, accompanying the dash to the house and into the bedroom, and one of dramatic foreboding, as Beethoven's purpose is originally unclear and then at best questionable. The music also helps convey a tension between Beethoven and Johanna that will not only be amplified with Beethoven's long battle of custody over Johanna's son Karl, but that eventually leads to the denouement, in which the Immortal Beloved is revealed to be Johanna herself and Karl to be Beethoven's son. In retrospect, we are to understand that Johanna had been Beethoven's lover, and through a mis-understanding at the hotel in Karlsbad, the early scene where Beethoven de-stroys the room, Beethoven had thought she had left him and vice versa. In ad-dition, Beethoven had a pathological need to protect, in reality to control, his two brothers' lives, which only heightened his anger at Casper's involvement with Johanna. Casper had for years served as Beethoven's secretary, so Bee-thoven saw Casper's devotion to her as a repudiation of the two brothers' rela-tionship.

Rose's solution to the Immortal Beloved question, entirely different but no less imaginative than Gance's, raises fundamental questions about historical accuracy and cinematic license. These are ultimately questions about film as genre itself, its complex relationship with the general public, and its role as creator, expositor, and mirror of its time. Because such issues transcend any single film, before addressing them another film about Beethoven needs to be considered; *Copying Beethoven* raises similar questions.

Copying Beethoven presents only the late Beethoven, and about two-thirds of it occurs in the week before the premiere of the Ninth Symphony in 1824. While the opening credits roll, we see a carriage in the countryside, but we do not know when or where it is traveling. When the carriage passes a country fiddler standing next to the road, we hear the principal theme of the *Grosse Fuge*. Is the music being scraped by the fiddler himself, or is it wholly nondi-egetic? Only as the other voices of the quartet enter does it become apparent that we are not hearing the fiddler alone but the fugue itself. Inside the car-riage is a young woman: Is the music inner-diegetic, that is, is she hearing the fugue in her head, because we quickly discover that she is rushing to Beetho-ven's deathbed? As Beethoven dies (accompanied by the thunderstorm that tradition has associated with his death), the relationship between these two characters remains to be clarified, but later the audience discovers that the fugue indeed was central to it.

The film reverts to 1824, to the shop of Beethoven's copyist and publisher Wenzel Schlemmer, who is old and dying of cancer and cannot keep up with Beethoven's last-minute compositional frenzy as the premiere of the Ninth Symphony approaches. He sends to the Vienna Conservatory for the best stu-dent they have to help copy the score and parts. To his surprise, Anna Holtz shows up. After she dispels Schlemmer's doubts that a woman can do the job, Schlemmer, desperate for someone, anyone, to help, agrees to allow her to work as Beethoven's copyist.

As in each of the previous films, Beethoven's first appearance establishes who he is. Hardly the sensitive, long-suffering Job of *Un Grand Amour* or the magnanimous neighbor of the three-minute *Moonlight Sonata,* he is the "beast," the term Schlemmer bestows on him at his first mention. As if to confirm Schlemmer's appellation, Beethoven soon bursts into the room ranting about the slowness of Schlemmer's copying; he dismisses Schlemmer's lament that he is dying as irrelevant. Beethoven is angry, uncaring, and bullying. The only thing he doesn't do is throw furniture.

When Anna shows up at Beethoven's house, Beethoven cannot believe that she is a copyist. He is at first half-amused and indulgent, but he becomes sarcastic later when she tells him that she is a composer herself: "A woman composer is like a dog walking on his hind legs: it's never done well, but you're surprised to see it done at all." Beethoven feels confirmed in his own gender prejudices when he examines her copying and finds that she has changed a B major passage to B minor. When she tells him she had neither made an error nor changed his manuscript but rather "corrected" it, he ridicules her. Later, however, he is forced to admit that she was indeed correct.

Thus begins a stormy but grudgingly respectful relationship. Anna herself has another important person in her life, Martin Bauer, a young, handsome, well-to-do engineer, to whom she is engaged. Martin is a man of the future, speaking of the new age of steel, and he has entered a competition to design a bridge that will span the Danube. He sees Beethoven as belonging to the world of the past.

Beethoven is portrayed as a man of many moods. He is unpredictable, sometimes thoughtful and aware when discussing art, sometimes loud and abrasive, sometimes sarcastic and at times cruel and cutting. Most of all he is mercurial, for instance switching suddenly from a calm discussion of his nephew Karl to fury when Anna contradicts him about the young man. He gets even angrier when she apologizes, insisting that she stand up to him and not assume a repentant stance. Beethoven is also crude, obnoxious, and adolescent in his desire to shock. Ascertaining that Anna has studied his sonatas at the conservatory, he then asks, "Which one is your favorite, the Waldstein, the Appassionata, or, I know, the Moonlight?" punctuating the last by mooning Anna.

Capturing Beethoven on the screen was a challenge for the director Agnieszka Holland and the writers Stephen Rivele and Christopher Wilkinson. Holland remarked that "Beethoven is one of those larger-than-life characters about whom you can say, 'Everything you've heard is true'—or at least most of it. He changed the very notion of music, destroying rules, conventions—and the nerves of some who worked with him—along the way."[10] The point is made explicit in the film; when Beethoven steps up to the podium to conduct the Ninth Symphony he mutters to himself, "Now music changes forever."

Venerable Hollywood screenwriter Ernest Lehman has stated that most Hollywood films can be broken down into three sections: "In the first act, who are the people, what is the situation of this whole story? Second act is the progression of that situation to a point of high conflict and great problems. And the third act is how the problems and the conflicts are resolved."[11] *Copying Beethoven* follows that pattern, but with a twist. It is organized around two large cycles, each leading up to a major event and each with a dramatic scene that underscores Beethoven's testiness and all but severs the relationship between the two principal characters. The relationship somehow survives these traumas, however, and continues. Thus each cycle contains Lehman's three sections, although the second cycle is briefer, as the principal characters need not be introduced but only further dimensions of their personae presented. The performance of the Ninth Symphony is the major event that closes the first cycle and the central moment in the film. The second cycle is less definitive in its final event, but shows Anna, who has apparently come to understand Beethoven's lofty vision of the nature of art and the artist, walking out of his house as he is dying, to pursue her own artistic ambitions. The scene is ambiguous but does suggest that she will succeed.

In the first cycle, where Beethoven's obtuse obnoxiousness is the spur to their moments of conflict, the climactic moment of tension comes when Anna shows him her own composition. He ridicules it in scatological terms, referring to one section as "fartissimo" and making flatulence sounds with his mouth as he plays it. The two reestablish their relationship only when Beethoven storms into the convent where Anna is staying and on his knees begs her to return. The climactic moment in the second cycle occurs when Beethoven arrives at the hall where the archduke will announce the winner of the competition to build the bridge over the Danube. Convinced that Martin's bridge has no soul and that Martin is not an artist, he smashes the model in front of Anna, the archduke, and the startled crowd in attendance. Anna, furious, returns to Beethoven's place only to retrieve her things, but Beethoven is able to convince her that art is about the soul, and that Martin may find his because of what he did. Anna, who had serious reservations about the beauty of Martin's bridge when he first unveiled it, finally agrees and stays on as his copyist, as Beethoven moves on to the late quartets.

Most of the dialogue in the first part of the film has to do with establishing the dichotomy between Beethoven as beast and his music as sublime. As Anna is climbing the stairs to Beethoven's apartment in one scene, she encounters an old woman sitting next to a window in the hall. Informed by the woman that she has no windows in her apartment and thus no respite from the rude

FIGURE 7.8

Copying Beethoven. Beethoven smashes Martin Bauer's bridge.

and tempestuous composer, Anna inquires why she doesn't move. "Move?" she replies. "I am the next-door neighbor to Ludwig van Beethoven. I hear all the pieces of Beethoven before they are premiered. I am the envy of Vienna. I have been with him since the Seventh." She then sings the second movement of the Seventh, which flowers into the full orchestral symphony as Anna goes upstairs.

Although music is not as closely tied to specific action in *Copying Beethoven* as it was in *Immortal Beloved*, Beethoven's compositions are still the heart of the film. The performance of the Ninth Symphony is the pivotal event. Its centrality is underscored by the sheer length of the scene; an uninterrupted eleven minutes of a symphonic performance is unusual in any commercial film. Fragments of all four movements are heard, and they are so joined that someone unfamiliar with the piece would not find the juxtapositions any more jarring than Beethoven himself intended, such as the "Schreckenfanfare" (terror fanfare) that begins the last movement.

Beethoven conducts the orchestra in the manner of a modern conductor, or in the manner that Michel Katzaroff portrayed in his 1930s lithograph, which the actor Ed Harris seems to consciously imitate (see Figures 7.9 and 7.10).

FIGURE 7.9

Lithograph of Beethoven conducting by Michel Katzaroff.

FIGURE 7.10

Copying Beethoven. Beethoven conducting the Ninth Symphony.
The similarity of the pose to the Katzaroff lithograph is unmistakable.

Much of the film's drama centers on whether the deaf Beethoven can conduct the performance. Beethoven is worried himself, so he places Anna in the
center of the orchestra to give him downbeats and cues that he relays to the
players. While necessary to the plot, this is an artifice that only detracts from
the message of the film, the sublimity of Beethoven's late music. In reality Beethoven did not conduct the premiere, but stood to the side beating time. The
situation, however, is largely rescued by Harris's performance as a conductor.
Harris demonstrates a surprising conducting ability, with a clear beat that,
although not always accompanied by the proper metrical pattern, displays
sensitivity to the music's moods. More important, his overall movement, demeanor, facial expressions, and reaction to the music shout in capital letters:
TRIUMPH. The power of the "Ode to Joy" of course has much to do with the effect of this scene.

The dialogue in the second part of the film shifts to a philosophical discussion of art, or rather Art, as Anna cannot accept the *Grosse Fuge*, which
she perceives as ugly. Here the repugnance of Beethoven's person that Anna
endured for a higher purpose—learning how to compose from Beethoven—

becomes a dialogue on the ugliness of Beethoven's music, with the *Grosse Fuge* as metaphor for Beethoven's personality.

The second part comes close to equating Beethoven with God, or at least seeing Beethoven as a vessel through which God sends music to man. When Anna, first confronted with the *Grosse Fuge*, says she does not understand it, Beethoven responds, "Of course you don't understand it, it's not about understanding, you must experience these works of mine. It's a language, a new language that I am inventing to talk about man's experience of God. My experience of God. That's why you are sent to me to write down this language. You are God's secretary." In another encounter:

> BEETHOVEN: Music is the language of God. Musicians are as close to God as man can be. We hear his voice. We read his lips. We give birth to the children of God who sing his praise. That's what musicians are, Anna. And if we are not that we are nothing.
> Everyone thinks I live in silence. It's not true. My head is constantly filled with sounds. It never stops. God infests my mind with music, and then what does he do. He makes me deaf and he denies me the pleasure he allows everyone else, hearing my work. Is that a loving God, is that a friend?
> ANNA: He is our father.
> BEETHOVEN: My father was a brutal drunken sod. If God is my father I disown him. Maybe I am losing my mind. That's what they think, all of them. What do you think?
> ANNA: I think God is speaking to you.

Beethoven's vision of music follows closely the Kantian contrast between the beautiful and the sublime. When Anna tells him that the *Grosse Fuge* is ugly, he says of course it's ugly, but it is beautiful. "You can't have your head in the clouds unless there's shit on the soles of your boots." Later he uses the word sublime. He also refers to the *Grosse Fuge* as "my bridge to the future of music," and he challenges her: "If one day you will cross over it, perhaps you will be free." The opening scene thus takes on added significance in retrospect, where the theme of the fugue is associated with the crudeness of a country fiddler, whether he's actually playing it or not. Beethoven's use of a bridge as a metaphor for art also reflects on his destruction of Martin's bridge, which he did not consider to be art.

Each of the above films about Beethoven stretches, bends, or distorts the truth, some more than others. What we know about Beethoven and what occurs in Beethoven films would bother any historian, fan, or musician familiar with Beethoven's life. As Mark Zimmer, reviewing *Copying Beethoven,* noted, "For some reason, filmmakers are more enamored with the idea of Beethoven than the actuality of Beethoven when making a film about the composer."[12] Some of the inaccuracies are minor, such as Beethoven conducting an orchestra as if he were a modern conductor, or suggesting that Beethoven was more or less completely deaf when he wrote the *Moonlight* or the *Kreutzer* Sonatas. These would bother only persons steeped in Beethoven biography. Others are more serious, such as the fake will in which Beethoven left his entire estate to the Immortal Beloved, and then identifying her as Johanna Reiss, or, in *Copying Beethoven,* the creation of an entirely fictional character, Anna Holtz.

Europe is no more faithful in its presentation of Beethoven than Hollywood. *Un Grand Amour de Beethoven* rivals any American film in that regard, creating a love triangle around Juliette Guicciardi and Thérèse de Brunswick with the Immortal Beloved letter in the middle, placing Beethoven in an abandoned mill and then an abandoned monastery, having his deafness occur suddenly and dramatically, and having him live in poverty with his compositions, including the *Eroica* and the Ninth Symphony, rejected until he is on his deathbed.

Yet to expect or complain about historical accuracy would be to misunderstand the film genre itself. Both Bernard Rose and Agnieszka Holland have readily acknowledged that their films are fiction, and that the writers and directors are simply using certain devices, such as the Immortal Beloved letter and the fake will, to allow the portrayal of the vision of Beethoven they wish to promulgate.

Rose defended his solution to the Immortal Beloved puzzle by stating that many candidates have been proposed as Beethoven's great love, but none have been universally accepted and probably never will be: "If you read 20 Beethoven biographies they will all give 20 different answers that reflect the prejudices of the writers and the era."[13] His film appeared just as the cultural battles that ran through many disciplines in the 1980s and 1990s reached an apogee in music scholarship. Postmodernism had confronted many fields of humanistic inquiry since the 1970s, but it was near the end of the 1980s that it had a significant impact upon music. For some in the musical community a strict positivism, characterized by a search for demonstrable fact, still prevailed, and for others all knowledge was brought under suspicion, leading to the argument that the past is what we make it to be. Any historical event or document allows multiple readings, and in that sense there is no objective truth. Thus, if this line of reasoning is carried to its logical conclusion, one interpretation is as good as another, and when the evidence is essentially circumstantial, as in the case of the Immortal Beloved letter, how can any solution be definitive?

Rose made precisely this argument: since we don't really know the name of the Immortal Beloved, why not Johanna? In a curious shift of the burden of proof, Rose stated, "I've researched it extensively, and I believe that it is completely plausible. That doesn't mean I could prove it, but I defy anybody to prove me wrong."[14]

After the movie critics gave generally positive notices to the film, the music critics weighed in. The difference in how these fraternities reacted to *Immortal Beloved* may be seen in two reviews that appeared in the *New York Times,* one by film critic Janet Maslin on December 16, 1994, and the other by music critic Edward Rothstein two weeks later. Maslin understood clearly what the film was about—the music. She opened with a line uttered by Beethoven: "It is the power of music to carry one into the mental state of the composer." She recognized that whatever the story, it is about Beethoven, and it is primarily about feeling, and she understood that these feelings were conveyed through the music: "'Immortal Beloved' is mostly feeling: grand, turbulent emotions meant to shed light on the music's meaning."[15]

Rothstein, apparently bothered by reaction to the film and by viewers taking it as historically accurate, felt compelled to set the record straight. In a column titled "How Can a Movie So Right Be So Wrong?" he acknowledged that there were moments of poetic power in the film, but too many events, both large and small ones, were simply incorrect historically. Most important was the entire premise of the movie: Beethoven did not leave his estate to the Immortal Beloved, and whoever she was it was definitely not Johanna. Other music critics responded with much the same argument: Lawrence Teeter observed that the film "makes a shambles of the truth," and Lewis Lockwood provided the longest and most thoughtful essay on the topic, titled "Film Biography as Travesty." Lockwood admits the film has value, but after enumerating the many ways it misses the mark historically, he focuses his ire primarily on the cynicism of the producers, specifically their notion, as expressed by the critic John Richardson about the movie *Surviving Picasso,* that "most people won't know what is authentic or not." As recent films have demonstrated, this attitude holds for *JFK* and *Nixon,* so for a figure as famous but as unknown to the general public as Beethoven, why expect anything different? Most people know Beethoven, but they don't know Beethoven.[16]

The screenwriters of *Copying Beethoven* felt a particular dilemma: according to Rivele, the essential problem they faced was where to put the camera. That is, how do you create someone that the audience can identify with? Rivele felt that could not be the Beethoven of 1824, who was isolated, testy, and "had no one to talk to." So Rivele and Wilkinson began with historical fact: Beethoven's copyist, Ferdinand Wolanek, had left him and, needing someone to help prepare the parts for the premiere of the Ninth Symphony, Beethoven asked the Vienna Conservatory to send someone. They sent two male students. Rivele and Wilkinson wondered, however, "What if it had been a woman?" That approach not only gave them the premise around which to build the plot, but at the most practical level it allowed the film to be made: "This is what enabled us to create a film about the late Beethoven that could actually get financed."[17]

Anna Holtz is more than a copyist; she is an observer and later in the film a confidante and caretaker of Beethoven. Beethoven makes no sexual advances, although they symbolically confirm the intimacy of their relationship when later in the film Beethoven sits down in his room without a shirt and says, "Wash me." Anna is startled but does so, while the *La malinconia* of the String Quartet op. 18, no. 6, plays. Anna also becomes his ghost composer, "correcting" the Ninth Symphony while convincing Beethoven that her changes were what he himself would do. The implication is that without her the Ninth Symphony would not be what it is today.

In one sense the question of historical accuracy is irrelevant. What matters is the vision that the directors present, the image of Beethoven that they perpetuate. The old cliché about suspension of disbelief in the theater applies, albeit in a different way here, as any discussion of Beethoven in film demands, as a sine qua non, suspension of any expectation of historical accuracy. These films are, to reiterate, fiction.

Each of the films starts with the character of Beethoven, then culls some real incidents in his life and uses them as the ingredients around which a fictional narrative is crafted. What is fact and what is fiction thus blur, and for this purpose do not matter. The choices each director makes in plot, tone, and even music are an illumination of the figure of Beethoven and, in virtually every instance, of what art is and what it means to be an artist.

Yet there may be a point when the viewer will stop and say "Enough!" and the suspension of disbelief necessary for any drama crashes, pulling the viewer away from any personal involvement in the story and creating an atmosphere of either outrage or bemused irony. The film must then be taken as either camp or failure, depending on how offended the viewer is. Where that tipping point occurs will of course vary greatly from viewer to viewer, depending on what the viewer brings to the film, in terms of both background knowledge and expectation. When it happens, however, then the film's artistic success must be questioned, but for our purposes, that is less important than another issue.

Does it fail because the image of Beethoven that the film presents is too out of line with that held by the American public?

Copying Beethoven raises this issue particularly. It was the least success-ful of the three films at the box office and was the most eviscerated by critics. "Beethoven Bio is Dum Dum Dum Dum," screamed one headline. Various critics referred to it as an "inelegant snooze," "the worst film about a composer since Hollywood's Golden Age," "boring and pointless," and "a dull and un-inspiring film."[18] Not all critics were so negative. Most of the reasons for the film's failure have less to do with the way Beethoven is presented than with an inferior script and logical inconsistencies that required no knowledge of Bee-thoven himself. Particularly glaring was the handling of Beethoven's deafness, which would come and go depending on the needs of the scene. At times he would refer to it, at times he would wear or hold a device, such as an ear trum-pet, at times he would be completely unable to hear any sound, even the thun-derous applause at the end of the premiere of the Ninth Symphony. Yet he never used a conversation book, and often he could hear even the softest whis-per from different parts of the room.

For the great majority of moviegoers the character of Beethoven in both *Immortal Beloved* and *Copying Beethoven* remains close to the general percep-tion of Beethoven. He is portrayed as Goethe described him, a "completely un-tamed personality," an egotistical, temperamental, explosive genius who has bad hair and scowls most of the time. *Copying Beethoven* goes further in pre-senting Beethoven as crude and scatological, with disgusting personal hab-its. Part of that has to do with the time: thanks in part to cable stand-up com-ics, twenty-first-century culture is more tolerant of or at least accustomed to scatological banter than in 1993, where it still retained some shock value. Such would have been inconceivable for a film about an artist in 1936.

Peter Shaffer's *Amadeus* had pioneered the use of vulgarity in the presenta-tion of an artist, but for a specific dramatic purpose: the dichotomy between Mozart's earthy, vulgar personality and his ethereal music formed the funda-mental dramatic tension throughout both the play and the film (1984). Pos-sibly influenced by *Amadeus*—virtually every film about a classical composer is compared to *Amadeus*—*Copying Beethoven* in particular parallels that film in characterizations and even some entire scenes. In the latter, Beethoven is portrayed as crude, inconsiderate, often unaware of his effect on people, and even as a vulgar adolescent, but he is also viewed or views himself as a vessel of God, his music approaching God. The closing scene in particular seems mod-eled on *Amadeus*. In *Amadeus* Mozart dictates his *Requiem* to Salieri on his deathbed. Here Beethoven is on his deathbed, dictating his "Heiliger Dank-gesang" (Hymn of Thanksgiving, from the String Quartet op. 132) to Anna as she writes it down. At the end both Beethoven and Mozart have entered into a spiritual realm that seems removed from everyday life. Beethoven articulates it specifically, whispering to Anna, "Earth does not exist. Time is timeless. And the hands that lifted you caress your face, molded to the face of God. And you are at one. Finally free." Anna sits there—for how long we don't know— then opens the door and, as the film ends to the finale of the Ninth, walks out into a field and the distance.

In spite of artistic flaws, *Copying Beethoven* is more successful in presenting Beethoven as a powerful personality, a force of nature, than either *Immortal Beloved* or *Un Grand Amour*. This is largely because Ed Harris is a more commanding presence than either Harry Baur or Gary Oldman; he is the only one of the three actors able to communicate the force of Beethoven's personality.

While Gance presents the idealized Beethoven typical of the early twentieth century, both *Immortal Beloved* and *Copying Beethoven* conceive Beethoven as somewhere between a Romantic god and a rock star. In the two later films he has the clichéd persona of a rock icon, but his music is that of the heavens. The first point is made with Beethoven's first appearance in each film, where he is trashing a hotel room and ranting at a dying man. The latter point is made through the reaction to the Ninth Symphony in both films, where everyone in his orbit, including Johanna and Karl, is moved. It is further reinforced cinematically in *Immortal Beloved*, where Beethoven as a boy is virtually transported to the stars during the choral finale, and in *Copying Beethoven* through much discussion that links Beethoven and his music directly with God, as well as in Harris's performance on the podium as conductor. Harris conveys an expression of one transported and transcended by the music.

The Romantic-rock connection may go beyond an attempt to sell Beethoven to the late twentieth and twenty-first centuries. Since the 1960s rock has been viewed by many as a special kind of music, as a Bacchanalian, hyper-emotional vehicle for personal expression, more of a cultural world than entertainment. It is music that comes from the gut, precisely the language Beethoven used to describe the *Grosse Fuge* to Anna. Although the means and approach of nineteenth-century German composers and twentieth-century Anglo-American rock musicians differ significantly, rock nevertheless embodies much the same aesthetic orientation perceived in nineteenth-century Romanticism. Bernard Rose may have been off in his choice of rock musicians

when he equated Beethoven with the Sex Pistols, but his broader point reso-nates not only in film but with much of the American public. To many, Bee-thoven was the rock star of the Napoleonic era.

Regardless of how one views the interpretations of Beethoven in *Un Grand Amour de Beethoven, Immortal Beloved,* and *Copying Beethoven,* they are clearly and obviously meant to be about Beethoven. One particular film, how-ever, may be read as a portrayal of Beethoven, but his presence is so shrouded that the connection is only suggested and must be teased out by the viewer. The film is *Five Easy Pieces,* which came out in 1970, the bicentennial of Bee-thoven's birth.

Five Easy Pieces features a searing performance by a youthful, hyper-charged Jack Nicholson, who plays the part of Bobby Dupea, a young man on the run from himself. In the opening scene Bobby appears to be just another roust-about on an oil rig somewhere in the southwest, a volatile, hard-working, hard-

FIGURE 7.11

Copying Beethoven.
Anna Holtz leaving
Beethoven's house
after he has died.

drinking tinderbox commonly found in a lifestyle that combines physical labor with challenge, exhilaration, and danger. Bobby has a girlfriend, Rayette, a vacuous blonde who ultimately turns out to be a genuinely feeling person. She idolizes Bobby, although it is not clear that she understands at all the volcanic forces brimming just below the surface of his personality.

We soon learn that Bobby is a fugitive from another world. Brought up in a well-to-do musical household, Bobby was poised to become a concert pianist when he abandoned his career, family, culture, and ambitions. News that his father is dying, however, brings him back into that world, and Bobby, with the ever-hopeful but clueless Rayette accompanying him on the journey, must reenter it and come to terms with it and himself. In the end he fails at both. Along the way he seduces his brother Carl's fiancée, Catherine Van Oost, and tries to persuade her to leave Carl and run off with him. Carl is the mirror opposite of Bobby, steady, civil, physically fragile, temperamentally rock-solid,

Five Easy Pieces. Bobby Dupea and his girlfriend,
Rayette (right), at a bowling alley.

and dull. In a climactic scene, Catherine realizes that she is better off with a
dullard than a psychopath, and rejects Bobby in no uncertain terms.

Since the sound track does not use a note of Beethoven's music, alternating
instead between Bach, Chopin, Mozart, and Tammy Wynette, and since there
are no direct references to Beethoven, even where one might be expected, the
Beethoven connection is admittedly speculative. Evidence in both the film
and the original script, however, suggests that the principal male character,
whose full name is Robert Eroica Dupea, was intended as a topus for the Beethovenian hero as seen through the lens of 1970, in particular through the political turbulence and the growing feminism that marked that year. The full
name of Bobby's brother is Carl Fidelio Dupea. Beethoven thus appears, but
only encoded. The encoding is deep enough that none of the critics addressed
the implications of the reference, probably because they were film rather than

music critics. Consequently, they missed an important connection, and based on the original script it is clear that the connection was intentional.

As a hero Bobby leaves much to be desired. He is unsettled, he is angry, he is out of control, he is running from himself—in short, he is lost. He remains in that state throughout the movie, including the final scene, when he leaves his car and, significantly, his wallet with Rayette at a gas station off the highway and after a brief conversation with a trucker jumps into the cab of a logging truck without knowing where the driver is headed. His sudden disappearance leaves Rayette alone but at least with a car and money; symbolically, however, he has shed not only his relationship but his identity, all the while trying to deny his situation. When the truck driver points out that it's cold where they are going and offers to loan Bobby a jacket, he replies:

BOBBY: No, it's okay.
DRIVER: Suit yourself. But I'll tell you, where we're headed it's gonna get colder'n hell.
BOBBY: It's all right. I'm fine.
I'm all right.
I'm fine.

The semi pulls out on the highway, heading north. A plume of smoke emerges from the exhaust. Rayette has returned to the car, puzzled, and the gas station attendant points toward the men's room. Rayette heads toward it, she and Bobby moving in opposite directions as the film ends.

There is as little subtlety in Bobby's character as there is resolution in the final scene, and Nicholson's performance is more hyperactive than nuanced. On the surface Bobby appears far from the Beethovenian heroic ideal. Yet Bobby may be the 1970s remnants of the traditional hero, a commentary on a time of division, soul-searching, and uncertainty. His character can be understood partly through a comparison with the principal characters in *Easy Rider,* Nicholson's previous film to which *Five Easy Pieces* was often compared. *Easy Rider* came out the year before and transformed the 1960s motorcycle movie, its direct ancestor, into a glorification of freedom, the road, drugs, and rock 'n' roll. It portrayed the protagonists—Wyatt, nicknamed Captain America (Peter Fonda), and Billy (Dennis Hopper), soon to be joined by George Hanson (Nicholson)—as emblematic of the freedom that the 1960s counterculture promised, pitting them against a conforming, disapproving, violent society. In the end all three characters are murdered, the victims of intolerance and fear of the lifestyle they represented. Even though Hopper and Fonda are drug

FIGURE 7.13

Five Easy Pieces. At the end of the film, the logging truck,
with its plume of smoke, heads toward the bridge as Rayette
walks away from Bobby's car toward the men's room to look for him.
Each character thus moves in the opposite direction from the other.

users and dealers, their trip financed by their cocaine business, and Nicholson
is an alcoholic attorney, they are portrayed positively in the film. They are non-
violent and well-meaning in their own ways, and they stand for the same sense
of freedom, albeit mixed with the self-centered irresponsibility found in 1960s
songs such as Bob Dylan's "Don't Think Twice, It's All Right," or John Har-
ford's "Gentle on My Mind." Their defiance of conservative society, particularly Billy's, contributes to their downfall, but their deaths more than anything
symbolize the darkness and viciousness that simmered just below the surface
of mainstream and, in this film particularly, southern society.

    Five Easy Pieces captures the same restlessness, the same rootlessness that
Easy Rider did, but the tone is different. In contrast to the fun-seeking heroes
of *Easy Rider,* Bobby Dupea is troubled, conflicted, and self-destructive. That
Five Easy Pieces appeared one year later may be no coincidence. *Easy Rider*
was released on July 14, 1969, three weeks before what would be the defining
event of 1960s youth culture: Woodstock. Before Woodstock, the dream of a
society of love and freedom still lived for many young people. That Woodstock
was both the culmination and the end of the era was all too soon apparent, al-

though the decline of the idealism represented by "flower power" had already begun after the "summer of love" in 1967. The turbulence of the 1960s, with riots, assassinations, and then the Vietnam War, had acted as a somber counterpoint to the optimism of the 1960s youth that they could change the world. By 1970 such optimism was rapidly fading; the mood of the country was darker.

For many in 1970 the country itself appeared lost. The Vietnam War, curiously ignored in both films, had stalled in an apparently endless quagmire in which thousands of young Americans were dying, and the nation's social fabric seemed irreparably torn. The riots in many cities following Martin Luther King Jr.'s assassination and the confrontation between protestors and the Chicago police at the 1968 Democratic National Convention were still on everyone's mind. That same year, 1968, a group of seven men and two women, calling themselves the Baltimore Interfaith Peace Mission, invaded Draft Board no. 33 in Catonsville, Maryland, and burned six hundred draft records. They then issued a manifesto advising registrants that their records may have been lost. It was captioned in large handwritten letters, "YOUR LIFE MAY HAVE BEEN SAVED." After spending eighteen months in prison for his part in the affair, the Catholic priest Father Daniel Berrigan wrote a free-verse play on the event, which was published in 1970. That spring, college protests erupted throughout the country, culminating in the shooting of four students on May 4 at Kent State University by the Ohio National Guard.

Five Easy Pieces thus came out just as protests and the New Left had reached a zenith. Although the Vietnam War crystallized much of the unrest of the late sixties, the New Left had a different and broader agenda. They embraced more overt and specific political goals than the flower children of Haight-Ashbury. They were committed to social revolution, and although one specific political ideology did not dominate, they encompassed various forms of Marxist-Socialist-Communist ideology. Some young people went to Cuba, believing that Fidel Castro represented the hope for the Americas in establishing a revolutionary regime there. Others espoused Mao or Trotsky. The most important organization, the Students for a Democratic Society, advocated nonviolent civil disobedience. Yet not even the SDS presented a single radical ideology, and it had begun to splinter by 1970. With the creation of organizations even more radical, such as Weatherman, opposition to the Vietnam War provided a single rallying point for many New Leftists and also gave them a broader base of support than they would have had otherwise.

With the civil rights movement taking shape and racial tensions still festering, the ubiquity of rock even on Broadway, the hippies, the flower children, the drug culture, the New Left and its calls for revolution, the assassinations of

John Kennedy, Martin Luther King, and Robert Kennedy, and, casting a pall over everything, the Vietnam War, Yeats's poem "The Second Coming" (often quoted at the time) seemed all too appropriate:

> Turning and turning in the widening gyre
> The falcon cannot hear the falconer;
> Things fall apart; the centre cannot hold;
> Mere anarchy is loosed upon the world,
> The blood-dimmed tide is loosed, and everywhere
> The ceremony of innocence is drowned;
> The best lack all conviction, while the worst
> Are full of passionate intensity.

Under such circumstances it is difficult to imagine a hero emerging, even a fictional one. Bobby Dupea, a confused, directionless powder keg, may have been the appropriate everyman for 1970.

For Beethoven, the Napoleonic hero ended with the *Eroica,* or at least seemed to. In *Five Easy Pieces,* the Napoleonic vision of a hero that motivated Beethoven is dead. Beethoven moved on to eventually assume a broader and more abstract heroism in the concept of the universal brotherhood of the Ninth Symphony and the intense spirituality of the late quartets, but this is not in the film.

Five Easy Pieces is ultimately a critique of the militaristic, all-conquering, self-absorbed, raging, brooding personality type of Beethoven's middle period, the image that has prevailed in American culture. Beethoven's actual intentions regarding the *Eroica* are complex and unclear: when did he change his mind about dedicating it to Napoleon, and whom did he have in mind when he added the subtitle "to the memory of a great man"? Was he really portraying himself, as some scholars have speculated? Bobby retains many of the characteristics found in both Beethoven's original Napoleonic vision and Beethoven himself: he is egocentric, quick to anger, unwilling to bend to society, but rather than conquering he is at core empty, unable to conquer even himself. He is militaristic only in his rage. Bobby is the shell that is left when the Beethovenian *Eroica* hero is stripped bare, much as Beethoven himself later saw Napoleon. Bobby is the post-Napoleon *Eroica* but with a twist. In *Five Easy Pieces,* the Napoleonic hero gives way to nihilism.

The Bobby-Beethoven connection is problematized, however, because of the ways the middle names of the two principal male characters are handled. Bobby's middle name is revealed at a significant moment in the drama: when his sister Tita meets him in a recording studio after not having seen him for some time, she quietly says in surprise, "Robert Eroica." It not only re-identifies Bobby but signifies the existence of Bobby's other world, which the viewer had no reason to suspect, although Bobby's impromptu piano performance on a spinet being carried on the back of a truck suggests that there is more to him than simply an oilfield laborer. Thus when Bobby reenters the world of his family, he is Robert Eroica, not Bobby or not just Robert, although later his family does refer to him as simply Robert. Tita's line, however, whispered but not stressed vocally, is easily lost if the listener is not expecting it. Carl's middle name is never mentioned in the dialogue itself.

Most viewers will be aware of the Eroica-Fidelio names only at the end of the film when the screen credits roll. Yet it wasn't intended to be that way. The original script had five brief scenes at the beginning to be played during the opening credits. In the first, the camera scans a series of Dupea family photo albums, pausing on different members of the household. The identity of the person in the photograph is carefully penned beneath each, and each child is given a name related to music: The oldest son is named Herbert Kreutzer Dupea, and Bobby's sister's full name is Elizabeth Partita Dupea, from which she derives her nickname, Tita. The final photograph is of the entire family, with Isabella, the mother, looking lovingly at the three-year-old in her arms. His figure is circled and beneath, preceded by a small heart, is written, "Robert Eroica Dupea."

The second scene shows a seven-year-old Bobby sitting on a piano bench with his mother among the various older Dupea family members who are engaged in music making. Next we see Bobby at ten, preparing to go on stage as part of a family recital. The camera pans the program and stops on "Five Easy Pieces—Grebner—Played by Robert Dupea." An overdub of "Five Easy Pieces" is then played haltingly over a scene in a chapel, where the funeral service of Isabella Dupea is held. As the service ends the various Dupea family members go to the casket to pay their final tribute. Bobby hesitates in the aisle and then turns and walks out the door.

Thus in the original version several things are already known about Bobby when the opening scene on the oil rig begins: his full name, his family background, his place in the family as the youngest and the favorite of his mother, his musical training, and the death of his mother when he was still young. The original opening also explains the title, which is never referred to or mentioned elsewhere in the film. That the director kept it nevertheless strongly suggests that the original conceptualization of Bobby, in which his middle name clearly connects him to a particular aspect of Beethoven, remained the intent of the movie. And even though Herbert and Elizabeth have music-related middle names, Herbert doesn't appear in the movie and it is difficult to discern much from the name Partita. Only Bobby and Carl, the two male children who appear in the film, have names that comment on their character. The obviousness of Carl's middle name—he is the steady, faithful one—reinforces the idea that Eroica was meant to be descriptive of Bobby and more than a convenient device to stress the closeness of the family to music.

While changing the opening left the audience unaware of the Bobby-Beethoven connection, in a more subtle sense it strengthened it. The traditional narrative trajectory, in which the issues, tensions, and characters are presented at the start, followed by further complications and ultimately resolution, is undermined as only later the viewer discovers things are not as they appear. With this change, *Five Easy Pieces* is consistent with some of the new directions that cinema was taking in the 1960s and 1970s, which sought to disrupt or even ignore narrative continuity. Film theorists have called this strategy narrative intransitivity, and associated it with the postclassical or New Hollywood filmmakers.[19] One can also read this change as bringing it closer to Beethoven's own approach to the classical structures he inherited. Beethoven would often begin a piece with ambiguity or blur the structural boundaries, leaving the listener uncertain about the basic outline or where the composition was going. The most famous example of this is the Ninth Symphony, which begins with a soft, elemental rumbling, as if molten forces of the universe had not yet come together to define clearly those sonic features that constitute a symphony. This ambiguity is also stressed in a number of places in the Third Symphony, the *Eroica,* particularly the moment of return in the first movement, where, according to standard classical form, the listener expects to hear the opening theme in the original key. This happens, but the clarity of the moment is challenged by the French horns that enter early, and by the flutes and horns that repeat the theme almost immediately in new keys, upsetting the sense of tonal stability that this moment normally demands. At a rehearsal of the *Eroica,* Beethoven's friend Ferdinand Ries was so astounded by this passage that he turned to Beethoven and commented, "Can't that damned hornist count—it sounds horribly wrong." According to Ries, "I think I came pretty close to receiving a box on the ear."

The screenplay to *Five Easy Pieces* was written by Carole Eastman under the pseudonym Adrien Joyce, at a time when there were few female screenwriters in Hollywood. In the Writer's Guild in 1974, for instance, there were 2,882 men and only 143 women. It also came out just before what is called Second Wave feminism crested, which raises the question of whether the film has a feminist subtext. While *Five Easy Pieces* is not entirely consistent with the feminist movement as it existed in 1970, it has its own feminist message and part of it is the deconstruction of the Beethoven hero.

First Wave feminism, in the late nineteenth and early twentieth centuries, had focused on legal issues, such as women's suffrage and other mandated inequalities. While Second Wave feminism, which dates from the 1960s, dealt with legal issues such as rape laws, it also stressed the personal lives of women, particularly the deep-seated sexual stratification that affected all aspects of women's lives: in the workplace, at home, and in the social and political arena. It sought to address subtler but no less real forms of discrimination.

Two events heralded the beginnings of Second Wave feminism. The Presidential Commission on the Status of Women, created by John Kennedy, issued a report in 1963 that documented the pervading discrimination that affected women in all aspects of their lives. That same year Betty Friedan's book *The Feminine Mystique* appeared. Friedan called upon women to reject the cultural straitjacket of the suburban housewife to claim "an identity of their own." Judith Hennessee described *The Feminine Mystique* as "the opening salvo in the most far-reaching social revolution of the century," and, according to the *New York Times*, it "ignited the contemporary women's movement in 1963 and as a result permanently transformed the social fabric of the United States and countries around the world."[20]

Following these two events, Title VII of the Civil Rights Act, which forbade employment discrimination by sex, was passed in 1964 and the National Organization for Women was formed. This led to the creation of a number of other feminist organizations in the 1960s, such as the National Women's Political Caucus, the Women's Equality League, and the National Black Feminist Alliance.

Five Easy Pieces thus sits between the burgeoning activity of the 1960s and several landmark actions that occurred in the early 1970s: the passage of the Equal Rights Amendment in Congress in 1972 (although three-fourths of the states failed to ratify it), the passage of Title IX of the Civil Rights Amendment in 1972, which forbade sexual discrimination in education, and the Supreme Court's *Roe v. Wade* decision in 1973. The 1970s also saw further growth and awareness of the feminist movement, with many new organizations and magazines.

There is much to argue against a feminist reading of *Five Easy Pieces*. Bobby is abusive, even misogynistic, yet he is tolerated, adored, and irresistible to women in the film. The women, essentially a canvas upon which the character of Bobby plays, fall into one of two cliché categories in movies of the era: either they are attractive and both attracted to and deferential to Bobby, or

FIGURE 7.14

Five Easy Pieces. The obnoxious intellectual Samia (left) at the
Dupea home. Carl Dupea and his fiancée, Catherine, are on the right,
Bobby seated in the background, left.

when assertive they are unhappy bitches with a chip on their shoulder. Rayette,
Catherine, and Tita fall into the former category; those in the latter category
appear only briefly and in many cases as caricatures: Samia, the strident intellectual who holds forth at the Dupea family home, the waitress in the diner
who will not bend the rules, and Palm, the more bitter of the two lesbians that
Bobby picks up after their car has broken down. In every case their attitude
is made to look harsh, absurd, and at minimum unpleasant. Eastman clearly
had little sympathy for this stereotype.

Yet Bobby is painted only slightly less negatively mainly because ninety
minutes of focus on him allow his personality to be explored in greater depth.
Occasionally he can be at least minimally thoughtful or sensitive, such as
when he defends Rayette against Samia's cutting remarks, but most of the time
he is even nastier than the women he puts down. Almost all the characters in
the movie are quirky and limited in some way. Carole Eastman, who was not
known for overt feminist views, was recognized for introducing odd and eccentric characters and for having an ear for working-class dialogue. Shy, re-
tiring to the point of agoraphobia, she was much aware of the power struc-

ture of Hollywood, and resented the sexual stereotyping of writers. When she discussed the possibility of directing her first film in 1972, a friend asked her, "What are you going to wear—a muumuu, a Gestapo uniform or a terry-cloth robe, mules and pin curls?" Angered by the remark, Eastman "turned to a man who had just directed his first picture and said, 'Did they ask you what you were going to wear?'" While not as vocal as the screenwriter Eleanor Perry—who screamed to a meeting of women in 1974, "Women have been silent about their recent mistreatment in films because women are programmed to be silent— it isn't nice for a woman to scream"—Eastman was furious when the director Bob Rafelson shared the writing credit with her for the screenplay of *Five Easy Pieces.* Judging from the way some of the women are portrayed in *Five Easy Pieces,* Eastman's sentiments were probably close to those of Sue Mengers, the 1970s Hollywood super-agent, who epitomized the time for many. In 1975 she told *Ms.* magazine: "I'm not against the Movement. Women who want to con- tribute to the impotency of men, let them go right ahead. But they're hurting our work progress. By beating their chests and shouting, 'We are equal,' they're convincing the men that we're a hysterical bunch of shrews." About her own work Eastman commented, "All of the people in my writing are different as- pects of myself, and each of us has feminine and masculine components in our nature."[21]

In spite of the extent to which the feminist movement is negatively por- trayed in *Five Easy Pieces,* one female character does stand out: Catherine. At first she seems only a slightly classier version of Rayette. She is devoted to Carl and appears to have no strong will of her own. She allows herself to be seduced by Bobby, whose approach is characteristically impetuous, almost violent. It is clear from when Bobby first returns to his family's home, however, that she finds him sexually attractive and is willing to indulge her own appetite when Carl is out of town. Yet Bobby is more attracted to her than she is to him. She knows that a momentary pleasure is all that she wants. In the end she turns out to be the only really self-aware person in the film.

In the critical confrontation between Bobby and Catherine, Bobby has ap- parently proposed that she run off with him. She decisively but diplomatically tells him no, and when he pleads further she is more direct: "I'm trying to be delicate with you, but you're not understanding me. It's not just because of Carl, or my music, but because of you. . . . If a person has no love for himself, no respect, no love for his work, his family, his friends, something, how can he ask for love in return? I mean, why should he ask for it?" Bobby, hurt, asks in- credulously if her choice is to live in this "rest home asylum," and Catherine tells him simply, "Yes."

FIGURE 7.15

Five Easy Pieces. Catherine after telling Bobby she won't go away with him.

Catherine's choice may not be Betty Friedan's, but she has demonstrated that she knows her mind and what she wants, both in the short and long term, and is willing to stand up for it and speak it clearly and directly. Unlike Samia at the dinner party, or Palm in the car, she is not angry and strident, but also unlike Rayette she is not a victim. She had the perception to recognize that an earlier marriage was psychologically damaging to her, and she had the strength to walk out of it. She is herself and is willing to accept herself. Catherine may represent Eastman's own feminist perspective.

The treatment of Bobby in *Five Easy Pieces* is not that different from Adrienne Rich's "The Ninth Symphony of Beethoven Understood at Last as a Sexual Message," in which the protagonist, Beethoven presumably, rages of impotence or possibly male menopause, "howling from the climacteric." Rich wrote this poem in 1971, one year after *Five Easy Pieces,* and its influence on later feminists, such as Susan McClary, was considerable. While Rich is talking about Beethoven, with specific references to his own deafness, "where every-thing is silence," she is, as the title indicates, speaking of Beethoven's music, and she could easily be speaking of Bobby. Eastman's message may very well be that anger and egocentrism can lead to great music, or to empires, but it can also destroy. Bobby is the Beethoven hero, the same hero presented in *Immortal Beloved* and *Copying Beethoven,* the Beethoven of the public imagination, deconstructed.

8

Beethoven's Music in Film

*B*EYOND THE BIOPICS AND THE FILMS in which Beethoven appears as a coded character, discussed in chapter 7, Beethoven's music may be found in literally hundreds of other films.[1] Certain patterns arise in them. As standards of filmmaking evolved with each decade, both the prominence of Beethoven's music and the manner in which it was incorporated rose and fell with Hollywood trends. The sheer number precludes consideration of more than a sampling here, but discussion of a few significant films demonstrates just how important Beethoven was for Hollywood and the impact of their joint ventures upon the American public's perception of Beethoven. Several key films, such as *A Clockwork Orange,* the most notorious to prominently feature Beethoven's music, were pivotal in challenging norms that not only defined Beethoven as a signifier in film, but also those that underlay the Beethoven image of the nineteenth and twentieth centuries.

Music in films began with the nickelodeons, small movie theaters that showed a variety of fifteen- to twenty-minute films, sometimes interspersed with vaudeville acts, sometimes with sing-alongs, where words and song illustrations were projected as slides onto the screen. Nickelodeons date from around 1905; most had a pianist in residence who would provide accompaniment to the films, although there is some controversy whether, how much, or what the pianist played during the film.[2] Gradually a bulk of literature built up, however, to provide the local musician music to play, with different excerpts in the compilations categorized by the mood they were meant to convey. The compilations leave no doubt about the role of the pianist in movie houses.

Because music at each theater depended on the whim and the ability of the house pianist, it is difficult to know just what was played where. Popular songs and dances were more common than the classics, and sometimes a simple improvisation would suffice for a scene, such as an arpeggio on a diminished-seventh chord to accompany a melodramatic moment. One early record mentions Arthur A. Barrow, who had studied music at the Berlin Conservatory, playing Beethoven in Harry Altman's theater in Manhattan in the spring of 1908. What piece he played is not known, but the writer complimented Barrow's musical choices as being "in company and proper mood with the story and scene portrayed on the sheet." Although Beethoven had undoubtedly appeared in other nickelodeons, the use of his music was rare enough that a correspondent from Chicago to *Motion/Moving Pictures News* expressed surprise on hearing Beethoven's *Moonlight* Sonata in 1909 at the Senate Theatre in Chicago: "The first time, indeed, we ever heard Beethoven in a five-cent theater."[3]

Other evidence reinforces the observation that Beethoven's music was not that common in such a venue. Between 1910 and 1912 theater musicians mostly limited their classical music offerings to a small number of pieces that had become familiar during the nineteenth century: Gounod's "Ave Maria," Mendelssohn's "Spring Song" from op. 62, Anton Rubinstein's "Melody in F," Schumann's "Träumerei," and a few operatic selections, such as the sextet from Donizetti's *Lucia di Lammermoor,* the barcarole from Offenbach's *Tales of Hoffman,* the Triumphal March from Verdi's *Aida,* and the Pilgrim's Chorus from Wagner's *Tannhäuser.*[4] These are the same pieces that populated the many collections of piano, violin, flute, and cello music for amateurs at the turn of the century, and many theater musicians had only nominal classical training. As late as 1915 one reader wrote to *Moving/Motion Picture News* for help locating a sonata by Kreutzer, which prompted this reply: "NO!! There is no sonata by Kreutzer, but there is a 'Kreutzer Sonata' written and composed by Beethoven for and dedicated to his friend Kreutzer."[5]

The situation regarding music in theaters began to change around 1915, spurred by two developments. In 1914 the Strand Theatre opened at Broadway and 47th Street in New York. It had the opulence and atmosphere of an opera house, with a seating capacity of nearly 3,000 and with boxes on the sides, and it was the first large house in the country devoted primarily to film. The Strand's manager, Samuel "Roxy" Rothepfel, established a concert orchestra to accompany films and to perform between showings. When the theater proved a rousing success, its innovations spread to other cities, including the presence of a theater orchestra, which was considered an important part of the audience experience. In Boston, the Park Theater was remodeled to duplicate the Strand, and in Buffalo the 2,500-seat New Victoria Theatre brought in Herman E. Schulz, conductor of the Buffalo Symphony Orchestra, to lead the theater orchestra. Many cities throughout the country not only borrowed the approach of the Strand but the name as well.[6]

The second development was the creation of the first cinematic blockbuster: D. W. Griffith's *The Birth of a Nation.* At a time when few films were as long as an hour and most were much shorter, *The Birth of a Nation* ran three hours and ten minutes. *The Birth of a Nation* premiered in Los Angeles with a twenty-two-week run. The score that accompanied it, compiled by Carli Elinore, was performed by forty instrumentalists, a chorus of twelve, and vocal soloists. Among other pieces, it used Beethoven's Fifth Symphony. For the New York production and the subsequent road show Joseph Carl Breil compiled a completely different score. It drew upon popular and folk music and used mostly classical pieces that had become common in the cinematic-accompaniment repertoire: Grieg's *Peer Gynt Suite,* Tchaikovsky's *1812 Overture,* Wagner's "Ride of the Valkyries" from *Die Walküre,* and the overtures to Suppé's *Light Cavalry,* Wagner's *Rienzi,* Hérold's *Zampa*, Bellini's *Norma,* and Weber's *Der Freischütz.* Beyond those silent movie warhorses, the fourth movement of Beethoven's Sixth Symphony was also used, as well as the "Gloria" from a mass previously ascribed to Mozart.[7] Unlike in Los Angeles, Beethoven's Fifth Symphony did not appear in this score.

The Birth of a Nation premiered in New York, not at the Strand but at the Liberty Theatre. Appearing at a legitimate theater gave the film more prestige than opening at a cinematic venue. It also allowed the producers to charge theater ticket prices, in this case two dollars, an outrageous sum at the time for a film. This was, after all, only a few years from the heyday of the nickelodeon. Following the Strand model, a fifty-piece orchestra accompanied the film. When *The Birth of a Nation* went on tour throughout the country, every effort was made that it be shown only with a large orchestra, no matter how small the town. Hollywood quickly learned that a prestigious film needed a large orchestra.[8]

As a consequence of the larger halls, the longer films, and the use of classical conductors in movie houses, Beethoven's music became more common.

Since music was under local control and played between screenings, it is difficult to know precisely how often his music was performed. The film studios attempted to impose some order on this situation by distributing scores and cue sheets, which indicate that Beethoven pieces were no longer rare or sporadic in movie houses. The composers most often chosen for filmic accompaniment in the late teens were Beethoven, Bizet, Liszt, Massenet, Mendelssohn, and Offenbach.[9]

One early film is worthy of note for its inclusion of Beethoven. In 1915 Hobart Bosworth directed *The Rugmaker's Daughter,* a film of approximately fifty minutes that featured Maud Allan, a pioneer of modern dance and a contemporary with Isadora Duncan. Born in Canada as Beulah Maude Durrant, she grew up in San Francisco and planned on a career as a concert pianist. While she was studying in Berlin at age twenty-two, her older brother was charged in the murder of two young women and, after a sensational trial, hanged. Because she was close to her brother, she never got over the event and the scandal, changed her name, and gave up a music career to pursue dance. Her trademark was "Visions of Salome," based on Oscar Wilde's play. It included, of course, the Dance of the Seven Veils. By 1915 she had become famous, indeed, notorious in Europe, North America, and Australia, and Bosworth's film was designed specifically to showcase Allan's dancing.

There are no extant prints of *The Rugmaker's Daughter,* but descriptions have survived. The plot is complex, revolving around a rugmaker in Turkey named Halib Bey, his beautiful daughter Demetra, played by Allan, and an important rug, promised to Demetra as her dowry. A young American customer, Robert Van Buren, falls in love with Demetra, but her father insists that she marry Osman, who had persuaded Bey to sell him the rug. After much intrigue that spans both Turkey and America, which includes Osman holding Van Buren captive and later luring Demetra into a trap, Van Buren rescues her in a finale that includes, among other film staples, an early automobile chase scene.[10]

Bosworth may have chosen an exotic setting because of Allan's association with Salome, but her Salome dance is not in the film. She is featured in three dances, one based on Mendelssohn's "Spring Song," from *Song Without Words,* op. 62, one on "Anitra's Dance," from Grieg's *Peer Gynt Suite,* and one on the *Moonlight* Sonata, presumably the first movement. As critics noted, all three dances were woven into the plot "as a natural part of the story."[11] Elizabeth Weigand has suggested that the *Moonlight* Sonata dance probably occurred in the second act, when Demetra and Robert meet secretly in the rose garden, a situation reminiscent of Wagner's *Tristan und Isolde.*

While *The Rugmaker's Daughter* had neither the popularity nor the historical impact of *The Birth of a Nation,* it was nevertheless an innovative film for its time, five reels long, with a tightly integrated music and dance element. Taking advantage of the new trends toward sumptuous movie houses and large orchestras, Bosworth posted the following notice in *The Moving Picture World,* on July 24, 1915, two weeks after its bicoastal premiere in New York, at the Strand, and in Los Angeles:

SPECIAL MUSIC FOR MAUD ALLAN

Bosworth, Inc. has arranged special music to be used in conjunction with the showing of its latest release, "The Rug Maker's Daughter," in which Maud Allan, the internationally famous dancer makes her first motion picture appearance. Orchestrations are to be sent out with each print and in this way the true effect of this wonderful dancer's offerings will be realized.[12]

Here the orchestration accompanies the print; the two work hand in hand.

The arrival of sound allowed the studios in the 1930s to take complete control of the sound track, which in turn created an entire music department in the larger studios. Preexisting art music lost favor to newly composed in-house music. Since such music could be tailored more closely to the filmic moments, music became part of the creative process of filmmaking. A set of film conventions developed, resulting in what has been referred to as "the classic Hollywood film score." The classic Hollywood style employed a large orchestra that drew more on the music of Romanticism than on Beethoven with the consequence that unless for a specific, usually diegetic situation Beethoven was not particularly favored. Preexisting music at this time was mostly drawn from popular sources, but because of the prevalence of musicals on both Broadway and in film and the prevailing style of Tin Pan Alley, there was little difference between a song composed for a film and a popular song incorporated into a film.

The diegetic situations where Beethoven's music appeared were frequently simple interpolations without significance to the plot, such as in *Give Me Liberty,* a film about Patrick Henry, where the guests at George Washington's house dance a minuet to Beethoven's Minuet in G, or *Dancing Co-Ed*, where girls dance to Beethoven's Ninth Symphony played on a record in the college gym. The *Moonlight* Sonata remained a diegetic favorite, whether played by a boy in a boarding school, as in *The Rains Came,* or by a concert pianist as an integral part of the plot, as in *Beethoven's Moonlight Sonata,* performed by Ignace Jan Paderewski, who plays himself in the film. This particular film has barely a thread of an improbable plot: Paderewski and several others are marooned at the home of a Swedish baroness after a plane crash. Each has personal problems, which it seems can only be solved by hearing Paderewski play the first movement of the *Moonlight* Sonata, which of course he does at the climax of the film.

A typical diegetic moment for the *Moonlight* Sonata that reveals the popular image of Beethoven occurred in the 1932 film *The Man Who Played God.* The story revolves around a concert pianist named Montgomery Royale, who suffers a tragic accident when playing the *Moonlight* Sonata. In an early scene Royale is waiting in a drawing room for a visiting king who has been delayed. Rushing in, the king apologizes to Royale for his tardiness and states, "I would have given you my ears to hear the *Moonlight* Sonata."

To which the pianist replies: "Well, if your highness will give me your ears you should hear it now."

The opening movement begins. About one minute in, there is an explosion at the window, an assassination attempt upon the king. Urged by his entourage to leave, the king says: "If Mr. Royale will be so kind I should still like to hear the *Moonlight* Sonata."

With a distressed look upon his face, Royale begins but stops in the second measure, puts his hands to his ears, starts to play again, this time pounding out the basic outline of the sonata in large fortissimo chords. He stops, shaken, stands up, and announces: "I'm unable to play." Grace, his potential fiancée, says, "It's the shock." Royale: "I can't hear you." He then announces in a melodramatic tone that tells us we are not far removed from the silent film era: "I shall never play again. I'm stone deaf just as our mother was."

Presented here is not just a fragment of diegetic music, but Beethoven of the early twentieth century. Later when Royale is bitter and angry at God for his fate, he exclaims, "Music was a sacred thing to me." At the time the *Moonlight* Sonata was *the* Beethoven piece, a Romantic identifier, appropriated especially by Hollywood, as in *The Rugmaker's Daughter,* the biographical moment in *Beethoven's Moonlight Sonata,* and several other films. Even the king pleads to hear the sonata. The first movement is instantly recognizable and its tragic tone becomes a reality to Royale, as the explosion interrupts the piece and robs him of his hearing. Deafness afflicts him as it did Beethoven, but he strikes a different path, abandoning his musical career entirely.

As the world focused on the rising power of Hitler's Germany in Europe in 1941, pro-Nazi fascist forces also posed an internal threat to many in the

FIGURE 8.1

The Man Who Played God. Montgomery Royale, suddenly deafened
by a bomb explosion, announces, "I shall never play again."

United States. Frank Capra's film *Meet John Doe* is a tense drama that addresses directly that issue. The first of Capra's independent films after he broke
with Columbia Studios, where he was often assigned comedy, it belongs with
two other populist films that Capra made in the 1930s, *Mr. Deeds Goes to Town*
and the best known, *Mr. Smith Goes to Washington. Meet John Doe* portrays
how fascism can gain power by masquerading under the guise of populism
and manipulating the people through control of the media.

About to be fired when a newspaper is taken over by a new owner, colum-
nist Ann Mitchell creates a fictitious story about a man, identified as John
Doe, who threatens to commit suicide on Christmas Eve by jumping off the
top of City Hall to protest the state of the country and the corrupt politics of
the time. Connell, the new editor of the paper, is convinced to exploit the story,
and they find an ex-baseball pitcher, a hobo, to pretend to be John Doe. Doe,
played by Gary Cooper, is portrayed as an idealistic populist standing up for
the average man, the John Does everywhere, through columns and speeches
written by Ann (Barbara Stanwyck). The movement catches on nationally as
John Doe Clubs are formed throughout the country. Too late, they discover
that the newspaper's owner, D. B. Norton, is using the clubs to launch a run for

president, and that his real plan is to install a fascist regime in America. Doe tries to speak to a massive John Doe convention but is thwarted by Norton's men, dressed as Nazi storm troopers, and is denounced by Norton as a phony. Doe thinks that Ann, who has fallen in love with him, is in on the plot, and he decides to write another letter revealing all and then go through with the suicide threat.

The final scene is set in the dark on the observation deck of City Hall. Doe emerges from the shadows, holds a letter in his hand, and looks down. He is interrupted by Norton and his men, who tell him his effort is useless, that Norton has arranged that no one will know of the event. Doe informs him that he has already mailed a copy of the letter. Ann, who has been ill with a fever, runs in and pleads with Doe and professes her love for him. She then faints in his arms. Members of the local John Doe Club arrive and argue that the movement cannot be stopped and that they still believe in him. Doe hesitates and then, with Ann in his arms and a faint smile on his face, walks toward the John Doe group and out the door. As he does so the church bells ring and the finale of the Ninth Symphony is heard.

Throughout the entire film there is little music, and what does occur are arrangements of popular and folk tunes. The only exception is the *William Tell* overture, but its classical stance is undermined by its performance by Doe and his hobo friend, the Colonel, on a harmonica and ocarina. The Ninth Symphony, in contrast, sounds in full orchestra accompanied by church bells. It is a sacred moment, its solemnity enhanced by the presence of the bells, and at the same time a moment of great triumph, a signification for which the "Ode to Joy" is eminently suitable. Like the *Moonlight* Sonata in *The Man Who Played God,* it recalls the Beethovenian image of Romanticism and the early twentieth century.

Meet John Doe was released before America entered World War II. The optimistic stance of the film was not universal, nor was there yet a sense that the country would pull together in an all-out effort to defeat two militaristic powers on opposite sides of the earth. The depression, which four years before had seemed on the verge of ending, still lingered. Unemployment had dropped to ten percent in 1937, but a year later had doubled; it finally dipped below ten percent, but barely, in 1941. Only with the entrance of America into the war in December 1941 did it return to pre-Depression levels.

World War II saw a significant rise in the use of Beethoven's Fifth Symphony, not surprisingly given that the opening da-da-da-dum motive became the symbol of Allied resistance. The motive equated to the dot-dot-dot-dash Morse Code symbol for "V." "V for Victory" became an important motto in

FIGURE 8.2

Meet John Doe, final triumphant scene.

Great Britain during the 1940–41 shadow war, when Germany was regularly conducting bombing raids on Great Britain and the island was bracing for a Nazi invasion. Prime Minister Winston Churchill would regularly flash the "V" sign with his first and second fingers, and the BBC broadcast the opening of the Fifth to the continent. The Allies began a "V campaign," suggesting the letter "V" be scratched as graffiti everywhere.

Hollywood quickly adopted the patriotic motif. Not counting the French biopic *Un Grand Amour,* only two films made between 1929 and 1941 used Beethoven's Fifth Symphony. From 1942 through 1945 the Fifth Symphony appeared in seven feature films and at least nine animated cartoons. Most had a war theme, such as *Reunion in France,* where Michelle 'Mike' de la Becque (Joan Crawford) hides a downed American pilot, Pat Talbot (John Wayne). The Fifth Symphony is heard on the radio in her lover's Robert Cortot's apartment. In *Sherlock Holmes and the Voice of Terror,* Holmes and Watson have been transported to England in 1942—a card at the beginning of the movie explains that they are "timeless"—to aid the war effort. Holmes is asked to investigate a Nazi propaganda broadcast, *The Voice of Terror*, in which the announcer predicts sabotage that will occur in Great Britain. As he sits pondering the case Holmes listens to the Fifth Symphony on the radio, then calls the BBC to request that Beethoven's Fifth be played on another station. When Watson questions about this, Holmes replies: "I like it."

Even more than feature films, cartoons took up the patriotic mantle of the Fifth Symphony. Daffy Duck, Tom and Jerry, Popeye, Barney Bear, and many other creatures contributed to the war effort spurred by Beethoven's Fifth Symphony. Sometimes, as in Popeye the Sailor Man, the war is specifically World War II, or sometimes a metaphorical war with strong satirical overtones, as in *Fifth Column Mouse,* where one mouse meets with the newly arrived cat and works out an appeasement agreement. He convinces his cohorts to try it, but in the end appeasement fails, and to avoid being eaten the mice are forced to go to war against the cat.

After World War II through the 1960s, Beethoven's music appears sparingly in Hollywood films. In some cases, such as the 1967 movie *Counterpoint,* it is virtually mandated by the plot. In *Counterpoint* a famous conductor is captured with his USO orchestra by the Germans and forced to give a concert for a Nazi general, appropriately named Schiller. The general is torn between his orders not to take prisoners and his love of culture, particularly his desire to hear Wagner. Most of the film's drama is the struggle between the two outsize personalities, the conductor and the general, about whether the concert will occur. With all the ingredients of the plot, World War II, a Nazi general, a conductor, and the presence of an orchestra, it is not surprising that Beethoven's Fifth Symphony would make an appearance. A similar situation occurs in *Taking Sides* (2002), set in postwar occupied Germany. U.S. Army Major Steve Arnold is charged with prosecuting conductor Wilhelm Furtwangler for his connections to the Nazis. Most of the drama centers around the tense and hostile meetings between Arnold and Furtwangler. While there are references to Beethoven's Ninth Symphony in the dialogue, the longest and most important musical episodes are diegetic performances of the first movement of the Fifth. These performances frame the film: a Nazi concert in an opulent concert hall at the beginning and Furtwangler's Telefunken recording of the Fifth played at the end.

In most other films Beethoven's music is less central to the story. Noticeable, however, is a shift in repertoire. The Fifth Symphony continues to be heard, but the Ninth Symphony and the *Moonlight* Sonata all but disappear.

Beethoven's Minuet in G appears several times, and the *Pathetique* Sonata remains popular. Music directors also draw upon the Second, Sixth, Seventh, and Eighth Symphonies as well as the String Quartet op. 131. *Für Elise* is not ignored, either.

The signifiers that surrounded Beethoven's music in film changed little until *A Clockwork Orange* appeared in 1971. *A Clockwork Orange* redefined Beethoven and particularly the Ninth Symphony for an entire generation of moviegoers, creating a set of associations regarding Beethoven's music that found its way into a number of later films. With *A Clockwork Orange* the Ninth Symphony in particular assumed an ominous tone that was completely at odds with its use in a film such as *Meet John Doe*.

A Clockwork Orange was based on a novel by the British author Anthony Burgess. Even though it was set in a mildly futuristic England and made in the UK, it did have American ties and a strong presence in the United States. Stanley Kubrick, who produced and directed it and took credit for the screenplay, was born in the United States and grew up in New York, although he became an expatriate. The film was distributed by Warner Bros., premiering in the United States on December 19, 1971, and was shown throughout the country. It received five Academy Award nominations, including Best Picture.

A Clockwork Orange is about irony, disillusionment, nihilism, and violence. Set in a vaguely future time somewhere in Great Britain, its plot centers around Alex, a British youth who leads a gang of four hoodlums or "droogs." The story is told from Alex's point of view with his narration. Completely without any conventional sense of right and wrong, the droogs find thrills in violence, including rape, and in one instance murder. Alex refers to their indulging in "the old ultraviolence." In the first half of the film Alex and his droogs gratuitously beat up a tramp, engage in a fight with another gang, enter the house of a writer, assault him, and rape his wife. Setting Alex apart from his droog brothers is his love of Beethoven. In an early scene Alex and his gang are sitting in the Korova milk bar where they obtain milk laced with drugs from the breast of a nude sculpture, which acts as a dispenser. A group from a local TV studio is seated nearby. One of the women among them pulls out a score and begins to sing the "Ode to Joy" in German. Alex is entranced. When she has finished, Dim, one of the droogs, makes a rude farting noise, which prompts Alex to reprimand him for disrespect by smashing him on his legs with a stick that each carries. Alex and Dim almost get into a scrap right there but Dim backs down.

The most revealing moment about Alex's love of Beethoven occurs when he has returned to his room after the night of beating, raping, and gang fight-

FIGURE 8.3 ABOVE

A Clockwork Orange. Alex and his gang of thugs, the droogs.

FIGURE 8.4 BELOW

A Clockwork Orange. Alex in his room with Ludwig Van.

ing. He explains: "It had been a wonderful evening and what I needed now to give it the perfect ending was a bit of the old Ludwig Van." Worn out by their evening's activities, "feeling a bit shagged and fagged and fashed," he puts on "Ludwig Van's lovely symphony" the scherzo to the Ninth, and its music conjures in Alex's mind fantastical images of sex, horror, and destruction, including a group of dancing crucifixes. Alex's expression soon resembles that of a giant portrait of Beethoven that he has on his wall.[13] In a world where eroticism and violence are conflated, Beethoven serves to stimulate Alex. He both respects him and is excited by him. In that sense this is the same Beethoven that John S. Dwight and Margaret Fuller encountered, although the specific effects are as different as the three persons themselves. Beethoven goes right to the core of Alex, but that core is in any conventional sense rotten, and consequently Beethoven's music becomes complicit in exciting Alex toward ends diametrically opposed to thoughts of universal brotherhood and freedom from oppression. In this scene, Alex explains the effect Beethoven has on him:

> Then, brothers, it came. O bliss, bliss and heaven, oh it was gorgeousness and georgeosity made flesh. The trombones crunched redgold under my bed, and behind my gulliver the trumpets three-wise, silver-flamed and there by the door the timps rolling through my guts and out again, crunched like candy thunder. It was like a bird of rarest spun heaven metal or like silvery wine flowing in a space ship, gravity all nonsense now. As I slooshied, I knew such lovely pictures. There were veeks and ptitsas laying on the ground screaming for mercy and I was smecking all over my rot and grinding my boot into their tortured litsos and there were naked devotchkas ripped and creeching against walls and I plunging like a shlaga into them.

The strange language that Alex speaks, Nadsat, is a combination of words derived from Russian and English and some that Burgess, a polyglot, invented himself. Burgess wanted to created an argot that only the droogs would understand. Using slang from his time would have dated the material: "Using a language of my own, would date too rapidly, would date in a year, would date even between the writing and publication of the book." Thus Burgess's fictional language remains timeless since it never existed beyond his own fiction. Prior to writing *A Clockwork Orange* Burgess had spent time in the Soviet Union and noticed the language that teens used there. He appropriated many of their terms, such as devotchka, meaning girl, or droog, which means friend. The term Nadsat itself is from Russian, and loosely means teen; it is a suffix for the numbers eleven through nineteen.

Throughout the film Alex never refers to Beethoven, except when necessary in conversation with someone else, but always to "Ludwig Van." Beethoven is more than a classical music composer; he is a person in Alex's life. He is defended by Alex twice, when Dim insults the singing of the "Ode to Joy" in the Korova Bar, and later after his arrest, when Beethoven's Ninth Symphony is used as part of the conditioning treatment to which Alex is subjected in order to cure him of his violent tendencies. Alex's connection with Beethoven is reinforced by Alex's position as narrator. Although Alex comes across as an arrogant, unfeeling insouciant, through the nature of first-person narration we tend to believe that Alex is at least speaking honestly about himself and his closeness to "Ludwig Van." At one point he calls him "our old friend."

In the second half of the film the tables are turned, and Alex becomes the victim of the violence he has inflicted on others. He had assaulted two of his droogs, Dim and Georgie, who had challenged his leadership. The droogs go to a house in the country, where a woman who lives alone with her cats runs a health farm. Alerted by newspaper reports of the previous night's violence she calls the police, but Alex manages to get into the house and confront her. In a scene choreographed to Rossini's *Thieving Magpie* overture, she tries to hit Alex with a bust of Beethoven. Alex, meanwhile, picks up a large sculpture shaped like a phallus and uses it as a shield while he dances around evading her swings. Alex finally knocks her down and kills her by battering her with the sculpture.

As Alex leaves the house, the other droogs attack him and leave him for the police to pick up. His murder of the woman leads to his conviction and a fourteen-year prison sentence. After two years, Alex is chosen for a new experiment in aversion therapy called the Ludovico treatment. He is put in a straitjacket with his eyes clamped open, forced to watch films of violence, and given drugs that make him ill when he sees the films. In one scene that begins with Nazi troops marching, the sound track has the Turkish march from the finale of the Ninth Symphony. The use of Beethoven is coincidental—the psychiatrists conducting the experiment are surprised that he even knows who Beethoven is. As Alex shrieks, "Stop it please, I beg you, it's a sin," the "Ode to Joy" theme appears, providing an unsettling counterpoint to Alex's screams of horror. The Ninth, heretofore Alex's stimulus to violence, has become a trigger that makes him not only ill but suicidal.

Having become abject, Alex is released only to encounter some of his past victims who now wreak vengeance upon him. Alex is unable to fight back. A critical moment occurs when Alex, having been beaten again by his old droogs, who are now policemen, stumbles to the house of the writer whose wife he had previously raped. The writer is crippled from his injuries and his wife has died.

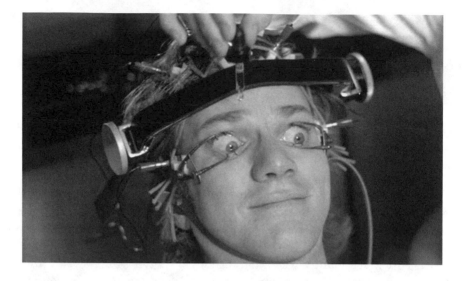

FIGURE 8.5

A Clockwork Orange. Alex receiving the Ludovico treatment,
an experimental conditioning procedure.

When he realizes who Alex is, he plans his revenge. Alex had become a prize
exhibit on the government's response to violent crime, his story detailed in the
media. Knowing about Alex's treatment in prison, the writer locks him in an
upstairs bedroom and puts the Ninth Symphony on the stereo at full volume.
Unable to stand it, Alex jumps out a window but survives, badly injured.

Alex awakens in a hospital, where he gradually discovers that he has been
cured from the aversion therapy. Public opinion has turned against both Alex's
treatment and the party in power that devised it. The government minister re-
sponsible for the experiment on Alex comes in to befriend him and to offer
him a job if he will help his party survive the next election. As a way of showing gratitude, the minister wheels in a gigantic stereo, accompanied by the
press. As the stereo plays the "Ode to Joy," Alex fantasizes having sex with a
beautiful woman while a crowd in Victorian-like dress looks on. The final line
in the film: "I was cured all right."

The political and moral message, assuming that there is one, has been debated ever since the film premiered. Is the film about free will, and is free will,
even when turned toward evil, more desirable than the state creating a society

of automatons, conditioned to respond mechanically, without choice? This question is raised directly by the prison priest whom Alex cynically befriends in hopes that this would better his stay. When Alex first hears of the Ludovico technique the priest observes, "The question is whether or not this technique really makes a man good. Goodness comes from within. Goodness is chosen. When a man cannot choose, he ceases to be a man." After he has been treated, Alex is humiliated by a bully and tempted by a nude woman before an assembled group of dignitaries to demonstrate the success of the program. The same priest, who watched Alex's abject and retching reaction when confronted by these two, stands up and reiterates his previous comment: "Choice! The boy has no real choice, has he? . . . He ceases also to be a creature capable of moral choice." The viewer is left with the question, never answered, of which is worse: someone like Alex, who commits heinous acts out of free will, or a state that drains its subjects of the opportunity to exercise free will.

In another sense the film is a refutation of Rousseau. Kubrick believes that Alex represents man's natural state when free of the restraining influence of civilization. He becomes a being capable of raping and murdering without guilt. He is in essence a savage, a reversal of the Rousseauian vision that man in his natural state is good, but by enslaving him civilization has made him a savage. Rousseau's ideas had long been discarded, as for example in William Golding's 1954 novel *Lord of the Flies,* which Peter Brook made into a film in 1963. There a group of boys are shipwrecked on an island and eventually revert to savagery even though some of the more rational ones strive to prevent it. Kubrick, however, carries the issue of man's nature one step further. To Kubrick the film establishes an internal conflict within the viewer: most people are repulsed by Alex's actions and the violence he provokes, but at the same time most subconsciously desire that guiltless freedom that Alex represents. In other words, Rousseau argued that man is good, and that society makes him bad. Kubrick finds this a "dangerous fallacy" and believes that "Alex's guiltless sense of freedom to kill and rape, and to be our savage natural selves," gives us "the true glimpse of man" and that "the power of the story derives" from that.[14]

Except for the final scene, each time the Ninth Symphony appears in the film it is associated with violence: the altercation between Alex and Dim, Alex's fantasies when he returns to his house, the Ludovico technique itself, and the writer's revenge on Alex. While the final statement conjures in Alex not atypical male sexual fantasies (it is apparently not a rape scene, but consensual sex), the implication is not far from the viewer's mind, that the cure of the cure returns Alex to his previous fondness for "the old ultraviolence."

Through these associations the moral, uplifting message of universal brother-hood is totally inverted; here the symphony is connected with gratuitous, un-restrained malevolence.

Kubrick's use of the Ninth Symphony was neither original nor revolution-ary; he was drawing on historical precedence. What was new, especially to Anglo-American audiences, was Kubrick's choice to emphasize the less com-mon associations of the Ninth Symphony and feature them in a major motion picture. The twentieth century in effect witnessed two Ninth Symphonies. The first was the more familiar, the Ninth as exemplar of universal brotherhood. This was an important theme in Europe, where it emerged with particular vigor in celebrations of the Beethoven Centenary in 1927. Europe in 1927 was still in a state of tension and adjustment. The war was over, but over fifty mil-lion casualties were felt throughout Europe.[15] Germany was reeling from hy-perinflation, Austria from the loss of its empire and the end of centuries of Hapsburg rule. Yet European countries came together to celebrate Beethoven's world vision. The Ninth Symphony was heard in cities throughout Europe. The most important event occurred, appropriately, in Vienna, where a multi-day celebration of concerts, speeches, and exhibitions revolved around March 26, the anniversary of Beethoven's death.

Thirty-three nations, including all of Europe and the United States, sent representatives; eighteen countries chose important government officials. The image of Beethoven portrayed at the commemoration was most visible in the special ceremony held at Beethoven's grave. Government officials and diplo-mats from the eighteen countries spoke, and all quoted the Ninth Symphony. Religious metaphors were common, reaching a climax when the Italian repre-sentative, composer Pietro Mascagni, literally equated Beethoven with Jesus: "Dead like Jesus! . . . But, like Jesus, redeemed! Resurrected in the dazzling light of his art. Resurrected for the good of Mankind! Immortal in History, Immortal in Art, Immortal in our hearts, which beat for him and for his Glory *per omnia saecula saeculorum*—world without end, Amen!"[16]

Beyond the actual deification of Beethoven, the Ninth Symphony became a metaphor that conflated brotherhood and the sacred. Austrian Chancellor Ignaz Seipel spoke of Beethoven's music leading "to the highest levels of a uni-versal Ethos," and exhorted "all men [to] follow the true path! Then will these words truly become reality: 'All men will be brothers.'"[17] Other speakers were less ecclesiastical in their tone, but in a time when the League of Nations was struggling to survive, they spoke of Beethoven's spiritual message as suggest-ing a united Europe.[18]

It would be two more decades and another world war before the first efforts toward a united Europe would occur, but when that finally happened the Ninth Symphony again held a privileged place. On May 5, 1949, the Council of Europe was formed with the goal of creating a unified continent. In 1955 Count Richard Coudenhove-Kalergi of Austria, who had first advocated European unity in 1929, proposed that the Ninth Symphony be adopted as the official anthem of a Pan Europa.[19] There was resistance to the anthem proposal as there had been to the idea of European unity itself, but after the Beethoven bicentennial celebrations of 1970 the "Ode to Joy" was officially adopted as the anthem of the European Union in 1972. At least in music, universal brotherhood triumphed over political nationalism.

Yet the Ninth Symphony has a second darker side in European history. It became associated with the Nazis and, unlike the Fifth, it was not appropriated by the Allies in their own war cause. For several reasons Wagner was Hitler's favorite composer, and Bayreuth, the opera house built for Wagner, became an official shrine under the Nazis. The first Bayreuth Festival under Nazi control, however, opened with a performance not of Wagner but of Beethoven's Ninth Symphony. The Ninth was also performed at the opening ceremonies of the Berlin Olympics in 1936, which Hitler envisioned as a display of German and hence Nazi superiority. Hitler's celebrated his birthday in 1937 with a performance of the Ninth Symphony, and the Ninth was again used to commemorate Hitler's assumption of the command of the Eastern front in 1942. In 1941–1942 the Ninth Symphony was the most performed orchestral work in Nazi Germany. As early as 1933, *Die Musik,* which had become an official Nazi organ, hailed Wagner and Beethoven as "the two poles of *urdeutsche* [pure German] music."[20]

In Alex's Ludovico treatment, the connection of the Ninth Symphony with evil is reinforced when Alex encounters it precisely as Nazi filmmaker Leni Riefenstahl's images of a Nuremberg rally are displayed. Other writers, such as Robert Griepenkerl and Susan McClary, have heard in the Ninth Symphony representations of violence, but in virtually every case it was in reference to the first movement. Kubrick, however, completely avoids the first movement in *A Clockwork Orange,* attaching violence instead to two other movements that seem least reflective of it, the scherzo and the finale.[21] The Nazi association in both the film and in events such as the 1936 Olympics was to the second and fourth movements, most notably the "Ode to Joy."

The contrast between the concept of universal brotherhood familiar to most movie audiences and the violence arising from the Nazi connection with the

Ninth Symphony bestows an ironic element on the music. Irony itself is a significant aspect of the film. Alex's voiceover has a continually ironic tone, as in his frequent references to "the old ultraviolence"; referring to the night of beating, raping, and gang fighting as a "wonderful evening"; describing his arrival in prison as "the real weepy and like tragic part of the story beginning, O my brothers and only friends"; and, as he begins to watch the first Ludovico film, of a man being brutally beaten, his comment that "so far the first tile was a very good professional piece of cine, looked like it was done in Hollywood."

Much like *Five Easy Pieces,* the turn toward irony was typical of the time. The idealism of the youth movement, the rejection of the hollowness of accumulation, had given way to anger and disillusionment brought on by many events of the late sixties: the assassination of John F. Kennedy was followed by those of Martin Luther King and Robert Kennedy. Police beatings of demonstrators at the Democratic National Convention in Chicago were carried live on primetime television interspersed with an angry Mayor Richard J. Daley inside the convention hall. This was at a time when a majority of Americans tuned into television coverage of the major parties' conventions. The Cold War continued as the Vietnam War dragged on, with America's military might supplied by a draft that affected virtually all young men under the age of twenty-six. Eventually over 50,000 Americans would lose their life in the war. On the home front, Second Wave feminism was at its height, only to suffer a setback when the proposed Equal Rights Amendment was rejected. The tone of optimism and determination that had characterized America's entry into both World Wars I and II had turned to cynicism and disillusionment; a darker view of American society prevailed. Such attitudes easily lead to a tone of irony, which became a common mode of expression for several decades.

The ironic use of Beethoven's Ninth Symphony in *A Clockwork Orange* affected its presentation in a host of other films. The most direct connection occurred in the film *Die Hard* (1988). *Die Hard* features Bruce Willis as John McClane, a New York City policeman who has come to Los Angeles to see his estranged wife, Holly, and their children. Holly has taken a position with the Japanese company Nakatomi, a career move that clashes with John's more traditional ideas of marriage. He arrives during the company's Christmas party. Hans Gruber, played by Alan Rickman, and his group of twelve soon arrive with a well-conceived plot to steal millions of securities in the company's vault. They seal the building and take everyone hostage on the thirtieth floor. Except McClane, that is, who is washing up in a private bathroom. Thus begins a cat and mouse game as McClane attempts to thwart the gang's plan. Eventually the LA police and the FBI become involved, though Gruber leads them to believe that a terrorist plot has been hatched. The ending is predictable: Gruber and the "terrorists" are defeated because of McClane's heroism and he and Holly are reunited.

What makes *Die Hard* more than a run-of-the-mill Hollywood action film is the contrast between the two principal characters: Gruber is a highly educated, erudite, aesthetically aware, charming German, McClane is a down-to-earth, blue-collar American. While Gruber is totally ruthless, without a shred of morality or regret, he is, unlike Alex in *A Clockwork Orange,* interested in violence only when necessary to achieve his ends. In one sense Gruber is the most fascinating and dominant character in the film.

The music underscores Gruber's importance. McClane has no defined thematic material, only what Robynn Stilwell, in a brilliant analysis, calls "stock suspense signifiers as low, indeterminate rumblings, string tremolos and figurations, percussive outbursts and screech brass interjections, but nothing so dignified as a fanfare."[22] As if to emphasize McClane's blue-collar status, the only time he is associated with a melody is when he whistles "Jingle Bells" on the way to the party. Gruber, on the other hand, is identified with the most important musical material in the film, the "Ode to Joy." It appears several times, as both source and underscore, and the composer Michael Kamen has also taken fragments of it to construct a complex polyphonic web of symbolic meaning to enhance and guide the dramatic structure of the film.

The "Ode" is first heard played by a string quartet at the Christmas party. As the bad guys arrive in a large truck, the first three notes, greatly augmented, sound in the bass. As they emerge from the elevator where the party is in full swing, the bass sustains the first two notes, against the string quartet melody, which is in a different key (A♭ versus E♭), creating a further dissonance. The music is interrupted as the gang fires gunshots in the air.

The next appearance of the "Ode to Joy" is when Gruber whistles it, in a sort of up-beat improvised version, just before he murders Takagi, who refuses to give him the code to open the vault. Gruber's whistling indicates both his supreme confidence and control as well as his familiarity with this iconic example of high art music. The "Ode" appears several other times during the ensuing conflict, but its most important appearance occurs when Gruber's gang finally succeeds in opening the vault. Here it is stated by full orchestra with Beethoven's harmonies, as Gruber and Theo, the computer expert whose responsibility it was to hack the systems of the building, slowly rise and stand awestruck before the open vault, whose innards glow with a brilliant blue

Die Hard. Hans Gruber, the sophisticated, intellectual thief, at
the moment his gang succeeds in opening the vault.

light. Undershots of each thief's head highlight the triumphant moment. As
they rush into the vault and begin to riffle through the contents, including, for
Gruber's appreciation, a Degas painting and an Asian statuary, the Turkish
March from the Ninth sounds.

If music is any indicator, this is the climactic moment of the film. It is
strictly Gruber's moment, however, as McClane is stuck in a bathroom tend-
ing to his bleeding feet after an earlier glass explosion. Partly for contrived plot
reasons and partly to show off McClane's machismo, he then runs around the
building barefoot, first in an undershirt and later with bared torso. The linger-
ing highlight on Gruber in this scene helps to evoke a favorable image of him,
in spite of his villain status, just as Alex's narration in *A Clockwork Orange* creates more sympathy for him than would otherwise have been the case.

Even after Gruber meets his inevitable demise, falling from the thirtieth-
floor window, he continues to dominate the film. As the credits roll at film's
end, it is Gruber's music the audience hears, the "Ode to Joy." This has an effect
similar to Kubrick's choice of "Singin' in the Rain" over the closing credits in *A
Clockwork Orange,* which Alex sang as he kicked and beat the writer and raped

his wife. Its reprise in the credits serves to remind the audience that Alex may be evil, but he has triumphed over the evil of the state. The credit music is less manipulative in *Die Hard*, but it succeeds in hinting that Gruber may be gone but is not forgotten. His death itself is highly choreographed: Holly pushes him out the window, but not before he is able to grab hold of the watch she is wearing, thus threatening to take her with him. As McClane holds onto her and tries to undo the watch, Gruber pulls a gun from his pocket, but the watch comes loose just as he is about to pull the trigger. His fall is filmed in slow motion from the window view. The audience never sees him hit the ground or his dead body afterward. He is last seen in free fall, in the air.

That *A Clockwork Orange* and *Die Hard* share a negative depiction of the Ninth Symphony might suggest either coincidence or influence, but the musical connection between the films goes beyond Beethoven. Theo, the computer geek, is the only other character in the latter film besides Gruber who has his own prominent theme: "Singin' in the Rain." In keeping with Theo's scientific, intellectual precociousness, the theme is subjected to several classical developmental techniques: mode change, octave displacement, extension by motivic repetition, as well as character transformations, such as when it appears as a fanfare.[23] The association of both "Singin' in the Rain" and the Ninth Symphony with weirdly sympathetic villains strongly suggests that *A Clockwork Orange* could not have been too far from the minds of *Die Hard*'s filmmakers. Indeed, composer Michael Kamen, who wrote the original music for the film, said in an interview that pairing the Ninth Symphony with Gruber was director John McTiernan's idea, and that he considered Gruber's gang "the lineal descendants" of Alex's gang. Sounding much like some of the responses to the Beethoven-was-black question that we will see in chapter 10, Kamen was bothered by the idea: "I actually said to him, please, if you want me to fuck with some German composer, I'm very happy to take Wagner to pieces. I'll do anything you like but can't we leave Beethoven alone."[24] When McTiernan persisted in connecting Alex's and Gruber's gangs through Beethoven's Ninth, Kamen decided to incorporate "Singin' in the Rain" into *Die Hard* as well, in a scene where its use parallels *A Clockwork Orange:* Theo disables a computer system by ripping out wires and at one point kicking the case, all the while humming "Singin' in the Rain." The reference is hard to miss.

Kamen held the traditional, romantic view of the Ninth Symphony: "This is one of the greatest pieces of music celebrating the nobility of the human spirit of all time and you want me to aim it at a bunch of gangsters in an American commercial film?" His concern was that having the "Ode to Joy" represent a criminal would demean the music, although Gruber's characterization should have lessened that fear somewhat. Gruber is not, after all, just another lowly criminal. In the one moment in the film that he loses his cool, he corrects Holly when she accuses him of being a common thief: "I am an *exceptional* thief, Mrs. McClane."

The use of the Ninth Symphony in *Die Hard* may be read in several ways. In an obvious sense it is ironic: one of Western culture's noblest monuments to the human spirit has been appropriated by a criminal, be he common or exceptional. Yet it is fitting for Gruber. He is cultured and sophisticated, and that quality is important to the overriding conflict of the film, that between the main antagonists. Gruber is also German, giving him legitimate claim to the work. This may also be considered a tribute to *A Clockwork Orange*, even though, as Stilwell has demonstrated, the two films as a whole and the principal characters are not at all similar.

However the use of the symphony is read in *Die Hard*, the film established an action formula that would be often repeated: a hostage situation, a sophisticated villain, and a misunderstood hero who will save the day while shedding his shirt. It also solidified a new role for Beethoven and particularly the Ninth Symphony. *A Clockwork Orange* and *Die Hard* both associate the Ninth Symphony with evil, whether it's the evil of Alex, who fantasizes rape and mayhem, the evil of the state that takes away free will, or the evil of Hans Gruber for whom human life is coldly expendable. In each case the Ninth Symphony is connected directly to these agents and their actions. The familiarity of the Ninth Symphony is critical to this reinterpretation. The audience must recognize it, or at least know that it is a classical icon. Since the traditional Hollywood score often sounds similar to the orchestral music of the common-practice era, the eighteenth and nineteenth centuries, a symphonic work by Liszt would not make the same point. Beethoven in such a situation, however, is recognized and carries a well-known idealistic message, hence the irony.

Several other films exploit the dark side of the Ninth Symphony that *A Clockwork Orange* introduced.[25] In several cases, such as *Sophie's Choice* and *Apt Pupil*, the connection with Nazism is direct and specific, in the sense that Nazis are an important element in the stories. In a film such as *Bowling for Columbine*, the use of the Ninth Symphony resembles even more closely *A Clockwork Orange*, although it is strictly underscore.

Bowling for Columbine (2002) is a Michael Moore documentary about the gun culture of America, seen in the aftermath of the Columbine High School massacre of April 1999, in which two students went on a rampage, killing twelve students and one teacher and injuring twenty-one other students, some critically. The Nazi connection with the Ninth Symphony is, as in *A Clockwork Or-*

ange, explicit. A sequence of episodes begins with the two student killers at Columbine bowling, something they allegedly did the morning of the shooting, followed by flashes of violent scenes, some from American movies, some from archival footage of the Nazis, the Japanese occupation of China, the French massacre in Algiers, and the British slaughter in India.

Throughout this sequence the Turkish March from the Ninth Symphony sounds, while Moore questions why, even when other cultures have a history of violence, America has so many more gun murders. The Ninth Symphony is thus associated specifically with disturbing, horrific scenes, bloodthirsty scenes, scenes of malevolence. The sequence first links the symphony to the two young men as they are engaged in a seemingly innocent activity, yet its presence suggests that they are on the same moral plane as Alex. Since the audience knows what lies ahead, the symphony assumes a portentous quality even for those unfamiliar with Alex. As if that were not clear enough, the continuation of this filmic sequence with scenes of mayhem while the Turkish March plays solidifies the dark (and in this case the Nazi) connection to the work.

A second film based on the Columbine massacre interpolates a different Beethoven. *Elephant* (2003), directed by Gus Van Sant, is a thinly veiled fictional account of a high school shooting whose parallels to Columbine are hard to miss. The film, shot in a Portland, Oregon, high school with real Portland students, follows various characters on the day of the shooting. The camera highlights one student and then another, providing personal interactions from multiple points of view and establishing what an ordinary day at school it is. The audience, of course, knows better, and this somber irony gives the typically commonplace student interactions the film's dramatic edge. The shooting and its aftermath occupy only the final twenty minutes of the film. The two killers, Alex and Eric, are shown truant earlier in the day, and while Eric plays a violent video game Alex plays Beethoven's "Für Elise" on the piano. They then watch a documentary on Hitler. Though the Ninth Symphony is not present, Beethoven, the killers, and Nazism are tied together in one scene, as in *Bowling for Columbine*. Van Sant tends to use the students' real first names, but the fact that he chose Alex as the name of the murderer who played Beethoven may not have been coincidental.

The success of *Die Hard* led to two sequels, *Die Hard 2* (1990) and *Die Hard: With a Vengeance* (1995). Neither sequel uses the Ninth Symphony, probably because Gruber's death necessitated a new villain, although the third film featured Hans's brother Simon, and another prominent character is named Schiller. When all three films were packaged together as DVDs, however, Warner Bros. assembled a *Die Hard Trilogy* trailer in which the "Ode to Joy" plays amidst various scenes of violence and mayhem from all three films: cars getting blown up and rolled over, people shooting each other, people falling out of airplanes.

The Ninth Symphony has a similar role in the *The Last Action Hero* (1993), a spoof on action films starring Arnold Schwarzenegger as both the action hero Jack Slater and as himself. In a complicated series of contrived events, a young fan, Danny Madigan (Austin O'Brien), is given a magic ticket that allows him to pass between the world of the Jack Slater film and the real world. The film is strewn with jokes about other action films. In one scene Madigan is shown the Laurence Olivier film version of *Hamlet*. He fantasizes Slater as Hamlet, who when addressed as "Fair Prince" by Polonius responds, "Who said I'm fair?" and instead of a sword pulls out an assault rifle and lays waste to his enemies. In the film this scene is accompanied by composed music associated with Slater. When the scene is excerpted in the film's trailer, however, it is accompanied by—the Ninth Symphony.

The Ninth Symphony can also have a nefarious undertone without any reference to Nazis or murder. *Cruel Intensions* (1999) is a remake of Pierre Choderlos de Laclos's 1762 novel *Les Liaisons Dangereuses*, transferred to Manhattan amidst a group of ultra-rich, cynical preppies. Sebastian Valmont (Ryan Phillippe) is a teenage playboy who prides himself on his conquests. He makes a bet with his equally callous step-sister, Kathryn Merteiul (Sarah Michelle Gellar), that he can seduce the newly arrived headmaster's daughter, Annette Hargrove (Reese Witherspoon), who has written an article in which she proclaims her virginity and advocates abstinence before marriage. In one scene Annette is in Sebastian's mansion and he uses the Ninth Symphony played at full volume to lure her to the indoor swimming pool where he can begin to work his charms on her. The Ninth Symphony thus becomes one of the anti-hero's tools of a wicked seduction.

In the swath of Ninth Symphony-as-evil interpretations that *A Clockwork Orange* unleashed, Hollywood did not forget the Ninth Symphony-as-triumphant-moral-uplift, the *Meet John Doe* treatment. In *Dead Poets Society* (1989), Todd Anderson (Ethan Hawke), a painfully shy student, is drawn out by an English teacher, Mr. Keating (Robin Williams); overcoming his fear, Todd stands on a desk and improvises a poem. The camera then cuts to an after-class soccer session that is underscored by a full orchestral rendition of the "Ode to Joy." In *Eight Days a Week* (1997), a nerdy high school student has a crush on a beautiful girl. Finally, after essentially hanging around outside her window all summer, she invites him to her bedroom at the end of the film. Reminiscent of *Meet John Doe,* this moment of triumph is celebrated with full orchestra and the chorus singing the "Ode to Joy." The Chinese film *Eat Drink Man Woman* (1994), which enjoyed considerable popularity in the United States, is the story of a widowed chef and his three grown daughters. In a climactic moment the husband of the oldest daughter, who has converted to Christianity, agrees to be baptized. The ceremony concludes with the hymn "Joyful, Joyful." Since the hymn is sung in Chinese, most of the audience likely registers it not as a hymn but as part of the Ninth Symphony.

One *Die Hard* spinoff to use Beethoven's Ninth differently was the low-budget B-minus film *Icebreaker* (2000). It might have been called "Die Hard at the Killington Ski Lodge." It has all the characters and plot twists one would expect in a *Die Hard* derivative: a hostage situation involving the hero's fi-nance, Meg, and her extremely wealthy father; a group of pure-evil terror-ists; ticking bombs disposed of at the last second; the poor ski bum hero who must prove his worth to his girlfriend's father; chase scenes on skies and snow-boards; and bad guys who can't hit a mountain with assault rifles. It even has a very similar *Die Hard* phone call between Matt, the hero, and Carl Greig, the vaguely German leader of the terrorists. The main difference is that the terror-ists turn out to be real terrorists, and it's too cold on the ski slopes for the hero to shed his shirt. The other major difference is the use of the Ninth Symphony. It appears twice, framing the movie. The Turkish March, with the first word, "Froh" (joy), is heard during the opening, which features a lengthy series of shots showing the lodge and the ski slopes full of vacationing skiers. Then at the end, after Matt has saved the day, is united with his fiancée, and receives her father's blessing, the triumphant conclusion of Beethoven's final move-ment sounds as underscore. The creators of the film, undoubtedly influenced by the presence of the Ninth in *Die Hard,* reject its villainous association and return to Capra's *Meet John Doe* usage, the exultant and expected one.

Few films have drawn upon the spiritual nature of Beethoven's music the way the television miniseries *Band of Brothers* (2001) did. Although ten epi-sodes in length, and thus not technically a movie, it many ways it was a World War II film in its script, characters, and cinematic treatment, and it was shown on HBO, the cable channel that regularly broadcasts movies. The opening of episode 9 features Germans solemnly sorting through the rubble of a ruined city after the Allies have occupied it. Amidst the rubble, four German musi-cians slowly raise their instruments and begin playing the opening movement of the String Quartet op. 131. One of the Americans watching thinks it's Mo-zart, but Captain Lewis Nixon walks up and says somberly, "It's not Mozart, *that's Beethoven.*" The opening movement of op. 131, a fugue marked by Bee-thoven "molto espressivo," is one of his most somber and at the same time most spiritual statements. A German quartet playing this amidst the ruins of their city, and indeed their nation, is a particularly strong testament to the human spirit.

With the increasing use of preexisting art music, the 1980s and 1990s saw a dramatic expansion of the Beethoven repertoire in film. To the moviegoing public Beethoven was no longer the composer who wrote possibly a half-dozen powerful or catchy "songs." Music directors begin to mine the entire Beethoven literature, including the quartets and many of the lesser-known sonatas, and some of the more familiar works were used in imaginative ways. In *My Life So Far* (1999), Edward Pettigrew (Colin Firth), the father of an eccentric family in a Scottish castle, is a Beethoven aficionado, and he plays Beethoven recordings on the phonograph for the entire family. In one nondiegetic moment, the Fifth Symphony becomes accompaniment as Pettigrew teaches his children to fly-fish by singing "da-da-da-dum," imprinting the rhythm of casting as he whips his pole back and forth. The Fifth then continues as Fraser (Robert Norman), the preadolescent boy who narrates the film, juxtaposes his love of fly-fishing and his discovery of some of his uncle's erotic books. Imagery follows narration, creating an odd blend of symbols for the symphony.

In *The Quiet* (2005), the *Moonlight* Sonata assumes the same ominous overtones that the Ninth Symphony did in *A Clockwork Orange*. The film centers on two teenagers, Dot and Nina. Dot's parents have died, and she is adopted by Nina's parents, the Deers, her godparents. Dot is a deaf-mute and Nina a popular high school teenager. Nina treats Dot cruelly and humiliates her at school, but Dot discovers that Nina is sleeping with her father, Paul. It's a love-hate relationship for Nina: she hates what he is doing but loves him doing it. Throughout the film we see both girls playing a grand piano in an otherwise empty room, mostly Beethoven. In Dot's narration she frequently comments on Beethoven's deafness. Eventually it comes out that Dot is not actually deaf. In a climactic scene when Nina tries to break away from her father, he slaps her and tries to rape her. Dot comes in with a piano wire, wraps it around his neck, and strangles him. Throughout the scene we hear the *Moonlight* Sonata, first being played by Dot downstairs, later nondiegetically during the murder.

A few Beethoven compositions newly brought to the silver screen in recent years are the Cello Sonatas op. 5, no. 1 (*The Horse Whisperer*) and no. 2 (*Along Came Polly*); the Piano Sonatas op. 31, no. 1 (*Search and Destroy*), op. 101, op. 26, op. 81a, and op. 49, no. 1 (*The Quiet*), and op. 2, no. 3 and the Bagatelle op. 126, no. 1 (*My Father, the Genius*); the Fantasy for Piano, Chorus, and Orchestra, op. 80 (*Oscar and Lucinda*); the String Quartets op. 18, no. 2, op. 59, no. 1 (*Sour*

FIGURE 8.7

V for Vendetta. "V," who leads a revolution against an
Orwellian state, in his Guy Fawkes mask.

Grapes), op. 130 (*One Night Stand*), and op. 131 (*I Heart Huckabees*); the Piano
Quartet op. 16 (*The Talented Mr. Ripley*); and Symphony no. 1 (*People I Know*
and *We Don't Live Here Anymore*).

Some films revert to the more traditional cinematic role for Beethoven
compositions. *V for Vendetta* (2006) is a film based on a comic book series,
set in a futuristic police state in Great Britain.[26] Reminiscent of Orwell's *1984*,
it abounds with totalitarian symbolism. One man, known only as "V," who
wears a Guy Fawkes mask and whose face is never seen, is set to lead a revolution.

The film recalls November 5, 1605, when Guy Fawkes, with a small band of
revolutionaries, attempted to blow up the House of Lords. The plot was discovered and Fawkes and his compatriots were brutally executed according to the

custom of the day. The attempt became known as the Gunpowder Plot, and Guy Fawkes Day is still celebrated in England, principally with fireworks and giant bonfires where Fawkes is burned in effigy. V's plan is to blow up Parliament on November 5, the tagline in the film being, "Remember, remember, the fifth of November." V dies in the end, but his plan succeeds and his message resonates, sparking the revolution against totalitarianism.

With a Brit who calls himself V fighting against a fascist-style government, the sound track not unexpectedly features the first movement of the Fifth Symphony. It occurs in a scene where V confronts Peter Creedy, the head of the government's secret police, threatens him with a knife, and sets up the final confrontation of the film.

In addition to the many composer biopics produced in Hollywood, films about classical musicians, either real or fictional, have also held a special attraction. Virtually all involve some sort of concert situation, and in virtually all Beethoven's music is heard diegetically at some point. For example, in the fictional films *The Competition* (1980), centering on an international piano competition, and *Mr. Holland's Opus* (1995), about a frustrated composer who eventually finds fulfillment as a high school music teacher, Beethoven's Piano Concerto no. 5 (the *Emperor*) and the Seventh Symphony, respectively, are heard. *The Pianist* (2002) tells the true story of Wladyslaw Szpilman (Adrien Brody), considered the finest Polish pianist of the 1930s. Because he is Jewish he sees his world collapse: his family is sent to concentration camps and he is forced into hiding in the Warsaw Ghetto. In his hiding place in an attic he hears Beethoven's *Moonlight* Sonata from below. *Shine* (1996) tells the story of piano prodigy David Helfgott (Geoffrey Rush), who, driven by his abusive father, eventually has a mental breakdown, is institutionalized, and after many twists returns to the concert stage. One of the pieces he plays is Beethoven's *Appassionata* Sonata. *The Soloist* (2009) is about a mentally troubled street musician, Nathanial Ayers (Jamie Foxx), befriended by journalist Steve Lopez (Robert Downey Jr.). Ayers is a trained cellist and Juilliard graduate, but because of his illness he cannot function in society. Much Beethoven music is heard: the Third and the Ninth Symphonies, the String Quartets op. 127 and 132, the Cello Sonata op. 102, no. 1, and the Triple Concerto.

There are, of course, many other films in which Beethoven's music is found. Whether diegetic or not, whether limited to the famous handful of iconic pieces or not, whether referencing the composer or not, Hollywood has done much not only for introducing Beethoven to many, but also defining and redefining his image in American culture. In 1925 Erno Rapeé, who compiled a massive index of music to be used to accompany silent films, credited the movie orchestras with doing much to spread the popularity of classical instrumental music.[27] He was also prescient in his description. Even after the talkies replaced the silent films, the symbiotic relationship between Beethoven and Hollywood continued. Hollywood has much to thank Beethoven for, and Beethoven has much to thank Hollywood for.

9

Beethoven in the Theater

$\mathcal{F}$OR SOME OF THE SAME REASONS that Beethoven appealed to Hollywood—a universally recognized icon, a tragic life, a volatile complex person, and emotionally powerful music—he has intrigued playwrights as well.
Beethoven has been a principal character in a number of plays ranging from
more or less straight biographies to avant-garde experimental works in which
Beethoven either appears in unusual places, such as Ghana or inside his own
head, is psychoanalyzed, or transcends time to descend upon the modern world.
Some plays focus on Beethoven's relationships, some on his music, and at least
one, *33 Variations,* on a specific composition. Certain fixtures from several
films, such as Beethoven's deathbed scene with the metaphorically rich thunderstorm, are also found in plays. Yet in spite of many commonalities, differences in approach between film and theater outweigh similarities.

The first play about Beethoven to appear in twentieth-century America was
Beethoven, by the French poet and playwright Rene Fauchois. It was translated into English by Henry Grafton Chapman and produced at The New Theatre in New York in 1910. Purporting to be a biography, it was closer to a loose
series of vignettes that touch on some of the events in Beethoven's life. Each
act more or less highlights one, the first on Beethoven's less-than-successful
relationships with women, the second on his growing deafness, and the third

on his relationship with Karl. Between moments of action there are scenes that show Beethoven composing: he rubs his forehead, grasps his temples, rushes about the room trying to construct the next composition, and when a thought comes to him the audience hears it played by an unseen orchestra. At other times Beethoven expresses his own thoughts on various topics in lengthy soliloquies.

Beethoven's music, of course, plays an important role throughout the play, not only as he composes it but also to enhance moods that the action demands. In the first act Beethoven is smitten by his pupil, the lovely Giulietta Guicciardi, and when she informs him that she has decided to marry Count Gallenberg, it is to the accompaniment of the *Moonlight* Sonata and a backdrop of silvery lights playing on a painting of a river. Here the legend of the sonata depicting moonlight on the river, which the poet Ludwig Rellstab invented and which had nothing to do with Beethoven, is brought to life on the stage. A similar scene minus the river is found in Gance's 1936 film *Un Grand Amour de Beethoven;* was Gance, a French filmmaker, influenced by Fauchois's play, or did the connection seem obvious, particularly since Beethoven dedicated the sonata to Guicciardi?

Music especially comes to life in the final scene of the play. As Beethoven lies on his deathbed, his symphonies appear in the form of nine young women in white robes. Each is accompanied by a poetic description from a voice offstage and excerpts from the symphony that she represents. According to contemporary reports, the scene, itself bordering on questionable taste, was made even more ludicrous by the lighting, which one reviewer called "atrocious" and "like that of a drunken sailor trying to pick up white buoys in a dense fog." This was the climactic scene of the play, marred even further by what was supposed to be the thunderstorm that occurred at the moment of Beethoven's death. Here it was represented by "one startling explosion of an over-loaded bomb which completely robbed the death scene of any impressiveness it might possibly have had."[1]

The language of the play lapses between prose dialogue and soliloquies in iambic pentameter, as if the author had been uncertain whether to emulate Shakespeare or Molière. The soliloquies allow Beethoven to be portrayed as the god of music himself, as Orpheus bringing music to mankind. At one point Anton Schindler, Beethoven's friend, secretary, and factotum, comments on the world prior to Beethoven:

Those days were like the days when the old Alps,
Locked in the bosom of eternal snows,

As yet sent down no river. From the dales
Among the mountains there arose no sound
But hoot of owls or the thin pipe of birds.
But when the time was come the wild young Rhine
Burst from St. Gothard's, black, untamable,
Carrying all before him. Trees and rocks
And blocks of ancient ice were tossed aside.
The noise of hooting owl and piping bird
Was all drowned out; and from that day the Rhine
Has silenced all less noises.
So it was
With Beethoven.

Many similar speeches by different characters, including several by Beethoven, appear throughout the play, creating a heightened poetic effect that at the same time retards dramatic action. This is a play of nineteenth-century Romanticism, with much the same pacing of a late Wagner opera. Its French origins are apparent in the use of poetic speeches and, as one reviewer noted, illustrates a difference between modern French and modern American theater. He refers to the interpolations as "dear to the French stage," but "tiresome" to American theater audiences who demand more direct and natural drama. Beethoven's music, which is specified exactly by the inclusion of scores, does much to help sustain the drama and the mood. Reviews suggest that this play may not be consistent with Victorian pre–World War I American stage values, but it does suggest the gulf that rests between what was feasible then and today as well as the hagiographic image of Beethoven that prevailed at the time.

The portrayal and interpretation of Beethoven's love relationships were more out of the nineteenth than the twentieth century. Guicciardi does not renounce Beethoven for Gallenberg, but like an obedient daughter she agrees to marry him because her father wishes her to. That Beethoven by the second act became interested in Bettina Brentano troubled the reviewer for the *New York Times*, who called Beethoven's actions "fickleness [which] in heroic lovers is one thing that audiences will not understand, or understanding, will not easily condone." He then explains that a proper stage lover should go on "eating his heart out for Giulietta to the end."[2]

It is hard to imagine that in the twenty-first century, Beethoven, having been cast aside by one woman, would be condemned for moving on to seek another partner. Victorian sentiment, if not Victorian reality, expected their hero to remain true to one love forever, whether requited or not. The reviewer's concerns help explain one song from the 1890s, "After the Ball," which by any statistical measure must be considered the most popular song ever written. At a time when 100,000 copies of sheet music defined a major hit, "After the Ball" sold somewhere between three and five million. The story tells of a young man who sees his betrothed hugging and kissing another man. Heartbroken, he departs and breaks the young woman's heart. When he is an old man he recounts the event to his niece to explain why he never married, only then to discover that the young man was his betrothed's brother. Such tragedy went right to the heart of Victorian sentiment.

Adrienne Kennedy's play *She Talks to Beethoven* is set in Ghana, and, like most of her work, much in it is autobiographical. In 1960 and 1961 she and her husband David were in Ghana where he was doing graduate work. She became pregnant and when she began bleeding, the doctor advised her not to travel. Her husband had to be gone for several days at a time for his work, she had never been away from her husband for any length of time, she was in a foreign culture, and she was afraid: "All of this produced growing tensions and unhappiness in me. . . . The long hours alone in the rented Accra home, at the guest home in Achimota or Kumasi, from dawn to late at night, filled me with fear."[3]

The principal character in the play, Suzanne Alexander, is an American playwright who is recovering from unspecified surgery. Meanwhile her husband, David, a prominent professor, has disappeared and is feared captured by rebels because of his political views. As Suzanne waits anxiously, the radio provides commentary and speculation on David's fate, and also informs the audience that David's wife is writing a play about Beethoven. Suzanne tries to distract herself from concern about David by working on the play. As she reads aloud from Beethoven diaries, the stage opens to Beethoven's room; Suzanne enters and begins a conversation with Beethoven. The rest of the play conflates Suzanne's place and time with Beethoven's. The radio acts as a constant reminder of Suzanne's situation, and her struggles to create a play are paralleled with Beethoven's struggles to produce *Fidelio*.

Suzanne's illness is also paralleled with Beethoven's own infirmary, his deafness, which he has kept secret but about which he confides to Suzanne. Suzanne's concern about David finds parallels with Beethoven's concern about Karl, who attempts suicide in the course of the play. Thus each character has an artistic crisis and two personal crises, one relating to health, the other to a loved one. Beethoven not only comforts Suzanne about David, but later he becomes a conduit by which David communicates with her. Mysteriously, messages from David in David's handwriting appear in Beethoven's conversation books that she is studying. At the end of the play, when David has survived his situation and returns, Suzanne rushes to the door to greet him:

> SUZANNE: David. You sent Beethoven until you returned.
> DAVID'S VOICE: (*Not unlike Beethoven's.*) I knew he would console you while I was absent.

We do not see David. It is David's voice, but is it? Was Beethoven speaking to Suzanne or was it David all along? Beethoven at the least was a surrogate for David, or, as Suzanne says, an imaginary friend sent by David. Beethoven may not have been David, but their identities commingle and become difficult to separate.

Identity conflation raises important ethnic issues, a theme found throughout Kennedy's oeuvre. Kennedy herself is of mixed background, with a black father and a white mother. Born in 1931 as Adrienne Lita Hawkins, she was raised at first in Mount Pleasant, a middle-class mixed neighborhood in Cleveland, then, as her father succeeded, in a more affluent one, Glenville. Society constantly reminded her of her racial heritage, however, and of the difficulties of being black in America. She speaks of riding in an all-black car on a train ride to visit her mother's family in Georgia, and of the racial hatred she faced in her dormitory at Ohio State University.

Beethoven became more than another type of sound to her. In the play David is an African American professor and Beethoven is a white German composer. But is he? Kennedy could not have been unaware of the "Beethoven is black" movement of the late 1960s, and there are hints of that argument in this play. Beethoven is described as "full of rude energy," with "strong and prominent features" and hair that "overshadowed his broad brow in a quantity and confusion to which only the snakes round a Gorgon's head offer a parallel." At one point the African music that Suzanne hears outside her window morphs into a Beethoven overture. Beethoven's death occurs in the Schwarzspanierhaus, the House of the Black Spaniard, named after the monks that once inhabited it, and while Kennedy avoids describing Beethoven as a black Spaniard, the placement of the reference in the play at the least alludes to descriptions others had of Beethoven, descriptions that formed the core of the Beethoven-was-black argument.

Yet Kennedy, it seems, never bought into that argument. Beethoven for her represented something different, namely, one aspect of her heritage. She had developed a special affinity for Beethoven's music and had used the image of Beethoven as inspiration. As a youth she studied piano with a Polish teacher, Miss Eichenbaum. Throughout those years Miss Eichenbaum gave her several busts of composers. As an adult Kennedy ordered an LP set of all the Beethoven string quartets, and both the music and the album covers remained vivid in her memory. In her collection of autobiographical vignettes, *Material from People Who Led to My Plays,* she remembers how "each record was wrapped in delicate paper and the record covers were in Romantic pale colors. How I treasured them." As far as the music itself, "His string quartets taught me that dark, impossible, unbearable moods could be transposed into work. A creative person could capture what he felt in andante, allegro, molta bella [*sic*]."[4]

Later she bought a foot-high ivory statue of Beethoven in New York and placed it on her desk. She read and reread Sullivan's book, *Beethoven, His Spiritual Development,* "and I listened to his string quartets." The statue in particular became an inspiration to Kennedy, but its purpose was shared by another image on her wall, a photograph of Queen Hatshepsut, one of the few female Pharaohs of ancient Egypt and one who enjoyed a long and successful reign. For her the two images represented "those forces of my ancestry . . . European and African . . . a fact that would one day explode in my work" [ellipses in original]. Thus Beethoven for her stands for Europe, in direct contrast to Queen Hatshepsut, who represents Africa, and there is no trace of the Beethoven-was-black idea in her comments.

Some ethnic ambiguity characterizes both Kennedy's plays and her own life. The ivory statue of Beethoven itself is multiply symbolic. It was, of course, an image of a major European artist. It reminded her of her European piano teacher, who kept composers' busts on her desk. It was made of ivory, a material often associated with Africa. But being of ivory it was light, almost white in color. In many of Kennedy's plays paleness is associated with decay, disease, or death. This theme occurs in *Funnyhouse of a Negro* and *The Owl Answers,* as well as *She Talks to Beethoven.* All three have to do with the metaphorical significance of a festering wound. In *She Talks,* Suzanne's wound, signifying an unspecified illness, is wrapped in white gauze, and when she unwraps her bandage to see if the wound has healed, she explains to Beethoven that "if the wound is pale white I'm still sick." It is, and even though David returns at the end, there is no reference to the wound or illness healing.

Asked if she identified herself as either a black writer or a woman writer, Kennedy emphatically rejected both. She made clear that she wanted to break barriers, but she did not want to be pigeonholed into an artistic ghetto. Curiously, when this question arose in the interview she was more emphatic about not being a woman writer than her denial of being a black writer. Her Beethoven fits into that realm of ambiguity. He is European, he is a surrogate for her husband, his music is intertwined with the European, but he is decidedly not limited to one or the other classification. He more or less floats above the ethnic divide that separated America in the sixties, just as Kennedy herself did. She made it clear that her voice was that of a black woman, but she did not want her work to be identified with any cause, ethnic or feminist.[5]

Beethoven's Tenth, a play written and performed by Peter Ustinov, is neither experimental nor ambiguous. It premiered in London and had a brief run in New York in 1983.[6] Billed as "A Comedy in Two Acts," it involves a dysfunctional twentieth-century family consisting of a pompous, rigid music critic, Stephen Fauldgate, his wife, Jessica, a mezzo-soprano who gave up her career for her family, and their son, Pascal, a whimpering twenty-two-year-old composer, who facilely turns out facile but insipid symphonies. In their house is also an Austrian au pair, Irmgard, who knows more about Bruckner and Mahler than Stephen thinks she should. The atmosphere is acrimonious, with Stephen calling Pascal's work banal, tepid, vapid, trivial, ingratiating, servile, and mincing, not necessarily in that order, with Irmgard about to be fired as she defiantly defends Pascal, and with Jessica trying as usual to mediate between her two men.

Into that melee strides Beethoven, with a da-da-da-dumm knock on the door. He has been mentally summoned by Irmgard. The rest of the play is about Ustinov playing Ustinov by playing Beethoven, as the other characters fade into the background. Critics were not kind about that situation: Benedict Nightingale described the matching of Beethoven and Ustinov as "a love match between a giant turtle and an old, stuffed sofa," and Frank Rich, somewhat more generously, referred to Ustinov as merely a "spectacular sight" and a "portly anachronism."[7]

The play itself, with its time-travel premise, delivers plenty of technological jokes as Beethoven confronts the modern world. Beethoven is given a hearing aid but is not sure of its worth, as "the great drawback about being able to hear is that sometimes you're tempted to listen." Most jokes are predictable: he cannot understand how you can get an entire symphony into a small black disc, especially one with a hole in it; he is frightened by those metal objects hurling themselves at him on the streets and flying through the clouds; and he is fascinated by chrome and leather chairs. There are an abundance of musical jokes, such as commentary on Schoenberg's dissonance, and Beethoven's observations about music critics: to Stephen, "you are a critic, and not a musicologist at all. In that case, perhaps you would rather talk about yourself first—or exclusively about yourself."

For the most part Beethoven acts as a wise counselor straightening out the dysfunctional dynamics of the Fauldgate family. Eventually father and son become reconciled, Irmgard and Pascal are officially paired, as they had been secretly behind everyone's backs, with Irmgard becoming pregnant, and Beethoven offers sage musical advice to Pascal. He also offers advice to Irmgard, who is not sure she loves Pascal: if Pascal has talent, make him miserable, and if he doesn't then at least make him happy. The family then turns the tables on Beethoven, summoning Giulietta Guicciardi and her husband Count Gallenberg as Irmgard had summoned Beethoven. There can be no reconciliation between Guicciardi and Beethoven, of course, so they have an awkward conversation in which she professes her love of Beethoven, Beethoven is aloof, Gallenberg, thinking Beethoven can't hear, insults him, and Beethoven tells him he is stupid.

The play itself is purely entertainment, a comedic romp enhanced by Ustinov's "elephantine splendor," coupled with his lunging thigh-slapping hyperactivity. It essentially boils down to a twenty-minute gag in which Beethoven encounters the modern world extended into a two-hour celebration of a "magnificent grouch."[8]

Beethoven in Denver, written by Burton Raffel in 1999, is not a theatrical piece but more an extended poem, or forty-eight short poems strung together into a quasi-narrative, but because it is based on the same premise as Ustinov's play the two deserve comparison.[9] It explores how Beethoven would react were he to experience America on the brink of the twenty-first century. He visits the Raffel family in their Denver home, although Raffel does not tell us how this occurred. Like the opening of the Ninth Symphony or the Piano Sonata op. 109, the conversation begins as if it had been ongoing, the opening scene depicting twentieth-century suburban bliss. Beethoven sits with the family and their labrador, Midnight, in the backyard, sipping piña coladas and viewing the Rocky Mountains while steaks cook on the barbecue. Unlike Ustinov's play, this poem deals less with Beethoven's reaction to modern technology than to Beethoven's observations about people, the social order, and the places around him. He is fascinated with the Rocky Mountains, although he insists they are not as big as the Alps; he is put off by American bureaucracy, such as the social security card and the forms he confronts when he visits a doctor's office with a bad shoulder. He is puzzled by the American academic system, and his occasional comments sound suspiciously like Raffel's own on the matter:

> I tried to introduce Beethoven to my colleagues—
> professional men,
> Well educated, some of them deeply fond of music,
> some of them still fond of books—
> But they could not understand him, his assertions
> about music were terribly absolute
> (And had no footnotes)

Or after Raffel comes homes tired after a day at the university, he recalls this encounter with Beethoven:

> He took my briefcase out of my hand and told me
> not to let students—
> Even graduate students, whose need is greatest of them all—
> trouble me as they did:
> "You must not let them feed on your insides," he
> smiled fiercely.
> "Prometheus is Prometheus, and you are Raffel."

The stress on academics is not surprising, reflecting Raffel's milieu; he is a poet, translator, and professor of English at the University of Louisiana at Lafayette. In many ways the university is where Beethoven's music has been most strongly cultivated in late twentieth- and twenty-first-century America.

Like Ustinov, Raffel portrays Beethoven as a man with a keen interest in the ladies. He is intrigued by the telephone because it allows him to hear female voices, or anyone's, whether they know him or not, a situation that he sees could lead to problematic results. He is rendered catatonic by a waitress in a restaurant wearing a mini-skirt and tight blouse, and he is more than happy to play a Beatles record if a young female poet who visits the Raffel's house would show him how to dance.

Raffel's Beethoven is not the angry "untamed personality" that has become a cliché. He is genial, good-natured, and childlike in his curiosity. He has his rages but they don't last. He is more bemused than angry. He is easily distracted, as when Raffel defuses a potentially tense situation by offering to show him his lilacs or to engage in a game of tennis. He is a fantasy Beethoven and, one suspects, Raffel's alter ego. Except for its reference to the Rocky Mountains, the piece could have taken place in any American city. It is a commentary on twentieth-century America and especially on American academia.

The one moment in which Beethoven displays real anger occurs when Raffel takes him to a Jean-Pierre Rampal concert. This is also the longest poem in the piece. There are various comments about the French fondness for the flute and about the program, which consists of a Mozart sonata, the Schubert Arpeggionne Sonata, an unidentified Kuhlau work, the Frank Sonata in A, and finally "a clever contraption of runs and trills." Beyond Beethoven's observations about the prevalence of transcriptions, however, his mood darkens as the concert wears on. He refuses to applaud and is visibly angry in the car. When Raffel approaches him, it comes out: there was no Beethoven on the program.

Beethoven's life has long been recognized as overflowing with material for psychological drama. Psychological issues, particularly in relation to Karl, have engrossed writers since Editha and Richard Sterba's 1954 book *Beethoven and His Nephew: A Psychoanalytical Study of Their Relationship*. Both authors were trained in psychoanalysis at the Vienna Psychoanalytic Institute, and they were well aware of both the potential and the limitations of psychoanalysis. In their book the Sterbas specifically avoid discussion of the music, focusing instead on Beethoven's inner and outer life. Twenty-three years later, Maynard Solomon published what has become the most famous English-language psychological study of Beethoven. Solomon, though not a psychiatrist or psychologist, applied Freudian theory to explain in particular Beethoven's attitudes toward himself and his family. He also discusses the music, although more as a general survey than in a detailed analytical study. With regard to the late music, however, Solomon mostly abandons psychological explanation; he discusses the music either in terms of specific situations that engendered it, such as a commission, or within the context of artistic currents in Europe, such as the Enlightenment or Romanticism.

It was with these antecedents that Frederick Kurth, a trained psychiatrist, wrote his play *The Beethovens* (1992). Although he admitted in an interview that he was writing when the age of psychoanalysis was virtually over, his play may have been an escape from the dreariness he felt from his subsequent professional work: "I finally went into psychoanalysis, and then that died. Psychoanalysis has perished from the earth in many respects—so much of my work now is just doing psychiatry, which is medicines and that kind of stuff. Now I'm in theater."[10]

Kurth's play engages the middle and late Beethoven, beginning in the 1810s. By this time Beethoven was psychologically a mess. His personal life, always in turmoil, had deteriorated further, and by the end of the decade he seemed to have abandoned any pretense of maintaining a presentable personal appearance. The Napoleonic wars had created both internal and tangible external conflicts, ranging from his angry denunciation of Napoleon to the devaluation of his pension due to inflation. His hearing had worsened significantly, a mysterious love affair had scarred him deeply, and he had become deeply involved in a battle for guardianship of his nephew Karl. Yet Beethoven managed to survive the tumult of this time to emerge into his third period, where he composed some of his most sublime music: the Missa Solemnis, the Ninth Symphony, and in particular the late string quartets.

The Beethovens directly addresses the question of what allowed the composer to resurface musically and enter into one of the most fallow periods of his artistic life. Kurth's answer is disarmingly simple: "It's sex." In his later compositions, "what he's talking about is sex, about needing a child, needing a woman. He was talking about these basic human dimensions." Specifically, says Kurth, Beethoven was saved by a woman "who kept him from becoming really cuckoo." Yet the playwright's identification of the woman is anything but simple: she was none other than his brother's wife, Johanna, whom Beethoven referred to as "that whore," and against whom Beethoven fought in court for custody of Karl, and against whom he used all legal means to deny even visitation rights. Kurth believes that Beethoven loved her deeply, that "he was confused by this rivalry for the child and having all these sexual feelings about her." Beethoven never acts overtly on these sexual attractions in the play, although there is hint of the attraction and tension when Johanna later gives birth to another son, whom she calls "Ludvica," and the end of the play suggests a reconciliation. In the penultimate scene Beethoven and Johanna care for Karl together after he has attempted suicide. The final scene returns to the court where much of the conflict had played out; the judge reads Beethoven's will, which names Karl as his sole inheritor, but gives the capital of his estate to Johanna.

According to Kurth, Beethoven's conflicting feelings about Johanna became the source of his later music: "He could not sort them out ('these sexual feelings about her'), but he did in his music." Kurth does not delve into that issue in any detail; there is no attempt at Freudian or other types of analysis of the late works themselves. The actual play and its stage presentation smacks less of deep Freudian analysis than of twentieth-century soap opera. It is conventionally American and works on two levels. According to one review it is "very big theater," with "action bursting up the scaffolds," and Richard Grove, in the role of Beethoven, turns "the tempestuous image we share of the composer into the human form of a pained lion."[11] On another level the play is subtler, providing a Freudian interpretation to motives and actions, although, to Kurth's credit, psycho-speech is avoided and there are no monologues or dialogues that probe Beethoven's psyche in any overt way.

Unlike other plays about Beethoven, which are either fantastical (*Beethoven 'N' Pierrot*) or erudite (*33 Variations*), *The Beethovens* is the least consciously intellectual of the Beethoven plays, with the exception of *Beethoven's Tenth*. The stage is set minimally, Kurth suggesting a "Brechtian or Shakespearean approach," with Beethoven's piano the focal point; at the beginning, as Beethoven plays the piano, we see Karl hanging from above, with blood from a head wound dripping on the piano. This type of gesture, highly effective in the theater where visual symbolism is important, would of course require considerable translation to work in film. Later there are scenes, such as Beethoven riding his friend Nikolaus Zmeskall as if he were a donkey and Zmeskall braying like one—a kind of slapstick that can be pulled off on stage but which would simply look silly in a movie. One of the more effective theatrical devices is Beethoven hauling a trunk around the stage to indicate his moving from one dwelling to another, something the geographic flexibility of a film would render unnecessary.

In the avoidance of heavily intellectual dialogue or deeply subtle symbolism, one can argue that this play and Beethoven films are aimed at the same audience. Kurth does raise psychological issues, such as the conflict between sexual desire and moral duty, the thin line between desire and hatred, and the destructive nature of obsession. These are themes easily understood by the majority of both the theatergoing public and film audiences. These are also themes that could appear in any American soap opera: love-hate, desire, lust, tangled family relationships, an obsessive male, and the suffering he inflicts. Kurth presents the psychological issues in a form that anyone can understand.

Because of its characterization of Beethoven and Johanna, one may wonder if the play influenced the film *Immortal Beloved*. The play premiered in Los Angeles two years before *Immortal Beloved* was released. In spite of Kurth's comments, the relationship between Beethoven and Johanna is only suggested in *The Beethovens,* however, and may be nothing more than a deep rumbling sexual attraction. Bernard Rose, who wrote and directed *Immortal Beloved,* seems to have taken that suggestion and amplified it. In *Immortal Beloved* the relationship moves from the Freudian subconscious to full consummation: Johanna becomes the immortal beloved herself, the object of the most intense love affair that Beethoven ever had, and Karl is revealed to be Beethoven's own son, the result of that liaison.

The closing scene of *The Beethovens* further suggests a connection between the two dramas. The will giving Beethoven's capital estate to Johanna, revealed at the end of *The Beethovens,* becomes the premise on which the action of *Immortal Beloved* occurs. In *Immortal Beloved* Schindler sets out to discover the Immortal Beloved's identity so that she may claim her inheritance. This will is pure fiction, however; Beethoven left his estate to Karl. Neither playwright nor screenwriter would have found this in the many Beethoven biographies.

Blake & Beethoven in The Tempest by Stanley Kenneth Freiberg is a long philosophical discourse about art, vision, religion, what the artist hopes to achieve, and the artist's place in society. In it, Beethoven and William Blake curse the fate of the artist and the artist's difficulty living in the real world. Beethoven, who understands the necessity of compromise and how to work the system, is less emphatic on this point than Blake, an idealist whose vision sees through reality to something beyond. Referring to "The Sun at the Eastern Gate," a painting of Blake's, Beethoven observes that the tree that dominates the work is a natural object "that must point toward some meaning":

> BLAKE: I never paint allegory! There is a mighty difference between vision and allegory. Can a tree and a vine point to something other than they are? These are the tree of life and the subtle serpent of experience. They are not objects at all!
> BEETHOVEN: I saw them as a tree and a vine; now they look a bit more like the tree of life and the serpent.
> BLAKE: At first you were trapped by visible forms, not instantly seeing bliss and corruption, God and Satan, Innocence and Experience, Eden and Hell.
> BEETHOVEN: You pass instantly beyond the objects that you paint?
> BLAKE: I do not look at them, but through them.
> BEETHOVEN: How is it possible to not see real and natural objects while painting them?
> BLAKE: Because they are illusion! Dross! Meaningless!

Near the end Beethoven speaks of occasional despair:

> Over the years, I must confess, I've destroyed my share of fiddles—and also a quantity of somewhat larger instruments. But I've always left the fragments behind and gone on. Why do we?
> BLAKE: Because Art is the overflowing of the Holy Spirit and we cannot deny her.

The writers Thomas de Quincey and Emily Brontë also appear in the play, which is interspersed with dialogue from Shakespeare's *The Tempest* and bits of poems from Blake sung by Ariel, a spirit in *The Tempest*. Paintings of Blake appear on the backdrop periodically, and Beethoven's music is heard. Both connect to the dialogue between the actors, who also at times assume the role of characters in *The Tempest*. De Quincy becomes Ferdinand and Brontë Miranda when they perform Beethoven's dream of finding a wife. The dialogue is taken directly from Shakespeare's act 3, scene 1. Later in Freiberg's act 2, when Caliban, Stephano, and Trinculo appear at Blake's exhibition, more lines are taken from Shakespeare, although the dialogue is truncated somewhat.

Blake seems to have some musical sophistication, or at least he resists some of the cliché other dramatists have imposed. Beethoven speaks of the grief of Baroness Dorthea von Ertman, a talented pupil of Beethoven, when she lost a child, how he came to see her and did not say a word, but sat down at the piano in a darkened room "full of shadows" and played. A perfect setup for the *Moonlight* Sonata, it is almost identical to James Fitzpatrick's scene in the 1920 short *Beethoven's Moonlight Sonata*. Unlike Fitzpatrick, however, Freiberg does not choose the *Moonlight* Sonata. Instead, the audience hears the second movement of the Sonata in D op. 28. The pianist Artur Schnabel, in his edition of the sonatas, labels the movement "serious, somewhat gloomy," to which the key of D-minor contributes, but the rhythmic motion, with a walking arpeggio in the bass, and crisp chords on downbeats create more a sense of a slow-duple time scherzo than either a statement of lament or even a funeral march.

Characters in the play assume the personages of others. The second act opens with Emily Brontë as Nelly Dean speaking to Beethoven, who has become Heathcliff. Both Dean and Heathcliff are characters in Brontë's novel *Wuthering Heights*. In the scene Beethoven is not only in the form of Heathcliff but has assumed his persona, that of an insecure, whimpering young man bemoaning his fate. In the second scene a member of the corp de ballet places a mask of Caliban on him and he assumes that persona. Freiberg directs him to continue Caliban's mood even after removing his mask, but his speech, where he angrily insists on his own nobility and upsets the banquet table, could just as well be Beethoven's. Unlike the dream scene about Beethoven finding a wife, this event only roughly parallels Shakespeare's act 3, scene 3, where Ariel disguised as a harpy magically causes the banquet table to vanish. Here there is no magic, just an angry, delusional composer.

Act 3 contains a long scene setup by Blake discussing how his Canterbury sketches were appropriated and taken to another engraver, who profited handsomely from them. Following this is a long scene in which his paintings are shown while Ariel quotes at length from Chaucer in Middle English.

Of all the plays about Beethoven, this one demands the most erudite audience. Freiberg has mixed in references and quotations from Shakespeare, Blake, Chaucer, and Brontë. It is not a stage work that even a typically sophisticated theater audience could follow. It is a play designed for highly literate audiences, and in order to follow the characters as they transform into others, it is probably better read than staged. Indeed, to this day it has never been staged.

Given that Freiberg is a Blake scholar, it is not surprising that Blake more than Beethoven is the central figure in the drama. Nevertheless, Freiberg understands Beethoven and his music. We see both the angry Beethoven and the dedicated artist. We also see the realistic side of Beethoven, his ability to maneuver through the thicket of aristocratic Vienna and multiple publishers to establish and maintain his reputation and his pocketbook. In that sense Beethoven is as much a foil to Blake's more fanciful vision as he is a character in his own right.

Beethoven 'N' Pierrot—the "N" in the title stands for "Napoleon"—takes the viewer on a journey through Beethoven's mind.[12] In the opening scene Beethoven is on his deathbed, lying on a piano, and in the penultimate scene he climbs onto a trapeze and is hoisted into the air all the while conducting the Ninth Symphony. The 105 minutes of the play conform to real time, the jumble of thoughts and hallucinations that run through Beethoven's mind during the roughly two hours that he is lying on his deathbed.

Those two hours are the only thing that is realistic in the play. The rest is a series of brief fantasy scenes in which various characters interact with Beethoven. Many of the characters, such as Napoleon, Beethoven's nephew Karl, Josephine and Therese Brunswick, Maria Erdödy, and Bettina Brentano, are persons out of Beethoven's life. Some, such as Napoleon, are historical figures figuring in his life, although Beethoven never interacted directly with them. Others, such as the Austrian Emperor and Empress, are symbolic characters bearing no relation to any real Austrian royalty. Finally there are Pierrot, the Alabaster Princess, Centaurs, and Mephistopheles, legendary persons or creatures that have a long tradition in European folklore and belief.

The writer and director of the play, Pavel Dobrusky, made clear that it was not a play but a "theater piece" or, if you wish, a "performance piece." It consists of fifty short scenes, most with a page or two of dialogue, a few with more, and some with no dialogue at all. Scene 29, titled "Beethoven Chases Napoleon," reads, "Napoleon enters running across the stage with Beethoven in hot pursuit. Napoleon's arms are trapped by his side by a big crown." While there is some plot progression, the work does not have the typical beginning, middle, and end, or the overriding conflict and character development of a traditional play. Dobrusky referred to Beethoven 'N' Pierrot as "process theater," and while he laid out the script and some of the basic dialogue, he encouraged the actors to improvise during rehearsals, which allowed the piece to evolve until opening night. It is only loosely structured: the fifty modules can be rearranged in any order, and the order they appear in the published script simply represents the order in which it was first performed.

Dance and movement are important elements in the play, partly dictated by the presence of Pierrot himself, who cannot speak. Pierrot was a stock figure from mime and commedia dell'arte, usually portrayed in a loose, white tunic, moonstruck, out of touch, and pining for the love of Columbine, which he never receives. He is the traditional sad clown. There are many dance moments in the play, some integrated into scenes with dialogue and other action, some standing alone. The entire text of scenes 36 and 41 is this:

36. MISSA SOLEMNIS DANCE
Three Dancers—two women, one man—perform the dance, a trio ballet, as Beethoven watches from the voms (vomitories, special passages for the actors).
41. ADAGIO DANCE
Two women Dancers perform an adagio dance. It is quite sensual and slow.

At least one critic called scene 38, where Countess Maria Erdödy, who has become crippled, is lifted up by Pierrot and eventually learns to fly, the high point of the evening. It is also depicted in the photograph on the cover of the published book. The emphasis on dance is not surprising because according to Dobrusky he originally conceived the work as a dance piece, although it was never produced as such.

In some ways the piece may be called theater of the absurd, although not in the Samuel Beckett sense. The Austrian Emperor, who has the emotional maturity of a two-year-old, drags a miniature throne around with him and wants Beethoven to write a mass for his dead elephant, Picola-ninona. The Emperor eventually explodes, literally. Karl is played by a marionette who mostly goes around whining "Mommy." In one scene reminiscent of Monty Python, a giant foot comes down and tries to squash Beethoven. According to Dobrusky, this is the foot of Godot, a reference to Estragon's sore foot and his attempts to remove his boot in Beckett's play *Waiting for Godot*. In another scene Napoleon enters in a miniature tank and then raps a song in praise of himself as he crowns himself emperor. Napoleon becomes more egomaniacal and psychotic as the play progresses.

Some of the longest scenes in the work are between Beethoven and Mephisto, who wants to make a Faustian bargain with him. Mephisto warns Beethoven that if he does not agree, history will judge him "the Barry Manilow of the 1800s." Mephisto continuously changes shapes, appearing as a psychiatrist and later a beautiful young girl who attempts to seduce Beethoven, but each time he is thwarted as Beethoven discovers Mephisto's tail. It is worth remembering that all the characters and events are products of Beethoven's

Pavel Dobrusky
Per-Olav Sørensen

Beethoven'N'Pierrot
A theatrical biography

Beethoven & Pierrot
Eine szenische Biographie

Translated into German by
Ins Deutsche übertragen von
Michaela Fisnar-Keggler

FIGURE 9.1

Beethoven 'N' Pierrot. Pierrot and Maria Erdödy dance.
Courtesy of Pavel Dobrusky, Per-Olav Sørensen,
Barbara Sellers of DCTC, Michaela Fisnar-Keggler,
and Agentura dell'Arte.

thoughts, hallucinations, and fantasies as he lies on his deathbed. In that sense the play is a psychological study, but it is not an overtly psychoanalytic interpretation as in the Sterbas' or Solomon's books. It is more a collective fantasy, a curious blend of central European and American thought: Dobrusky is Czech, although he has lived in the United States for several years, and the actors who contributed considerably through their improvisation are predominantly American. Pierrot and the Alabaster Princess and the depiction of the Emperor seem European, while references to Barry Manilow and Napoleon's rap performance are distinctly American.

The conclusion of the play as first performed could be out of Hollywood or opera buffa. The entire cast gathers on stage and sings the "Ode to Joy" while spiral ribbons and confetti drop down onto the stage. Beethoven from the previous scene continues to conduct while standing atop the piano. It is an emotional and a triumphant moment, symbolic of Beethoven's success in overcoming all odds to create the symphony; its impact here is primarily due to the power of the piece itself.

In spite of the zaniness of the play, or maybe because of it, *Beethoven 'N' Pierrot* was a hit with critics and audiences when it premiered in Denver on December 7, 1995. The *Denver Post* commented that there was "never a dull moment in daring romp through composer's mind," and observed that the audience was left "dumbfounded." Susan Froyd in *Denver Westword* acknowledged that audiences were "confounded" but also "delighted." It was a play for the late twentieth century: confusing, maybe, but quick-paced, outlandish, utterly unpredictable, fantasy-laden, rollicking in oversized humor, and, in the collage of many short fast scenes, never taxing the spectator's attention span by dwelling too long on a single subject. It was a play designed to entertain and to engender curiosity about Beethoven, not to elucidate. There was nothing didactic here. It was twentieth-century collage at its best, from beginning to end.

33 Variations, the most recent play on Beethoven, is unique in several respects. It is an extended examination of a single work of Beethoven, the *Variations on a Waltz by Diabelli*. On the surface this hardly seems promising material to keep today's demanding and restless theater audience engaged for more than two hours, but Moises Kaufman, an experienced and successful playwright, manages to do just that. Of all the Beethoven plays, *33 Variations* has had the most box office success. It premiered in Washington, D.C., on August 24, 2007, and on Broadway on March 10, 2009.

Kaufman became interested in this particular piece of Beethoven while browsing in Tower Records near Lincoln Center. According to Kaufman, "I was looking for an album with Beethoven and the salesperson said to me, 'Why don't you look at the Diabelli Variations?' And then he proceeded to tell me the story of how they were made. As soon as I heard the story, I said, 'That's my next play.'"[13]

In 1819, Anton Diabelli, a music publisher, composed a waltz and sent it to fifty different composers, asking each to contribute a variation on it. He then planned to publish all the variations as a set. Beethoven apparently thought the theme trivial and put it aside. Then for some reason he began to compose variation upon variation, either to demonstrate his contempt for the group process or because he saw a myriad of possibilities in this seemingly banal waltz. After three years he had completed thirty-three variations, and Diabelli was only too eager to publish Beethoven's efforts as an entity in itself. The *33 Variations on a Waltz by Diabelli* today stands as Beethoven's most extended exploration of the variation form, and, along with Johann Sebastian Bach's *Goldberg Variations*, as two of the most profound sets of variations ever written.

Kaufman was intrigued: Why would a composer of Beethoven's stature spend so much time and energy on what originally seemed an inconsequential and unpromising theme? He discovered the work of William Kinderman, who more than any other scholar has explored the *Diabelli Variations*, as they are sometimes called, and not only read his book but spent considerable time discussing it with Kinderman and his wife, Katherine Syer, a musicologist. For dramatic purposes he created a character, a musicologist who becomes obsessed with this question, and is determined to find an answer by examining the sketches. This eventually takes her to the Beethoven-Haus in Bonn, where many of the sketches are found.

Kaufman recognizes his debt to Kinderman and Syer in the play. The musicologist, who is the central figure, is named Katherine, and in order to gain entrée to the Beethoven archives, she must be approved by the librarian Gertie Lansberger, who is the guardian of the sketches. In this she is successful because she has a letter from "Dr. Kinderman." Gertie comments, "Dr. Kinderman must think highly of you. His recommendation is the only reason you're allowed in here."

There are complications: most notably, Katherine is dying from amyotrophic lateral sclerosis (ALS), and she is in a race to discover the answer before her body gives out. As the play develops Katherine and her daughter Clara become closer, and Clara and Mike, Katherine's nurse, development a relationship that begins awkwardly but blossoms into a full-blown romance.

Using a technique similar to Tom Stoppard's *Arcadia*, where stage lighting provides instant juxtaposition between two different times, the play flashes between centuries, showing Beethoven, Diabelli, and Anton Schindler during the time of composition of the variations, as well as Katherine and her contemporaries. The audience sees both Diabelli and Schindler in discourse and in soliloquy as they reveal their own feelings about the waltz. Later in a climactic scene, as Katherine lies ill, Beethoven crosses the time line and speaks directly with her. The jolt caused by the violation of seemingly absolute temporal boundaries is palpable because Kaufman has blurred reality: what is seemingly real may be Katherine's own hallucinatory state.

Much of the success of the play in New York had to do with Jane Fonda in the role of Katherine. It was her first appearance on the Broadway stage in forty-six years. In fact, most reviews of the Broadway production were less about the play than about Fonda. Reviews of the play itself were mixed, but Fonda's presence was sufficient to keep the play running for six weeks. Yet its success cannot be attributed to star power alone. Its Washington premiere and its run at the La Jolla Playhouse in San Diego were both successful without Fonda.

In spite of the several subplots and Katherine's valiant struggle against her illness, Beethoven's composition lies at the core of the play, in more ways than one. As the audience enters the theater it sees a stage with several movable screens in front that contain musical scores. On closer examination these are photographs of Beethoven's sketches, presumably for the *Diabelli Variations*. On the side walls are sets designed to look like library shelves, with several rows of many manuscript boxes lying horizontally. The screens are moved around during the play to establish sub-sets of the stage, and the library shelves are integral to the extensive discussion about Beethoven's music that occurs between Katherine and Gertie in the Beethoven archives. When Katherine and Gertie discuss a particular sketch, it is projected on the back wall of the stage, allowing the audience, at least those who can read music, an immediate sense of the excitement of historical discovery. The sets were designed by Derek McLane and used with some "variation" throughout all the productions.

One of the more effective stage decisions was to employ a live pianist rather than pre-recorded music. Whenever a variation is discussed, the pianist on stage plays the specific passage. This brings a presence to the music that heightens the dramatic importance of the piece and the sketches. As Kaufman says, the pianist playing the variations and the sketches are characters in the play. The importance of the sketches are stressed again and again, even romanticized. Katherine claims that they are more important than the finished product because "they are closer to the original inspiration of the artist." The implication is that art comes to the creator in a single inspiration. Through the sketches Beethoven comes to life and he and Katherine develop an intimacy.

FIGURE 9.2

The set of *33 Variations*, showing the library atmosphere
and pages of Beethoven sketches. Katherine and
Gertie are on the left, Clara and Mike on the right.
Courtesy of Derek McLane and Shoko Kambara.

As Katherine and Gertie examine the sketches in a long scene, they examine
the early sketches with the sketches projected and the pianist playing them
at the same time. Katherine says, "I feel like I'm looking over his shoulder as
he's composing." Later Gertie and Katherine are at a train station, and when
Katherine discovers that Gertie is reading a book on Mozart she asks, "Don't
you feel like you're cheating on Beethoven?" The intimacy reaches a climax
when Beethoven actually visits Katherine on her sickbed.

Kaufman organized the play around three parallels: illness, family relationships, and obsession. Katherine's illness is paralleled with Beethoven's.
Katherine is the more serious—ALS is virtually always fatal—but Beethoven
suffers in two ways: his deafness, which was permanent, and which by the
time of the *Diabelli Variations* was total, and a second, immediate illness that
occurred in the years between 1819 and 1822, which was not fatal but serious
enough to incapacitate him for a time. Documentation is scant about Beetho-

ven's medical situation, but he apparently suffered from rheumatic fever and an attack of jaundice in 1820–1821.[14] His creative production dropped precipitously and even most of the conversation books from the period have disappeared.

Katherine has to deal with her never-satisfactory relationship with her daughter and the mutual distance they have kept from each other, and Beethoven with the even less satisfactory relationship with his nephew Karl and his sister-in-law Johanna. Beethoven fought viciously both in and out of court to have complete guardian rights to Karl and to keep him from seeing his mother, whom he regarded as immoral and unfit. It was a long saga that began when Beethoven's brother Kasper Carl died in 1812, and did not end until Beethoven softened his stubbornness on his deathbed in 1827.

Obsession is a principal theme in this play. Kaufman specifically stated as much in an interview.[15] Beethoven was obsessed with Diabelli's waltz; over a period of three years he kept returning to it and adding more variations, after first dismissing it as unworthy of attention. Katherine was obsessed with discovering why Beethoven was obsessed, to the point of undertaking a trip to Germany in spite of her deteriorating health, and of maintaining her work to the very end.

How obsessed was Beethoven with this waltz? Kinderman discovered that he worked on it for at least three years. Given that it was interrupted with his illness, we don't know exactly how long he worked on it and how consistently he worked on it when he did. Was it something that occupied his every waking moment, as true obsession does? Was it something he would come back to every now and then, and add a variation or improvise around it? The waltz did hold some fascination to Beethoven, but was it musical or competitive? It was not unusual for Beethoven to get a musical idea in his head and pursue it doggedly, often through more than one piece. The first sketches for the Ninth Symphony appear some ten years before the work itself, and Schiller's "Ode to Joy" interested him for at least thirty years before it came to fruition in the finale. The famous eight notes that make up the principal theme of the *Grosse Fuge* op. 133 also appear in the String Quartet op. 132, and became something of a leitmotif of his final three years. What has been called the Neapolitan incident, a motivic statement followed by its repetition a half-step higher, is found in several Beethoven pieces—the *Appassionata* Sonata op. 57 and the string quartets, op. 59, no. 2 and op. 95. Often Beethoven would latch onto a musical idea and work and rework it. Katherine and Kinderman are right about Diabelli's waltz in one respect: Beethoven was determined to take this theme and wring it dry, to explore every musical possibility it contained.

It may be better to refer to dedication rather than obsession in this case. Obsession implies an overwhelming interest or desire that is irrational. Katherine's dedication may be excessive, but it has a rational quality to it. In that regard Kaufman's choice of Beethoven is important. Katherine's determination to discover the secret of the *Diabelli Variations* must seem rational for the play to work. Beethoven is probably the only composer that the American public would deem of sufficient importance for one to literally give one's life for. Were it Mendelssohn or Haydn, her fortitude in the face of a fatal illness, her willingness to alienate her family, would seem at best questionable. But because of Beethoven's stature and image in American society, her pursuit does not seem unreasonable, and consequently Kaufman need not spend time in the play establishing a justification for her decisions.[16]

Why Beethoven chose to spend so much time on Diabelli's waltz is a puzzle that can be answered only by speculation. Of course it is possible that Beethoven saw this as an opportunity to reestablish his reputation. Diabelli had contacted most of the well-known composers of the age. Beethoven was feeling neglected, a relic that time has passed by. Vienna was more interested in the melodious, tuneful operas of Rossini than the heavy, somber style of Beethoven. And with few exceptions, the big pieces upon which Beethoven's reputation rested were almost a decade in the past. With Diabelli's entrée, Beethoven, in his best testosterone-competitive mode, had the opportunity to show all the younger upstarts just what he was still capable of doing.

That is not the Beethoven of Kaufman's play, however. The play is also about transcendence and transformation, a view of Beethoven that persists in our society today. Clara reads Katherine's final paper to an important musicological conference, as she announces her mother died three weeks before. In the paper Katherine rejects the standard perceived reason that Beethoven "wanted to demonstrate how he could transform the most prosaic piece of music into an epic work of splendid beauty." Her conclusion: Beethoven saw the waltz not as a trivial composition, but as a beer-hall piece people danced to. Beethoven's final variation is a minuet. He has thus transformed the beer-hall waltz into an aristocratic eighteenth-century court dance. The play concludes not with the dramatic reading of Katherine's paper but with the whole cast dancing the minuet.

33 Variations has striking parallels to Kennedy's *She Talks to Beethoven*. In both plays, the heroine deals with an infirmity and in both Beethoven visits them to support them in their struggles. In both cases Beethoven is portrayed as sympathetic and helpful, and in both cases the women hold a fascination with Beethoven. And yet the situations could not be more different: Suzanne

Alexander's illness is never specified in Kennedy's play, and Kennedy uses it as a metaphor. Suzanne is concerned particularly with the disappearance of her husband; Beethoven is used both to comfort her and as a conduit through which David can communicate with her. Katherine, in 33 *Variations*, is a musicologist who has both a professional interest in and a fascination with Beethoven's music, in particular the *Diabelli Variations*. As she investigates the piece she uncovers parallels between Beethoven's life and her own, particularly with illness. Katherine's situation is of course far worse than Beethoven's. ALS is a disease for which the only prognosis is steady deterioration, loss of muscular control, and death, all while the mind remains intact, able to record what is happening to the body.

Beethoven thus becomes not only a source of strength for both women but a real presence, a time-crossing psychological image, in which he is more than an inspiring historical figure. He is there and both women can communicate with him directly. In both plays we anticipate that direct interaction will occur, and when it comes it creates a moment of high drama. Is it more, however, a view of the female psyche, an experience akin to that of Margaret Fuller, who, while not ill but nevertheless in a trying time emotionally, poured her heart out to Beethoven in a private letter after hearing his Seventh Symphony?

The parallels are there; what they mean is another question. All three women were enamored with his music, and through it felt his physical presence as something real, powerful, and ultimately comforting. Possibly they recognize that Beethoven has the capacity to hear without the sense of hearing—that he listens so deeply that he hears what hasn't been said. Beethoven is hearing sound in his head that hasn't been sounded. They recognize Beethoven's ability to hear and understand that which is inaudible. Verbalization is thus informed by his ability to listen deeply, and when he speaks it is with a depth of understanding that a lot of people with normal hearing don't achieve. It is the difference between hearing what people say and what people are saying. Deprived of the former, Beethoven was forced to hear at a different level.[17]

Beethoven in the theater occupies an entirely different cultural space than Beethoven in films. Beethoven films are aimed at a broad, general audience, whereas with the exception of *Beethoven's Tenth* and possibly *The Beethovens*, plays featuring Beethoven are aimed at a much more elite, sophisticated audience. They are experimental, complex, and best understood by those with some familiarity with both Beethoven's music and persona. They are not plays that would become successful films, as *Amadeus* was, but the image of Beethoven they present shares many features with the Beethoven of film.

PART FOUR

Beyond Classicism: Beethoven in
American Society & Culture

10

"Beethoven Was Black"

Why Does It Matter?

*A*s a young man on the streets in Roxbury, Massachusetts, and Harlem, New York, Malcolm Little pursued a number of illegal activities, including gambling, drug and prostitution rings, and burglary. The burglary attempt landed him in the Massachusetts State Prison in 1946, an event that became the turning point in his life. He read copiously in the prison library, and through his brother Reginald was converted to the Nation of Islam, a religious organization that advocated a separate state for American blacks. Following his release in 1952 he rejected his "slave name," Little, in favor of X and became Malcolm X. He quickly distinguished himself as an important spokesman for the NOI, and by the early 1960s his influence was second only to that of Elijah Muhammad, the longtime leader of the movement.

Malcolm X broke with the Nation of Islam in 1963 and adopted a more moderate tone regarding racial relations in the short remaining years of his life, but before he did he gave a controversial interview that appeared in the May 1963 issue of *Playboy*.[1] In it he asserted that Western history as written by Western historians reflected a "history-whitening process," in which black accomplishments were either left out or blacks who succeeded "had gotten whitened" in the historical record. He cited a long list of Western historical figures who were black, including Jesus Christ, Columbus, and Beethoven.

Four years later, on April 19, 1967, Stokely Carmichael addressed the predominantly black Garfield High School in Seattle, Washington. Carmichael had been a founder of the Student Nonviolent Coordinating Committee (SNCC), and later became a leader in the more radical organization the Black Panthers. The principal point in his address was the same as Malcolm X's in the interview, that virtually all important accomplishments of Western culture either came from Africa or were achieved by people of African descent, that white culture has stolen the black legacy and claimed it as its own. His rhetoric was purposely inflammatory and his reference to Beethoven was specific and pointed:

> The problem is that our culture is not legitimatized. They have made us ashamed of it. Forget it! They have never had any culture! They have always stolen ours. That's a fact. The blues ain't theirs. Come on, be serious! Ha! Be serious. Don't let them get away with that. The Blues . . . We might let them get away with Bach. Beethoven was black. They won't tell you that in school. He was a Spanish Moor—black as you and I, but they don't tell us that. It's calculated, it is calculated.[2]

Calls for black power, black pride, and black nationalism were heard frequently in the 1960s, and Malcolm X and Stokely Carmichael were important voices in the world of black radicalism. Yet among the many historical figures whose African heritage was asserted, why was Beethoven so embraced by the Black Power movement? Why was a German composer who epitomized the Western European classical canon so important to their argument? Carmichael was willing to concede Bach, but Beethoven seems to have been an important symbol to the black community. How did this come about and what did he signify?

Both the historical evidence about Beethoven's ethnicity and the broader one of the validity of Afrocentrist assertions about Western culture have been discussed thoroughly in the literature.[3] How claims about Beethoven arose and the nature of the Afrocentrist argument must be considered, but the important question is why his ethnicity matters in connection with American society, and particularly in the 1960s and 1970s among black nationalists and separatists such as Malcolm X and Stokely Carmichael. In other words, how and why within 1960s American culture did it advantage certain groups to claim that Beethoven was black?

The notion that Beethoven had an African heritage was voiced as early as 1907 by the African British composer Samuel Coleridge-Taylor. Coleridge-Taylor based his theory on Beethoven's appearance, his friendship with the mulatto violinist George Polgreen Bridgetower, and, according to his biographer Berwick Sayers, "many little points in his character." Sayers never elaborated on what those traits were, but he did refer to a "remarkable likeness," "in brow and the outlines in general expression," between Coleridge-Taylor and Beethoven. Coleridge-Taylor was of mixed race, with an African father and an English mother. Although Coleridge-Taylor was English, he traveled in the United States and was familiar with African American writers, such as W. E. B. Du Bois and Frederick Douglass. Regarding Beethoven's appearance he commented, "I think that if the greatest of all musicians were alive today, he would find it somewhat difficult, if not absolutely impossible, to obtain hotel accommodation in certain American cities."[4]

Coleridge-Taylor's remark underscores his understanding that he himself could not get a hotel room in the Jim Crow–era South. That he drew significance from Beethoven being a friend of Bridgetower seems less compelling than the statement about Beethoven's appearance, but the logic, that because Beethoven befriended a black he must have been black himself, may not have been an unreasonable conclusion for a British subject of African descent who had witnessed the racism of the United States in the early twentieth century.

There is little additional reference in print to the idea that Beethoven was black until the 1940s, when Joel A. Rogers gave it its most extended argument, one that laid the basis for the claim that many other writers and speakers adopted. Rogers (1868–1963) was a native of Jamaica who immigrated to the United States in 1906. He worked for a time as a Pullman porter and then became a journalist in the 1920s. He considered his real life's work, however, to refute racist beliefs common in the early twentieth century, particularly those that held blacks to be inferior. An autodidactic scholar, Rogers sought through extensive research to counter what he considered a Eurocentric bias in Western writings and to highlight the achievements of people of African ancestry. His first book, a novel, consisted of a dialogue between a black Pullman porter and a bigoted politician-passenger on the subject of race. In the end, the erudite porter convinces the politician, identified only as a senator from Oklahoma, of the error of his views. One wonders if such a conversation ever took place, and if it did whether it actually had such a happy ending. In several later books Rogers sought to demonstrate that many important figures in European history had African roots. This was especially true of the ancient world, in which he considered Egyptians themselves to be "Negroid." He identified a number of prominent modern figures, including Aleksandr Pushkin, Alexandre Dumas, Charlotte Sophia of the British Royal Family, five American presidents, and Beethoven, all of whom according to Rogers had some African blood in them.

Rogers's case for Beethoven appeared in several of his books, but the most detailed version was in his three-volume work *Sex and Race*.[5] He based his conclusions on two principal arguments: the geographic origins of Beethoven's family and Beethoven's appearance. The latter was especially important to Rogers, who relied heavily on visual sources, either drawings or paintings of Beethoven, and on reports from Beethoven's contemporaries about how he looked. Rogers addressed that point in two separate volumes of *Sex and Race*: in the first he juxtaposed a photograph of the African American composer Clarence Cameron White and an engraving of Beethoven by Blasius Hofel (Figure 10.1).

In the two images Beethoven is clearly seen as darker, and his hair, long and out of control, appears especially curly. Hofel's engraving was reproduced frequently in Beethoven's time and exists in various shades of light, darkness, and color. The Beethoven-Haus in Bonn has put six versions online and the chiaroscuric variety can easily be seen.[6] The engraving was originally taken from an 1814 pencil drawing by Louis Letronne, but Hofel, feeling that the drawing was not sufficiently accurate, revised it in a further sitting with Beethoven.[7] Because Hofel used Letronne's sketch only as a starting place and completed his image from life, Letronne's sketch is of less-than-critical importance to the ethnic issue. Beethoven was quite pleased with Hofel's engraving and sent copies of it to several of his old friends.

Rogers recognized that the tint of an engraving does not always correlate to the color of the subject, and that different versions of this print vary in shade. He justified his conclusion based not just on the color of the image but rather the effect the color has on enhancing other visual features: "A dark tint, however, will bring out Negroid features, if there are any, as they do in this picture of Beethoven—a reason, perhaps, why this one is often reproduced in a shade much lighter than the original."[8]

To support his argument Rogers quoted numerous contemporaries who described Beethoven's appearance: Franz Grillparzer, "dark"; Bettina von Arnim, "brown"; Weber, "dark red"; Schindler, "red and brown"; Rellstab, "brownish"; Gelinek, "short, ugly, dark"; Ludwig Fischer, "rounded nose, black-brownish complexion"; and Carl Czerny, "his beard—he had not shaved for several days—made the lower part of his already brown face still darker."[9] He then quoted from various Beethoven biographers and memoirists. Among them he cited

FIGURE 10.1

From Joel Rogers, *Sex and Race,* a comparison of Beethoven
and the African American composer Clarence Cameron White.

Carpani's story of Prince Esterhazy referring to Haydn on first meeting him
as a "Blackamoor" because of his dark color, and then Thayer's comment that
Beethoven "had even more of the Moor in his features than his master."[10] Rogers
also refers to Frederick Hertz's statement that "one may easily trace in Beethoven slightly Negroid traits," and Emil Ludwig's observation that he was so
dark that he was dubbed "Spagnol," because according to Rogers he "was certain that there was a mixture of Spanish blood in this half-Netherlander."[11]

The second pillar of Rogers's argument, regarding Beethoven's family background, may be summarized as follows: Beethoven's family was from what is
now Belgium, a fact on which virtually all scholars agree. Belgium, or Flanders as it was known, was controlled by Spain in the sixteenth and seventeenth
centuries, and in the Spanish army were many Moors. Rogers cites Theophile
Gautier, who describes dark-skinned and dark-haired Belgians as "a second
race which the soldiers of the Spanish Duke of Alva have sown between Brus-

sels and Cambrai."[12] Thus through the Spanish military occupation, Moorish blood could easily have slipped into Beethoven's family, as it did for many Flemish.

Rogers produced no documents to prove that Beethoven had Moorish ancestors, and it should be stressed that he asserted only that it is a reasonable possibility. Yet beyond evidentiary considerations his contention raises thorny questions about racial definitions, which themselves are as much cultural as biological. What determines someone's racial or ethnic composition has also been a legal and especially a political issue, affected as much by hegemonic bias as by any scientific evidence. For instance, what defined someone as black in twentieth-century America and what defined someone as black in nineteenth-century France are not the same.[13] Within Africa itself, should a distinction be made between northern (Mediterranean) and sub-Saharan Africans? Is it legitimate to speak of all Africans as one race? These questions do not even address the broader one, whether the term itself has any biological meaning, and how it differs from ethnicity. Rogers's point that somewhere in Beethoven's background there may have been Moorish or even, as others have suggested, Sephardic blood can never be fully denied, but barring advances in DNA testing or some as yet unknown scientific methodology, they can probably never be completely resolved. Even should DNA testing become much more precise about pinpointing ancestry, given the absence of consensus on what defines race or ethnicity the question will almost certainly remain open.

Thus, in this case, advocacy for a particular position and its social impact assume a life unto themselves, and consequently the very assertion that Beethoven was black and the acceptance of this idea within a social group become the more important historical issue. Even though Rogers marshaled considerable source material to support his claim, the fact that he planted the belief that Beethoven was black in the African American community was more important than whether his arguments met a rigorous standard of scientific evidence. The existence of that belief and its social consequences are the subjects under consideration here. This distinction can also be framed another way. On first hearing the assertion that Beethoven was black, many people respond, "Is that true?" The more important question is, "Why does it matter?"

Particularly in the 1960s, 1970s, and 1980s, there was no doubt in many segments of the black community that Beethoven at the very least had some black blood. Patricia Williams, writing in 1991, claimed that "blacks have been teaching white people that Beethoven was black for over one hundred years now." Black musicians who grew up in the 1960s and 1970s remember hearing about it, as did many others in the black community. Several events in the late 1960s did much to spread this belief beyond black culture, however.

FIGURE 10.2

Rolling Stone drawing of Beethoven made to look black.

Sometime in 1968 or 1969, Doug Cass, a disc jockey at KDIA, the top-rated soul station in San Francisco, began to recite "Beethoven was black" constantly between recordings, almost as a mantra. In reaction, mail poured in from all over the country, from clergy, from supportive blacks, from outraged whites, and from scholars. Spurred by the maelstrom he had stirred, Cass formed "Beethoven was Black, Inc.," with the intention of marketing educational materials, bumper stickers, and sweatshirts.[14] Talk shows in both San Francisco and Los Angeles debated the question. Soul Publications featured a story on this phenomenon in a fan magazine. The International issue of *Life* magazine ran a story in its May 1969 issue. The *Rolling Stone* issue of July 14, 1969, contained a story titled "Beethoven Was Black and Proud" with a line drawing of Beethoven that made him look African American.

This publicity caught the attention of Charles M. Schulz, who incorporated it into his *Peanuts* comic strip on July 7, 1969.

While almost everyone who weighed in on the issue cited Rogers as their principal source, if they cited a source at all, most went from Rogers's qualified conclusion to a definite assertion, as Carmichael did. Malcolm X was even more specific: "Well, Hannibal, the most successful general that ever lived, was a black man. So was Beethoven; Beethoven's father was one of the blackamoors that hired themselves out in Europe as professional soldiers." Others, when confronted with evidence about Beethoven's paternal ancestry, have stated that his mother was a Moor or from the Caribbean.[15]

Although the issue of a possible African heritage for Beethoven crested in the 1960s and 1970s, it did not disappear. In 1991 Molefi Asante referred to "that great Negro composer Beethoven." In 1990 Detroit Piston power forward John Salley was asked to recite "Casey at the Bat" with the Detroit Symphony. When asked about appearing with a symphony, he laughed, "Hey, Beethoven was black." The absence of records about Beethoven's maternal ancestry was used as proof of his African ancestry, the argument running that the records disappeared because the Nazis did not want the truth known.[16] And in the early twenty-first century, the web is filled with claims, often providing striking fictitious details, such as the following: "People whom [sic] specialise in Beethoven all agreed that he was Black. Women whom have had sex with him say that he was of Blackish-Brown complexion. . . . The most reputable Beethoven historian said that he was Black. If Alexander W. Thayer, 'perhaps the foremost authority on Beethoven' isn't 'anybody special,' then please tell us which historian, who specialises in Beethoven, is somebody special."[17] In another case this particular syllogism appeared on the web:

> Beethoven was indeed black. We can derive this through the simple formula:
>
> 1. Only oppressed people make great music.
> 2. Beethoven had no other means of being oppressed.
> 3. Beethoven made great music.
>
> ∴. Beethoven was black.[18]

One reads the above syllogism and asks, is this serious or ironic? While Wilson Moses and Marcus Garvey, both prominent black intellectuals, believe there is considerable irony, even sarcasm within the black community over the issues of Beethoven and of racial identification, the overall tone of the many claims suggest that indeed most writers and bloggers are serious.[19] In many

FIGURE 10.3

Peanuts comic strip. 2010 Peanuts Worldwide LLC.

such arguments any trace of Rogers's nuance is gone; what was a possibility has become a certainty. Beethoven *was* black.

The question of Beethoven's racial mix came to a head at Stanford University in 1988, in what has been called the Ujamaa House incident. It merits a close look for several reasons. It received national publicity; Beethoven's ethnicity was at the heart of the situation; it raised fundamental questions about racial perceptions and their impact on different ethnic and social groups; and it had aesthetic ramifications in relation to Beethoven's music.

Because of the investigation that Stanford undertook about the incident, a detailed record of the principals' feelings and actions was preserved. The Ujamaa House was a black culture–theme residence hall at Stanford University. At the time it housed sixty-five black and sixty-two nonblack students.

On September 29, 1988, several students there were having a heated conversation about a number of racial and cultural issues. Three students in particular, identified only under fictitious names—Fred and Alex, who were white, and QC, who was black—then got into an argument about music.[20] QC argued that "all music is black," and when questioned about Beethoven asserted that Beethoven was a mulatto. Fred was disturbed by the assertion. The next night, after Fred and Alex had been drinking, they found a poster of Beethoven advertising the Stanford Symphony, transformed it into a crude black caricature with kinky hair, big lips, and red eyes, and posted it outside QC's room.

Black students were outraged. QC was "flabbergasted." Rebecca, a resident assistant at the house, called it "hateful, shocking." Another, Baldwin, said, "The Afro was a black stereotype. To me the red eyes had an evil connotation. No human being has eyes like that. The whole being looked very evil—devilish."[21] Fred and Alex eventually admitted defacing the Beethoven poster and, after much discussion among the resident staff, they agreed to address a meeting of the entire Ujamaa House. It did not go well. Racial tensions were high, and the meeting ended in chaos, with QC so upset that he had to be literally carried out of the room.

Of particular interest is Fred's explanation about his motivations and his own background. He was from Canada and had gone to school in England. His family was Jewish, and part of the ritual at his English school was for older students to tease new ones about their weaknesses, the object being for them to come to terms with them. When Fred said his was considered being Jewish, he had to endure many stereotypical remarks about his religion. Eventually he learned to "see the humor as a release." Fred also said that not being from the United States, he was unaware of the depth of racial feelings, and that he had done the poster in the same spirit as he had been teased in England. He was bothered by "all this emphasis on race, on blackness," and wanted to send a message: "Why can't we just all be human—I think it denies one's humanity to be racial."

Yet Fred's reaction to race seems at odds with his reaction to Beethoven. Some time after the original discussion in the Ujamaa House that had triggered the poster incident, another student had shown Fred a book that dis-

---

FIGURE 10.4 FACING

Poster defaced as a prank by
students at the Ujamaa House,
Stanford University.

Uncle Ludwig wants You!

to audition for the Stanford Symphony Orchestra and Chamber Orchestra

**Monday and Tuesday
September 26 and 27**

Come by Braun Music Center to sign up.
Call 725-2694 for information.

cussed Beethoven's ethnic background.[22] It convinced Fred that Beethoven was indeed black and, according to reports at the Ujamaa House meeting, he said that "before [he] knew Beethoven was black he had had a certain image of Beethoven and hearing he was black changed his perception of Beethoven and made him see Beethoven as the person he drew in the picture." Thus even though Fred believed that race was not an important issue, the idea that Beethoven was black caused him to see Beethoven in terms of crude black stereotypes. Since Beethoven and his music are so often conflated, by implication this may have affected the way Fred heard Beethoven after that, although he did not state so.

The Stanford Disciplinary Board eventually decided against serious disciplinary action for the students, a decision based on a finding of no injury to QC, and of Fred's First Amendment rights. The incident, however, had several ramifications: legal ones regarding first amendment rights and the nature and limits of injury, aesthetic ones regarding how the racial construction of Beethoven affects the perception of his music, and finally semantic ones, particularly on the nature and definition of race.

Although the issue never came before a court of law, and even though Stanford as a private university was immune from First Amendment issues, the incident became a hot topic in legal scholarship. In separate books, Patricia Williams and Richard A. Posner addressed the issue in detail. For Posner the legal implications were his principal concern, but he also investigated the Beethoven literature to determine if indeed it could be demonstrated that Beethoven was black. He used the analogy of Beethoven's racial makeup to the breed of his cat: "Of course the student may simply have been incredulous that Beethoven had a black ancestor, just as I would be incredulous to discover that my cat was Siamese, though I know that some cats are. The student may not have been a racist in any illuminating sense, although the defacing of the poster was, at the least, insensitive."[23]

For Williams, the case was more than a legal abstraction; it was also personal. While she is the James H. Dohr Professor of Law at Columbia University, she is also an African American woman, which she readily admits affected her sense of the case. She took affront at the finding of no injury, arguing that by limiting the issue to the three students involved, the Stanford Disciplinary Board did not take into account the broader question of "extrinsic" injury to the Stanford community, and particularly to the "group identity of blacks." She also thought that First Amendment rights must be weighed against forms of (verbal) abuse "that may lurk behind the 'defense' of free speech."[24]

Clark Freshman, reviewing Posner's study in the *Columbia Law Review,* called attention to a significant semantic shift in Posner's argument from what

Williams stated: Fred was not "incredulous" as Posner concluded but found the idea "preposterous," the term Williams, who had examined the Stanford report, used. There is considerable irony in this legal argument: we have three attorneys arguing over the semantics of two words, but neither word is used in the original report. It is also unclear to what extent a determination of Beethoven's ancestry would have upon the legal issues surrounding the two students actions. While I am not qualified to discuss the legal intricacies and implications of this issue, what is of interest is the amount of attention legal scholars devoted to this case. Following the lead of Posner and Williams, other attorneys discussed it in the *Duke Law Journal*, the *California Law Review*, the *Michigan Law Review*, the *University of Pennsylvania Law Review* as well as assorted books.[25]

Williams and other legal scholars who were concerned about the racist aspects of the incident had no doubt about Beethoven's own heritage. Richard Delgado, writing about it in 1997, observed that "the black students correctly maintained that he was a mulatto." In the flow of his legal argument about constitutional free speech and whether hate speech should be governed, this statement seems to slip in as an established fact. Later, possibly after a lengthy exchange on the legal issues with Steven G. Gey in the *University of Pennsylvania Law Review*, Delgado decided to drop the assertion. In 2004 he referred to the Stanford incident without taking sides on the historical question: "At a top-flight private university in 1988, some students argued over whether the composer Ludwig van Beethoven was mulatto."[26]

Beyond the legal questions, the other issues that this incident raises need to be placed in an even broader context, that of Afrocentrism and Black Power, both of which came to prominence in the 1960s. The two are closely related. The basic premises of Afrocentrism are that African Americans as well as African Europeans have a rich cultural heritage derived from Africa, and that the Eurocentric bias of Western culture has prevented much of this heritage from receiving the recognition that it deserves. The term Afrocentrism itself was probably first used by W. E. B. Du Bois in 1961 or 1962 and was brought to prominence by Molefi Asante, one of the strongest advocates of the theory in the 1980s.[27] The basic idea, however, is much older and can be traced back at least to the early nineteenth century.

For many writers, Egypt lies at the heart of the Afrocentrist argument, although some scholars distinguish between Egyptocentrism and Afrocentrism.[28] Rogers himself stressed the importance of Egypt as the gateway through which African culture passed to Europe. He and many others believed that Egyptian culture was derived from sub-Saharan African culture, particularly Ethiopian, and that many of the pharaohs had strong Negroid traits. This theme far predates Rogers and may be found in the nineteenth-century writings of Samuel Ringgold Ward, William Wells Brown, and Frederick Douglass.[29] It was later elaborated in particular by Martin Bernal in his book *Black Athena: The Afroasiatic Roots of Classical Civilization*. The work elicited an impassioned response, especially from Mary Lefkowitz in her book *Not Out of Egypt: How "Afrocentrism" Became an Excuse to Teach Myth as History*.[30] Subsequent reviews and references confirm just how controversial this idea is.

Afrocentrism is hardly a monolithic movement, as it comes in many varieties and degrees, as several scholars have elucidated. Gerald Early wrote of a "range of ideas and stances" that characterize Afrocentrism, from those that are "demagogic and even fascist or racist in their assertion" to others that are more "nuance[d]" and "thoughtful."[31] Robert Elliot Fox distinguished between soft and hard Afrocentrism. Soft means that blacks have a rich African cultural heritage that remains an important part of African American culture. Hard Afrocentrism means that most (for some, all) of Europe's accomplishments came from Africa, and their African origins or sources were purposely suppressed by whites. Soft Afrocentrism, according to Fox, merges with multiculturalism; hard Afrocentrism "is a mirror image of Eurocentrism."[32] Within Fox's binary division, of course, there are many further distinctions, which the historian Wilson Moses has categorized.[33]

Few would deny the fundamental assertion of soft Afrocentrism, but it will not be explored here. On the other hand, hard Afrocentrism has generated considerable controversy, particularly in its form that attributes virtually all the advances in Western civilization to Africa. Hard Afrocentrism relates directly to the type of radicalism that prevailed in the 1960s and was advocated by Malcolm X and Stokely Carmichael. Since it was within that context that the Beethoven-was-black idea took root, most of the discussion here is about this assertion in relation to hard Afrocentrism.

Earlier writers, such as Du Bois, had touched on the debt that Europeans owe to Africans, mainly through Egypt, but the work that most directly articulated the position of hard Afrocentrism was George James's *Stolen Legacy*, published in 1954.[34] James claimed that virtually all Western culture was "stolen" from Africa. With its mixture of historical argument, mystical tone, and anger at the irrationality of southern race laws, *Stolen Legacy* became "the Bible of a small coterie of African Americans, especially young males on the campuses of urban, working-class colleges."[35]

As the civil rights movement gained momentum in the 1960s, books such as *Stolen Legacy* began to have an impact, and partly in response a group of young blacks began to question the integrationist goals of leaders such as

Martin Luther King. They felt that the only way African Americans could enhance their position in the dominant American culture was to create a separate strong economic and cultural base within the black community. Some began to champion the phrase "Black Power" in 1966.[36] Afrocentrism, Black Power, black nationalism, and black separatism were not synonymous, and as movements each had different goals and means. They were all related in at least one sense, however: each in its own way stressed African American political and economic independence within the black community, with an emphasis upon African culture as a unifying as well as a distinguishing element. Each wished to distance African Americans from the dominant white culture. In the 1960s a number of different organizations embraced these principles in various ways: the Nation of Islam, US Organization, the Congress of Racial Equality, the Student Non-Violent Coordinating Committee, and the Black Panthers among them. The political goals, methods, and evolution of these groups have been discussed extensively in the literature, and the complexities of their activities and their relative successes resist easy summarization.[37] Of importance in relation to Beethoven is the cultural dimension, which, as Austin Algemon has observed, has received less attention than might be expected.[38]

The most concrete result of the cultural emphasis within the framework of Black Power was the Black Arts Movement (BAM), which from the beginning was closely aligned with theater. In contrast to Afrocentrism, whose legacy can be traced back at least two centuries, the Black Arts Movement has been given a more precise and concrete origin, in New York in 1965, although recent scholarship has questioned that assertion. Rather than a monolithic movement with a single beginning, some scholars view it more as an outgrowth of developments of the 1930s and 1940s, with many regional variations. According to James Edward Smethurst, it had "no real center."[39]

Other scholars, while acknowledging its grassroots beginning, point to the founding of the Black Arts Repertoire Theatre School (BART/S) in New York in the spring of 1965 as the catalyst from which a national movement sprang.[40] Among the several founders of BART/S, the most important was LeRoi Jones, later known as Amiri Baraka. At a minimum this group had a major impact because of its relatively early founding within the framework of the rise of Black Power, the influence of Jones in the black nationalist movement, and the theoretical writing of Larry Neal, poet, playwright, literary writer, editor, and associate of Baraka. By 1965 Jones had become a controversial but recognized playwright, and his play *The Toilet* had just completed a run off Broadway. Jones referenced the BART/S as early as February 10 at a Village Vanguard event and made a more formal announcement about it on February 23. By

May 30 the school had announced instruction in playwriting, poetry, painting, music, dancing, acting, remedial reading, mathematics, psychology of migration, the social history of the West, and cultural philosophy. Theater was still the focus of the organization, and during the summer BART/S presented a number of street events, including poetry readings, lectures, jazz concerts, and plays. This activity was made possible by a grant from the Office of Educational Opportunity through HARYOU-ACT, the organization formed from the merger of the Harlem Youth Opportunities Unlimited and the Associated Community Teams, both social activist organizations. The latter was sponsored by Adam Clayton Powell, then the congressman from Harlem. BART/S received $44,000 to present "cultural field demonstrations."

A lack of funding after the OEO summer grant had ended and "internal problems" caused the theater to close sometime in late 1965. The precise date is difficult to determine; Baraka himself refused to divulge much information to the press when interviewed. Yet the idea of a black nationalist arts movement had gained attention, and soon BAM groups sprang up throughout the country, in Detroit, Philadelphia, Jersey City, New Orleans, Los Angeles, and Washington, D.C., as well as in several colleges and universities.[41] The movement flourished for approximately ten years until ideological drifts, internal dissension, new external issues, and a softening of many blacks' radical positions weakened the radical focus of the movement. These positions had softened due to assimilation and, according to Kaluma ya Salaam, who has written extensively about the Black Arts Movement, "capitalist co-option." Even Baraka later rejected the Black Power movement, considering it racist.[42] This development was part of a broader movement away from black nationalism in general. The more radical groups, such as the Black Panthers, had been driven underground or "rendered ineffective" by enhanced powers the Nixon administration granted to the FBI's counter-intelligence program, and blacks were gaining power within the American political system. According to sociologist Manning Marable, 3,499 black men and women held political office in the United States by 1975, including 18 members of Congress, 281 members of state legislatures, and 135 mayors. This compared with approximately 100 black elected officials in 1964. In Congress itself, the Congressional Black Caucus, founded in 1969, gave powerful voice to black interests.[43]

While Baraka was the acknowledged driving force behind BART/S, Larry Neal gave it its theoretical manifesto. In an article written in 1968, he makes clear the close connection that BAM had with the Black Power movement, calling Black Art "the aesthetic and spiritual sister of the Black Power concept." He refers to the "Black aesthetic," whose motive "is the destruction of the white thing, the destruction of white ideas, and white ways of looking at the world." "We must destroy Faulkner, dick, jane, and other perpetuators of evil."[44] He calls the Harlem Renaissance of the 1920s a failure, because "it did not address itself of the mythology and the life-styles of the Black community." To both Neal and Baraka, black separatism was important, and BAM was to be for blacks only. Baraka had gone so far as to stipulate that, when invited to lecture, "no whites [were] to meet him at the plane, no whites to be on stage, the blacks to have a special seating area down front."[45]

Within this separatist environment, it is hard to see where Beethoven would fit. Which returns to the earlier question: Why did it advantage Afrocentric blacks to claim Beethoven? The most obvious answer might be that to claim Beethoven was black was to claim metaphorically the entire Western musical heritage, which would be consistent with Afrocentrist assertions. Throughout the nineteenth century Beethoven was so venerated and influential that many composers considered him a force that they had to fight against to keep from being enveloped. When writing his first symphony, for example, Johannes Brahms had commented, "You have no idea how difficult it is to write a symphony when you hear the footsteps of a giant like Beethoven treading behind you." After it was finished the conductor Hans Von Bülow allegedly referred to Brahms's symphony as "Beethoven's Tenth."[46] In the twentieth century a popular biography by Robert Haven Schaufler was titled *Beethoven, The Man Who Freed Music*.[47] If Beethoven had been black, then all of Western music for the past two centuries derived from African culture. That was QC's point at Stanford when he was arguing with Fred and Alex.

Yet while there is considerable truth in that position, such an answer oversimplifies a highly complex situation. Beethoven was not a figure of great political power, nor was he a religious icon or god. The position also undercuts the strongest cultural argument within black culture. The impact of black artists has been substantial in many fields, but African American contributions to American music especially stand out, providing a voice unique from the music of European heritage. The history and the evolution of American musical culture would hardly be recognizable without the contributions of black artists. Remove them and American music loses much of its identity. Simply put, American music would not be American music without the African American imprint. Yet if Beethoven is included as well, then the distinctiveness of American black music from European music would come under question.

The importance of African American music as a cultural identifier was clearly recognized within the black community, sometimes implicitly and

sometimes more explicitly, particularly when it was coupled with strong political overtones. Jazz especially became a statement of the black experience
after World War II and a voice for black separatism in the 1960s. In one of the
key documents about the movement, *Black Aesthetic,* Hoyt Fuller discusses
how writers in a workshop of the Organization of Black Culture in Chicago
defined the black aesthetic as "the distinctive styles and rhythms and colors of
the ghetto, with those peculiar qualities which, for example, characterize the
music of a John Coltrane or a Charlie Parker or a Ray Charles."[48]

At least one writer tried to connect Beethoven with African American
music through rhythm. Deborah D. Moseley associated the syncopation that
is typical of Beethoven's style to the offbeat accent that "is intrinsic and integral to Black people's music making, which gives it a unique vitality and ki-
netic energy." She then cites specific Beethoven compositions. According to
Moseley, the second movement of Beethoven's Piano Sonata, op. 111 "sounds
like the genesis of jazz," and the finale of the *Waldstein* Sonata, op. 53, "has
a syncopated bass, which might inspire clapping in gospel music. It is also
the same off-beat pattern used in reggae and Hip-Hop music." She further
cites the "use of the syncopating drum" in Beethoven's Fifth Symphony and
the Piano Concerto no. 5, the *Emperor.* While syncopation is a principal trait
of both Beethoven's music and of jazz, the connection or the logic behind it
seems to end there. Syncopation, or offbeat accents, can be found in many
musics throughout the world, as well as many other Western composers, and
beyond the fact of its existence in both Beethoven and jazz, there is little stylistically to suggest a direct influence, least of all on which to build an ethnic
argument.[49]

Post–World War II jazz, however, did become a statement of black condition. Be-bop musicians such as Dizzy Gillespie and Charles Parker often
showed an overt disdain for the usually white audience, either refusing to acknowledge them or even turning their back to them when playing. Free jazz,
which developed in the 1960s, was connected directly with the "black aesthetic" and the black power movement. Central to the black aesthetic was the
removal of all traces of white culture, to create a black art for blacks: "The
black artist must construct models which correspond to his own reality. The
models must be non-white. Our models must be consistent with a black style,
our natural aesthetic styles, and our moral and spiritual styles."[50] Musically,
free jazz accomplished that purpose: all vestiges of European music, scales,
harmonic patterns, the structure of the popular song, were removed. With free
jazz the musical and the political blended; it was "freed of the popular song.
Freed of American white cocktail droop, tinkle, etc. The strait jacket of Ameri-

can expression *sans* blackness. . . . It wants to be freed of that temper, that scale. That life. It screams. It yearns. It pleads. It breaks out (the best of it)."[51]

Given the heavy cultural load that music carried within virtually all segments of the black community, Beethoven would seem to be the epitome of European colonialism and a white patriarchal society, something that feminists would also soon argue. Why appropriate such a Eurocentric figure? Possibly in part because Rogers and others had established plausibility. That a stronger case can be made for Beethoven being black than most classical musicians allows the argument at least to proceed. Even Fred was eventually convinced. It would be much harder to argue that point about Mozart, or about Bach, as Carmichael acknowledged. The two-pronged argument about his origins in Belgium and his appearance provides at least a conceivable basis to sustain a position that Beethoven had black blood in him. In addition, Beethoven's personality was suitable to the movement: he is the angry outsider, the person standing up to and defying the dominant society.

A more compelling reason that the Beethoven-was-black argument resonated resides in Beethoven's ubiquity in American culture. Beethoven's presence is so strong that he is hard to ignore. He is better known to the entirety of American society than probably any other classical musician. To claim Beethoven is to claim not just European musical culture but an American icon. When the rap group Soulja Boyz invoked Beethoven, it was as a symbol, not in regard to his music. In their song, "Beethoven," they claimed that for the song they needed a little help: "I'm going to have to get Beethoven to help me out on this one man." The song began with a quote from Beethoven's *Für Elise* but soon morphed into Mozart's Rondo alla Turca from the Piano Sonata in A minor K. 331. There was no mention of Mozart. Here Beethoven was more important as a metaphor for the incorporation of some sort of classical music than an identification of precisely what was used. Yet Soulja Boyz appears to have bought into the notion of a musical hierarchy: Beethoven is mentioned with both irony and respect, as someone special, who can do the heavy lifting and can pull together what in the song would otherwise be problematic.

Yet the contradiction still remains. Beethoven is European; the black nationalists and black separatists wanted to purge themselves of European culture. If European culture were African, then the philosophical argument could be solved, but that would not solve the political argument. The white, stolen legacy won't do; it must be purely African, or at the minimum freed from the Eurocentric layer that has been imposed on American blacks.

Maybe the contradiction cannot be solved; maybe it should not be. According to Moses, Afrocentrism itself was not a rational but rather a charismatic movement. For 1960s radicals, Beethoven was useful. The claim that he was black was sure to draw a backlash and to provide a point of pride for all African Americans. If he could be claimed as part of the African community, then the whole European world was topsy-turvy. It was also a claim certain to gain notice. Blacks were on more solid ground claiming that Pushkin and Dumas had been black, but how much resonance would that have had throughout American culture? Beethoven, in contrast, was everywhere. A thick square face with heavy eyebrows, long hair out of control, and a deep scowl, Beethoven's image is almost as familiar as da-da-da-dum. It is imprinted in American society far beyond its classical music locus, in popular songs and videos, in film and television commercials. Even as the role of classical music has moved from representing a transcendent moral standard toward a seeming irrelevance for many Americans, Beethoven remains one of the most recognizable figures in American culture.

It might be best to think of the Beethoven-was-black claim as less an argument than a verbally improvised explosive device, or as a Molotov cocktail. It was incendiary, and that was the point. That it embraced contradictions may in the end be pedantic. The answer to the problem perhaps lies with that most American of poets, Walt Whitman:

> I contradict myself?
> Very well, I contradict myself.

The Beethoven-was-black question, however, raises another issue, again exemplified by Fred. If Beethoven were proven to be black, or if a listener became convinced that he was, how would that affect the way his music is heard? This point raises fundamental questions about history, aesthetic response, and transcendence, namely, whether the aesthetic response encompasses the historical situation of the composition. For Fred apparently it did; for many listeners it is difficult to disassociate Beethoven's music from the European tradition, if not Germany per se.

Since the early 1800s there has been a tension between place and transcendence in Western music, as Romantic philosophy posited a transcendent quality for some music. At the other end of the spectrum musical nationalism by its very nature asserted a strong connection with place. Can what Denise Von Glahn termed the "essential musicness of the music" be separated from "placedness"?[52] This leads to two major philosophical issues, the autonomy of the artwork and the nature of the transcendent artwork. The two, while not synonymous, are related in the notion that the artwork exists independent of time and place. The former is more an ideological or philosophical stance, the latter a historical judgment, the former an approach to perception, the latter an evaluative ideal. As much as any composer, history has bestowed on Beethoven a universality to his music. While American Romantics such as John S. Dwight quickly elevated Beethoven's music to a special, literally sacrosanct position in the musical firmament, and while this attitude expanded to include Beethoven the person in the early twentieth century, it has not abated even in the twenty-first, long after historical writing has moved beyond the history-as-hero approach and postmodern inquiry has substituted an ironic detachment for any veneration or reverence. In 1998 William Kinderman wrote that "the last half-century has increasingly demonstrated the universal scope of his legacy," and as late as 2005 the belief in the universality of Beethoven's music was emblazoned in the title of Edmund Morris's book *Beethoven: The Universal Composer.*[53]

While the philosophical issues broach the question of whether Beethoven's ethnicity should matter to Fred and affect his aesthetic response, particularly if transcendence is assumed, historical reality is that for whatever reason it did. Is Fred, then, an isolated example, or is this an issue that more generally pervades American society? Can he be dismissed as a naïve twenty-year-old with only a limited understanding of art?

Fred was not alone in one sense: many whites were outraged by the Beethoven-was-black assertion. By 1970 Doug Cass's "Beethoven was black" mantra on KDIA had reached Los Angeles radio and was used as a signoff by a Los Angeles disc jockey. When Sandra Haggerty, reporter for the *Los Angeles Times,* heard the signoff one day while sitting in a coffee shop, she noticed the response of the woman sitting next to her: "Oh brother! What next? They're carrying this black thing too far." Her curiosity piqued, she wrote a column on it, including some informal street reaction. The response to her column was so strong she later published another column about that. Some of the reactions were blatantly racist in the most insulting way: "Beethoven was black? Ridiculous! Transplant a human brain into an ape and he could play basketball—not compose!" "Beethoven was black! Yeah, and so was Adolf Hitler!" Others took a somewhat different but no more rational tack: "Who ever heard of a Negro with the name of Ludwig? Black what a laugh." "Only a Communist would dare to suggest that Beethoven was black." Finally there were those whose feelings resembled Fred's; the racism is less overt, but the idea that Beethoven could be black somehow disturbed the bond between the listener and the composer: "Keep your cotton-picking hands off Beethoven!" "Madam, claim anyone else you want. But please NOT my beloved Beethoven."[54]

These inflammatory remarks and Fred's more lengthy description of his own feelings raise the question of the emotional triggers to a composition and the extent that external factors contribute to it. Many musicians do respond to a piece of music based upon what they hear, strictly within the sonic world presented. Does the work draw the listener in, is it inspired, does it hang together, is there a sense of inevitability, do the sounds have an interest or fascination in their combinations, does it move in a way that holds the listener? These questions are independent of who wrote it, or where, or when.

For some, Beethoven's music is universal, and under such circumstances color is irrelevant. One respondent to Haggerty's article invoked a thoroughly Romantic image: "Beethoven, musically in his soaring language, speaks of the power of the human spirit, the sad and lonely heights of the romantic individual. And what would poor Beethoven say today to the masses? Love is not a color." Another said, "Beethoven's music proved him to be of the universe."

Yet in spite of claims to a purely musical modality and a universality, from the most educated professional musician to the most naïve listener cultural associations cannot be dismissed when hearing a piece of music. Memory, no matter how unformed, is inseparable from the listening experience. For highly trained musicians memory may embrace the sounds of many styles and types as well as a wealth of more specific information about composers, periods, and history in general. Such as person will know that Beethoven's *Eroica* Symphony is related to Napoleon, and know that Beethoven was influenced by both the music and the ideals of the French Revolution. On a more abstract level she will be able to anticipate a structure such as sonata form as it unfolds, based on familiarity with many other pieces that at least in a general way follow the same pattern. Or he may, as Beethoven's student Ferdinand Ries did, cry out that the horn player came in at the wrong time, at the anticipated entrance of the recapitulation in the first movement. Others, such as Fred, will probably know that Beethoven as well as classical music with roughly similar sounds has something to do with Old Europe, and possibly conjure specific visual images. The extent that a listener will shut out external associations when hearing a piece of music and confront the work purely on its own terms varies, but seldom will the associations disappear entirely.

From Soulja Boyz to Lincoln Center, the notion of high art and the association of it with certain iconic names matter. When Soulja Boyz invoked Beethoven, it was partly tongue-in-cheek, but it was said with an ironic reverence designed to titillate. Yet Lincoln Center has been known to play the composer card itself. The most prominent example would be the Mozart year of 1991, when Lincoln Center set out on the ambitious project to play the entire corpus of his compositions to commemorate the bicentennial of his death. The Lincoln Center audience was confronted with many minor and in some cases trivial compositions whose purely musical value must be questioned and which would probably never have been placed on a Lincoln Center program had they not carried the name Mozart.

This issue also arises in cases of attribution. What if a piece believed to be by Mozart or Beethoven was suddenly discovered to be by Süssmayr or Archduke Rudolf? Does this impact the value of the composition? Leonard Meyer raised this question in his article "Forgery and the Anthropology of Art" in 1963, which was originally spurred by the Metropolitan Museum of Art's discovery that some Etruscan sculptures were discovered to be forgeries. Is their value then lessened? Meyer quotes the art critic Clive Bell, who holds the position that "great art remains stable and unobscure because the feelings that it awakens are independent of time and place, because its kingdom is not of this world. To those who have and hold a sense of the significance of form what does it matter whether the forms that move them were created in Paris the day before yesterday or in Babylon fifty centuries ago."[55]

Meyer responded much as a twentieth-century modernist: what matters is originality, and hence primacy. Without agreeing with or disputing the validity of Meyer's argument, what may also matter is what mattered to Fred. The artwork itself carried cultural associations; remove those associations and one's perception of the artwork changes. For some the idea that Beethoven was black posed a threat on many levels. Racially, Beethoven would no longer be part of the line of European and especially German musicians whose creations created the classical canon that is still venerated, even though for many individuals hierarchical distinctions are no longer important in the twenty-first century. Remove Beethoven from his German-Austrian-Viennese provenance and the glory and magnificence of the classical edifice begins to crack if not crumble.

This argument cannot bear much scrutiny, either from its premises, in which racial attitudes are clearly central, or from its logic, in which the leap from place to ethnicity is at best questionable, but like its mirror counterpart, hard Afrocentrism, it is less about logic and more about underlying currents and feelings that at the very least pervaded American culture through the 1960s, 1970s, and 1980s.

In the end the question "Why does it matter?" remains, which is not the same question as "Should it matter?" True, for many it did not matter, even in the 1960s and 1970s.[56] But for many on both sides of the racial divide it did matter, and it mattered a lot.[57] Right or wrong, the biographical fallacy has been an important component of the classical music audience in the United States. As we have seen, venerable institutions cater to it, sometimes going too far, as in the case of Mozart at Lincoln Center in 1991, a situation that was encouraged by the relative success of the Beethoven bicentennial year of 1970. The nineteenth century had its own monster concerts that grew until the World Peace Jubilee in 1872 featuring Johann Strauss Jr., after which they finally collapsed under their own weight.

By the 1990s the Beethoven-was-black issue occupied a less and less central position in the American cultural world. Josephine Wright, an African American musicologist now at Worcester College in Massachusetts, remembers the issue was "very much in the air" specifically in the 1960s, 1970s, and 1980s."[58] At one time Lawrence Schenbeck, who taught at Spelman, a historically black college, could count on being asked that question at least a couple of times a year, but "I can't recall having been asked about Beethoven's race or ethnicity even once in the last six or eight years."[59] William Meredith, director of the Ira F. Brilliant Center for Beethoven Studies at San Jose State University, recalled that it was one of the most frequent if not the most frequent question the center was asked, prompting Patricia Stroh, whose responsibility is also to field such questions, to remark that "it certainly was a few years ago" but that she had not heard much of it in recent years.[60] Beethoven-was-black was directly connected to radical movements that sprang up in the 1960s, and as they began to splinter in the 1970s the racial makeup of Beethoven became less a concern for mainstream American culture, probably because it was less often asserted.

Beethoven's racial fate was also tied to that of Afrocentrism. While some black intellectuals in the 1990s and beyond continued to argue for a hard Afrocentrism, others looked back on the movement, saw its value, and attempted to put it in perspective. Wilson Moses saw it as a "cultural anchor" for its followers, a sort of "cultural mythology" deeply ingrained in black culture, a movement beyond intellectual debate: "Afrocentrism is among the masses of the black people and it's very deeply rooted in their consciousness. So I don't think you're ever going to oppose it. It may be wrong, but that's sort of like attacking George Washington and the cherry tree." Cornel West recognized Afrocentrism as "a contemporary species of black nationalism," "a gallant yet misguided attempt to define an African identity in a white society perceived to be hostile."[61] To Henry Louis Gates, Afrocentrism was based on a "superstitious faith in the power of 'race' or 'blood' to determine destiny." He then referred specifically to Beethoven: "Why else would anyone care if one of Beethoven's ancestors was a Moorish soldier in the Spanish Army?"[62]

Gates's question is of course the central issue. Clearly for a time it did matter to a lot of people. Ever since John S. Dwight began to champion his music in the 1840s, Beethoven has been useful for many reasons. In some instances Beethoven's very iconicity has been an important factor in how he has been used; that was certainly true for black nationalists in the 1960s, in spite of the seeming contradictions in logic that his appropriation raised. The Beethoven-was-black argument has never disappeared, as witnessed by the many current web sites that reiterate Rogers's and other's arguments, and as witnessed by the continuing presence of advocates of a hard Afrocentrism into the twenty-first century, such as Leonard Jeffries, Molefi Asante, and Asa Hilliard, who died suddenly in 2007 while leading students on a trip to Egypt. Asante and Hilliard both argued that Beethoven was black. Yet Gates may come closer to current thinking about Beethoven: Why would anyone care?

Gates's position regarding the significance of Beethoven's ethnicity is similar to that of Michael David Cobb Bowen, a black architect and writer, who politically occupies the opposite end of the spectrum from Jeffries and Asante. Bowen describes himself as a "Moderate Republican, Fiscal Conservative, Civil Libertarian," and member of the Conservative Brotherhood, a group of black, conservative writers. On his web site he has a list of seventy-seven questions that address black identity. Question sixty-eight is "How black was Beethoven?" He then quotes a lengthy answer by Bryan L Crudup, dated August 1995, in which Crudup cites Rogers in some detail. Crudup acknowledges that Beethoven may not have been a mulatto in the strict sense of the term but that he was "AT LEAST of African descent." Bowen then provides his own summary: "Politically and culturally, it's impossible [to know]. Genetically, maybe, but who cares?"

The assertion that Beethoven was black is ultimately a political statement. Political positions determined the importance of the argument as much as veracity did. The fate of Beethoven's ethnicity in the twentieth century was closely tied to the fate of black radicalism, and the certainty of Beethoven's heritage is directly proportional to the political stance, on either the left or the right, of the person making the argument. Since what happened in sixteenth-century Flanders will probably stay in sixteenth-century Flanders as far as Beethoven's ancestry is concerned, Beethoven will continue to be what he has become in American culture, more than a musician but an icon who serves many purposes.

11

Beethoven in Popular Music

*H*OW HIGH SHOULD THE BARRIER be that separates art music from popular music? Should it exist at all? Throughout American history this issue has arisen time after time and the answers have been varied and controversial. The distinction between the two types of music appeared nonexistent in early America, seemingly insurmountable in the late nineteenth and the early twentieth centuries, and all but shattered from the postmodern attacks of the late twentieth century. Throughout this time Beethoven's music has been appropriated by musicians of many stripes and used in a myriad of ways, sometimes to purposely transgress the barrier, sometimes to take advantage of a rich symbolism that different Beethoven pieces have acquired. Almost before the earliest performances of Beethoven's music in America, his name was used to sell sheet music of dubious authenticity. Later his music or his name was borrowed by musicians working in many styles—swing, rock 'n' roll, hard rock, metal, disco, rap, and even country. In many cases name recognition played an important role in the borrowing. The variety and extent of Beethoven's uses in popular music and their occurrence over many decades speaks both to his attraction by musicians and to his deep presence in American culture.

It would be difficult to distinguish art music from popular music in Federal-era America, less because the lines were not clearly drawn than because an art-music culture did not exist throughout most of the country. Even formal concerts, such as found in Charleston, consisted of mostly potpourris, combining symphonic movements with glees, comic songs, and variations on popular tunes. The kind of mass media later associated with popular culture had not yet formed at the time. Yet within the framework of a burgeoning popular culture Beethoven's music could be found, mostly in the form of sheet music.

In the early nineteenth century, as the waltz craze began to take hold in America, many waltzes were attributed to Beethoven. Beethoven may have been Beethoven but he was not Johann Strauss. Beethoven wrote only two waltzes, in 1824, minor pieces for the Viennese actor Carl Friedrich Müller, both of which would have been unknown to American publishers who thought that combining Beethoven with waltz guaranteed success. This, however, did not stop publishers from printing many supposed waltzes by Beethoven. Any piece by Beethoven in three-quarter time was fair game, and if the music bore no relation to anything Beethoven composed, that mattered little also. That is particularly true after he had become well known.

Beethoven waltzes first appeared in America in 1807, well before he wrote the two we know about, and only two years after the first American public performance of a work by Beethoven. In New York, J & M Paff published "Bonuparte's Waltz," and in Baltimore Carr's Music Store brought out "Prince Blucher's Grand Waltz." Neither is by Beethoven, although at least one waltz, "Le Souvenir," may be traced back to the German publisher Schott.[1]

Following those, a flood of Beethoven waltzes appeared throughout much of the century. They had many titles, some descriptive, such as "Beautiful Waltz," "Beethoven's Much Admired Waltz," or "The Celebrated Grand Waltz," some specific, such as the aforementioned "Prince Blucher's Grand Waltz" or "Gertrude's Dream Waltz," and some quasi-autobiographical, such as "Beethoven's Dream" or "Beethoven's Last Waltz." Most of the music for these pieces is unknown, although a few can be attributed to other composers: "Le Desire" is a waltz by Schubert, and "Beethoven's Dream" is by Carl Maria von Weber. Virtually all these waltzes were printed by different publishers in different cities, and titles alone are not reliable. Different publishers would assign different music to the same title, or use different titles for the same music. The presence of these waltzes stands less as testament about Beethoven's music than it does the state of music publishing in the nineteenth century, the popularity of the waltz throughout the century, and the reputation that Beethoven had ac-

FIGURE 11.1

A waltz allegedly by Beethoven, printed by an American publisher.

quired even before his music became familiar. The latter may have been due to the music publishing industry in England where Beethoven was better known. In the days before strict international copyright, many American publishers simply lifted their pieces from imprints in England, assuming that what was popular there would be popular in the United States. Since scruples about attribution were nonexistent, one should not expect scruples about borrowing. This was simply the state of the industry at the time.

Other types of music ascribed to Beethoven could also be found in the nineteenth century. At least two funeral marches existed. The first, a tribute to the death of the Latin American revolutionary leader Simon Bolivar, simply added words to the funeral march of the *Eroica*. The second, published on the death of Daniel Webster in 1866, bears no relation to Beethoven's music at all.

By the late nineteenth century, a music industry began to coalesce around Union Square in New York City, facilitated by several changes in the music business. Touring groups or vaudeville acts, an outgrowth of the minstrel shows earlier in the century, spread throughout the country thanks to the widespread railroad network. Less expensive printing methods of sheet music developed, and almost every middle- and upper-class home had a piano in it. Consequently, demand for sheet music was high, and, most important, copyright laws were strengthened so the composer and publisher could be guaranteed financial rewards should a song become popular. With the development of less expensive printing methods and with pianos, demand for sheet music songs was great.

Because New York was the center of vaudeville, it was advantageous for a publisher to be located there. Performers would often tour the publishing houses looking for the next hit to sing. The publishers would have song pluggers who would play or sing the songs for a singer and try to convince him to buy it, or if he was famous to incorporate it into his act, knowing that this was the way to sell sheet music. The jangling of dozens of pianos out the windows along a short block gave the area the name Tin Pan Alley.[2]

Even though Tin Pan Alley declined in the 1930s as records began to replace sheet music, its real demise came in the 1950s as rock 'n' roll displaced the ballad, dance, and novelty style that Tin Pan Alley composers favored.[3] For approximately sixty years a particular type of music had dominated American popular culture, although Tin Pan Alley's longevity had much to do with its composers' abilities to incorporate new elements, particularly rhythms, into their songs, such as waltz, ragtime, and jazz.

During this long reign of Tin Pan Alley, Beethoven was virtually ignored. Only a few fleeting instances of reference to Beethoven may be found in Tin

Pan Alley songs, and practically none of his music was used. Composers did not hesitate to mine classical music for what they could use, however. Songs based on the music of Chopin, Rimsky-Korsakov, and Tchaikovsky immediately come to mind, and may still be found in many anthologies.[4] Why, then, did Tin Pan Alley shy away from Beethoven? Part of the answer lies in Beethoven's position in the late nineteenth and early twentieth centuries. As we have seen, the music as well as the man had been thoroughly sacralized by the second half of the century, not only his music but his person. He was a god to be revered and worshiped. His music was not simply to be enjoyed, but was a spiritual experience. He loomed over this time in a way that was both inspirational and intimidating. Metaphorically, a large sign had been placed on him: "Keep Off My Melody."

Tin Pan Alley was after the immediate; its goal was to entertain, either with catchy, foot-tapping music, or to indulge in heartrending sentiment that was direct and on the surface, not to probe spiritual depths or to pile on elaborate and powerful structures. Harmonies could become quite complex, as they did in the early and mid-twentieth century (e.g., Hoagy Carmichael's *Stardust*), but it was the harmony of Romanticism, the thick, lush chords and the chromaticism that came after Beethoven, not the hard-driving enhanced dominant-tonic polarity that Beethoven never left, even when he expanded its scope. Beethoven did begin to move past that in his late works, especially the quartets, but not toward the Romantic school. That is partly why the music of late Beethoven to this day confounds scholars who try to place it stylistically. It stands apart.

Tin Pan Alley was interested in melody, a flowing, singable melody that moved and was eminently vocal. This was not Beethoven's forte. Beethoven was a composer of short, punchy motives molded into large powerful structures. His lyrical movements did not lend themselves to the voice as well, and they were not primarily melodic. For instance, two of the best known of Beethoven's lyrical moments are the first movement of the *Moonlight* Sonata and the second movement of the *Pathetique* Sonata. Both have a long flowing quality about them, but the mood is a product of the overall sound scheme, not the melody alone. The melody of the *Moonlight* Sonata by itself is not particularly memorable. It is the melody against the triplet chord patterns and the descending bass that creates the overall affect or mood. The same is true with the *Pathetique*, although the melody alone has more to offer than that of the *Moonlight*. The *Pathetique* melody, however, is neither catchy nor easily singable, two sine qua nons for the Tin Pan Alley composer. Two other famous Beethoven melodies, the "Ode to Joy" and *Für Elise*, simply did not fit the mold of the Tin Pan Alley song. The "Ode to Joy" was too close to a hymn, and indeed it was adapted for several hymns, most famously in 1912 by the Presbyterian clergyman and author Henry Van Dyke.[5] *Für Elise* was too instrumental, with its arpeggios and the repeating chromatic neighbor note at the beginning. One other possibility comes to mind among Beethoven's oeuvre, the opening theme of the *Archduke* Trio. The opening, however, is only one phrase, repeated, that does not lend itself to an AABA completion. Beethoven moves on to other material after that, and the shape of the melody is not that of a Tin Pan Alley song.

When not focused on sentimental song, Tin Pan Alley was interested in dance music, which meant contemporary dances. In the late nineteenth century waltz time dominated the music industry, although the height of the waltz craze had long passed. While new dances such as the polka had begun to replace the waltz as early as the 1840s, it nevertheless remained popular in America, receiving a shot in the arm with Johann Strauss's visit to Boston in 1872.

With the advent of ragtime, an entirely new set of dances came into vogue. While a number of waltzes were attributed to Beethoven in the nineteenth century, despite the fact that his music was not conducive to the type of waltz song popular later in the century, neither was Beethoven easily adaptable by ragtime composers. Syncopation was very much a part of Beethoven's music, but it was of a different nature, a broader metric syncopation embedded in a larger structural purpose, not the catchy beat-oriented syncopation of ragtime.

Even though Tin Pan Alley wanted to steer clear of Beethoven, he still managed to work his way into another genre of popular music in the first half of the twentieth century, namely swing. At least three swing pieces made use of Beethoven's music, two of which referenced Beethoven in the title. The first, "The Beethoven Bounce" by Al Donahue's Orchestra, appeared in 1940. This was quickly followed by "Sonata by L. van Beethoven" by Jimmie Lunceford's Orchestra and "Beethoven Riffs On" by John Kirby's Orchestra. Although exact release dates of these recordings are not clear, they all appeared in 1940 or 1941.

Swing, which began to emerge around 1930, was originally an expansion of 1920s jazz, as more instruments were added to the jazz band, a development that demanded greater control over what each member played. Written arrangements became necessary and a swing style evolved, characterized by thick, sometimes smooth, sometimes biting harmonies within each section or instrumental group, such as reeds, trumpets, or trombones; interplay between the sections; a fast, upbeat tempo propelled by a strong rhythm section; improvisatory solos built into the arrangements; and a special rhythmic swing feel. Count Basie, when asked to define swing, said that beyond being music you can pat your foot by, he couldn't define it. Louis Armstrong's comment was pithier. Although he said it about jazz, it applied equally to swing: "Man if you gotta ask, you'll never know."[6]

The question of raiding the classics was controversial in the swing genre. Musicians and critics both within and outside the jazz community had reservations about "jazzed classics," as they were called. In 1940 Count Basie remarked, "They're desecrating America's beautiful old melodies and favorite music. Mine is an out and out swing band, but I'll not go on the air if I have to resort to those beautiful compositions for my swing material." Like others, he felt that drawing on classical music suggested that the swing bands had run out of material. Although Basie spoke shortly after Lunceford's and Donahue's Beethoven-derived arrangements, he was probably not referring specifically to them. There had been a long tradition of drawing upon classical music, including Tommy Dorsey's "Song of India," based on Rimsky-Korsakov's opera *Sadko*, in 1937, Benny Goodman's "Spring Song," based on Mendelssohn's *Song Without Words*, and many others.[7]

Devotees of classical music were particularly outraged about "the daring and unashamed theft of 'classical' tunes to be incorporated into the 'latest hits,' which must be cause for grave concern," as the composer Solomon Pimsleur protested. Alfred Dennis, president of the Bach Society of New Jersey, was so offended when he heard a swing arrangement of Bach's *Toccata in D minor* on the radio that he made a formal request to the FCC "to make the 'swinging' . . . of masterpieces a misdemeanor punishable by suspension of license on the first offense and a revocation of license on the second." His protest reeked not only of outrage but out-and-out racism: "All the beautiful fugue effects were destroyed by the savage slurring of the saxophones and the jungle discords of the clarinets." The FCC, in its wisdom, declined to rule officially on Dennis's petition, but it did urge radio stations to use "a high degree of discernment" in their broadcast of jazzed classics. *New York Times* music critic Olin Downes devoted two lengthy columns to the incident, in which he pointed out the difficulty of deciding where to draw the line with classical adaptation. He observed that "more than rhythm was involved" and raised the question of free speech. The issue soon faded as a legal controversy, and bands continued to incorporate the classics; in fact, all three of the above-mentioned Beethoven arrangements were released after this controversy.

Al Donahue's background was unusual for a bandleader of the swing era. He studied violin, his principal instrument, at the New England Conservatory, and then received a law degree from Boston University. During that time he played on various cruise lines, and when his own band played at the Bermudiana Hotel the owners asked him to supply music for all their hotels and cruise ships. Donahue became a big-band entrepreneur and at one time had thirty-seven bands under his direction. The violin was seldom heard, and Donahue's main music contributions were his arrangements.

Donahue's "Beethoven Bounce," recorded January 24, 1940, is an adaptation of *Für Elise*. After a brief introduction, the sax section states Beethoven's main theme in unison but rhythmically alters it to give it a swing bounce. This chorus becomes the basis for the piece, with solos by the tenor saxophone and muted trumpet; also, saxophone and trombone improvise on it followed by a new melody by the trumpet section before the original opening statement returns.

Jimmie Lunceford's Orchestra recorded his version of Beethoven's *Pathetique* Sonata in Los Angeles on February 28, 1940. Although the recording swings the first movement of the piece, it essentially preserves its integrity. Even the original sonata form with introduction is roughly present in the arrangement by Chappie Willet. The original piano runs near the end of the introduction are given to the clarinet, creating a passage reminiscent of the opening of Gershwin's *Rhapsody in Blue,* which by 1940 had already become a classic. The allegro that follows is especially fast and driving in Lunceford's recording, and the entire arrangement is marked by interplay between full orchestra and solo or instrumental group passages. Modulations do not follow the original score, but they do emphasize the two key areas that Beethoven features, C minor and E-flat major.

With few exceptions, bands were rigidly segregated in the 1940s, and Lunceford's was considered one of the best black bands. It was often compared favorably with Duke Ellington's. The band began as a high school ensemble, the Chicksaw Syncopators, at Manassas High School in Memphis, Tennessee, where Lunceford was the band director. They began touring and cutting records and soon dropped all affiliation with the school as the band began to play at some of the most prestigious venues in the United States, such as the Cotton Club in New York.

The Paul Whiteman Orchestra, which premiered *Rhapsody in Blue* in 1924, was considered one of the most symphonic of the jazz ensembles, and as a consequence it was one of the whitest. Lunceford's evocation of *Rhapsody in Blue* and his use of Beethoven seems unusual for a black orchestra, although it should be noted that Lunceford also drew upon Chopin for another piece. It is impossible to know what occurred on stage when Lunceford's band played the Beethoven number, but Lunceford was noted for humorous antics and satire, which was an established tradition with black musicians and bands of the 1930s. Fats Waller and Cab Calloway's band engaged in it, and one can only speculate that a certain amount of satire accompanied this piece as well.

John Kirby was another black bandleader who borrowed from Beethoven. During the thirties Kirby was known primarily as a bass player with a number of prominent bands, those of Benny Carter, Fletcher Henderson, and Chick Webb. In 1937 he joined a small ensemble that, after some fluctuation in personnel, became a sextet in 1938 with Kirby as the leader. Until World War II decimated its ranks in 1942, it was one of the finest small jazz groups of the swing era.

"Beethoven Riffs On," from 1941, probably arranged by the sextet's trumpeter, Charlie Shavers, draws upon two Beethoven compositions, the *Moonlight* Sonata and the Seventh Symphony. Instead of the famous first movement of the *Moonlight* Sonata, the piece uses a portion of the more frantic third movement, measures 42–56, played by the trumpet and with harmony added by the saxophones. It is a short, punchy motive that makes an ideal swing riff. The ensemble then expands freely on the motive before switching to the smoother sounds of the second movement of the Seventh Symphony. Here, the clarinet and saxophone play the two contrapuntal themes straight and legato at first; then the trumpet joins in with a higher-pitched and more swing-like version of the principal theme. Other instruments follow with improvisations. Later, when the *Moonlight* Sonata motive returns, it is inverted.

Elements of satire are heard throughout the piece. Unlike with Lunceford, whose works included satirical acts onstage that could not be represented on recordings, with Kirby the satire is built into the arrangement. The introductory motive played by the saxes at the beginning hints of the opening triplet turn in Donahue's *Für Elise*, the arrangement played by a society orchestra for the well-heeled cruise set. Later there is a break in which the muted trumpet gives some well-placed raspberries, although for whom it is not clear: Beethoven, high art music, or the society of the New York Philharmonic, perhaps. Finally at the end we hear the over-repeated chords and several attempts to reach a final cadence. It is Beethoven's reiterated dominant-tonic coda, made absurd as it is tacked onto a jazz sextet arrangement.

After the brief flurry of Beethoven swing adaptations in 1940–1941, he disappears from popular music until the advent of rock 'n' roll in the 1950s. On April 16, 1956, Chuck Berry recorded "Roll Over Beethoven" in the Chess Records studios in Chicago. No Beethoven music was in the song, and, as Berry himself stated, it was less about Beethoven than about memories of his childhood when his sister Lucy would hog the piano playing classical music, while he wanted to play other things. Berry stated that Lucy's actions "delayed rock-n-roll for twenty years."[8] The lyrics suggest no revolution, no attempt to reject classical music, but are rather an entreaty to notice rhythm 'n' blues. It sings of the excitement of the genre and how it infects the listener: "You know my temperature's risin' . . . I got the rockin' pneumonia . . . I got the rollin' arthritis." It is also refers to songs of Elvis Presley and Bo Diddley. The lyrics alone, however, don't tell the whole story; it is the total aural package that delivers the song's message. Here we need to go back to Berry's brief recording career.

Rock 'n' roll was in its infancy as a national phenomenon. Fats Domino's "Ain't Dat a Shame" and Little Richard's "Tutti Fruitti," their first recordings to cross over onto the pop charts, had appeared only the year before, and Elvis Presley's first major hit, "Heartbreak Hotel," did not appear until 1956. Jerry Lee Lewis had not even recorded at the time. In 1955 Chess Records issued Berry's first recording, "Maybelline," on one side of an LP and "Wee Wee Hours" on the other. "Wee Wee Hours" was meant to be the hit. It is a blues recording through and through. It has a slow, strong beat; the voice ends halfway through the phrase, allowing the band, mainly the lead guitar, to answer, creating the traditional call and response structure of traditional blues. Especially important is Berry's singing style. He sings in a black dialect with the slides and inflections typical of African American blues singing. The lengthy instrumental section two-thirds of the way through the song echoes the African American voice. It is no wonder that Berry was particularly fond of this recording, and that the black audience at the Cosmos Club in St. Louis, where Berry performed, preferred it over "Maybelline."

"Maybelline" had its roots in Western swing, being based on an old Bob Wills song, "Ida Red." Berry sings in an obviously black dialect, but the diction is clear and there is little blues inflection in the voice. Berry considered the song more a joke, an amusing novelty number. Yet it also had roots in the black music tradition, where both songs about cars and double entendres were common.[9] Thus when Berry "caught Maybelline at the top of the hill," is he referring to the car or the person? The opening guitar riff—strong beat, driving rhythm, syncopation—sets the tone for the piece. The band has a raw rhythmic edge that distinguished it from early rock 'n' roll white bands such as Bill Haley and the Comets, even though Haley attempted to be just as pounding and driving.

By the time Berry recorded "Roll Over Beethoven" a year later, his guitar playing had improved and he was aiming his music at white as much as black audiences. The opening guitar riff does what it did in "Maybelline," creating a mood and a beat before the drums enter to continue it. This time Berry's guitar triplets add a sense of urgency to the music. Berry's delivery, supported by the powerful beat, flings out each word, with clear enunciation and an assertiveness that challenges Beethoven—here a metaphor for the classical music world—to notice rhythm and blues. The message is clear: the music is here to stay and you better pay attention. This point in driven home in the final verse, where the title phrase "Roll Over Beethoven" is repeated five times, with the final admonition, "Dig these rhythm and blues."

Yet why did Berry choose Beethoven? Could not any other dead white European male composer "roll over" just as well? On the one hand, Beethoven is the perfect symbolic choice. His name is universally recognized, and probably more than any other composer conjures images of serious, no-nonsense classical music, of culturally important high art, of the classical canon itself. Yet there may be another equally important reason: Beethoven's name scans. Once one has heard the song, the name and the rhythm fit perfectly; even without having heard it previously the phrase has a natural rhythm that grabs. "Roll OVer BeeTHO-O-Oven, roll OVer BeeTHO-O-Oven." Just try saying aloud, "Roll over Brahms."

Berry's song might have remained a big 1950s hit that was soon forgotten had not the Beatles done a cover version in 1963. The Beatles cover, which remains close to Berry's, spawned a host of others. Tom Jones, The Flying Burrito Brothers, Gene Vincent, Gerry & the Pacemakers, Jerry Lee Lewis, Carl Perkins, Johnny Rivers, George Jones and Johnny Paycheck, the Karaoke All Stars, Kerry Kearney, Leon Russell & New Grass Revival, Done Again (in the style of the Beatles), Mountain, Prima Donnas, Rock Circus Feat, Herbert Hildbrandt, Roger Matura, Routers, The Byrds, The Singing Penguins, and Sleepy LaBeef all recorded "Roll Over Beethoven." Some of these covers, such as those of Carl Perkins and Jerry Lee Lewis, themselves creators of rock 'n' roll in the 1950s, go back to Berry's original. Yet for most musicians it was the impact of the Beatles recording that provided the main impetus.

The Electric Light Orchestra's own 1973 recording expanded Berry's original into an eight-minute piece by adding numerous riffs from Beethoven's Fifth Symphony, creating a curious amalgam of Beethoven and Berry. This version no longer projects Berry's R&B challenge to classical music, but, in the best postmodern manner, attempts to blend the two together, although the blend sounds less like a marriage than an awkward blind date. The black accents, too, which had long disappeared on the many earlier covers, particularly of British singers, sound less than authentic here. Since the ELO belongs to a genre sometimes referred to as symphonic rock, its choices and arrangement seem appropriate. Significantly, this also became their signature piece, the work that invariably closed their concerts.

Yet the ELO demonstrates precisely what Zubin Mehta and Frank Zappa discovered at virtually the same time: rock and symphony do not mix. On May 15, 1970, Mehta, music director of the Los Angeles Philharmonic, and Frank Zappa, with his band the Mothers of Invention, put on a joint program that was televised nationally. The goal was to bridge the divide between the two cultures. In that regard the result was not successful, less because the two musical worlds were so disparate than because each saw their roles in a completely different light. To Zappa live shows meant theater, while to supporters of the Philharmonic the fiction that a concert is strictly an aural event persisted. Although some Philharmonic musicians seemed to enjoy the antics Zappa wrote for them—to burp and grunt, throw confetti, twirl a bass, or stuff a giraffe under one's dress—the actions seemed incongruous to those watching a large ensemble in formal attire. Many members of the audience also noted the disjunction.

When Berry recorded his song, the division between high and low culture was more a chasm, a cultural situation that provided Berry the bite for his satire. With Mehta and Zappa and the ELO, the division seemed artificial, and classical musicians, seeing the impact of 1960s rock and possibly feeling the heat from youth who wished to reject the past as no longer relevant, sought to bridge the gap between the two cultures. By incorporating Beethoven into a rock idiom the ELO clearly succeeded, if measured by audience approval. Approaching it from the opposite direction, bringing rock music into the symphonic environment turned out to be forced and awkward. The experiment would not be repeated for many years, until young composers themselves began to incorporate the rock idiom into their compositions, and orchestras, desperate about declining revenue and prestige, began to broaden their musical horizons.

Ultimately Berry's song had a cultural impact far beyond the song itself. The title took on a life of its own, to become a code word for postmodernism and any challenge to the status quo. A recent Google search of "Roll Over Beethoven" produced 550,000 hits. Many were online retailers pushing Berry's or the Beatles' or a few others' recordings. Most had nothing to do with the song itself, but rather were metaphorical uses of the phrase, such as Alex Ross's lengthy 1998 portrait in the *New Yorker* of the young British composer Thomas Adès. Other than Adès seeing himself as a new voice in contemporary music, there seems to be little or no connection with Chuck Berry. Dozens of newspaper articles about music and musicians have used the title, ranging from Frank Zappa to Awadagin Pratt, the black classical pianist with dreadlocks, to American evangelicals incorporating rock into their services. The phrase went far beyond music, as well. Stanley Aronowitz's entitled his book extolling cultural studies and postmodern approaches to culture *Roll Over Beethoven: The Return of Cultural Strife*. Peter Gabel and Duncan Kennedy published a lengthy article in the *Stanford Law Review* about the use of theory in Critical Legal Studies; their title was "Roll Over Beethoven."[10]

Within three years of Berry's recording, the first phase of rock 'n' roll was over. February 3, 1959, provided a dramatic *Götterdammerung* to fifties rock, as Buddy Holly, Richie Valens, and J. P. Richardson, known as the Big Bopper, were killed when the small plane they had chartered crashed in an ice storm. Don McLean, in his song "American Pie," called it "the day the music died." Soon almost all the stars that created the genre were no longer active. In December 1959, Chuck Berry was sentenced to prison for violating the Mann Act,[11] Little Richard found religion and vowed to record only religious music, Jerry Lee Lewis became ostracized when news broke that he had married his thirteen-year-old cousin, and Elvis Presley was drafted into the army.

Conservatives who saw rock 'n' roll as a serious threat to youth's morals had triumphed, and a new group of young, cute, squeaky clean white singers, mostly named Bobby, appeared.[12] At the same time, a folk music boom had begun on college campuses, and it soon spread throughout the country. New names emerged: the Kingston Trio, Peter, Paul, and Mary, Joan Baez, Bob Dylan. None of this music, neither that of the Bobbys or the folk singers, made use of Beethoven. He had to await another major turning point in American popular music.

That occurred on February 7, 1964, when the Beatles arrived at Kennedy Airport in New York, greeted by a crowd of three thousand fans. Their first single had already sold over two million copies in the United States and their appearance on *The Ed Sullivan Show* two days later was estimated to have attracted seventy-four million viewers, or forty percent of the American population at that time.[13] The rest of their first tour was a blur of sold-out houses, screaming teenagers, and extensive media coverage. Beatlemania was in full bloom, and soon other groups from England followed. With the British invasion a new type of rock appeared, which would dominate American popular music throughout the decade, and would then begin to splinter into a plethora of styles and types: psychedelic, heavy metal, hard rock, punk, grunge, progressive, alternative, indie, and symphonic rock were only some of the types that appeared in the 1970s and 1980s.

FIGURE 11.2

A collection of headlines: "Roll Over Beethoven"
becomes a journalistic cliché.

None of the new trends in popular music was strictly American, for by the second half of the twentieth century popular music had become international. The "Beatles invasion" of 1964 was the pivotal event that solidified and confirmed that trend. Their reception was not entirely unique in American culture; Johann Strauss had received almost the same treatment when he visited Boston in 1872. That his impact was mostly local had more to do with the absence of a wired world than lack of interest in his music and person. In 1964 the media amplification chamber, particularly television, could steamroll the Beatles arrival into national rather than local hysteria. Early rock 'n' roll had impacted Europe, not only among youth, but among scholars as well. In the 1960s, when American musicologists would not come close to Elvis Presley, German scholars were writing articles about him.

Thanks to the impact that 1950s American rock 'n' roll had on European youth, by the 1960s European bands had absorbed American vernacular, rock, blues, and rhythm 'n' blues well enough to easily make the leap into the American market, and the Atlantic Ocean became just another highway in the Euro-American world of popular music. Like the railroad in the nineteenth century, transportation factored into that change. Transatlantic jet travel, inaugurated on October 4, 1958,[14] cut distances so that a band could play one night in Great Britain and appear on an American television show the next.

Thus when discussing the importance of Beethoven in popular music, some of the examples are drawn from American musicians, some from European, especially British. All the musicians discussed below, however, had an impact on American soil; some, such as Ritchie Blackmore, a British guitarist, originally found a more fertile reception in America than in the United Kingdom.

Beethoven's music was found in several types of rock, as well as in other types of popular music of the time such as disco, country, and hip-hop. The most famous Beethoven borrowing was Walter Murphy's disco version of Beethoven's Fifth Symphony, "A Fifth of Beethoven." It was released on May 29, 1976, and remains the only song based on Beethoven's music to reach number one on the Billboard charts, where it resided for one week.[15] For the entire year Billboard listed it as number ten on their Top 100. It became even better known the next year when used in the film *Saturday Night Fever*.

The piece is only part Beethoven. The opening four notes, the da-da-da-dum motive repeated, mimic the original almost exactly. Only then the disco beat enters and the listener becomes aware that this is not unadulterated Beethoven. The beat itself changes Beethoven's meter from $\frac{2}{4}$ to $\frac{4}{4}$. Above the beat and an added disco bass line, Murphy continues with the original score through what is the first half of Beethoven's sonata form exposition. Where a classical listener would expect the second theme of Beethoven's symphony to appear, Murphy adds his own funky tune to the continuing four-note motive accompaniment. Murphy also avoids the modulation that occurs in Beethoven at this time and stays in the home key. In the place of a normal Beethovenian development, repetition of earlier phrases creates an overall pattern (AABBA) that is closer to popular song form than to classical symphonic structure.[16]

"A Fifth of Beethoven" was sampled extensively by Robin Thicke for his 2002 song "When I Get You Alone." Murphy's disco piece is heard as background throughout Thicke's song, with Thicke adding a straight $\frac{4}{4}$ drum beat, a pop melody with rap overtones, and, at climactic moments, further instrumentation that underlines the words of the singer. It blends well into a single package, although beyond Thicke's borrowing of Murphy there is no reference to Beethoven. While Thicke is an American songwriter, the piece had more success abroad than in the United States, particularly in Australia. Guy Sebastian, the first winner of the *Australian Idol* competition, performed it during the finals, and later included it on his first single, "Angels Brought Me Here," which went four times platinum. Although "Angels" was recognized as the hit, the presence of "When I Get You Alone" on the same recording and Sebastian's performance on *Idol* guaranteed its success. It later reached the popular music charts in Belgium, Italy, the Netherlands, Austria, and Switzerland, but not in the United States, although Blake Lewis sang it on *American Idol* in 2007.

Probably the most famous adaptation of Beethoven in hard rock was Rainbow's use of the "Ode to Joy" in their song "Difficult to Cure," also the title of the album, released in 1981. Rainbow was a hard rock group whose leader was the English guitarist Ritchie Blackmore. The band went through many personnel changes, as Blackmore was difficult to please musically. He was also a founding member of Deep Purple before leaving it to establish Rainbow. Like many British groups, Rainbow had considerable success in the United States.

Blackmore was known for his fondness for classical music, and "Difficult to Cure" is the most famous example of this. It is strictly an instrumental number that draws heavily on the last movement of Beethoven's Ninth Symphony, but unlike other uses of the Ninth's finale, it is not limited to the "Ode to Joy" theme itself. The recording opens with the recitative from the last movement of the Ninth, followed by improvisation on the recitative. Then comes the "Ode to Joy" statement with slight rhythmic changes—triplets where eighth notes are expected, and modulations on repetitions of the theme. This is followed by guitar and then keyboard improvisation on the tune. The keyboard and cymbal then introduce a fantasy-like section that contains hints of the opening theme and the instrumental fugue on the Ninth that follows the Turkish March. Rainbow then concludes with more statements of the theme and more modulations.

On the recording the listener hears heavy laughter at the end, although it sounds like it is added, not spontaneous. Is this a statement about what they have done to Beethoven, is it a continuing recognition of the resonance of Chuck Berry, or is it Rainbow insouciantly telling Beethoven to "roll over"? It may suggest an element of both irony and respect, respect only if the position of Beethoven as a continuing force in Western musical culture is acknowledged.[17]

Different versions of this piece are available on YouTube, and from them one can see how Blackmore used the Ninth Symphony version in various ways. In a performance in San Antonio, Texas, with only the core band, probably in the 1980s, he preceded it with a lengthy blues riff, alternating between himself and the keyboardist, then played only the "Ode to Joy" section of his version.[18]

If YouTube statistics are any indication, the most watched version of this piece is Rainbow's live performance in Japan in 1984. Here the band is augmented with an orchestra, including strings, and another segment from the finale is added. The piece opens with a guitar riff and an elaborated version of the recitative, followed by the modulating versions of the "Ode to Joy." After that, the orchestra states the latter part of the fugue that occurs following the Turkish March, before specific statements of the "Ode to Joy" return. All this with pounding drums and Blackmore's virtuosic guitar licks embellishing the orchestra.

Curiously, the "Ode to Joy" theme does not appear when it is most expected. Rainbow interjects the last part of the fugue that follows the Turkish March in the last movement of the Ninth Symphony, including the anticipated dominant extended anacrusis to the big tutti statement of the theme in D major. Beethoven extends the tension for twenty-five measures, as the orchestra first arrives on a unison, syncopated F-sharp, teasing the listener with the first three notes of the theme in B major and minor, before adding a bass A, which creates a short dominant pedal before moving up the scale to the anticipated D major statement of the theme. Rainbow does all of that, and anyone familiar with the Ninth will be holding their breath expecting the D major explosion. With Rainbow, it doesn't happen at that moment. Instead, we get a drum break and an improvisatory passage on the guitar before the "Ode to Joy" returns. Beethoven's passage is so rife with expectation and release that one need not know the symphony to experience this moment. But while Beethoven had created the anticipation, Blackmore and his drummer extend it, toying with the listener's minds, sowing doubt and frustration as to whether the expected will occur—in other words, delaying the orgiastic moment and making the climax even more satisfying.

Of all popular music genres, heavy metal in particular has shown an affinity to Beethoven. Some sub-types, such as symphonic metal, would appear to be an obvious choice, but use of Beethoven's music is not limited to that alone. Classifying metal bands is as complex as identifying the chemical properties of metal elements and compounds themselves, and is made even more difficult by the lack of the hard-and-fast definitions that pertain to the physical objects. Metal groups never stand still (both metaphorically and literally), and both their products and the classifications are constantly in flux. This extends beyond metal itself, as the line between hard rock and metal is both thin and porous. Blackmore's Rainbow, for instance, has been considered hard rock, heavy metal, and at times symphonic metal. Dragonland, a group that wrote a song about Beethoven, has been identified as both a power and a symphonic band, or a symphonic power metal band, and has also been called a goth metal and a neo-classical metal band.

Metal groups in both the United States and Europe have gravitated toward Beethoven's music. In the United States, the Great Kat and the Trans-Siberian Orchestra have drawn on Beethoven as have the two Scandinavian groups, Dragonland, from Sweden, and Apocalyptica, from Finland. The Swedish guitarist Ingwei Malmsteen has also used Beethoven, suggesting both the popularity of metal in Scandinavia and an affinity with Beethoven among Scandinavian metalists. In this day of iTunes, MP3, YouTube, file sharing, internet web sites and magazines, international touring, and, for the troglodytes, online CD purchase, all these performers have had some impact on American culture regardless of their national origins.

On his album *Odyssey,* Yngwie Malmsteen acknowledged his debt to J. S Bach, Paganini, Vivaldi, Beethoven, Jimi Hendrix, and Ritchie Blackmore. Each fits into the pattern of influence that characterizes metal. Like other rock musicians, metal players were drawn to Baroque music (Bach and Vivaldi) at least in part for musical reasons, such as "conventional harmonic progressions, melodic patterns and structural frameworks," and the way it operates "through imaginative combinations, elaborations and variations of these, rather than developing extended, through-composed forms."[19] In addition, its strong beat and driving motoric rhythm, as well as underlying improvisational quality, provide another level of affinity. Paganini is an obvious choice as he demonstrated not only what could be done on the violin, but what virtuosity could do to an audience. No metal guitar player could escape the influence of Hendrix and Blackmore: they transformed the instrument by doing for the guitar what Paganini did for the violin.

For many rock musicians Beethoven was a powerhouse not to be ignored. The four-note opening motive of the Fifth was the ultimate power-chord-opening-attention-getter in a world that traded in power. The fifth was also universally known. Once those four notes were heard, the audience knew what to expect, and they would wait to see what the performer would do with them. The key of the symphony was also important. Heavy metal favored modal keys, shying away from the major mode. In that respect, Blackmore's use of the Ninth Symphony, which is in D major, was an exception. The Fifth, in the key of C minor, allowed an Aeolian flavor to creep in as well as possibilities for the harmonic minor, a trademark of Malmsteen's playing.

Malmsteen never recorded Beethoven's Fifth Symphony, but he performed it frequently in concert. Several videos of live performances may be found on the internet, and at least one bootleg recording can be found, taken from his Fire and Ice Tour of 1992.[20] One internet version, assuming that it is authentic, follows Beethoven's first movement rather closely, with Malmsteen mostly doubling the instrumental parts with some embellishment. Another version, a video of a young Malmsteen in live performance, follows the Beethoven score in a hyper-speed guitar statement of the main theme only until the beginning of the second theme, at which point Malmsteen launches an extended improvisation. The version itself is short, and Malmsteen never returns to the symphony; the beginning serves mainly as a launching pad.[21]

Dragonland, founded in 1999, incorporates a wide range of literary, scientific, and fantasy sources in its lyrics. Its fourth album, *Astronomy,* released in 2006, contains references to astronomy, antimatter, supernovas, and Queen Cassiopeia, wife of King Cepheus, of the mythological Phoenician realm of Ethiopia. It also contains a song about Beethoven, "Beethoven's Nightmare," which explores the horror and the frustration of Beethoven's deafness. Virtuosic guitar riffs and keyboard excerpts from Beethoven sonatas support a set of powerful lyrics to create a nightmarish tone so real the listener can imagine Beethoven waking in the night to feel the horror of his affliction:

See my hands
Conducting a Nightmare
The symphony of a tragedy
So great it devours me
These notes are just fantasy

The opening of the song, a sudden powerblast of sound followed by Olof Mörck's blazing guitar riffs, creates the tone before the voice introduces the subject matter. Most of the keyboard material is taken from the first movement of the *Pathetique* Sonata and the first and third movements of the *Moonlight* Sonata. The vocal line is somewhat reminiscent of Andrew Lloyd Weber's forays into rock and is in keeping with European metal, which tends to have a more lyrical melody than American metal, in which growls and screams are more prevalent. It should be stressed, however, that use of the word "lyrical" in this context is only relative.

After the seventh verse a lengthy instrumental break beginning at 2:48 fluidly integrates Beethoven's music into the improvisational tapestry of Dragonland's power metal. Two moments stand out: Olof Mörck's guitar improvisation over Nicklas Magnunsson's relatively straight statement from the opening movement of the *Moonlight* Sonata, then Magnunsson's arpeggios imitative of the last movement of the *Moonlight* Sonata, which when reaching the top notes elide into a piano statement of the vocal melody of the song.

The most extensive treatment of Beethoven in heavy metal or any popular music genre was done by the Trans-Siberian Orchestra in 2000 with their concept album *Beethoven's Last Night*. It is a rock opera that tells a fantasy story of Beethoven as he nears death. He has just completed his Tenth Symphony when he is visited by Mephistopheles, who has come for his soul. Beethoven pleads that he needs time to complete what will be his greatest work. Mephistopheles calls his bluff and then proposes that he will give Beethoven back his soul if he will allow Mephistopheles to wipe out all of Beethoven's music from the memory of mankind. Beethoven hesitates and is given one hour to consider. Fate, a beautiful spirit, and her dwarf son, Twist, arrive, as Beethoven tries to imagine what he did to deserve damnation. With Fate he reviews his life and comes to realize that he would change nothing, that the pain he suffered inspired his most powerful musical moments. He cannot allow that music to be taken away.

Beethoven informs Mephistopheles that his offer is rejected, and Mephistopheles then offers to release Beethoven's soul for the Tenth Symphony. Beethoven is ready to say no again, when Mephistopheles points to a child sleeping outside in the gutter. She belongs to Mephistopheles and he tells Beethoven of the horrors she will suffer under him. For the Tenth Symphony he will release both the child and Beethoven. Moved, Beethoven agrees.

Fate then asks Beethoven how he can be sure that Mephistopheles will honor his agreement. She will write a contract for both to sign. It reads:

> It is agreed upon this night, March 26, 1827, between the undersigned, that the music of the Tenth Symphony, composed by Ludwig van Bee- thoven, firstborn son of Johann and Maria van Beethoven, in the city of Bonn, shall henceforth be the property of Mephistopheles, Lord of Dark- ness and first fallen from the grace of God. . . .

They both sign the contract, then Mephistopheles grabs the symphony's score and holds it over a lit candle. It is engulfed in flames but not consumed; it re- mains unscathed. Fate then informs a furious Mephistopheles that Beethoven the composer was actually the second-born Ludwig, that Mephistopheles has just signed a contract for the firstborn son who died in infancy. After Mephis- topheles storms off, Fate informs Beethoven that he never had any claim over Beethoven's soul, and so Beethoven, quiet and peaceful, hides his symphony behind a wall, waiting for future generations to find it.

Paul O'Neill, founder of the Trans-Siberian Orchestra, described it as "'Phan- tom of the Opera' meets The Who with Pink Floyd's Light Show." It was an outgrowth of the metal or progressive rock band Savantage, which created two rock operas in the 1990s. In one sense TSO can be considered Savantage with a symphonic string section. TSO was founded in 1996 when O'Neill, who had worked with Savantage as a producer and writer, suggested they add a symphonic orchestra and chorus to create an album of Christmas songs, a move panned by critics. Its success and several similar follow-up albums led to TSO's identification with Christmas music. The rock opera legacy remained, however, and combining that with the larger ensemble resulted in *Beethoven's Last Night,* which appeared in 2000.

The music in *Beethoven's Last Night* is essentially a juxtaposition of rock and classical. Rock has been toned down. It doesn't have the hard edge of most metal, and it does not integrate the two styles—Beethoven and metal—as well as Dragonland's "Beethoven's Nightmare," even though some classical music on *Beethoven's Last Night,* such as the overture to Mozart's opera *The Marriage of Figaro,* Beethoven's *Pathetique,* or the scherzo from the Ninth Symphony, is played with rock instrumentation. The keyboard, central to the piece, is more protean; at times it plays straight Beethoven, at other times other classi- cal music such as Chopin, and it plays original music that has the sound of a mellowed-out Beethoven with a hint of New Age. Yet there are moments when the juxtapositions work, particularly when the soft sounds of the piano are suddenly interrupted with metal blasts, or when the Fifth Symphony motive is combined with choral moments from Mozart's *Requiem.* There are also some surprises, such as when Mozart's well-known Sonata in C (K. 545) is played on guitar, not on piano.

The album is less like a rock opera than a prospectus for a rock opera, or a compilation of songs from a rock musical. The drama is not in the music but rather the liner book, and it can be followed only if the listener reads the book with the CD. Virtually all the action occurs in the printed text, which is neither sung nor spoken on the CD. The songs are the equivalent of operatic arias, moments of reflection or expressions of feelings about the events unfolding. There is no dialogue. One would either have to take a course in speed-reading or have the pause button handy to follow the action, however, as the few instrumental interludes are not sufficient to allow the listener to digest the plot before the next song starts.

Apocalyptica is unusual in its instrumentation, with three, sometimes four cellos and drums. It was founded in 1993 by four cellists at the Sibelius Academy in Helsinki, Finland, Eicca Toppinen, Paavo Lötjönen, Max Lilja, and Antero Manninen. It originally played covers, particularly by Metallica, but gradually began to introduce original work. On June 14, 2008, it introduced an excerpt from the first movement of Beethoven's Fifth Symphony at a Greenpeace concert in Rio de Janeiro. It consisted of only a portion of the exposition, but it was played straight and without drums. It was a serious treatment of Beethoven designed to underline the seriousness of the environmental message that underlay the concert: "Because today is the birth of environmental day we play something special for you."

Beethoven here is not metalicized, but treated as a symbol of respect and seriousness. Apocalyptica never recorded the piece, possibly because it was too removed from their stylistic norm, or because they did not attempt to alter or add to Beethoven. It is not the composition one would normally associate with the environmental movement, but within the context of the concert and the contrast from their normally pounding, driving wall of sound, it created a noticeable contrast, almost as a moment of meditation surrounded by the apocalyptic fury of power metal. Even though it was only a single minute of a single concert, it has gained wide circulation through the internet and on MP3.

No one in heavy metal has exploited Beethoven to the extent of Katherine Thomas, known as "The Great Kat." She does not just play Beethoven. If you believe her, she is Beethoven reincarnated: "The Great Kat is the famous Juilliard graduate violin virtuoso turned Guitar Shredder/METAL MESSIAH/ Reincarnation Of BEETHOVEN!!" Her act consists of three elements: sexuality, loud, blisteringly fast guitar riffs accompanied by screams, and an aggressive hyper-dominatrix persona. The latter extends not only to her stage acts but her interviews as well, where her modus operandi is to deluge the interviewer with a stream of curses and insults, insisting that he is unworthy of approaching her, much less interviewing her. She expects everyone to grovel at her feet, both the press and her fans. Her web page now lists her as The Great Kat Shred Guitar Virtuoso/Violin Goddess.

As advertised, Kat is a graduate of Juilliard with a degree in violin, which she often mentions to prove her superiority. Even at Juilliard some of her performance tendencies were evident. Reviewing her debut recital at Carnegie Hall, Edward Rothstein found her performance of Fritz Kreisler's "Liebesfreud" "too furiously played," parts of Sarasate's "Carmen Fantasy" "overstated," but noted her "strong technique, strong ideas, and strong will."[22]

Kat exploits her sexuality and then turns it on edge. She is a long-haired, long-legged busty blonde who flaunts sexuality much as many male rockers and metalists do. She usually appears onstage in scanty leather fetish gear, and even sells underwear on her web site. She is not a Tina Turner or a Madonna, however. While being provocatively female in appearance, and having the animal attractiveness that would appeal to a testosterone-laden, heavily male audience, she makes clear that she is ready to shred more than the guitar if you do not accept her as the dominant goddess she claims to be. Onstage she whips her fans and expects them to bow down to her and lick her feet. Her DVDs, such as "Metal Messiah," end as she is encircled by worshipers genuflecting toward her as she shreds her guitar. She describes one of her songs, "Castration," as a "1 Minute, 12 Second Psychotic Mini-Opera with The Great Kat seducing and castrating males in 4 Outrageous Acts." In the various acts she poses as a Geisha, Salome, and Black Widow before pulling out the knife.[23] Using the same manner with which men portray machismo in metal, her goal is to empower women, although her approach is not exactly mainstream feminism.

Her act is not subtle. She is direct and flamboyant about her intentions, and most of what she does is accompanied by screams; even when being interviewed she screams at rather than speaks to the interviewer, and in her DVDs if she is not screaming, her mouth is wide open as if she has channeled her scream into her guitar. Her theatrics are as over the top as hard rock groups such as Gwar, to which she has been compared. Her virtuosity is for real, however. *Guitar One, Guitar World, Classic Rock, Gibson Lifestyle,* and *Elle* have all placed her among the "fastest shredders" on the guitar. She claims to play one of her signature pieces, Rimsky-Korsakov's "Flight of the Bumble Bee," at 300 BPM, or beats per minute. Without quibbling about numbers, suffice it to

FIGURE 11.3

The Great Kat, Juilliard graduate (violin),
heavy metal artist, self-proclaimed "Goddess."
Courtesy of Great Kat.

say that she does play it fast. Her "Bloody Vivaldi" stays relatively close to the *Four Seasons,* blending classical instrumentation with heavy metal sounds. The "bloody" in the title refers to her being covered with "blood" as she plays.

Kat insists on the mantle of genius, and given the way she has manufactured a career, she well may deserve it. Her assertion puts her in company with Yngwie Malmsteen, who not only considers himself a genius, but links himself to classical musicians of past centuries. He also disdains most popular musicians. Kat differs mainly in that she links herself to a specific musician, Beethoven, rather than the "good old days of the seventeenth century," and brings a Juilliard diploma to validate her claims.[24]

Kat is World Wrestling Federation riding on the coattails of Beethoven. She can play fast and noisily, as can many graduates of Juilliard and dozens of other universities and conservatories. Her persona fit well with 1990s media, where shouting, insults, and aggressiveness prevailed, especially in political shows as found on cable TV. Civility disappeared, replaced by a pumped up in-your-face aggressiveness. Gangsta rap was at its height, and even the dance floor became a place of violence with rave and slam dancing. It was a small step from there to the choreographed violence of the professional wrestling ring, where even if the events were staged, 250-pound muscle-laden hulks tossing each other about from overhead to the floor could not disguise the potential for real damage that the antics embodied.

Kat's Beethoven repertoire consists principally of the Fifth Symphony. Two versions of it appeared on her second album, *Beethoven on Speed* (1990), "Beethoven on Speed" and "Beethoven Mosh." The latter was closer to a disco version, while the former was a full-bore heavy metal statement. Since then she has recycled this piece, most recently on her 2009 DVD *Beethoven's Guitar Shred.* The details vary, particularly the guitar solos, but it's still the same da-da-da-dum Beethoven. In an interview she stated that she would soon expand her Beethoven repertoire to include a shred version of the various *Fidelio* overtures and the Razumovsky string quartets.

In her stage persona and musical creations, Kat, more than any other performer, raises two issues central to heavy metal: Who is the heavy metal Beethoven, and what role does sexuality play in the genre? Although Kat's classical credentials exceed most, many heavy metal instrumentalists have studied classical music, some extensively. The four cellists in Apocalyptica began experimenting with Metallica songs at the Sibelius Conservatory as a release "from playing all those shitty scales." Ritchie Blackmore studied classical guitar briefly and later studied cello. Edward Van Halen studied classical piano when quite young before taking up the guitar. Randy Rhodes studied piano, classical guitar, and music theory from the age of six. Yngwie Malmsteen, given a guitar at the age of five, also had piano, ballet, voice, flute, and trumpet lessons.

Like much of the popular music world, only a limited selection of Beethoven appears in heavy metal, a handful of tunes that have permeated Western musical culture: "Ode to Joy," the Fifth Symphony, *Für Elise,* the *Pathetique* Sonata. As perceived by many in America, Beethoven is a symbol: the rebel, the genius, deaf guy, the omnipresent long-haired dude scowling down at us from the chest up. He epitomizes the society to be attacked, the statue (or at least bust) to be knocked off the pedestal. Yet to heavy metal fans, Beethoven himself creates conflict. He *is* the musical establishment, the classical canon personified, all the blue-haired ladies and pompous musicians and audiences rolled into one. At the same time he is a source of music that is universally recognized and sure to draw a cheer when quoted, and he is the Napoleonic-era image of the metalist himself: the defiant rebel with pounding music. He is someone that the metalist can both attack and identify with.

Heavy metal is about bravura, transgression, and power, especially power. Originally with an audience mainly of teenage males, it addresses their insecurities about patriarchy and their own masculine roles. It is a place where they can exercise their unrepressed masculinity and at least briefly absolve their insecurities about masculinity. Because these insecurities never go away, they must be reenacted time and again. Metal scholar Robert Walser sees three gender strategies characterizing heavy metal into the mid-1980s: misogyny, exscription, and androgyny. After that he detects a softening, with the introduction of songs that deal with romance.[25]

Exscription, the absence of female performers in early heavy metal, allowed "a world of action, excess transgression but little real violence, one in which men are the only actors, and in which male bonding among the members of a 'hero-team' is the only important social relationship."[26] It was a fantastic world, the performers themselves often donning elaborate costumes that recalled a mixture of science fiction and myth, with elements of doom, gloom, and goth either permeating or blatantly flaunted. Walser stresses the importance of male bonding, which is accomplished by symbols of masculinity, in the clothes, stances—the writhing, strutting, and pelvic thrusts with the guitar—and the music itself, with the pounding rhythm, super-high volume, and overt displays of instrumental virtuosity. It is music designed to overwhelm and intimidate, the ultimate male display of patriarchal power.

This leads to questions of homoeroticism, particularly as some of the performers' costumes suggest an overt androgyny, and the large numbers of gay fans of heavy metal suggest the presence of this element. Such has not limited metal's appeal to heterosexuals, however, as straight fans, according to Walser, can look past this dimension to identify with the power and the freedom that heavy metal promises.

Walser discusses the seductive woman who appears in some videos and explains that, beyond inciting heterosexual desire, they also function to remind the viewer of the threat to their freedom that she poses. Abuse of women, and violence in general, implied by the genre, seldom actually occurs.[27]

By the mid-1980s audiences included many females, and by 1987 the distribution was roughly even. As with much hard rock, women were attracted to heavy metal virtuosi for various reasons, including their macho nature. There was also a message of empowerment to women in this misogynist genre. The band Dokken's song "Heaven Sent" (1987) is about a woman who is both seductive and threatening. In the video—this was at the height of MTV videos—she never says a word but continuously appears in the collage of images, at first walking quietly outside at night, alone, later inside wearing a thin flowing gown surrounded by candles. The lyrics reflect desire and anxiety: "Heaven Sent, thought you would set me free," "Heaven sent, I feel desire." Women could identify as the one who could disturb the all-male fraternity of the metal world, and ultimately gain control of the power and energy that the music evoked.

Women as performers appeared only later in metal bands, and most of the time in traditional female roles, as singers who stressed their own sexuality with alluring and revealing outfits. They remained the seductress, even though many, such as Dora Pesch or Karyn Crisis, were strong-willed with voices whose power equaled that of any metal guitar.

The Great Kat was one of the first women in metal, appearing in the 1980s when the genre still had its hard-edge male-fraternity atmosphere. She was also unique at the time, establishing her reputation primarily as a guitar player, not a singer. After graduating from Juilliard in 1982 she appeared as a violin soloist in the United States, England, and Mexico. Somewhere along the way she heard Judas Priest's "You've Got Another Thing Coming" and began listening to metal. She picked up a guitar in 1985 and by 1986 had put together a demo LP of three songs. In 1987 she recorded her first CD, "Worship Me or Die," and her first stage appearance as a guitarist was in Albany, New York, in 1989.

With her over-the-top stage persona, she makes no attempt to soften the edges of metal, but rather adopts the power of thrash metal bands while inverting its sexual message. The metalhead male is now the one expected to

FIGURE 11.4

From Dokken's video "Heaven Sent." The unnamed woman is the object
of desire whose image appears throughout the video.

worship, and she is the goddess to be worshipped. She has drilled to the very
macho core of metal and vividly personified the male fear of the female taken
to its extreme. This is not the subtle message of Dokken's "Heaven Sent," where
the female is attractive but mysterious, suggesting a danger that may lie below
the surface. This is a frontal assault on the very nature of heavy metal. It succeeds because she also flaunts her sexuality in her costumes and general appearance. She is to be desired and feared, the fear stemming from the desire.
As outlandish as her act may appear, there is a consistency to it, and within the
framework of the 1980s and 1990s it both appropriates and transgresses the
genre, which is itself about transgression.

Since rap makes heavy use of sampling, it is not surprising that Beethoven's music appears in the genre, sometimes fleetingly, sometimes as the basis of the piece itself. Here we will do our own sampling: we will discuss three rap or hip-hop songs, two of which specifically mention Beethoven's name in the title and a third based on Beethoven's music.

VHB Beethoven's Fifth (Street) Symphony appeared in 1984. Recorded by DJ Chuck Chillout, member of the B-Boys, a Bronx hip-hop group, and produced by Vincent Davis, owner of Vintertainment Records, it was released as a 33⅓ single on Vintertainment in the United States and Streetwave in the United Kingdom. Included were four versions: a long version, short version, hip-hop version, and an a capella hip-hop version. An Electronic-techno piece, one detects in it the influence of Murphy's Fifth, although it has a hip-hop beat and uses less of the symphony itself. It consists mostly of the four-note motive repeated with long breaks between the statements. In the hip-hop version the hip-hop rhythm is stronger and one hears a voice repeating the word "Beethoven" while another occasionally repeats the word "Fifth" and other voices laugh in the background. The a capella version contains the rhythmic background and the voices.

In one respect this may be considered the black answer to 1970s disco. The 1980s were the height of the break-dance phenomenon, and the word "b-boy" stood for break-boy, a male dancer who engaged in breaking, which itself was closely associated with hip-hop. Beethoven's Fifth was taken from disco, with its glamorous club scene populated by beautiful (white) people, and brought to the street, to a more robust and athletic dance style. The title of the song implies as much: this is the Beethoven of the street, Beethoven merged with the hip-hop sound of the African American community.

The rapper group Soulja Boyz—not to be confused with DeAngelo Way, the rapper known as Soulja Boy—released a CD in 2007 that included a song titled "Beethoven." Soulja Boyz is based in Sacramento, California, and consists of DeAngelo Jenkins, known as D., Norrie Ray Whitaker, known as N. O., and David Lowery, known as D. A.

Their song "Beethoven" begins with an appeal for some help from Beethoven: "I have to get Beethoven to help me out on this one man." The song consists of a rap verse and chorus. As the rappers lay down the vocal, *Für Elise* plays in the background. Then they all break into a chorus based on the melody from the Turkish rondo in the last movement of Mozart's Piano Sonata in A minor, K. 331. There is no distinction between Mozart and Beethoven and no mention of Mozart. Beethoven here is the ur-classical composer, a mythological name to be drawn on when something classical is invoked. Curiously, the two classical pieces, *Für Elise* and the A minor sonata movement, fit together well.

Nas, short for Nasir bin Olu Dara Jones, grew up in the housing projects of Queens, New York. The release of his first album, *Illmatic,* in 1994, displayed his poetic gift as well as his street cred and instantly established him as a major presence in gangsta rap. After *Illmatic* he purposely cultivated a more mainstream pop style, but he never denied his strong hip-hop roots and his connection to the African American community. He has been involved in several controversies, with the rapper Jay-Z (they settled their feud amicably and subsequently collaborated), with Bill O'Reilly (they did not), and with Al Sharpton, Jesse Jackson, and his own record label when he wanted to entitle his 2008 album *Nigger.* Faced with the possibility that the title would limit distribution or worse, he changed it, allowing the recording to reach his fans.

His most successful piece, "I Can," appeared on his album *God's Son* in 2002. Panned by some critics—*Rolling Stone* called it a "boring-ass filler . . . a silly stay-in-school ad"[28]—it was an inspirational message addressed to children and young people of the black community: Keep away from drugs, don't try to be older than you are, be proud of yourself and your African heritage, and you can succeed. Near the beginning of the video we see a ghetto field with housing projects in the background and a spinet piano in the middle. A black adolescent girl begins to play *Für Elise.* As Nas unwinds his rhyming message and many children and young people respond, "I know I can," the Beethoven tune continues as musical backdrop. The young girl playing the piano at the beginning signifies that with work and dedication to your task you too can play Beethoven. Here Beethoven is equated with success.

Beethoven's music has little presence in country music, but Beethoven as a symbol of high culture does. When the Gatlin Brothers played a country music gig at Billy Bob's, a mega nightclub in Fort Worth, Texas, that claims to be the "the world's largest honky-tonk," they not only ironically interjected parts of Beethoven's Fifth Symphony into their piece "Boogie and Beethoven," but teased the audience with side comments about its presence: "trying to bring a little culture to Billy Bob's here" and "too much culture for some of you." And when George Jones and Johnny Paycheck recorded Berry's "Roll Over Beethoven," they began with some introductory banter:

(Spoken with a heavy country accent):
PAYCHECK: *Hey George.*
JONES: *Haaaiiy.*
PAYCHECK: *Do you know who . . . Bay-TOE-vin is?*

JONES: *Ha-ha-ha-ha-ha, Johnny I don't even know who . . . Cha-KOW-ski is.*
PAYCHECK: *Well we're gonna do a song about both of 'em.*
JONES: *We're gonna larn somethin' here.*

In both cases Beethoven is an icon used to situate the singer and the audience, while at the same time the singers satirize both classical music and their own followers. The world of Beethoven is not the world of the country boy, but from a distance it is to be respected, as it is to be mocked. Like most country music, usage is not subtle, and references are direct and specific. Here the high-low divide is shown at its most transparent, and the role of Beethoven, whose music is either nuanced, masked, or transformed in many other popular styles, is laid bare: he is a symbol and a myth, representative of a class far removed from the common world of the working-class American, yet he is hardly liminal; he is a familiar presence throughout all levels of society.

12

Beethoven Everywhere

*B*Y THE LATE TWENTIETH CENTURY, Beethoven seemed to be everywhere, defying the many laments about the death of classical music much
as he himself defied the aristocracy in the early nineteenth century. His bust
had become omnipresent in American culture, accruing the same universal
recognition accorded figures such as George Washington or Jesus. One need
not be a musician or classical music buff to recognize Beethoven's image any
more than one has to be a Christian to recognize Warner Sallman's painting
of *The Head of Christ*, or an American citizen to recognize Emanuel Gottlieb
Leutze's painting of *Washington Crossing the Delaware*. While many of the
Beethoven images belong to the same "velvet Elvis" tradition as Sallman's portrayal of Jesus, their importance lies not in historical fidelity but in the degree
that they have permeated American culture. Beethoven may not be a religious
figure, although some writers have tried to deify him, but he is an icon, the
subject of myth and veneration.

Precisely because he is not connected with any religion, Beethoven is fair
game for commercial purposes of all stripes, and his music is available for borrowing, sampling, and satire. Beyond the musical world Beethoven has been
used in television, magazine, and newspaper advertising, has been glorified or
satirized in comic strips, and has seen an entire industry of images connected

to him, with reproductions ranging from rag dolls to moveable action figures. He is heard on television sound tracks and in theme songs, has been used to market everything from hamburgers to fine watches, and has been appropriated by many a visual artist as well. His music has become a political symbol deemed appropriate for patriotic purposes and events. His name has been associated with commercial enterprises as well as dogs in movies. Buildings, both connected to music and outside the musical world, have been named after him. The internet has only magnified Beethoven's presence, with internet artists and composers manipulating his music to striking effect. He is even found buried in computer hardware. Beethoven has become deeply embedded in American culture, as much an icon as the founding fathers, although only a few sound bites of his music are generally recognized.

Reviewing Edmund Morris's popular biography of Beethoven, Greg Sandow observed that we know Beethoven but we don't really know Beethoven, because "he has slipped out of our culture."[1] Rather, he has shrunk as he has grown. He is now deeply rooted in the American consciousness, universally known and recognized. But the iconic Beethoven is only a small part of Beethoven. Sandow is correct that we don't know the full Beethoven; what we know are the barest framework of biography—"that deaf guy"—or the image—the hair, the scowl, the square jaw—and a handful of musical fragments. Even the six or seven pieces that the public recognizes are only known in small parts. Da-da-da-dum, the "Ode to Joy," the opening of the *Moonlight* Sonata, the first two phrases of *Für Elise*, this is the Beethoven embedded in the American psyche. These are the big four, the ones most likely to garner recognition. To that, one can add the second movement of the Seventh Symphony, some of the Sixth Symphony, and the *Pathetique* Sonata, which is in one way unique: all three movements have been used in popular culture, although to my knowledge they have never been used or associated together outside the classical music world.

A striking demonstration of public attitudes toward Beethoven occurred in the early seventies on late-night television. One evening I caught a TV commercial in which the announcer was hawking an LP collection along the lines of "the 100 greatest classical melodies," a type of recording that has appeared in many variants. To clinch his sales pitch he bragged, "Now you can hear Beethoven's famous 'Ode to Joy' without having to sit through an entire symphony." Well before politics degenerated into an occasional punch line, well before the internet fragmented the attention span, and while comedy shows such as those of Carol Burnett and Flip Wilson depended on lengthy sketches, America in its music was already into the sound-bite world. Anyone familiar with late-night TV of that era will recognize that this was not an improbable comment for a commercial.

Many Americans in fact know Beethoven's music through its appearance on TV programs, either as theme song or for dramatic accent. The Scherzo of the Ninth Symphony has been used for two news broadcasts, NBC's *Huntley-Brinkley Report* in the 1960s and 1970s and, from 2003 to 2011, *Countdown* on cable television's MSNBC. *The Huntley-Brinkley Report* was broadcast from October 29, 1956, to July 31, 1970, when Huntley retired. The closing credits featured the first part of the Beethoven scherzo; because of the popularity of the program and, in the days before the ubiquitous remote control and 200 channels, the tendency to leave one station on, millions became familiar with it. The vast majority of the public was unaware that this was Beethoven, only that they heard an upbeat, catchy tune played by an orchestra. That Beethoven would be played on network television usually elicited disbelief.[2] Keeping it all in the family, the network used the studio recording of the Ninth by Arturo Toscanini and the NBC Symphony.

Befitting the faster pace and more fragmented character of television in the twenty-first century, *Countdown* used only the opening two-second flourish of the Ninth at the beginning of the program. Whether the choice of the theme came from its original host, Keith Olbermann, or from an NBC executive, it does not seem coincidental.[3] The allusion tied the program to the most successful news program in television history and reminds the viewer of NBC's long heritage in delivering news.

The "Ode to Joy" appeared in the introduction to the third season of the CBS sitcom *Everybody Loves Raymond*. Since the introduction ran before each episode, it served as a quasi-theme song. Ray and his wife, Debra, live across the street from Ray's parents and his brother Robert. Ray's mother, Marie, is a fastidious housekeeper, manipulative and invariably critical of Debra, whose approach to things is looser than Marie's, but who is frustrated by trying to keep a household together with three small boys and not much help from her husband. Ray's father, Frank, is crass and macho. Neither Ray nor Debra are happy to have Ray's family so close. In the skit, Ray looks out his window to see his parents and his brother leaving their front door and heading toward them. "They're coming!" he shouts as the "Ode to Joy" begins to play, apparently on the stereo, and the family rushes to get organized. Ray dashes to lock the door as Debra throws a stuffed animal at the stereo, exploding it and shutting off Beethoven. Ray collapses in front of the door, relieved at getting to the latch before his parents do, when a hand goes through the mail chute and touches his hair; the "Ode to Joy" returns, this time nondiegetically. In this brief segment the "Ode to Joy" becomes an ominous march as Ray's and Debra's panic is interspersed with shots of Marie, Frank, and Robert moving steadfastly toward the house in time with the music, with close-ups of Marie's stern demeanor almost suggesting the arrival of an executioner. In this appropriation of the symphony, the ghost of *A Clockwork Orange* lives on.

It should come as no surprise that the opening motive of the Fifth Symphony has had an extensive life on American television. Several episodes of *The Simpsons* have used different Beethoven pieces, including *Für Elise,* the Sixth Symphony, and the "Ode to Joy." The Fifth Symphony alone has appeared in three contexts on the show. In the episode "The Seven-Beer Snitch," which originally aired on April 3, 2005, Marge convinces the architect Frank Gehry to design a concert hall for Springfield in order to raise what she considers the abysmally low cultural level of her town. Unfortunately, the citizens' disinterest in culture drives them out of the concert hall in droves on opening night, when Beethoven's Fifth Symphony is played.

Another use of Beethoven's Fifth Symphony is on an answering machine of Bart's friend Barney, in which the four-note motive is accompanied with the words "Nobody's here." This appeared in the episode "One Fish, Two Fish, Blowfish, Blue Fish," which originally aired on January 24, 1991.[4] The idea for the answering machine likely came from a commercial that aired in the late 1980s for "Crazy Calls," a tape that included seven different songs for an answering machine, ranging from an Andrews Sisters parody to Jacques Offenbach's "Can-Can," to rap and Beethoven's Fifth. Created by Mitch and Ira Yuspeh, it sold over one million units in two years and was followed by others, including a Christmas holiday set. Probably to avoid copyright issues, Barney's machine has a different voice, a more upbeat rendering of the symphony's motive, and a different text, "Nobody's here" rather than the original "Nobody's home." In another episode, "Lisa's Wedding," based on a fortuneteller's view of the future, Lisa is twenty-three and becomes engaged to a young Englishman, Hugh Parkfield. Martin Prince, the class nerd, who had supposedly died in a science fair explosion at the Simpsons' school, had not actually died and now lives under the school playing a pipe organ, like the Phantom of the Opera. When he hears of Lisa's engagement he responds by playing Walter Murphy's pop arrangement of Beethoven's Fifth.

Among other *Simpsons* episodes, "Dog of Death" is a direct parody of the use of the Ninth Symphony in *A Clockwork Orange.* The Simpson's dog SLH (Santa's Little Helper) falls ill and needs an operation. Forced to sacrifice essentials, such as beer for Homer, in order to pay for the operation, the family is in an angry mood. SLH senses that and runs away, eventually to be picked up by Mr. Burns, who trains him to be an attack dog. As part of the training,

SLH is connected to a helmet with electrodes and is forced to listen to the "Ode to Joy" while seeing scenes, some universally horrific, some especially horrific to a dog. There is an atomic explosion and the Hindenburg in flames, as well as Fido being rapped with a newspaper, someone kicking over his water bowl, the toilet lid crashing down on him as he drinks, and Him, Lyndon Johnson's dog, being picked up by the ears. The scene even has someone putting moisture drops in SLH's eyes as they did for Alex in *A Clockwork Orange*.

The Fifth Symphony is an integral part of the *Judge Judy* program, which recreates a real trial with former judge Judith Sheindlin. Although not an official court of law, the cases are culled from people who have actually filed for judgment in a small claims court and who have agreed to have the case heard on the show as binding arbitration. The action is unscripted and unrehearsed. Beethoven sets the somber tone, as the opening motive of the Fifth Symphony is heard whenever a judgment is made. The motive is thus Judge Judy's gavel amplified, a signal that justice has been rendered.

In all instances the Fifth Symphony motive portends something ominous. In *Judge Judy* it is the verdict. In the *Simpsons* episode "One Fish" Homer is in jail and has used his one phone call to phone his friend Barney to bring money for his bail. That Homer hears the answering machine is not good news, although it turns out that Barney is there and soon picks up the phone. In "Lisa's Wedding," it is prophetic, as the wedding never takes place and the relationship ends disastrously. These uses parallel Abel Gance's 1936 film *Un Grand Amour de Beethoven*, in which menacing or fateful twists in the plot are accompanied by the portentous four notes. This pattern occurs so often in Gance's film that critics derided it as cliché.

Only rarely has a television program used an entire movement of the Fifth Symphony. On January 27, 1951, Sid Caesar and Nanette Fabray play a married couple pantomiming an argument to the first movement of the Fifth on *Your Show of Shows*. This has become an internet classic today, having received over one million views on YouTube in its first three years on the site, as well as appearing on many other sites. Facial expressions, body language, and finger pointing follow closely the lines and rhythms of the music. Finally Caesar packs a bag and is about to leave when Fabray convinces him not to. As they make up, however, she notices a hair on his jacket—not hers—and furiously sends him out the door. After the door slams to a Beethoven sforzato, Fabray calls the dog over and while petting it notices a hair exactly like the one on Caesar's jacket. She then runs to the door as Caesar comes back and to the final chords they embrace.[5]

I mention this sketch because it is emblematic of early television. Well before *Laugh-In* pioneered the quick punch-line pacing and jokes, well before the age of the short attention span and internet surfing, comedy routines on television were more leisurely and were expected to encompass some narrative. Beethoven, of course, determined the length of this routine, but in a strictly informal and unscientific survey I found that some people today complain that it is too long. The routine also demonstrates the comedic talent of Caesar and Fabray, as this was done before a live audience, well before the existence of videotape and any possibility of a retake.

Beethoven's music is also found in many television commercials. In a McDonald's commercial that aired in the mid-1980s, a little girl is to play in a piano recital. She is scared and doesn't want to play, but her reluctance is assuaged by her father's promise to take her to McDonald's after the performance. As she plays *Für Elise* she sings to herself a jingle about McDonald's, the burger and fries and chocolate shake that she will soon eat.

A Reebok commercial that aired in 2007–2008 features a number of young athletes and other individuals engaged in various activities, ranging from playing basketball to jogging to sitting in an outdoor café. They all look up and see raindrops starting to come down. They wear Reebok shoes, of course, and the entire commercial is filmed in black and white and slow motion. There are no voices heard and the only text comes at the end when the words "Don't get caught" appear on the screen. In the last second the Reebok name and logo appear. Throughout the entire commercial the Andante of Beethoven's Seventh Symphony plays. For sheer beauty of sound and melody, few Beethoven compositions match this movement: with its steady, methodical pace, combined with black-and-white photography and the semi-abstract beginning, the slow-motion balletic movement of the athletes and their continual glances upward as they observe individual drops of rain falling, the commercial stands as an individual moment of *Gesamtkunstwerk* poetry that conveys to the viewer "class." Reebok is thus associated not only with sinuously graceful athletes but also with the finer things in life.

One of the more recent uses of the "Ode to Joy" appeared in a General Electric commercial that aired during the 2010 Winter Olympics. The screen flashes to several doctor's offices of children and adults, all saying "ah" as the doctor checks their throat with a tongue depressor. The "ahs" gradually merge into a richly harmonized version of the "Ode to Joy," as the announcer intones about "healthy imagination." Like the Reebok commercial, there is no direct verbal reference to a product; as the chorus of "ahs" grows into a symphonic statement, the camera pans out toward a panoramic, almost global view. The overt message is that GE is working through technology toward better health for millions; the only slightly more subtle message is that GE is everywhere.

Hyundai used Beethoven's Fifth Symphony in a manner similar to the GE commercial. In a series of "Duh" commercials released in 2007, a chorus intones various pieces of music to the syllable "duh." Given how well the syllable fits with the opening motive of the Beethoven symphony, it was inevitable that a commercial would exploit that. As three Hyundai's are driven through water, creating an almost abstract pattern, the "duh" symphony begins. Lest there be any doubt about the symbolism, a voiceover soon explains the colloquial meaning of the phrase: "The word 'duh,' meaning it's obvious, a no brainer." Of course, what is obvious is the wisdom of buying a Hyundai. Continuing the motoring theme, Lexus also used Beethoven in advertising but in a very different way. Elvis Costello is seen sitting in the back seat of a Lexus listening to the Scherzo of Beethoven's Ninth Symphony. Costello admits that Beethoven "wrote a few toe-tappers," and after a bit of biographical musing about Beethoven's deafness, he further admits that while it "doesn't start like a rock 'n' roll record, it's exciting like a rock 'n' roll record." The "money" line of the commercial is that "this is music you can see," equating Lexus with Beethoven.

Particularly telling is a Vitamin Water commercial that opens with a sumptuous concert hall seen in the background as two distinguished older men in tuxedos in the balcony announce that Beethoven's Ninth will be played, but that the conductor will be replaced by Curtis Jackson, otherwise known as the rapper 50 Cent. The orchestra rises as 50 Cent walks in with a Vitamin Water bottle. The other announcer, puzzled, looks at his note card as he states, in a quizzical, bemused voice, that 50 Cent considers Beethoven a "True OG."[6] 50 Cent then summarily dismisses the first violist and replaces him with the rapper DJ Whoo Kid, who also keeps the first violist's viola. The first theme of the first movement sounds before the orchestra breaks into a symphonic hip-hop version of 50 Cent's first big hit, "In Da Club," and all the while the announcers continue to comment on the action in their deep, mellifluous voices. Cut to an image of Vitamin Water and an exhortation to try it.

Few commercials exploit as well as this one the dichotomy between the pompous, stuffy, elite image of high culture, here epitomized by Beethoven's Ninth Symphony, and the world of the street, epitomized by 50 Cent and DJ Whoo Kid. It is about the clichés that once surrounded Beethoven to a broad segment of Americans, although Beethoven here is only the most visible symbol for a set of attitudes about classical music in general that persisted throughout the twentieth century. The deep monotone of the announcers highlights this point, as they recall a time when classical broadcasters did their best to convince listeners that they were about to have the Holy Grail revealed to them.

Because of his value as a symbol of status, Beethoven has proven to be particularly effective in selling wine. From the largest, mass-produced California mega-wineries to small, cult vintners, Beethoven's name has lent a cachet to a product in which image and perception are all important, and the manner in which Beethoven is used is directly related to the winery's target audience.

Beethoven's music has been used by at least two wineries. The best-known enomusical appropriation of Beethoven was in a 1978 wine commercial for Paul Masson that featured Orson Welles. The thirty-second spot opens with Welles sitting at a table with a bowl of fruit, a wine glass, and a bottle of wine. In the background is an expensive stereo receiver playing the beginning of Beethoven's Fifth Symphony. As Welles turns down the volume, he explains, "It took Beethoven four years to write that symphony. Some things can't be rushed: good music and good wine." Pouring a glass, Welles describes the wine and finishes with a quote purportedly from Paul Masson himself: "We will sell no wine before its time." Paul Masson wine, Orson Welles and his deep, rolling voice, surrounded by emblems of success and sophistication, and of course a Beethoven symphony created with the same care as the wine—all these create a rich pageant of symbols that belong together. Chuck Berry had argued that rock 'n' roll was on a par with classical music; here Orson Welles argues the same for a mass-marketed California wine.

Moving beyond television commercials, Arietta wine aims for a completely different audience and uses Beethoven much more subtly. Arietta is the brainchild of wine auctioneer Fritz Hatton and the winemaker John Kongsgaard. They shared more than just a fondness for classical music, however; they were directly involved in it. Kongsgaard was the director of Chamber Music in Napa Valley, where Hatton appeared on some of their programs as a pianist along with a roster that included Isaac Stern, Garrick Ohlsson, Emanuel Ax, several prominent string quartets, and, appropriately, the Santa Fe Chamber Music Festival Wine Hounds Piano Quartet. While "arietta" literally means a short aria or song, the winery takes its name from the Arietta section of Beethoven's last piano sonata, op. 111. When accessing their web page one hears the Beethoven arietta,[7] and the wine label features a Beethoven sketch of the opening of this movement.

The arietta's inclusion is a gesture that operates on several levels. For most people the name and the graphic seem appropriately related in a general way; arietta sounds like a musical term, and there is a handwritten musical score on the label. It should be pointed out, however, that there is no mention of Beethoven anywhere. Some will recognize the term arietta as operatic and associate the wine with music of the highest class. There are also those who will get

FIGURE 12.1

Label of the California winery Arietta.

the connection with Beethoven by recognizing the passage from a late Beethoven piano sonata. One can only imagine how small and select that group is. This is a long way from Orson Welles commenting on the opening motive of the Fifth Symphony.

In 1987, the journal *19th-Century Music* reprinted an entry from a Berkeley wine importer's brochure in which three vintages of a wine are explained. The vintages are compared to Haydn, Mozart, and Beethoven:

> 1981, the most classic of the three vintages, recalls Haydn's music. 1982 is something divine. Mozart springs to mind. . . . They possess a god-given

perfection, and if the angels drink wine (what else?) they'll be drinking 82s. It follows that the 1983 is our Ludwig van Beethoven vintage, a bit too wild and tempestuous for angelic circles. Fist shaking is not permitted in heaven. These 83s are far from tame or timid. As a new piano was developed to withstand Beethoven's thunderous passages, so a wineglass seems barely able to contain these audacious 1983 clarets.

The stormy Beethoven. Were sound included, surely this would be accompanied by the *Pathetique* Sonata, the Fifth Symphony, or the last movement of the *Moonlight* Sonata. Were the copywriter a musical sophisticate, maybe even the last movement of the *Appassionata* Sonata would be used.

Beethoven has proven to be a boon to marketing throughout American commerce. Businesses and buildings, ranging from a plethora of music stores to a Kansas City steakhouse, bear his name. Baltimore and Detroit have Beethoven apartments, and the promoters of both complexes have leveraged his name in their promotions. The Baltimore Beethoven apartments is located in Bolton Hill, one of the first areas in Baltimore City to undergo urban renewal more than a half-century ago. Originally consisting of mostly elegant town houses, the area appealed to culturally conscious urban dwellers even before the major push to restore inner Baltimore City in the 1970s and 1980s. When the owner put the Beethoven Apartments on the market in 2009, he stressed its proximity to Meyerhoff Hall, the home of the Baltimore Symphony, and the Lyric Opera House. The principal attraction of the Beethoven Apartments in Detroit, which was renovated and literally rescued from decay in 2010, is its proximity to Wayne State University. This, however, did not stop the developer, Scott Lowell, from taking advantage of its name: "The symphony is tuning up in Detroit as the newly renovated Beethoven Apartments open this summer."

On an even grander scale, Symphony Village in Centreville, Maryland, a designed community for persons fifty-five and up on the Eastern Shore near Annapolis, has an entire composers' collection of individual homes available. One can choose from the Bach, the Strauss (which Strauss not identified), the Schubert, the Gershwin, the Vivaldi, the Mozart, and the Beethoven. These vary in size from 1,700 to 4,000 square feet. While there is no evidence that house size is a critical commentary of the importance of these composers, Beethoven does stand at the top of this hierarchy, with his name attached to the largest, most expensive model. Equating size with musical reputation unfortunately breaks down, however, when one realizes that the smallest house is the Bach, suggesting that he is somehow a lesser composer than Vivaldi or Gershwin. Whatever the motivation or the musical preferences of the developers, Beethoven's association with the most gigantic is almost certainly a statement about how Beethoven is perceived within the broader framework of American culture.

Who is she? The great mystery of Beethoven's life, and one of the great mysteries of Western cultural history, is the recipient of a passionate love letter that Beethoven wrote when he was forty-two years old. The question ranks with the identification of the dedicatee of Shakespeare's sonnets. Thanks to much detailed investigation by scholars for over a century, we know a lot about the events surrounding the letter and can narrow the field of candidates down to a few. Yet in spite of some intense detective work, no consensus has emerged.[8]

In the summer of 1812—even the date was originally uncertain as Beethoven did not put the year on the letter—Beethoven was vacationing in Teplitz, where he expected to meet a woman who had already been his lover. They apparently did not meet, and virtually nothing is known about subsequent events. The letter itself, written over several days, displays a passion far exceeding any other correspondence of Beethoven. What happened? Why did we not hear anything further of her? The letter was found in a secret drawer in Beethoven's desk after he died, some fifteen years later. Was the letter sent and returned, or did Beethoven decide not to send it? She is not named in the letter, although some initials may hint at her identity. From a phrase that Beethoven used in the letter, she is known to history as his "unsterbliche Geliebte," "immortal beloved."

Thanks to the watchmaker Steinhausen, the mystery has been solved in a way that no scholar could have imagined. Steinhausen's 2008 magazine advertisement for their "Beethoven Skeleton Watch" proudly proclaims: "We found Beethoven's Immortal Beloved! And now it belongs on your wrist." To my knowledge, this solution has not been accepted by the scholarly fraternity. Steinhausen is not finished with the Beethoven analogy, however. On its web site, without referencing a particular piece of music, it states that the watch is "to the eyes what Beethoven's composition is to the ears." Thus Beethoven is now available for your wrist.

It is strictly a man's watch. There is no female version, for wearing the "Immortal Beloved" somehow seems inappropriate for a woman's wrist. The ad is especially clever as the insertion of the "Immortal Beloved" into the copy further enhances the masculine quality of the item. It is also a skeleton watch, which in this context means the workings are visible through the crystal. The visibility of the movement, the steel and gold inside, and the "sturdy leather

FIGURE 12.2

The Immortal Beloved discovered. Steinhausen watch advertisement.

band" are all designed to serve the same purpose as an expensive German sports car, to project a rugged yet sophisticated masculinity. In that sense, the choice of Beethoven is almost certainly no accident.

In America of the late twentieth and early twenty-first centuries, the predominant mode of popular culture and commodity is irony. In commercials irony sells, engages the perceiver, and embeds an object in her memory. The more absurd, the greater the success. Such irony in relation to Beethoven is dependent on the continuing notion of high culture as special, no matter the extent that it has been undermined by the reality of the postmodern revolution. Almost all the uses of Beethoven beyond the art music world depend on the beliefs that arose in the nineteenth century about that world, and of Beethoven's place at the apex of the canon. Thus Beethoven's tragic affair with the Immortal Beloved can be reduced to a wristwatch. The ad works, however, only on the assumption that the reader knows something about the "Immortal Beloved" story. That the ad appeared in an airline magazine means a targeted audience, a group of middle- and upper-middle-class travelers, many of whom are businessmen. Other ads in the same magazine are aimed at either young professionals, such as high-end dating sites, or well-heeled retirees, such as expensive condominiums, or the electronically obsessed, those who must have the latest gadgets. Possibly Steinhausen believed that readers would be old enough to remember the movie *Immortal Beloved.* With so many watches on the market, here is one that promises not only an exotic-looking watch with a Swiss name, but a bit of Beethoven too.

Instruments other than watches are part of the story as well. In 1850 Heinrich Englehard Steinweg immigrated to America from Germany with his family. He continued what he had begun in Germany, building pianos—he had already built some 482. One son stayed behind and continued to make pianos, but in America Steinweg and his other sons changed their name to Steinway and formed Steinway and Sons. Within a few decades they were the most successful piano manufacturer in the world and their name became synonymous with quality instruments. By the second half of the twentieth century, however, financial problems mounted and the remaining family members were less interested in continuing the tradition. They sold the company to CBS in 1985, which then sold it to a group of investors who formed the corporation Steinway Musical Properties. Through a series of mergers and acquisitions, the name then became Steinway Musical Instruments. Owners of the company decided to go public, and on August 2, 1996, they made an initial public offering of stock.

There was one problem, however. The new company was destined for the New York Stock Exchange and needed a symbol of one, two, or three letters. The two obvious choices, S&S and SMI, were already taken. Steinway wanted something that would convey the nature of their business, their mission, and a sense of prestige to who they were. The choice: LVB. It was a symbol that even the most culturally challenged stockbroker or hard-nosed financial expert would recognize. The word Beethoven was no longer necessary; the initials themselves conjured the entire range of aural and visual images associated with him, and Steinway, by appropriating the most visible symbol of classical culture, immediately set its pianos and other musical ventures apart from the Asian imports that were threatening its market position. Once again, Beethoven proved to be good business.

Given the millions of hits from any internet search on Beethoven, it is not surprising that he would even be part of a classical music baseball team. In the online game "Beethoven's Baseball,"[9] the player chooses five composers from among Stravinsky, Schumann, Mozart, Mahler, Copland, Brahms, and Bach (each is shown on screen as a baseball player holding a bat, with an identifiable approximation of the composer's head), and the game is Beethoven versus the other players. He thus takes on the entire classical spectrum, from Baroque to twentieth-century, German, Russian-French, and American. When cued by the mouse Beethoven makes an improbably involved windup, pitches, and while the ball is in the air the player has to answer a classical musical question. If answered correctly the player is rewarded with a hit, and answered incorrectly it is a strike. After three strikeouts or five runs scored, the inning is over. As the game is played the viewer sees the composers moving around the bases and hears the sounds of a baseball game, the bats and the crowd. There is no classical music to accompany the game, and the questions are mostly biographical. While listed as a kid's game, the questions are not for kids. Some are quite difficult.

Beethoven has invaded the computer far beyond the internet, however, as the following situation attests. Assume that you are sitting at your computer and it suddenly begins to play *Für Elise,* unexpectedly, unbidden, over and over. It won't stop. Have you been hit by a virus? *PC Magazine* reported receiving multiple calls and emails about a "Beethoven Virus" in 2001, in which the computer begins to play *Für Elise* incessantly. It turned out not to be a virus at all, but an integral part of the computer hardware. Diamond Flower International, a manufacturer of motherboards, inserted the tune into their BIOS as a warning that either the computer was overheating or the voltage from the power supply was off. Inquiries to DFI failed to ascertain who chose *Für Elise* or why Beethoven was deemed appropriate to warn the user of impending disaster. I was unable to find a single employee who had been there in the mid- to late 1990s when this motherboard was made. Representatives with whom I discussed this were stunned that DFI would do such a thing. The tune itself, with its childlike innocence, is known throughout the world, which may be one reason for its choice, and possibly DFI did not want to frighten the user too much. Da-da-da-dum or Chopin's *Funeral March* would not have been a good choice.

Given Beethoven's striking appearance, familiar music, and almost universal name recognition, it is no surprise that he has appeared in many cartoons. Most of the time he is mentioned without comment, usually in connection with the high-low culture divide or his deafness. The strip *Drabble* makes jokes about the inappropriateness of using Beethoven's music as a ringtone (May 9, 2005). In *Arlo and Janis* (October 18, 1997), Arlo has a Beethoven bust that came with his newly purchased piano. As he and a friend examine it, Arlo comments, "I think it's Meat Loaf."[10] In *Motley* (July 23, 2004), Joey's mother

asks him about his piano lesson, to which Joey replies that his teacher thinks that Beethoven would have been pleased. Delighted, Joey's mother asks, "That you played so well?" To which Joey responds, "No, that he was deaf."

Without question the most sustained use of Beethoven in cartoons occurred in *Peanuts,* arguably the most popular cartoon of the past fifty years. Between 1950 and 2000 Charles M. Schulz created 17,897 *Peanuts* strips. How many Americans know Schroeder with his toy piano and his love of Beethoven? It was a long-running gag that appeared in over 250 strips with many permutations. Schulz was not a musician, but he developed a love of classical music while an instructor at the Art Instruction School in Minneapolis. Schroeder is the virtuoso and Beethoven fanatic who plays on a toy piano that has only painted-on black keys. Neither Schroeder nor the piano appears in the first strip that mentioned Beethoven, however. Charlie Brown attempts to play the violin, and, characteristic of Charlie Brown, does so badly. In the last strip he comments to Snoopy, who has been holding his ears in pain (see Figure 12.3).

Later, as Schroeder takes over the musical duties of the strip, Schulz depicts his playing by including scores in balloons above the piano. The music is not random; the balloons are fragments of specific Beethoven pieces and the piece chosen is often related to the cartoon itself. For instance, several strips show variants of Schroeder exercising before leaping to the piano to play the opening notes of the *Hammerklavier* Sonata. This sonata is the longest and arguably the most challenging sonata that Beethoven wrote, metaphorically demanding great dexterity and stamina. Thus while the cartoon is funny for anyone reading it, as it suggests Schroder's absolute dedication to his piano, knowing what piece is depicted adds another level of humor. William Meredith, director of the Ira F. Brilliant Center for Beethoven Studies at San José State University, explained this in a major exhibit of *Peanuts* Beethoven cartoons he curated with Jane O'Cain of the Schulz Museum; the exhibit was seen at both institu-

FIGURE 12.4

Peanuts, March 25, 1952. Schroeder plays the *Hammerklavier* Sonata, op. 106. 2010 Peanuts Worldwide LLC.

tions. Titled "Schulz's Beethoven, Schroeder's Music," it featured many of the Schulz Beethoven cartoons along with commentary by Meredith. The exhibit was featured in a lengthy article in the *New York Times*.[11] The strips were also posted online with the music in the cartoons available as audio files.

Schulz later admitted that his favorite composer was Brahms, but that the name Beethoven worked better in the strip because of its three-syllable sound. His decision, reminiscent of but preceding Chuck Berry's, was wise in another way: Beethoven has drilled deeply into American culture, a figure of almost universal name recognition who instantly conjures an image, a great advantage for a visual medium. Brahms, although revered by many in the classical music world, is known outside it, if at all, only vaguely, one of those older European composers who may have written a lullaby. For most of the American public it is much easier to identify with Beethoven than with Brahms.

Going back to an earlier era, World War II saw comics of an entirely different tone than the light-hearted frustrations characteristic of *Peanuts*. Some became war propaganda, as the cover of *Real Life Comics* of January 1943 illustrates. A white, square-jawed American soldier is about to kill a Japanese soldier who is essentially a buck-toothed caricature, dark, evil-looking, almost nonhuman. The cover sports the heading "True Adventures of the World's Greatest Heroes" printed with the admonition, "Buy War Bonds and Stamps for Victory." The issue tells the story of four heroes: Alexander, William Tell, Giraud, and Beethoven. Alexander is the American major general Robert Alexander, a hero during World War I, Giraud is the French General Henri Giraud, who was captured by the Germans in World War I and again in World War II but who managed to escape both times, and William Tell is the Swiss folk hero of the fourteenth century, best known for being forced to shoot an apple off his son's head. Tell also assassinated the hated Austrian-appointed ruler of his vil-

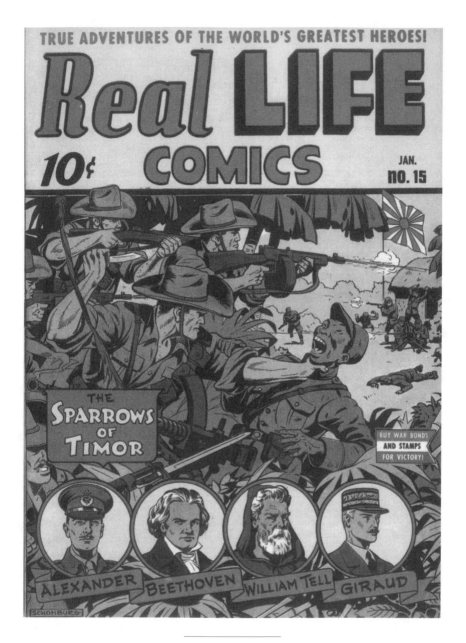

FIGURE 12.5

The cover of *Real Life Comics*, January 1943.

lage, Albrecht Gessler, and helped inspire a revolution that created the Swiss Confederation.

In this comic book Beethoven is depicted as a hero dedicated to the struggle for liberty. In the four biographical pages, Beethoven's defiance of the aristocracy is stressed. He confronts his teacher Haydn, symbol of the old order, claiming that he may not be a Mozart, but "I shall be Beethoven"; he forces the nobility to accept his rudeness as the price of genius; when walking with Goethe he refuses to bow to the nobility, claiming "my nobility is here" as he points to his head. His change of the dedication of the *Eroica,* scratching Napoleon off the title page, and the composition of the Ninth Symphony are both depicted as the result of his love of liberty.

The opening box connects Beethoven directly to the war effort. Next to his portrait is an American soldier with bayoneted rifle, ready for action, a tank, an orchestral conductor in tails, and, below Beethoven's name, the opening four measures of the Fifth Symphony. Beneath this scene are the words, "With a passion for freedom and music endowed by his staunch Belgian ancestry, he composed the mighty 'V Symphony'—Tocsin of Democracy!"

Symbols pile upon symbols here. While the Nazis claimed Beethoven as their own, second only to Wagner in their musical firmament, Americans are reminded of his non-German heritage, representing one of the countries overrun by the Nazis. In the cartoon the symphony is referred to as the "mighty 'V symphony,'" a convenient double entendre, referring both to victory, the da-da-da-dum motive equated with the Morse Code letter "V," and the Roman numeral V, for five.

Even young music students in the United States were enlisted in the war effort: the September 1941 issue of *Etude* magazine, a journal dedicated to piano music and piano pedagogy, ran an article titled, "Will Beethoven Stop Hitler?" The issue contained an arrangement of the Fifth Symphony, and in 1942 young piano players were referred to in *Etude* as "Our Young Musical Army." Few events in U.S. history did more to introduce Beethoven and the Fifth Symphony to Americans outside the concert world than his association with "V" and "Victory."[12]

Beethoven's image and his music have been the inspiration for many works in the art world, ranging from the monumental to the bizarre. During the nineteenth century, massive statues were erected in both the United States and Europe. The two best known in America are the Crawford statue that originally occupied the Boston Music Hall, and the Baerer bust that still resides in New York's Central Park.

FIGURE 12.6

Real Life Comics. Beethoven as World War II hero.

Thomas Crawford (1814–1857) was born in New York but went to Rome to study at age twenty-one and remained there the rest of his life. He acquired sufficient reputation in the United States that he was commissioned to execute several statues for the U.S. Capitol in Washington, D.C. In 1856 C. C. Perkins, a wealthy Bostonian, asked him to create a statue of Beethoven, which was unveiled in the Music Hall on March 1, 1856. It was accompanied by a lengthy program, including an extended poem by William Wentworth Story and several Beethoven compositions. The program included the Ninth Symphony, but for some reason only the first three movements, even though there was a large choir on stage.[13] The statue, mentioned above in chapter 2, is now in the foyer of the New England Conservatory.

Henry Baerer (1837–1908) was a German immigrant who settled in New York in 1866 after studying there in 1854. His bronze bust of Beethoven was completed in 1885 and given to the city of New York by the German-American Choir Society. The city placed it in the south part of Central Park, just below the 72nd Street Traverse. It is massive, four feet high, and sits on a six-foot base. At the foot of the base is Beethoven's muse, a robed figure holding a lyre.

Beethoven busts are among the most ubiquitous objects of popular art, appearing in a variety of sizes and material. Most busts today are modeled on the later Beethoven, with the fuller face and long hair. He is inevitably scowling, his brow furrowed as if in deep thought, and he is often looking slightly down as a Roman god might look down upon his subjects. Baerer's bust fits that description. In some of the most famous statues of Beethoven, such as that of Max Klinger in Vienna, he is indeed portrayed as a Roman god.

None of the more familiar busts are modeled on the three known to have been made during Beethoven's lifetime, although Franz Dietrich's is still seen sometimes today. It was based on the life mask that Klein himself made in 1912, portraying a younger Beethoven with shorter hair. While it is considered one of the most accurate depictions of Beethoven, it is not today's iconic Beethoven.[14]

Beethoven busts have also served a variety of artistic and commercial uses. Ross McBride, an American designer who moved to Tokyo in 1985 after graduating from the California Institute for the Arts, put a set of Vuarnet sunglasses on one, except on closer examination the glasses are there to project the time. Each contains an LED, the hours displayed in the left eye, the minutes in the right eye. Few Beethoven representations combine multiple symbols as well as this clock. He remains easily recognizable as Beethoven, but has been transformed into a cool jazz dude who also just happens to thrive on digital technology. He is at once the classical icon of both twentieth-century America and the new digital world. McBride originally conceived the idea around 1984 when he was in college, and first showed it in 1997 at a solo exhibition of proto-

---

FIGURE 12.7

The Beethoven statue in
New York's Central Park.
Photo by the author.

FIGURE 12.8

Ross McBride, Beethoven digital clock, with LED numbers in the lenses
of the sunglasses. Courtesy of E&Y Co., Ltd.

type clocks. The Japanese company E&Y then produced a limited edition of one hundred in 1999. McBride is uncertain why he conceived it, because "it didn't follow any of my standard design methodology. It most likely came from a dream." He chose Beethoven "simply because I thought it was the most iconic bust there is," and remembers "seeing it on Schroeder's piano in the Peanuts comic strip."[15] McBride has since become celebrated for unusual clock designs, and his work has appeared in museums worldwide.

Fiona Thomson, a UK artist, also combined the classical and the modern, in this case a bust that actually produces sound. She created an "Ode to Beethoven" MP3 player, which consists of a bust of Beethoven with an opening in the head that holds an iPod. As an iPod, complete with hidden speakers, the owner can thus partake the artistic effect through his choice of music. The meaning of the sculpture can change dramatically, from situational irony to reinforced grandeur, whether rap or a Beethoven symphony comes out of the speakers. According to Thomson, "My collection re-visits a selection of 19th century iconic forms, which I have adapted and utilized for modern 21st century products. Each piece embodies hidden technology, transforming an ornamental object into a functional and practical object. Or as I like to say intelligence beneath the elegance!"[16]

Frank Kozik created a particularly controversial and disturbing Beethoven bust in which the images of Beethoven and Alex from *A Clockwork Orange* are melded. We see Beethoven's face and hair, but he has on Alex's derby and his right eye is closed, with a black painted Alex-style eyelash under it. Kozik began making concert posters for the underground music scene in the 1980s and has since produced records and created vinyl toys. In 2007 he created the company Ultraviolence, from which the Beethoven sculpture came, along with others such as one of Ho Chi Minh and one blending Josef Stalin and Joe DiMaggio.

How could Andy Warhol's silkscreen series of famous persons not include Beethoven? As part of his pop-art work, Warhol often chose images that would be instantly recognizable, including Mao Zedong, Mick Jagger, and Marilyn Monroe. For each person he took an iconic image and added bright unrealistic colors to it, especially to the face. He then produced from four to ten variants of each. For Beethoven he chose four, all based on the 1820 Joseph Karl Stieler portrait. In Warhol's pop-art milieu, the colors must be bright, striking, and artificial, as he himself acknowledged. When asked in a 1981 interview whether he tried to make the prints look lifelike he replied, "Gee, I don't know how."[17] Mina Yang found a particular irony in Warhol's treatment of Beethoven, as the colors distort the iconic image and create a surreal quality to the

composer. The colors suggest the "sheen and banality of commercial advertising imageries," while aggressively attacking Beethoven's status as *the* symbol of high culture, as "the Ubermensch of Western music," and bringing him
down from his elitist position into the world of the "capitalist marketplace."[18]

Surreal might best describe Kris Kuksi's Beethoven. His sculpture, *A Tribute to the Madness of Beethoven,* has the familiar bust set within a quasi-Goth
arch. Across the bottom frame is what appears to be a concert hall balcony,
with suggestions of a concert hall ceiling below. Two skulls hang over the balcony and there are many small figures throughout the piece. Nail-like objects
hang from Beethoven's eyes and a chain goes through his closed mouth to two
large bolts on each side of his neck, creating a Frankenstein effect. Yet there
is a dignity to Beethoven amidst the grotesque. It may be madness, but Kuksi
seems to be asking, "Who is mad?" Kuksi's work thus appears satanic and
macabre, made all the more so by the children's toys that seem to have little
to do with childhood, though this may reflect the artist's experience since he
grew up with an alcoholic stepfather.

Kuksi often refers to historical or mythological figures, such as Napoleon or
"The Three Disgraces," a takeoff on the Three Graces, the Greek goddesses of
charm, beauty, and creativity, but in this world Beethoven seems an anomaly,
unless it's the Beethoven of *A Clockwork Orange* or Susan McClary. An aura
of death surrounds Beethoven, suggested by the two skulls flanking him just
below his image. Skulls often appear in Kuksi's work, with various meanings. His most obvious association of skulls with death is his 2007 sculpture
Through Death United, which depicts the remains of a couple. All that is left
are two skeletons and the male's genitals.

"Macabre" and "grotesque" are two words that Kuksi uses on his official
web site biography. He readily admits his dissatisfaction with the modern world,
in which "today much of mankind is oftentimes frivolous and fragile, being
driven primarily by greed and materialism." He believes he belongs to an old
world, never defined, but he sees his work, in spite of its disturbing quality,

FIGURE 12.9

Frank Kozik, *Ludwig Van,*
bust of Beethoven as Alex in
Clockwork Orange. Beethoven
has Alex's trademark hat
and one false eyelash.
Courtesy of Sharon Kozik.

FIGURE 12.10

Kris Kuksi, "A Tribute to the Madness of Beethoven."
Photo courtesy of Kuksi and Joshua Liner Gallery.

to be "about a new wilderness, refined and elevated, visualized as a cultivation emerging from the corrupt and demoralized fall of modern-day society.
A place where new beginnings, new wars, new philosophies, and new endings
exist."[19]

Writer and critic Yasim Bilbeise refers to Kuksi's choice of small plastic objects as "using the flotsam and jetsam of consumerism."[20] This may be a key
to Kuksi's work and its appeal to the twentieth and twenty-first centuries. It is

a critique on the consumerist Beethoven. As consumerism has made Beethoven a commodity, it has transformed him into a Frankenstein's monster. Much more than any other classical composer, he is changed and enslaved by the world of pop consumerism to which he has been consigned in the past half-century.

Musicologist David Patterson has recently discussed the importance of music and of Beethoven in particular in the work of Frank Lloyd Wright.[21] Wright not only saw music and architecture as twin disciplines coming from the same root—"Music is architecture . . . just as architecture is a kind of music"—but, as Patterson ironically commented, "in his typically shy and self-effacing way" Wright equated himself with Beethoven: "Since the mind required for greatness in either art is the same, [had I taken up music] I should have ranked with Beethoven."[22]

To Wright, his fondness of Beethoven went beyond idle recreation to become an important factor in his own work. In the broadest sense, organic form was central to both artists, but such was too common to ascribe a direct influence. Wright several times explicated a more direct relationship. He viewed the growth of an idea in musical terms: both composer and architect "always [keep] with the nature of materials . . . materials used in such a way as to reveal the beauty in tone and texture they possess . . . planned progressions, thematic evolutions, the never-ending variety in differentiation of pattern." He saw Beethoven as a builder: "When you listen to Beethoven you are listening to a builder. You are seeing him take a theme, a motif, and building with it. . . . Architecture is the same thing."[23]

An important aspect of Wright's approach to organic form was the relationship between the large and the small parts, that is, between the overall construction and the ornamental details. According to Wright, each is essential to the other: the ornaments were part of the structure, not added details. He called them "integral ornaments," in which "the character of structure [was] revealed and enhanced."[24] In discussing this concept, Wright articulated his most specific comparison between his creations and Beethoven's:

Integral ornament is founded in organic simplicities, just as Beethoven's Fifth Symphony, that amazing revolution in tumult and splendor of sound, was built upon four tones, based upon a rhythm a child could play on the piano with one finger. Imagination supreme reared the four tones repeated in the simple rhythms into a great symphonic poem that is probably the noblest thought-built edifice in the world.[25]

Wright felt that when you look at one of his buildings you not only hear music, but you hear Beethoven. Given when Wright developed his architectural aesthetic, it is not surprising that the Fifth Symphony in particular had an impact on him. The short, sturdy four-note motive, its many repetitions contributing to a towering edifice, find an architectural realization in the rhythmic repetition of the many right angles and cubes in Wright's architecture.

The conceptual artist Leif Inge took a different approach to Beethoven, using his music rather than his image. In *9 Beet Stretch* he digitally expanded a recording of the Ninth Symphony to last twenty-four hours. Other than length, no other parameters of the music, pitch, timbre, or dynamics are altered.[26] Although Inge is a Norwegian artist, the premiere occurred on April 17–18, 2004, at the Kupfer Ironworks, an abandoned building in Madison, Wisconsin. In this and subsequent performances, the audience brings blankets, furniture, sleeping bags, whatever allows them to be comfortable for an extended period of time. In some ways the event resembles a giant sleepover. Inge expects audience members to come and go during the performance, although some stay the entire time.

Inge was inspired to create the piece from viewing a similar stretch of Alfred Hitchcock's 1960 film *Psycho,* done by Douglas Gordon in 1993. In Gordon's work the standard projection rate of twenty-four frames per second was slowed to two, transforming the viewer's perception of the piece from smooth motion to an awareness of rapidly changing individual stills. Thus the famous shower scene, which is one minute long in the film, is extended to ten. Any sense of overall narrative is lost and the listener becomes more aware of the passage of time, particularly if he is familiar with the original film. The absence of sound in Gordon's recreation further distances the viewer from being pulled into the narrative framework of the movie.

Inge felt that slowing down the film exposed the film's "unconscious," and he was interested in trying the same with sound.[27] He is not a musician and was not familiar with the Ninth Symphony, but he chose it for its composer's iconic stature, much the same way that Gordon chose *Psycho.* Each wanted to use a piece to which the audience would bring some background and familiarity. This allowed Inge to assert, "I haven't only stretched a piece of music. I've stretched music history."[28] As a conceptual artist the concept is more important than the material. Inge also stated that in the (unlikely) event that a recording of the Ninth Symphony is not available, Mozart's *Requiem* may be used. Although not as well known as the Ninth, the *Requiem* has an iconic status in the West because of its use in the film *Amadeus.*

Curiously, the reception of Inge's Ninth differed among musicians and others less familiar with the entire symphony. As several blogs attest, many felt the stretched experience to be transcendent.[29] Some critics heard it differently. Kevin Ferguson noticed technical issues, how each tiny mistake by the performers was magnified.[30] Ben Sisario was disturbed that the "Ode to Joy," "lasting 5 or 10 seconds becomes minutes of slowly cascading overtones,"[31] and to Kyle Gann, "the rasp of horsehair against strings while sopranos hold forth on high Gs . . . has a noticeable fingernail-on-the-blackboard quality."[32] Yet the experience allowed other critics to get inside the piece and to connect with Beethoven in a more intimate way: Mark Swed was engulfed by "the pure, concentrated essence of Beethoven" and felt that it is "the closest we can ever come to experiencing what the deaf Beethoven heard, or experienced, in his head" because the listener is "inside the sounds, inside the harmonies."[33] Greg Sandow felt that he was "looking inside the cells of [his] own body,"[34] and by extension, Beethoven's. To these critics the message of brotherhood took on an entirely new dimension. At the crudest level, Inge's work may be a distortion, but at a deeper level it is revelatory.

Given the extent of Beethoven's popularity, it might be appropriate to close with a party. The same day that *Beethoven 'N' Pierrot* premiered in Denver, the classical radio station KVOD held its annual Beethoven birthday gala, a vivid, colorful event attended by 10,000 people. KVOD had been hosting a birthday party since the bicentennial year of 1970, when it began as an informal event; it was the brainchild of Charley Samson, who was an on-air host, known to some as the voice of classical music in Denver. Samson himself had been a Beethoven fan since his youth: "I was such a geek in high school I would have Beethoven parties at my house. My mom would make a cake and we'd play all nine symphonies."

The first parties were simple: someone brought a cake, someone brought punch, there were a few hors d'oeuvres, and the station opened its doors to the public and displayed birthday cards submitted by listeners while Beethoven's music played in the background. By 1989 the event had become so popular it was moved to the Colorado Convention Center. It reached its apogee in the 1990s, drawing crowds of between 6,000 and 10,000 people. The Colorado Symphony Orchestra played, the Colorado Ballet performed, and local merchants, mostly KVOD advertisers, set up booths allowing attendees to do their Christmas shopping. School children were invited to send in Beethoven birthday cards with prizes for the top entrants. The event would end with an hour and a half of waltzing on a special parquet floor with music provided by the Colorado Symphony Orchestra. Attendees were encouraged to come in period costume and participate in an opening grand march. There was a prize for the best costume, which in 1993 was won by Keven and Kathleen O'Connor in handmade period outfits, complete with powdered wigs, and the following year by the Shady Ladies of Central City, described by Dawn Denzer of the *Rocky Mountain News* as "an octet of outrageously bawdy babes representing tavern wenches."

For some, such as Sherry Afshar, who was a regular attendee since the first bash in the studios, the party presented a rare opportunity to waltz to the Colorado Symphony: "How else could I live a fantasy like that?"[35] For most, however, the high point of the evening was the appearance of Ludwig himself. Or herself: as the entire crowd sang "Happy Birthday, Ludwig," pianist Zoe Erisman, dressed as Beethoven, bounded onstage and entertained the crowd with selections from Beethoven's piano sonatas. The last such party was held in 1999, after which, through a complex series of corporate changes, KVOD was sold and its frequency reassigned. After a brief tenure on the AM band, it reemerged as a public radio station, where it is today. Although Erica Stull, vice president for community relations at Colorado Public Radio, attempted to revive at least the tradition of birthday cards in 2006 and 2007, staging any sort of elaborate event has proved impossible for the station.

What do all the different images of Beethoven tell us about him as an American icon? Some present a Romantic bohemian, the smoldering titan of the popular imagination, struggling with tones, his own fate, and society around him. In spite of the many changes in American culture, this remains the Beethoven most familiar to the public. Others present a gentler Beethoven, an observant figure who is fascinated and curious about the world. We have Beethoven the poet, who is fiercely proud of his accomplishments. There is the egocentric Beethoven, the rebel who recognizes his worth, is bothered by disturbances, and views the elite as hopelessly juvenile and anachronistic. He is the artist who can create immense works while his life is in chaos. And there are the Beethoven images, the busts, paintings, and drawings, in art museums and on T-shirts, in music stores and cartoons, and resting on pianos throughout the country. They are so fixed in the American imagination that his face is as recognizable as the four-note motive that has long been his trademark.

For many, Beethoven is transcendent, beyond time. In poems and plays he literally travels through centuries, free of the limits of both time and place. His music is eternal, unconnected to its cultural underpinnings. For others his music, or at least a small subset of it, is there, along with the man, as more symbol or myth than the tracings of a real historical figure.

The parties described above speak volumes about Beethoven in America. They were, first of all, just that, parties. According to Erica Stull they may have originated because KVOD wished to have some sort of celebration in December and Beethoven's birthday fit very well. Yet it would not have grown to the magnitude it did had it been simply a KVOD open house or a birthday party for Schubert, Bach, or Brahms, not to mention Schoenberg or Milton Babbitt. This bespeaks the Beethoven of the people, the Beethoven of popular thought. The birthday party became a major event because Beethoven has captured the American imagination in ways that no other classical musician has, not even Mozart—in spite of *Amadeus*. In one sense Beethoven stands for classical music, but in another he transcends it; he is a figure of the imagination who can be a genial companion, a rebel genius, or a fantasy image capable of inciting the minds of thousands in disparate ways. Beethoven may be German, Austrian, Belgian, an old-world classicist, a Promethean hero, a revolutionary, or black, but he remains familiar because he can be what we want him to be. He is a protean icon in American culture, the man and his music deeply embedded in the American consciousness far beyond the concert hall.

NOTES

INTRODUCTION

1. Arlene Naylor Okerlund, "Beethoven at San José State University," *Manuscript* 57, no. 4 (Fall 2005), 281–90. Okerlund was dean of the College of Arts and Humanities when the center was formed.

2. E. T. A. Hoffmann did much to establish that image with his review of the Fifth Symphony in the *Allgemeine musikalische Zeitung* 12, nos. 40 and 41 (July 4 and 11, 1820), 630–42 and 652–59. At Beethoven's funeral Franz Grillparzer's funeral oration presented a clearly Romantic image, quoted in *Thayer's Life of Beethoven,* rev. and ed. Elliot Forbes (Princeton, N.J.: Princeton University Press, 1967), 1057–58.

1. ARRIVAL IN AMERICA

1. Nicholas Michael Butler, *Votaries of Apollo: The St. Cecilia Society and the Patronage of Concert Music in Charleston, South Carolina, 1766–1820* (Columbia: University of South Carolina Press, 2007), 6–7.

2. Ibid., 8–9.

3. Ibid., 217–18, 223, 335.

4. See Michael Broyles, *"Music of the Highest Class": Elitism and Populism in Antebellum Boston* (New Haven, Conn.: Yale University Press, 1992), 317–18, for a discussion of the problems relating to the determination of professional status of musicians in the early nineteenth century.

5. Specifically, "only twenty-seven families had pianos." It is highly unlikely than any had more than one. Arthur Loesser, *Men, Women and Pianos* (New York: Simon and Schuster, 1945), 445, cites only "a newspaper" as his source.

6. Ibid., 456–57.

7. Lowell Mason, Address on Church Music: Delivered by Request, on the Evening of Saturday, October 7, 1826 (Boston: Hilliard, Gray, Little, and Wilkins, 1827).

8. A nonet is a piece for nine instruments. Otto E. Albrecht, "America's Early Acquaintance with Beethoven," in *Music, Edition, Interpretation, Gedenkschrift Günter Henle* (Munich: G. Henle Verlag, 1980), 14.

9. William Treat Upton, *Anthony Philip Heinrich, A Nineteenth-Century Composer in America* (New York: Columbia University Press, 1939), xi.

10. Cremona was the most important center of violin making in the seventeenth and eighteenth centuries. Heinrich's violin was unfortunately destroyed on one of his transatlantic voyages.

11. Upton, *Heinrich*, 23.

12. Joy Carden, *Music in Lexington before 1840* (Lexington, Ky.: Lexington Fayette County Historic Commission, 1980), 8.

13. Benefit means for the benefit of the named person. The performer arranged the concert, hired the hall, and, after expenses, pocketed the profits, if any.

14. Rum was the favorite drink of colonial and Federal America, in some cases more popular than water. In some areas it was safer than the water.

15. Vernon L. Parrington, *The Colonial Mind, 1620–1800*, vol. 1 of *Main Currents in American Thought* (New York: Harvest Books, 1954), 162.

16. The Boston Handel and Haydn Society, founded in 1815, was by far the most successful. It is still active, presenting Bostonians with important concerts each year. The New York Handel and Haydn Society seems to have expired around 1821. The Lexington Handel and Haydn Society was active as early as 1818, but its fate is unknown. Whether Heinrich had anything to do with it is also unknown.

17. Anne Hui-Hua Chen, "Beethoven in America to 1865" (Ph.D. diss., University of North Carolina, Chapel Hill, 1976), 198.

18. Quoted from *New Music Review* in "Minor Topics," *Magazine of History* 8 (January-June 1908), 249. A brief history of the society was also published: Ira Berry, *Sketch of the History of the Beethoven Musical Society of Portland, Maine, 1819–1825* (Portland, Maine: Stephen Berry, 1888).

19. Albrecht, "America's Early Acquaintance with Beethoven," 17. Albrecht does not list the printer of the 1818 version.

20. Broyles, *"Music of the Highest Class,"* 162–65. "Euterpeiad" comes from the Greek Euterpe, who was one of the nine muses, the goddess of music, lyric poetry, and dance.

21. "Modern Music," *Euterpeiad* 1, no. 4 (April 22, 1820), 14

22. "Beethoven," *Euterpeiad* 1, no. 24, 94.

23. "Programs of Concerts in Boston, 1817–1863," manuscript collection in the Boston Public Library; Robert A. Gerson, *Music in Philadelphia* (Westport, Conn.: Greenwood Press, 1970), 57.

24. These quotations are taken from Vera Brodsky Lawrence, *Strong on Music: The New York Music Scene in the Days of George Templeton Strong, 1836–1875*, vol. 1, *Resonances, 1836–1850* (New York: Oxford University Press, 1988), 57–60,

which summarizes and quotes critical reception. The words "perplexed" and "bewildered" are hers.

25. *American,* September 10, 1839, reprinted in the *Corsair,* September 14, 1839, 423, and in Lawrence, *Strong on Music,* vol. 1, 60. The author is not identified in any of these sources.

26. Thomas Wentworth Higginson, *Cheerful Yesterdays* (Boston: Houghton, Mifflin and Company, 1898), 18.

27. Samuel Jennison, "Reminensces [*sic*] of an Ex-Pierian," in scrapbook at the library of the Harvard Musical Association, Boston.

28. This figure is taken from "Measuring Worth, "http://www.measuringworth .com/ppowerus/result.php. At this writing, the last year for which calculations are available is 2009. The only thing missing from Jenny Lind's arrival in America was the television hysteria that would later surround the Beatles. What might have happened if Barnum had had the modern media at his fingertips?

29. John S. Dwight, letter to Lydia Marie Child, quoted in George Willis Cooke, *John Sullivan Dwight, Brook-Farmer, Editor, and Critic of Music* (Boston: Small, Maynard, 1898), 80–82. The date of the letter, which Cooke does not give, is October 1844.

30. First Annual Report of the Boston Academy of Music (Boston: Isaac R. Butts, 1833), 3. Quoted in Broyles, *"Music of the Highest Class,"* 163, from which most of the discussion of the Academy and of Samuel Atkins Eliot is taken.

31. Allen Johnson et al., *Dictionary of American Biography,* vol. 6 (New York: American Council of Learned Societies, 1928–1937), 81–82.

32. Fifth Annual Report of the Boston Academy of Music (Boston: Perkins, Marvin, 1937), 9–10.

33. John S. Dwight, "The History of Music in Boston," in *The Memorial History of Boston,* vol. 4, ed. Justin Winsor (Boston: James R. Osgood, 1881), 426–27.

34. John S. Dwight, "Music as a Means of Culture," *Atlantic Monthly* 26 (September 1870), 322.

35. James M. Bergquist, *Daily Life in Immigrant America, 1820–1870* (Santa Barbara, Calif.: Greenwood Press, 2008), 167.

36. Edward J. Lowell, *The Hessians and the Other German Auxiliaries of Great Britain in the Revolutionary War* (New York: Harper and Brothers, 1884), online at http://www.americanrevolution.org/hessians/hess4.html, accessed June 22, 2009.

37. Lawrence, *Strong on Music,* vol. 1, 111. "Saxon" was a term commonly used in the United States to refer to Britons or their descendants. It excluded Celts, Germans, Italians, and other Europeans, hence the term Anglo-Saxon.

38. Broyles, *"Music of the Highest Class,"* 172–73.

39. Lawrence, *Strong on Music,* vol. 1, xli.

40. This is based on relative GDP growth from 1824 to 2008, the latest year for which such figures were available at the time of writing. http://www .measuringworth.org/datasets/usgdp/result.php, accessed June 25, 2009.

41. Lawrence, *Strong on Music,* vol. 1, liii.

42. John Erskine, *The Philharmonic-Symphony Society of New York, Its First Hundred Years* (New York: Macmillan, 1943), 6–7.

43. Henry Edward Krehbiel, *The Philharmonic Society of New York* (New York: Novello, Ewer & Co., 1892), 95–96.

2. DEFINING BEETHOVEN

1. *Allgemeine Musikalische Zeitung* 12 (July 4 and 11, 1810), 30 and 41. It has been reprinted many times. One English translation appeared in *Beethoven, Symphony No. 5 in C minor,* ed. Elliot Forbes (New York: Norton, 1971), 150–63.

2. John Gatta, *Marking Nature Sacred: Literature, Religion, and Environment in America from the Puritans to the Present* (New York: Oxford University Press, 2004), 88–89.

3. Ernest Lee Tuveson, *The Avatars of Thrice Great Hermes* (Lewisburg, Pa.: Bucknell University Press, 1982), 4–5; "Pantheism," *Oxford English Dictionary,* http://dictionary.oed.com.proxy.lib.fsu.edu/cgi/entry/00340790?single=1&query_type=word&queryword=panentheism&first=1&max_to_show=10; accessed July 22, 2009.

4. Barbara Novak, *Nature and Culture: American Landscape and Painting, 1825–1875* (New York: Oxford University Press, 1995), 15–17.

5. John S. Dwight, "The History of Music in Boston," in *The Memorial History of Boston,* ed. Justin Winsor, 4 vols. (Boston: James R. Osgood, 1881), 4:425.

6. Margaret Fuller, "Entertainments of the Past Winter," *Dial* 3 no. 1 (July 1842), 61.

7. John S. Dwight, "Concerts of the Past Winter," *Dial* 1, no. 1 (July 1849), 124.

8. Novak, *Nature and Culture,* 18–29.

9. Immanuel Kant, *Observations on the Beautiful and Sublime,* trans. John T. Goldthwait (Berkeley: University of California Press, 1960). Kant distinguished between the beautiful and the sublime, considering the beautiful pleasant but more superficial than the sublime, which was associated with a sense of awe.

10. Margaret Fuller, "Youth Autobiography," in Margaret Fuller, William Henry Channing, Ralph Waldo Emerson, James Freeman Clarke, *Memoirs of Margaret Fuller Ossoli,* 3 vols. (Boston: Phillips, Sampson and Company, 1857), vol. 1, 15.

11. Abby Slater, *In Search of Margaret Fuller* (New York: Delacorte Press, 1978), 19.

12. The summaries are actually in the hand of Elizabeth Hoar, although Nancy Craig Simmons believes they were originally made by Peabody. Nancy Craig Simmons, "Margaret Fuller's Boston Conversations: The 1839–1840 Series," in *Studies in the American Renaissance* (Charlottesville: University Press of Virginia, 1994), 195.

13. Only twelve were recorded in the manuscript, numbers 9–15 being omitted. Ibid., 223.

14. Ibid., 213.

15. *The Letters of Margaret Fuller,* ed. Robert N. Hudspeth, 6 vols. (Ithaca, N.Y.: Cornell University Press, 1983), 2:98.

16. Ibid., 2:147

17. Ibid., 2:206.

18. Fuller, "Entertainments," 61–62.

19. Fuller, *Letters,* 2: 225.

20. Margaret Fuller, "Lives of the Great Composers," *Dial* 2, no. 2 (October 1841), 150–51.

21. Bell Gale Chevigny, *The Woman and the Myth: Margaret Fuller's Life and Writings* (Boston: Northeastern University Press, 1994), 61–62.

22. Slater, *In Search of Fuller,* 4.

23. Fuller, *Letters,* 4:263.

24. Slater, *In Search of Fuller,* 2–3.

25. John S. Dwight, "Academy of Music—Beethoven's Symphonies," *Pioneer* (January-February 1853), 26.

26. John. S. Dwight, "Music Review: Music in Boston during the Past Winter. No. IV," *Harbinger* 1, no. 12 (August 30, 1845), 194.

27. John S. Dwight, "The History of Music in Boston," in *The Memorial History of Boston,* ed. Justin Winsor (Boston: James R. Osgood, 1881), 4: 427.

28. By 1841 it had severed all ties with Harvard University.

29. John S. Dwight, "Address Delivered before the Harvard Musical Association, August 25, 1841," *Musical Magazine* 3 (August 28, 1841), 259, 263–64.

30. John S. Dwight, "Music," in *Aesthetic Papers,* ed. Elizabeth P. Peabody (Boston: the Editor; New York: G. P. Putnam, 1849), 31–32, 36.

31. Letter, Albert Brisbain to John S. Dwight, December 2, 1845, quoted in Walter L. Fertig, "John Sullivan Dwight: Transcendentalist and Literary Amateur of Music" (Ph.D. diss., University of Maryland, 1952), 111.

32. Quoted in George Willis Cooke, *John Sullivan Dwight, Brook-Farmer, Editor, and Critic of Music* (Boston: Small, Maynard, 1898), 115–16.

33. So dubbed in Theodore Thomas, *A Musical Autobiography,* ed. George P. Upton (New York: Da Capo Press, 1964), 93.

34. Ibid., 58. The word "menagerie" is Thomas's.

35. His summer concerts were meant to be lighter, which he agreed to.

36. Thomas's quote is contained in a letter from Julius Fuchs to George Putnam Upton, editor of Thomas's *Autography,* and printed therein, 233. Fuchs does not cite the source of the interview.

37. Leslie Petteys, "Theodore Thomas's 'March to the Sea,'" *American Music,* vol. 10, no. 2 (Summer 1992), 174.

38. Quoted in the frontispiece in Thomas, *Autobiography.*

39. John S. Dwight, "Musical Review," *Harbinger* 5, no. 21 (October 30, 1847), 327.

40. Thomas, *Autobiography,* 256–57.

41. The statue now stands in the lobby of the New England Conservatory in Boston.

42. The old Metropolitan Opera House in New York had burnished on the proscenium the names of six composers, including Beethoven, even though he wrote only one opera.

43. "Modern Music," *Euterpeiad* 1, no. 4 (March 22, 1820), 14; "Beethoven," *Euterpeiad* 1, no. 24 (September 9, 1820), 94. The first article originally appeared in *Gentleman's Magazine,* the second in the *Edinburgh Pamphlet.*

44. William W. Story, An Address Delivered before the Harvard Musical Association in the Chapel of the University at Cambridge, August 24, 1842 (Boston: S. N. Dickinson, 1842); J. S. Dwight (?), "Beethoven in Boston," *Dwight's Journal of Music* 34, no. 11 (September 5, 1874), 294; J. K. Paine, "The New German School of Music," *North American Review* 116 (April 1873), 217–45.

45. W. J. Henderson, "Beethoven after a Hundred Years," *Musical Quarterly* 13, no. 2 (April 1927), 164.

46. Park Benjamin, "The True Rights of Women," *Godey's Lady's Book* 28, no. 6 (June 1844), 272.

47. D. H. Barlow, "Music," *Godey's Lady's Book* 44, no. 5 (May 1852), 305.

48. Robert H. Wiebe, *The Opening of American Society* (New York: Alfred A. Knopf, 1984), 278.

49. Edith Woodley, "Aunt Tabitha's Fireside. No. II. -Paul's Impromptu," *GLB* 43, no. 2 (August 1851), 106.

50. "Records of the Arionic Sodality, Cambridge: N. E. 1813," manuscript book, Harvard Musical Association Library, Boston, record dated September 12, 1830.

51. Samuel Jennison, "Reminensces [*sic*] of an Ex-Pierian," in scrapbook at Harvard Musical Association; Lowell Mason, *Address on Church Music: Delivered by Request, on the Evening of Saturday, October 7, 1826* (Boston: Hilliard, Gray, Little, and Wilkins, 1827), 17. I have addressed this point before in "*Music of the Highest Class": Elitism and Populism in Antebellum Boston* (New Haven, Conn.: Yale University Press, 1992), 295.

52. Margaret Fuller, "Lives of the Great Composers," *The Dial* 2, no. 2 (October 1841), 150.

3. DEIFICATION AND SPIRITUALIZATION

1. Eugen D'Albert, "Ludwig van Beethoven," in *The International Library of Music for Home and Studio,* vol. 1, *Music Literature* (New York: University Society, 1927), 103.

2. "Beethoven Services Today," *New York Times,* March 27, 1927, 23.

3. They were Harry Moore of New Jersey, Albert C. Ritchie of Maryland, John E. Weeks of Vermont, A. J. Rothier of Rhode Island, I. I. Paterson of Oregon, Fred W. Green of Michigan, and H. N. Spaulding of New Hampshire.

4. Olin Downes, "The Workshop of Beethoven," *New York Times,* March 20, 1927, X8.

5. Edward J. Dent, "Beethoven and a Younger Generation," *Musical Quarterly* 13, no. 2 (April 1927), 317.

6. David Bradshaw, "The Best of Companions: J. W. N. Sullivan, Aldous Huxley, and the New Physics," *Review of English Studies,* n.s. 47, no. 186 (May 1996), 189–90.

7. Unpublished autobiographical sketch, MS A. A. Knopf Misc, n.d. [1931], in the Harry Ransom Center, University of Texas at Austin, quoted in ibid., 190.

8. J. W. N. Sullivan, "Beethoven the Man," *John O'London Weekly* 6 (February 11, 1922), 611.

9. J. W. N. Sullivan, *Beethoven, His Spiritual Development* (1927; New York: Vintage Books, 1960). Following the tone of the early twentieth century, the cover of earlier editions bore the subtitle *A Study of Greatness,* which was dropped in the Vintage edition.

10. Ibid., 37, 35, 27.

11. Ibid., 77.

12. *Thayer's Life of Beethoven,* 2 vols., rev. and ed. Elliot Forbes (Princeton, N.J.: Princeton University Press, 1967), 221.

13. Sullivan, *Beethoven, His Spiritual Development,* 91.

14. Ibid., 93.

15. Some important pieces did appear during the supposed compositional hiatus, particularly the two cello sonatas, op. 102, in 1815.

16. Sullivan, *Beethoven, His Spiritual Development,* 115.

17. Ibid., 121.

18. Ibid., 128, 140.

19. While several writers addressed the nature of the sublime, the most important studies were Edmund Burke, *A Philosophical Enquiry into the Origin of Our Ideas of the Sublime and Beautiful* (London: J. Dodsley, 1757); and Immanuel Kant, *Observations on the Feeling of the Beautiful and Sublime* (1764), trans. John T. Goldthwait (Berkeley: University of California Press, 1960).

20. Daniel Gregory Mason, *The Quartets of Beethoven* (New York: Oxford University Press, 1947); Robert Haven Schauffler, *Beethoven: The Man Who Freed Music* (Garden City, N.Y.: Doubleday, Doran & Company, 1935); Lewis Lockwood, "Beethoven, Florestan, and the Varieties of Heroism," in *Beethoven and His World,* ed. Scott Burnham and Michael Steinberg (Princeton, N.J.: Princeton University Press, 2000), 27–47. William Kinderman acknowledges the importance of Sullivan to modern writers in *Beethoven* (Berkeley: University of California Press, 1995), 323.

21. Ralph Wood, "The Meaning of Beethoven," *Music and Letters* 15, no. 3 (July 1934), 209–21; Robert S. Hatten, *Musical Meaning in Beethoven* (Bloomington:

Indiana University Press, 1994), 3; Kevin Korsyn, "J.W.N. Sullivan and the Hei-liger Dankgesang: Questions of Meaning in Late Beethoven," *Beethoven Forum* 2 (1993), 133–74.

22. "Toscanini-Beethoven," *Time,* February 14, 1927, http://www.time.com/time/magazine/article/0,9171,730012,00.html, accessed August 17, 2010.

23. Leonard Bernstein, *The Joy of Music* (New York: Simon & Schuster, 1957), 29.

24. Joseph Kerman and Alan Tyson, "Beethoven," *New Grove Dictionary of Music and Musicians* (Oxford: Oxford University Press, 1980), 3, 382. The identical paragraph still appears in Grove Online.

25. Scott Burnham, *Beethoven Hero* (Princeton, N.J.: Princeton University Press, 1995), 65.

26. Scott Burnham, email to author, May 6, 2009; Joseph Kerman, email to author, May 13, 2009. Alan Tyson has unfortunately passed away.

27. Joseph Kerman, *The Beethoven Quartets* (New York: Alfred A. Knopf, 1967), 194.

28. For a discussion of Blavatsky's theories and their sources, see Siv Ellen Kraft, "To Mix or Not to Mix: Syncretism/Anti-Syncretism in the History of Theosophy," *Numen* 49, no. 2 (2002), 142–77.

29. *The Secret Doctrine* (London: Theosophical Publishing Company, 1888), and *The Voice of the Silence* (London: Theosophical Publishing Company, 1889).

30. Stephen Prothero, "From Spiritualism to Theosophy: 'Uplifting' a Democratic Tradition," *Religion and American Culture* 3, no. 2 (Summer 1993), 215.

31. David Tame, *Beethoven and the Spiritual Path* (Wheaton, Ill.: Theosophical Publishing House, 1994), after 234.

32. Ibid., 2, 3.

33. Ibid., 33.

34. Ibid., 65.

35. Ibid., 74.

36. Ibid., 195.

37. Ibid., 199.

38. Robert S. Ellwood, *Religious and Spiritual Groups in Modern America* (Englewood Cliffs, N.J.: Prentice-Hall, 1973), 111.

39. All her books are now available in editions published through the New Age Bible and Philosophy Center, with which she was associated.

40. Corrine Heline, *Beethoven's Nine Symphonies Correlated to the Nine Spiritual Mysteries* (Santa Barbara, Calif.: J. F. Rowny Press, 1963), 23.

41. Ibid.

42. I want to thank Christian Savage for pointing this out to me.

43. Ibid., xi, 15.

44. Ibid., xi.

45. In a graduate seminar I taught, the following question came up during a discussion of Sullivan: Can a confirmed atheist feel the spiritual power of Beethoven's music? One student answered, "Yes, and yes. I am and I can."

4. BEETHOVEN, MODERNISM, AND SCIENCE

1. "Cubists and Futurists Are Making Insanity Pay," *New York Times,* March 16, 1913, SM1.

2. Denise Von Glahn and Michael Broyles, "Musical Modernism before It Began: Leo Ornstein and a Case for Revisionist History," *Journal of the Society for American Music* 1, no. 1 (February 2007), 29–56.

3. Michael Broyles, *Mavericks and Other Traditions in American Music* (New Haven, Conn.: Yale University Press, 2004), 102.

4. W. J. Henderson, "Concert Ends in Uproar," *New York Herald,* March 5, 1923, in Carl Ruggles folder, Irving S. Gilmore Music Library, Yale University, New Haven, Conn.

5. Paul Rosenfeld, *An Hour with American Music* (Philadelphia: J. P. Lippincott Company, 1929), 83.

6. Harriete Brower, "Leo Ornstein, an Ultra Modern Pianist and Composer," *Musical Observer* (August 1915), 467.

7. Leila Chevalier, "The Battle of the Music-Makers between the Ultra-Modernists and the Reactionaries Rages War to the Death," *Arts and Decoration* 17 (October 1922), 405.

8. Harry Partch, *Bitter Music: Collected Journals, Essays, Introductions, and Librettos,* ed. Thomas McGeary (Urbana: University of Illinois Press, 1991), 12.

9. Charles Seeger, "Carl Ruggles," in *American Composers on American Music: A Symposium,* ed. Henry Cowell (New York: Frederick Ungar, 1933), 30; Ray Wilding-White, "Remembering Ruth Crawford Seeger: An Interview with Charles and Peggy Seeger," *American Music* 6, no. 4 (Winter 1988), 443; Carlos Chávez, "The Music of Mexico," in Henry Cowell, ed., *American Composers on American Music: A Symposium* (Palo Alto, Calif.: Stanford University Press, 1933), 168.

10. Linda Whitesitt, *The Life and Music of George Antheil, 1900–1959* (Ann Arbor, Mich.: UMI Research Press, 1983), 70.

11. Olin Downes, "The Workshop of Beethoven," *New York Times,* March 20, 1927, X8.

12. Daniel Gregory Mason, *Beethoven and His Forerunners* (New York: Macmillan, 1930), 295; Colin McAlpin, "Musical Modernism: Some Random Reflections," *Musical Quarterly* 16, no. 1 (January 1930), 4–5.

13. Guido Adler and Theodore Baker, "Schubert and the Viennese Classical School," *Musical Quarterly* 14, no. 4 (October 1928), 473–85; Olin Downes, "Regarding the Ring," *New York Times,* February 7, 1937, 167.

14. Lawrence Gilman, *Toscanini and Great Music* (New York: Farrar and Rinehart, 1938), 60.

15. Joseph Szigeti, liner notes for *Early Recordings of Fritz Kreisler* (Berkeley, Calif.: Music and Arts Programs of America, 1988), CD-290(2).

16. Robin Stowell, *Beethoven, Violin Concerto* (New York: Cambridge University Press, 1998), 39. Flesch does not indicate exactly when he heard Ysaÿe, but Ysaÿe began performing the concerto c. 1888.

17. As with all significant change, there were precursors. In this case, developments in mathematics formed the foundation upon which Einstein, Planck, and others built the new physics. See William R. Everdell, *The First Moderns: Profiles in the Origins of Twentieth-Century Thought* (Chicago: University of Chicago Press, 1997), 159–76, 227–40.

18. Quoted in Paul Griffes, *Modern Music and After: Directions Since 1945* (Oxford: Oxford University Press, 1995), 4, and Joan Peyser, *Boulez* (New York: Schirmer, 1976), 19.

19. Babbitt claims to have developed many of his ideas about serialism in a treatise written in 1946: "The Function of Set Structure in the Twelve-Tone System." It was never published, however, and only later became known to other musicians as Babbitt's reputation spread.

20. Cole Gagne and Tracy Caras, *Soundpieces: Interviews with American Composers* (Metuchen, N.J.: Scarecrow Press, 1982), 198.

21. Pierre Boulez, "Sonata, que me veux-tu," in *Orientations: Collected Writings of Pierre Boulez,* ed. Jean-Jacques Nattiez, trans. Martin Cooper (Cambridge, Mass.: Harvard University Press, 1968), 154; Earle Brown, "The Notation and Performance of New Music," *Musical Quarterly* 76, no. 2 (1986), 181; Anthony Tommasini, "Composers Mining the Music of Their Youth," *New York Times,* April 18, 1999.

22. Kate Hevner Mueller, *Twenty-seven Major American Symphony Orchestras: A History and Analysis of Their Repertoires, Seasons 1842–43 through 1969–70* (Bloomington: Indiana University Press, 1973), 28–44, and Chart 6, xlvii.

23. "Records," *High Fidelity* 3, no. 6 (January-February 1954), 52.

24. William S. Newman, *The Sonata Since Beethoven* (New York: W. W. Norton, 1972), 7.

25. Charles Rosen, *The Classical Style* (New York: W. W. Norton, 1971), 384.

26. As Harry Haskell has pointed out, interest in early music goes back considerably further, but what was to become the twentieth-century movement took shape around the time that Arnold Dolmetsch and Wanda Landowska began to advocate a different approach in the early 1900s. Harry Haskell, *The Early Music Revival: A History* (London: Thames and Hudson, 1998).

27. John Rockwell, "Music: In-Depth Beethoven Experience," *New York Times,* February 10, 1987, C18.

28. John Rockwell, "Old Instruments May Herald the Future," *New York Times,* February 22, 1987, H1.

29. Richard Taruskin, "The Spin Doctors of Early Music," *New York Times,* July 29, 1990, H1; Nicholas Temperley, "The Movement Puts a Stronger Premium

on Novelty than on Accuracy, and Fosters Misrepresentation," *Early Music* 12, no. 1 (February 1984), 17.

30. Richard Taruskin, "The Authenticity Movement Can Become a Positivistic Purgatory, Literalistic and Dehumanizing," *Early Music* 12, no 1 (February 1984), 6.

31. Ibid., 7–8.

5. "THE WARM TROPICAL SUMMER OF SKETCH RESEARCH"

1. A list of Beethoven's addresses may be found in *Thayer's Life of Beethoven*, rev. and ed. Elliot Forbes (Princeton, N.J.: Princeton University Press, 1967), 1109–10.

2. Lewis Lockwood, "On Beethoven's Sketches and Autographs: Some Problems of Definition and Interpretation," *Acta Musicologica* 42, fasc. 1/2, special issue, "Preliminary Papers of the Colloquium at Saint-Germain-en-Laye (September 1970)," (January 1970), 42.

3. Douglas Johnson, Alan Tyson, and Robert Winter, *The Beethoven Sketchbooks: History, Reconstruction, Inventory* (Berkeley: University of California Press, 1985), 10.

4. Paul C. Squires, "Beethoven's Concept of the Whole," *American Journal of Psychology* 48, no. 4 (October 1936), 684.

5. Oswald Jonas, "An Unknown Sketch by Beethoven," *Musical Quarterly* 26, no. 2. (April 1940), 186–91.

6. Joseph Kerman, "Beethoven Sketchbooks in the British Museum," *Proceedings of the Royal Musical Association,* 93rd sess. (1966–1967), 77–96, 93.

7. Joseph Kerman, "Beethoven's Early Sketches," *Musical Quarterly* 56, no. 4, "Special Issue Celebrating the Bicentennial of the Birth of Beethoven" (October 1970), 515–38; Ludwig van Beethoven, *Autograph Miscellany from Circa 1786 to 1799,* 2 vols., ed. Joseph Kerman (London: Trustees of the British Museum, 1970).

8. Beethoven, *Autograph Miscellany,* xvii–xviii.

9. Ibid.

10. Ernest Sanders, "Form and Content in the Finale of Beethoven's Ninth Symphony," *Musical Quarterly* 50, no. 1 (January 1964), 59–76; Karl Geiringer, "The Structure of Beethoven's 'Diabelli Variations,'" *Musical Quarterly* 50, no. 4 (October 1964), 496–503.

11. Alexander L. Ringer, "The Art of the Third Guess: Beethoven to Becker to Bartók," *Musical Quarterly* 52, no. 3 (July 1966), 304–12.

12. Lockwood, "On Beethoven's Sketches and Autographs," 32–47.

13. Joseph Kerman, "Sketch Studies," *19th-Century Music* 6, no. 2 (Autumn 1982), 175.

14. Alan Tyson, "Introduction," *Beethoven Studies,* vol. 1 (1973), ix–x.

15. Douglas Johnson, "Beethoven Scholars and Beethoven Sketches," *19th-Century Music* 2, no. 1 (July 1978), 3–17, 12.

16. These points, which have been raised by many scholars, were summarized early by William Drabkin, in "Viewpoint: On Beethoven Scholars and Beethoven's Sketches," *19th-Century Music* 2, no. 3 (March 1979), 274–76.

17. Brandenburg's comments were published in the same issue as Drabkin's: Sieghard Brandenburg, "Viewpoint: On Beethoven Scholars and Beethoven's Sketches," *19th-Century Music* 2, no. 3 (March 1979), 270–74.

18. Joseph Kerman, email to author, December 12, 2007.

19. Donal Henahan, "Do You Speak Classical or Pop?" *New York Times*, August 9, 1981, D1.

20. Benjamin DeMott, "Rock as Salvation," *New York Times*, August 25, 1968, SM30. DeMott, it should be pointed out, was critiquing this point of view.

21. Milton Babbitt, "Who Cares If You Listen," *High Fidelity* (February 1958), 38–40, 126–27.

22. Jonathan Eberhart, "Commentary: The Day the Sky Was Opened," *Science News* 122, no. 14. (October 2, 1982), 220–21.

23. Carol Schulz Slobodin, "Sputnik and Its Aftermath: A Critical Look at the Form and Substance of American Educational Practice Since 1957," *Elementary School Journal* 77, no. 4 (March 1977), 259.

24. Arthur Flemming, "The Philosophy and Objectives of The National Defense Education Act," *Annals of the American Academy of Political and Social Science* 327 (January 1960), 132.

25. Austin E. Fife, "Research in Folklore under the National Defense Education Act," *Journal of American Folklore* 74, no. 292 (April–June 1961), 146.

26. Peter Kivy, "Communications," *Journal of the American Musicological Society,* 28, no. 2 (Summer 1975), 397–98.

27. Quoted in Forbes, *Thayer's Life of Beethoven,* 851.

28. Philip Gossett, "Beethoven's Sixth Symphony: Sketches for the First Movement," *Journal of the American Musicological Society* 27, no. 2 (Summer 1974), 260.

29. Alan Tyson, "Stages in the Composition of Beethoven's Piano Trio Op. 70, No. 1," *Proceedings of the Royal Musical Association* 97 (1970–1971), 1–19, 11; Amanda Glauert, "The Double Perspective in Beethoven's Opus 131," *19th-Century Music* 4, no. 2 (Autumn 1980), 113–20, 118.

30. Lewis Lockwood, "Eroica Perspectives: Strategy and Design in the First Movement," *Beethoven Studies 3,* ed. Alan Tyson (Cambridge: Cambridge University Press, 1982), 85–105.

31. Gustav Nottebohm, *Ein Skizzenbuch von Beethoven aus dem Jahre 1803* (Leipzig: Peters, 1880).

32. Particularly since Manfred Bukofzer provided his compelling narrative about his search for the Caput Mass, detective work retained cachet in the musicological world. Manfred Bukofzer, "Caput: A Liturgico-Musical Study," in *Studies in Medieval and Renaissance Music* (New York: Norton, 1950), 217–310.

6. REACTIONS TO MODERNISM

1. Adrienne Rich, *Diving into the Wreck, Poems of 1971 and 1972* (New York: W. W. Norton, 1972).

2. Adrienne Rich, "The Ninth Symphony of Beethoven Understood at Last as a Sexual Message." Copyright © 2002 by Adrienne Rich. Copyright © 1973 by W.W. Norton & Company, Inc., from *The Fact of a Doorframe: Selected Poems 1950–2001* by Adrienne Rich. Used by permission of the author and W. W. Norton & Company, Inc. Rich specifically dates this poem to 1972.

3. Letter from Adrienne Rich to author, July 17, 2010.

4. Susan McClary, "Getting Down Off the Beanstalk," *Minnesota Composer's Forum Newsletter* (January 1987), 7. The article was revised and reprinted in McClary, *Feminine Endings: Music, Gender and Sexuality* (Minneapolis: University of Minnesota Press, 1991), 112–31, but without that sentence.

5. The most strident critique has come from Peter Van den Toorn, "Politics, Feminism, and Contemporary Music Theory," *Journal of Musicology* 9, no. 3 (Summer 1991), 1–37; and the most detailed defense from Robert Fink, "Beethoven Antihero," in *Beyond Structural Listening? Postmodern Modes of Hearing,* ed. Andrew Dell'Antonio (Berkeley: University of California Press, 2004), 109–53.

6. *The Rubaiyat of Omar Khayyam* by Edward FitzGerald, stanza 51, first ed. 1859, available at http://www.therubaiyat.com/fitzindex.htm, accessed August 5, 2010.

7. McClary, *Feminine Endings,* 123, italics in original.

8. Ibid., 123–24.

9. Leonard Meyer, "Some Remarks on Value and Greatness in Music," in *Music, the Arts, and Ideas: Patterns and Predictions in Twentieth-Century Culture* (Chicago: University of Chicago Press, 1967), 26.

10. This discussion is taken from Anne K. Mellor, *Romanticism and Gender* (New York: Routledge, 1993), 95–96.

11. Ibid., 91, 96–97.

12. Paula Higgins, "Women in Music, Feminist Criticism, and Guerrilla Musicology: Reflections on Recent Polemics," *19th-Century Music* 17, no. 2 (Autumn 1993), 185.

13. Robert Griepenkerl, *Die Musikfest, oder die Beethovener* (Leipzig: O. Wigand, 1838), quoted in Fink, "Beethoven Antihero," 113–14.

14. Ibid., 116.

15. Ibid., 118–19.

16. Donald Francis Tovey, *Essays in Musical Analysis,* vol. 2 (London: Oxford University Press, 1935), 6.

17. For example, see Ernest Sanders, "Form and Content in the Finale of Beethoven's Ninth Symphony," *Musical Quarterly* 50 (1964), 59–76; James Webster, "The Form of the Finale of Beethoven's Ninth Symphony," *Beethoven Forum* 1

(1991), 25–62; Ernest H. Sanders, "The Sonata-Form Finale of Beethoven's Ninth Symphony," *19th Century Music* 22, no. 1 (Summer 1998), 54–60; Michael C. Tusa, "Noch einmal: Form and Content in the Finale of Beethoven's Ninth Symphony," *Beethoven Forum* 7 (1999), 113–37. For a summary of different formal attachments, see Michael Broyles, *The Emergence and Evolution of Beethoven's Heroic Style* (New York: Excelsior Music Publishing, 1987), 260.

18. Lawrence Kramer, "The Harem Threshold: Turkish Music and Greek Love in Beethoven's 'Ode to Joy,'" *19th-Century Music* 22, no. 1 (Summer 1998), 78–90.

19. Byron, *Don Juan,* quoted in ibid., 85.

20. Ibid., 85–86.

21. I realize that I am engaging in some post-positivistic thinking in speculating what a modernist historian would do.

22. Kramer, "Harem Threshold," 89.

23. Paul Rosenfeld, *Discoveries of a Music Critic* (New York: Harcourt, Brace & Co., 1936), 5–6.

24. Herman Kretzschmar, "Anregungen zur Förderung musikalischer Hermeneutik," *Jahrbuch der Musikbibliothek Peters* (1902), 45–66; reprinted in *Gesammelte Aufsätze über Musik und Anderes,* i (Leipzig, 1911), 168–92; quoted in Ian D. Bent, "Hermeneutics," *Grove Dictionary of Music and Musicians Online,* http://www.oxfordmusiconline.com.proxy.lib.fsu.edu/subscriber/article/grove/music/12871?q=hermeneutics&search=quick&pos=1&_start=1#firsthit, accessed July 12, 2010. Much of the discussion of hermeneutics here is based on Bent's article.

25. Arnold Schering, *Beethoven und die Dichtung* (Berlin: Junker & Dünnhaupt, 1936).

26. Jérôme-Joseph, *Cours complet d'harmonie et de composition,* 3 vols. (Paris: chez l'auteur), 1806, vol. 2, 109, vol. 3, 602.

27. Joseph Kerman, "How We Got into Analysis, and How to Get Out," *Critical Inquiry* 7, no. 2 (Winter 1980), 311–31; Joseph Kerman, *The Beethoven Quartets* (New York: Alfred A. Knopf, 1971); Rey M. Longyear, "Beethoven and Romantic Irony," *Musical Quarterly* 56, no. 4 (October 1970), 647–64; F. E. Kirby, "Beethoven's Pastoral Symphony as a *Sinfonia caracteristica*," *Musical Quarterly* 56, no. 4 (October 1970), 605–23. Anyone masochistic enough to plow through these endnotes will notice that the last two articles are from the same issue. That is because in 1970 *MQ* published a "Special Issue Celebrating the Bicentennial of the Birth of Beethoven."

28. Scott Burnham, *Beethoven Hero* (Princeton, N.J.: Princeton University Press, 1995).

29. Cf. Wilhelm Lenz, *Beethoven et ses trios style* (Paris: G. Legouix, 1909). One of the later books to follow in the old Adlerian tradition of strict style analysis was Broyles, *Emergence and Evolution of Beethoven's Heroic Style.*

30. Burnham, *Hero,* 25.

31. Ibid., 110.

32. Ibid., 111.

33. The quotations are from ibid., 147, 150.

34. Maynard Solomon, *Beethoven* (New York: Schirmer Books, 1977); William Kinderman, *Beethoven* (Berkeley: University of California Press, 1995); Lewis Lockwood, *Beethoven: The Music and the Life* (New York: W. W. Norton, 2003); Edmund Morris, *Beethoven: The Universal Composer* (New York: HarperCollins, 2005).

35. Solomon, *Beethoven*, 200, quoted in William Drabkin, "New Beethoven Insights," *Musical Times* 120, no. 1634 (April 1979), 304.

36. Lockwood, *Beethoven*, 100–101.

37. Probably a Norton editor chose to translate the title as the *Grand Fugue,* which is an accurate translation but not how the piece is known. Given Lockwood's reputation as a precise and careful scholar, I think he would have preferred the more usual title, *Grosse Fuge.*

38. Lockwood, *Beethoven*, 463.

39. One exception is movement-plan three, which consists of the fugue, an allegro in C-sharp major, and a finale in C-sharp minor.

40. Kinderman, *Beethoven*, 1.

41. Ibid.

42. Ibid., 287–90.

43. Ibid., 63.

44. Ibid., 116.

45. Ibid., 8–9.

46. Ibid., 124.

47. Morris, *Beethoven*, 108–109.

48. Kerman, Beethoven Quartets, 167.

49. Morris, *Beethoven*, 152.

50. Ibid., 210.

7. BEETHOVEN ON THE SILVER SCREEN

1. Both the film and documentary information may be found at http://www .lvbeethoven.com/Fictions/FictionFilmsMoonlightSonata.html#Film, accessed September 28, 2010.

2. References to characters in the film are as they are spelled in the film. References to the historical characters are as they are normally spelled in Beethoven scholarship.

3. Frank S. Nugent, "The Screen," *New York Times,* November 22, 1937, 15.

4. Beethoven's letter is quoted from *Thayer's Life of Beethoven,* rev. and ed. Elliot Forbes (Princeton, N.J.: Princeton University Press, 1967), 286.

5. Quoted in Anton Schindler, *Beethoven as I Knew Him,* trans. Donald MacArdle (Chapel Hill: University of North Carolina Press, 1960), 47.

6. Mary Kunz, "Ludwig in Love," *Buffalo News,* January 9, 1995.

7. Christopher Bagley, "Tea and Symphonies," *Premiere* (January 1995), 69; comments by Kevin on The Beethoven Reference Site Forum, http://www.gyrix .com/forums/archive/index.php/t-137.html, accessed June 20, 2007.

8. Mick LaSalle, "Well-Composed 'Beloved' Looks at Ludwig's Loves," *San Francisco Chronicle,* December 16, 1994, C3; Janet Maslin, "The Music Almost Tells the Tale," *New York Times*, December 16, 1994, C4.

9. David Rocks, "Beethoven Movie Has Mystery Role," *San Francisco Chronicle,* August 5, 1994, C13.

10. *"Copying Beethoven,* Full Production Notes," Verve Pictures, http://www .vervepics.com/copyingbeethoven.shtml.

11. Joseph M. Boggs and Dennis W. Petrie, *The Art of Watching Films,* 7th ed. (New York: McGraw-Hill, 2008), 55.

12. Mark Zimmer, http://www.digitallyobsessed.com/showreview. php3?ID=9329.

13. Quoted in Bruce Britt, "Isabella Rossellini Stands In for Her 'Immortal Beloved,'" *San Francisco Chronicle,* December 15, 1994, E3.

14. *Premiere* (January 1995), 69.

15. Maslin, "The Music Almost Tells the Tale."

16. Edward Rothstein, "How Can a Movie So Right Be So Wrong?" *New York Times,* January 1, 1995, H31; Lawrence Teeter, "Thanks to Filmmakers, Composer's Life Still a Mystery," *Los Angeles Times,* February 13, 1995, F3; Lewis Lockwood, "Film Biography as Travesty," *Musical Quarterly* 81, no. 2 (Summer 1997), 195.

17. Stephen Rivele, "An Introduction to the Film 'Copying Beethoven,'" http:// www.lvbeethoven.com/Fictions/FictionFilmsCopyingBeethoven.html, accessed November 28, 2007.

18. Many newspaper reviews of *Copying Beethoven* may be found at "Rotten Tomatoes," http://www.rottentomatoes.com/m/copying_beethoven/?critic= creamcrop, accessed October 7, 2007.

19. Derek Nystrum, "Hard Hats and Movie Brats: Auteurism and the Class Politics of the New Hollywood," *Cinema Journal* 43, no. 3 (Spring 2004), 31.

20. Judith Hennessee, *Betty Friedan, Her Life* (New York: Random House, 1999); Margalit Fox, "Betty Friedan, Who Ignited Cause in 'Feminine Mystique,' Dies at 85," *New York Times,* February 5, 2006, http://www.nytimes.com/2006/ 02/05/national/05friedan.html, accessed November 13, 2007.

21. Dennis McLellan, "Carole Eastman, at 69; Wrote 1970 Classic 'Five Easy Pieces,'" *Los Angeles Times,* February 28, 2004.

8. BEETHOVEN'S MUSIC IN FILM

1. The most complete list of films that use Beethoven's music is the ongoing IMDb (Internet Movie Database), at http://www.imdb.com/name/nm0002727/, accessed September 5, 2008.

2. Rick Altman, *Silent Film Sound* (New York: Columbia University Press, 2004), 181–201.

3. The Barrow citation is from "Music and Films," *Views and Film Index,* May 16, 1908, 4; the Chicago quotation is from "Notes From Chicago," *Motion/Moving Picture News* (March 13, 1909), 300. Both are quoted in Altman, *Silent Film Sound,* 205.

4. Altman, *Silent Film Sound,* 267.

5. Ibid., 269.

6. Ibid., 291.

7. Martin Miller Marks, *Music in the Silent Film: Contexts and Case Studies, 1895–1924* (New York: Oxford University Press, 1997), 199–207.

8. Altman, *Silent Film Sound,* 293.

9. Ibid., 313.

10. The film was summarized by C. S. Walters in the trade journal *Motography,* July 14, 1915, which is quoted in Elizabeth Weigand, "'The Rugmaker's Daughter', Maud Allan's 1915 Silent Film," *Dance Chronicle* 9, no. 2 (1986), 241–42.

11. Lynde Denig, *Moving Picture World,* July 24, 1915, 670. Quoted in Weigand, "Rugmaker," 248.

12. *The Moving Picture World* 25, nos. 4–6 (July 24, 1915), 627. Taken from http://books.google.com, accessed April 19, 2010.

13. Alex's picture of Beethoven is an etching done by Ludwig Michalek (1859–1942).

14. Bernard Weinraub, "Kubrick Tells What Makes 'Clockwork Orange' Tick," *New York Times,* January 4, 1972, 26.

15. The precise death total cannot be determined, but estimates range from roughly 50 to 70 million. Including Russia, the death total in Europe may have been as high as 40 million.

16. Quoted in Esteban Buch, *Beethoven's Ninth: A Political History,* trans. Richard Miller (Chicago: University of Chicago Press, 2003), 192.

17. Quoted from ibid., 192–93.

18. Ibid., 191. Unfortunately, the French minister Édouard Herriot who suggested this was criticized for a "Franco-Napoleonic vision of a united Europe."

19. Ibid., 203.

20. Ibid., 205.

21. Barring the opening chord of the last movement.

22. Robynn J. Stilwell, "'I Just Put a Drone under Him . . .': Collage and Subversion in the Score of 'Die Hard,'" *Music and Letters* 78, no. 4 (November 1997), 562. Much of the following discussion is indebted to Stilwell's analysis.

23. Stilwell discusses these transformations and provides some musical examples, ibid., 561–62.

24. The quotations are taken from ibid., 568–69.

25. For a discussion of a number of films that use Beethoven's Ninth Symphony, including an extended analysis of *A Clockwork Orange* and *Die Hard*, see James Wierzbicki, "Banality Triumphant: Iconographic Use of Beethoven Ninth Symphony in Recent Films," *Beethoven Forum* 10, no. 3 (Fall 2003), 113–38.

26. The original episodes appeared in the British series *Warrior*, published by Quality Comics between 1982 and 1985. They were written by Alan Moore and illustrated by David Lloyd. DC Comics reprinted the series in 1988, adding the final two episodes. Later they were published as a book by DC Comics (New York, 1989) and by Titan Books (London, 1990).

27. Erno Rapeé, *Encyclopedia for Motion Pictures* (New York: Belwin, 1925), 24.

9. BEETHOVEN IN THE THEATER

1. "Drama: Musical Biography and Musical Farce," *Life*, April 21, 1910, 55.

2. "Life of Beethoven at the New Theatre," *New York Times*, April 12, 1910, 11.

3. Adrienne Kennedy, *People Who Led to My Plays* (New York: Alfred A. Knopf, 1986).

4. Ibid., 86, 87.

5. Adrienne Kennedy, "A MELUS Interview: Adrienne Kennedy, Wolfgang Binder, Adrienne Kennedy," *MELUS* 12, no. 3, "Ethnic Women Writers IV" (Autumn 1985), 108.

6. It played between October 7 and November 27 at the Nederlander Theatre in New York City.

7. Benedict Nightingale, "Stage View; It Should be Called 'Ustinov's Twentieth,'" *New York Times*, April 29, 1984, H5; Frank Rich, "Theater: 'Beethoven's Tenth' With Peter Ustinov," *New York Times*, April 23, 1984, C11.

8. The quotes are from Nightingale, "Stage View."

9. In this study I have avoided any extended discussion of literary works, such as novels, based on Beethoven, in part because it would be almost impossible to cover that field in as wide-ranging a volume as this. It is a topic that awaits treatment.

10. T. H. Mcculloh, "All in Ludwig's Family, 'The Beethovens,'" *Los Angeles Times*, Valley ed., January 12, 1992, 87.

11. Robert Koehleer, "Grandiose 'Beethovens' Twists the Myth," *Los Angeles Times*, January 24, 1992, 22.

12. In the only published edition, an English-German dual language version published by kfmVerlag, Switzerland (n.d.), the title at the bottom of the page, *Beethoven & Pierrot*, is simply incorrect. The proper title *Beethoven 'N' Pierrot* is given at the top of the page.

13. Elise Winter, interview with Moises Kaufman, March 3, 2009, http://gothamist.com/2009/03/09/moises_kaufman_playwright_and_direc.php, accessed December 29, 2009.

14. *Thayer's Life of Beethoven,* rev. and ed. Elliot Forbes (Princeton, N.J.: Princeton University Press, 1967), 775–77.

15. Winter, interview with Kaufman.

16. I want to thank Douglass Seaton at The Florida State University for this observation.

17. I want to thank Denise Von Glahn for this particular insight.

10. "BEETHOVEN WAS BLACK"

1. "Playboy Interview: A Candid Conversation with the Militant Major-Domo of the Black Muslims," *Playboy,* May 1963, 53–63.

2. Available as a transcript and as a wav file at "African American Involvement in the Vietnam War, Speeches and Sounds," http://www.aavw.org/special _features/speeches_speech_carmichae101.html, accessed March 14, 2010.

3. Dominique-Rene de Lerma, "Beethoven as a Black Composer," *Black Music Research Journal* 10, no. 1 (Spring 1990), 118–22; Wilson Jeremiah Moses, *Afrotopia: The Roots of American Popular History* (Cambridge: Cambridge University Press, 1998), offers the most detailed historical investigation of each of these subjects as well as extensive bibliographies.

4. W. C. Berwick Sayers, *Samuel Coleridge-Taylor, Musician: His Life and Letters* (London and New York: Cassell and Co., 1915), 92, 203.

5. It is mentioned in volume 1 and then discussed more fully in volume 3. Joel A. Rogers, *Sex and Race,* vol. 1, *Negro-Caucasian Mixing in All Ages and Lands* (New York: Helga M. Rogers, 1942), vol. 2, *The New World* (New York: Helga M. Rogers, 1942), vol. 3, *Why White and Black Mix in Spite of Opposition* (New York: Helga M. Rogers, 1944).

6. http://www.beethoven-haus-bonn.de, search term "Hofel." Accessed July 27, 2008.

7. The original Letronne portrait is in a private collection in Paris and is unavailable, although reproductions of it may also be found on the internet.

8. Rogers, *Sex and Race,* 1:289.

9. Ibid., 3:306. Rogers takes all these quotations except for Gelinek's and Fischer's from Oscar Sonneck, *Beethoven: Impressions of his Contemporaries* (New York: G. Schirmer, 1926). The Gelinek quote is from Ludwig Nohl, *Beethoven Depicted by His Contemporaries* (London: W. Reeves, 1880), and the Fischer quote is from Robert Haven Schauffler, *Beethoven: The Man Who Freed Music* (Garden City, N.Y.: Doubleday, Doran & Company, 1935).

10. *Thayer's Life of Beethoven,* rev. and ed. Elliot Forbes (Princeton, N.J.: Princeton University Press, 1967), 146.

11. "Mann kann in Beethoven Physiognomie leicht negerahnliche Zuge finden," in Frederick Herz, *Rasse und Kulter* (Leipzig: A. Kröner, 1925); Emil Ludwig, *Beethoven, Life of a Conqueror,* trans. George Stewart McManus (New York: G. P. Putnam's Sons, 1943), quoted in Rogers, *Sex and Race,* 3:307.

12. Rogers, *Sex and Race,* 1:169.

13. I want to thank Gayle Murchinson for pointing this out to me.

14. There is no record of any actual activities of this organization, and I have been unable to locate Doug Cass. Since 1969, KDIA has undergone several changes of ownership and format, and twice disappeared from the air for a period of time, mainly for economic reasons. As of this writing the station has a Christian talk format. It has no connection to the station from the 1960s except having inherited its call letters.

15. Dominique René de Lerma, "Beethoven as a Black Composer," posted on the Myrtle Hart Society web page, September 27, 2007, http://myrtlehart.org/content/view/182/174/, accessed June 17, 2008. In spite of the same title, this is not the same article that appeared in the *Black Music Research Journal* (BMRJ).

16. "14 Emmy Nods for 'Twin Peaks,'" *Detroit Free Press,* August 3, 1990, 1C, http://forums.civfanatics.com/showthread.php?t=102277, accessed June 17, 2008; de Lerma, "Beethoven as Black Composer," Hart Society web page; Kwaku Person-Lynn, "Thanks to Filmmakers, Composer's Life Still a Mystery: Beethoven's Racial Ties Misrepresented Again," *Los Angeles Times,* February 13, 1995, 3.

17. Posted by BOTP on Civilization Fanatics' Center blog, http://forums.civfanatics.com/showthread.php?t=102277, accessed June 17, 2008. Thayer states that "Beethoven had even more of the Moor in his looks than his master [Haydn]." Forbes, *Thayer's Life of Beethoven,* 134.

18. Posted by S. R. Prozak, November 2, 2004, on http://chris.quietlife.net/2003/03/13/was-beethoven-black/, accessed July 6, 2008.

19. Moses, *Afrotopia,* 187–88. Moses quotes Marcus Garvey on 188.

20. The report of this incident comes from the "Final Report on Recent Incidents at Ujamaa House," Board of Trustees of the Leland Stanford Junior University, Stanford, California, 1989. In order to protect the students, the Board substituted fictitious names in the report for all persons involved.

21. Ibid., 15.

22. The book was not identified. It was likely Rogers's.

23. Richard A. Posner, *Overcoming Law* (Cambridge, Mass.: Harvard University Press, 1995), 375.

24. Patricia J. Williams, *The Alchemy of Race and Rights* (Cambridge, Mass.: Harvard University Press, 1991); Williams also consistently misspells Ujamaa throughout her discussion.

25. Clark Freshman, "Were Patricia Williams and Richard Dworkin Separated at Birth?" *Columbia Law Review,* 95, no. 4 (October 1995), n. 20, 1573; Charles R. Lawrence, "If He Hollers Let Him Go: Regulating Racist Speech on Campus," *Duke Law Journal* (June 1990), 431–83; Richard Delgado, "Rodrigo's Thirteenth Chronicle: Legal Formalism and Law's Discontents," *Michigan Law Review* 95, no. 4 (February 1997), 1105–49; Richard Delgado and Jean Stefancic, "Campus Anti-Racism Rules: Constitutional Narratives in Collision, Or, Why There

Are Always Two Ways of Looking at a Speech Controversy," in *Must We Defend Nazis? Hate Speech, Pornography and the New First Amendment* (New York: New York University Press, 1997), 46–70.

26. Delgado and Stefancic, "Campus Anti-Racism Rules," 46; Steven G. Gey, "The Case against Postmodern Censorship Theory," *University of Pennsylvania Law Review* 145, no. 2 (December 1996), 193–297; Delgado, "Are Hate-Speech Rules Constitutional Heresy? A Reply to Steven Gey," *University of Pennsylvania Law Review* 146, no. 3 (March 1998), 865–79; Gey, "Postmodern Censorship Revisited: A Reply to Richard Delgado," *University of Pennsylvania Law Review* 146, no. 4 (April 1998), 1077–95; Delgado and Jean Stefancic, *Understanding Words That Wound* (Boulder, Colo.: Westview Press, 2004), 113.

27. Moses, *Afrotopia*, 2; Molefi Asante, *The Afrocentric Idea* (Philadelphia: Temple University Press, 1987); Molefi Asante, *Kemet, Afrocentricity, and Knowledge* (Trenton, N.J.: Africa World Press, 1990).

28. Moses, *Afrotopia*, 3.

29. See ibid., 24n20, for a list of writings.

30. Martin Bernal, *Black Athena: The Afroasiatic Roots of Classical Civilization* (New York: Basic Books, 1987); Mary Lefkowitz, *Not Out of Egypt: How "Afrocentrism" Became an Excuse to Teach Myth as History* (New York: Basic Books, 1996).

31. Gerald Early, "Afrocentrism: From Sensationalism to Measured Deliberation," *Journal of Blacks in Higher Education* (Autumn 1994), 86.

32. Robert Elliot Fox, "Afrocentrism and the X Factor," *Transition*, no. 57 (1992), 19.

33. See "Varieties of Black Historicism," in Moses, *Afrotopia*, 18–43. Some of the types that he discusses are "sentimental Afrocentrism," "Vindicationist and Contributionist Traditions," "Heroic Monumentalism," "A Grand Center of Negro Nationality," "African Redemptionism," and "Romantic Racialism."

34. George James, *Stolen Legacy* (New York: Philosophical Library, 1954).

35. See Moses, *Afrotopia*, 92–93, for a discussion of James's work and influence. The quotation is from 93.

36. Gene Roberts, "Why the Cry over 'Black Power,'" *New York Times*, July 3, 1966, 89. The term "Black Power" had been used at least as early as 1954 by Richard Wright in *Black Power: A Record of Reactions in a Land of Pathos* (New York: Harper, 1954). His book referred not to the United States, however, but to Ghana.

37. Cf. Clayborne Carson, *In Struggle: SNCC and the Black Awakening of the 1960s* (Cambridge, Mass.: Harvard University Press, 1981); Komozi Woodard, *A Nation within a Nation: Amiri Baraka (LeRoi Jones) and Black Power Politics* (Chapel Hill: University of North Carolina Press, 1999); William J. Van Deburg, *New Day in Babylon: The Black Power Movement and American Culture, 1965–1975* (Chicago: University of Chicago Press, 1992); Jeffrey O.G. Ogbar, *Black Power: Radical Politics and African American Identity* (Baltimore, Md.: Johns

Hopkins University Press, 2004); Jama Lazerow and Yonhuru Williams, eds., *In Search of the Black Panther Party: New Perspectives on a Revolutionary Movement* (Durham, N.C.: Duke University Press, 2006); Judson L. Jeffries, *Huey P. Newton: The Radical Theorist* (Jackson: University Press of Mississippi, 2002).

38. Austin Algernon, "Cultural Black Nationalism and the Meaning of Black Power," paper presented at the annual meeting of the American Sociological Association, Atlanta Hilton Hotel, Atlanta, August 16, 2003, available at http://www.allacademic.com/meta/p107842_index.html.

39. James Edward Smethurst, *The Black Arts Movement: Literary Nationalism in the 1960s and 1970s* (Chapel Hill: University of North Carolina Press, 2005), 15.

40. Kalama ya Salaam, "Historical Background of the Black Arts Movement (BAM)," in *The Magic of Juju: An Appreciation of the Black Arts Movement (BAM)* (Chicago: Third World Press, forthcoming), available at The Black Collegian Online, http://www.black-collegian.com/african/bam1_200.shtml, accessed October 17, 2008.

41. Larry Neal, "The Black Arts Movement," *Drama Review: TDR* 12, no. 4 (Summer 1968), 33.

42. William J. Harris, ed., "Introduction," in Amiri Baraka, *The LeRoi Jones, Amiri Baraka Reader* (New York: Thunder's Mouth Press, 1991).

43. Manning Marable, *Race, Reform and Rebellion: The Second Reconstruction in Black America, 1945–1982* (Jackson: University Press of Mississippi, 1984); for a more general discussion of the decline of black nationalism, which cites the Marable statistics, see John D. Baskerville, *The Impact of Black Nationalist Ideology on American Jazz Music of the 1960s ad 1970s* (Lewiston, Maine: Edwin Mellen Press, 2003), 129–33.

44. Baraka refers to the white Mississippi novelist William Faulkner and to the Dick and Jane of the *Elson-Gray Basic Readers,* from which almost all children in America learned to read. The series of readers, originally written by William H. Elson, was first published in 1930 and ran until 1965.

45. Gerald Weales, "What Were the Blacks Doing in the Balcony?" *New York Times,* May 4, 1969, SM38.

46. Harold C. Schonberg, *The Lives of Great Composers* (New York: W. W. Norton, 1981), 298.

47. Robert Haven Schauffler, *Beethoven, The Man Who Freed Music* (Garden City, N.Y.: Doubleday, Doran & Company, 1935).

48. In Addison Gayle, ed., *The Black Aesthetic* (Garden City, N.Y.: Doubleday-Anchor, 1971), 9.

49. Deborah D. Moseley, "Beethoven, the Black Spaniard," *ChickenBones: A Journal for Literary & Artistic African-American Themes,* http://www.nathaniel-turner.com/beethoventheblackspaniard.htm, posted February 15, 2007, updated October 2, 2007, accessed March 3, 2008.

50. James T. Stewart, "The Development of the Black Revolutionary Artist," in *Black Fire: An Anthology of Afro-American Writings,* ed. LeRoi Jones and L. Neal (New York: William Morrow, 1968), 3–10, quotation from 3.

51. LeRoi Jones (Amiri Baraka), *Black Music* (New York: William Morrow, 1970), 209.

52. Personal conversation with Denise Von Glahn, September 10, 2008. Her recent book examines the role of place in Western music: *The Sounds of Place: Music and the American Cultural Landscape* (Boston: Northeastern University Press, 2003).

53. For a discussion of Dwight's views on Beethoven, see Ora Frishberg Saloman, *Beethoven's Symphonies and J. S. Dwight* (Boston: Northeastern University Press, 1995); William Kinderman, *Beethoven* (Berkeley: University of California Press, 1995), 1. Kinderman's statement is the opening sentence in his book. Edmund Morris, *Beethoven: The Universal Composer* (New York: Atlas Books/ Harper Collins, 2005).

54. Sandra Haggerty, "Beethoven and Negro History Week," *Los Angeles Times,* February 11, 1970, and "'Beethoven was Black'—???," *Los Angeles Times,* May 13, 1970. Unfortunately, Haggerty does not identify either the radio station or the disc jockey that she heard in the coffee shop.

55. Leonard Meyer, "Forgery and the Anthropology of Art," *Journal of Aesthetics and Art Criticism* 15, no. 4 (June 1957), reprinted in Leonard Meyer, *Music, the Arts, and Ideas, Patterns and Predictions in Twentieth-Century Culture* (Chicago: University of Chicago Press, 1967), 54–67, quotation from 55.

56. Haggerty, "'Beethoven was Black.'"

57. The issue was controversial even in Europe. Julia Ronge of the Beethoven-Haus in Bonn informed me that it came up on the Beethoven-Haus Forum, and the discussion at one point became quite heated and degenerated into personal accusations. The accusations apparently came from someone who lived in Germany. Email from Julia Ronge, Beethoven-Haus, July 11, 2008.

58. Telephone interview with Josephine Wright, August 6, 2008.

59. Email from Lawrence Schenbeck, June 8, 2008.

60. Telephone interview with William Meredith and Patricia Stroh, August 20, 2008.

61. F. C. G., "Afrocentrism," *American Journal of Economics and Sociology* 52, no. 2 (April 1993), 192, http://www.jstor.org/stable/3487056, accessed June 26, 2008.

62. Quotes in Jerry Adler, "African Dream—Days of Empire," *Newsweek,* September 23, 1991, 42.

11. BEETHOVEN IN POPULAR MUSIC

1. Georg Kinsky and Hans Halm, *Das Work Beethovens: Thematisch-Bibliographisches Verzeichnis Seiner Sämtlichen Vollendenten Kompositionen* (Munich: G Henle Verlag, 1955), 727. Kinsky lists the waltz in Anhang 14.

2. The exact origins of the name are not clear. The locale also later changed, from Union Square to 28th Street, between Sixth Avenue and Broadway.

3. H. Wiley Hitchcock, "Tin Pan Alley," *Grove Music Online,* http://www.oxfordmusiconline.com, accessed January 13, 2010.

4. Chopin, "I'm Always Chasing Rainbows," taken from his *Fantasie-Impromptu;* Rimsky-Korsakov, "Song of India," from *Sadko;* and Tchaikovsky, "None But the Lonely Heart," number six from *Six Romances,* op. 6.

5. "Joyful, Joyful We Adore Thee."

6. Count Basie interview, in Charles Dance, *The World of Swing* (New York: Charles Scribner's Sons, 1974), 13; Louis Armstrong in *The Jargon File,* ed. Eric S. Raymond and Guy S. Steele, http://www.gutenberg.org/etext/3008, accessed January 18, 2010.

7. Rimsky-Korsakov, "Song of the Indian Guest," from *Sadko;* Mendelssohn, *Song Without Words,* op. 62, no. 6. Sony has collected twenty-three swing songs taken from classical material on the CD *Beethoven Wrote It But It Swings,* Sony B0000029ON.

8. Chuck Berry, *Chuck Berry: The Autobiography* (New York: Harmony Press, 1987), 150.

9. Paul H. Fryer, "Brown-Eyed Handsome Man, Chuck Berry and the Blues Tradition," *Phylon* 42, no. 1 (1981), 64.

10. Peter Gabel and Duncan Kennedy, "Roll Over Beethoven," *Stanford Law Review* 36, no. 1/2 (January 1984), 1–55.

11. The Mann Act was a federal law that made it illegal to transport a woman across state lines for prostitution or immoral purposes. Berry was convicted for having taken a fourteen-year-old girl with him across state lines.

12. Bobby Darrin, Bobby Rydell, Bobby Vinton. Probably the most talented, Paul Anka, was not named Bobby.

13. Jonathan Gould, *Can't Buy Me Love: The Beatles, Britain and America* (London: Piatkus, 2008), 3.

14. "Transatlantic Jet Flight Celebrates Fifty Years," *London Telegraph,* October 6, 2008, http://www.telegraph.co.uk/travel/3146988/Transatlantic-jet-flight-celebrates-50-years.html, accessed February 15, 2010.

15. The week of October 9, 1976.

16. For a detailed discussion of this piece see Ken McLeod, "'A Fifth of Beethoven': Disco, Classical Music, and the Politics of Inclusion," *American Music* 24, no. 3 (Autumn 2006), 347–63.

17. Robert Walser, *Running with the Devil: Power, Gender and Madness in Heavy Metal Music* (Hanover, N.H.: University Press of New England, 1993), 66–67, discusses this piece in some detail.

18. The piece is available at http://www.youtube.com/watch?v=tKf7oYywdS8, accessed January 29, 2010

19. Richard Middleton, *Studying Popular Music* (Philadelphia: Open University, Press, 1990), 3, quoted in Walser, *Running with the Devil,* 267.

20. At http://www.guitars101.com/forums/f90/yngwie-malmsteen-fire-and-ice-tour-92-a-48399.html, accessed February 22, 2010.

21. At http://www.youtube.com/watch?v=rrhdx5W8GFI, accessed February 22, 2010.

22. Edward Rothstein, "Music: Debuts in Review," *New York Times,* November 21, 1982, 70.

23. Wil Forbis, "An Interview With the Great Kat," *Acid Logic,* June 1, 2001, http://www.acidlogic.com/great_kat.htm, accessed February 8, 2010.

24. John Stix, "Yngwie Malmsteen and Billy Sheehan: Summit Meeting at Chops City," *Guitar for the Practicing Musician,* March 1986, 59; quoted in Robert Walser, "Eruptions: Heavy Metal Appropriations of Classical Music," *Popular Music* 11, no. 2 (October 1992), 297.

25. Walser, *Running with the Devil,* 111.

26. Ibid., 111–12.

27. Ibid., 116–17.

28. Christian Hoard, "Album Reviews," *Rolling Stone* online, posted December 30, 2002, http://www.rollingstone.com/artists/nas/albums/album/99319/review/6067946/gods_son, accessed February 24, 2010.

12. BEETHOVEN EVERYWHERE

1. Greg Sandow, "The Concise Beethoven," *New York Times,* November 6, 2005, http://www.nytimes.com/2005/11/06/books/review/06sandow.html?pagewanted=print, accessed May 11, 2009.

2. This statement is based on a number of conversations and informal interviews I had in the late sixties with students who were not music majors and whose families were not involved in classical music, either as performers or listeners.

3. Queries to the program yielded no answer about who decided on the theme and whether it was a direct allusion to *The Huntley-Brinkley Report.*

4. Another instance of Beethoven and the telephone occurs in *The Simpsons,* season 18, episode "Little Big Girl," in which Bart, having saved the city from a fire, is granted a driver's license. Homer gives him a cell phone with a special ringtone so that Homer can call when he needs Bart to drive him somewhere. The ringtone is *Für Elise.*

5. As of this writing (April 5, 2011), this routine may be seen on YouTube, http://www.youtube.com/watch?v=EEhF-7suDsM.

6. "OG" in this context stands for "original gangster, meaning a person who came up through a tough environment to succeed and remain true to himself."

7. Played by William Kinderman.

8. Maynard Solomon's candidate, Antonie Brentano, is the most widely accepted solution today. Solomon, *Beethoven,* 2nd rev. ed. (New York: Schirmer Books, 1998), 207–46.

9. At http://www.dsokids.com/games/baseball, accessed April 14, 2010.

10. Meat Loaf is the rock singer Michael Lee Aday, who first achieved success in the 1970s.

11. April Dembosky, "Listening to Schroeder: 'Peanuts' Scholars Find Messages in Cartoon's Scores," *New York Times,* January 13, 2009, online at http://www.nytimes.com/2009/01/14/arts/design/14pean.html, accessed February 19, 2010.

12. I want to thank William Meredith, director of the Ira F. Brilliant Beethoven Center at San José State University, for sharing with me "Fate, Joy, and Propaganda: Beethoven from 1938 to 1945," a lecture he delivered at "Joy's Legacy: Beethoven's Ninth," a Beethoven Festival and Symposium at Wake Forest University, Winston-Salem, N.C., March 1, 1997, from which the "V" references came.

13. "The Grand Musical Festival in Boston, Inauguration of Crawford's Statue of Beethoven," *New York Times,* March 3, 1856. The anonymous reviewer found Story's poem, delivered in rhymed couplets, "interminable," and the Ninth "well played" even though it was "mutilated."

14. The Beethoven-Haus online has photographs of all the pre-1827 busts. http://www.beethoven-haus-bonn.de; click on "Digital archives," "Pictures and objects," and "Busts." Accessed June 24, 2010.

15. These quotations are taken from an email interview with Ross McBride, June 22, 2010.

16. At http://www.dezeen.com/2008/08/21/fiona-thomson-at-new-designers, accessed June 22, 2010.

17. Unidentified interview, probably with the BBC in 1981, at http://www.webexhibits.org/colorart/marilyns.html, accessed April 5, 2010.

18. Mina Yang, "Für Elise, Circa 2000: Postmodern Readings of Beethoven in Popular Contexts," *Popular Music and Society* 29, no. 1 (February 2006), 2.

19. These quotations are written in the third person, but as they are part of his "biography" on his official web site, we can assume that he had a hand in the statements if he did not actually write them himself. See http://kuksi.com/biography, accessed June 24, 2010.

20. Yasim Bilbeise, "Not in Kansas Anymore," *Hi Fructose Magazine,* December 5, 2009, http://www.hifructose.com/index.php?option=com_content&task=view&id=442&Itemid=56, accessed April 15, 2010.

21. He used Béla Drahos's recording with the Nicolaus Esterházy Sinfonia and Chorus, Naxos 8.553478. I want to thank Elisa Weber for sharing with me her unpublished paper, "9 Beet Stretch," from which much of the material for this discussion comes.

22. Ben Sisario, "Beethoven's Ninth around the Clock," *New York Times,* April 11, 2004, 2:25.

23. David W. Patterson, "Frank Lloyd Wright: Musical Intersections and the Shaping of the New American Architecture," paper presented at the National Conference of the Society for American Music, Cincinnati, March 12, 2011.

24. First quotation in "Daily Rhythms," *Frank Lloyd Wright Quarterly* 9, no. 2 (Spring 1998), 13; second quotation in Frank Lloyd Wright, "An Autobiography, Book Five: Form" (1943), in *Frank Lloyd Wright Collected Writings: Volume 4, 1939–1949*, ed. Bruce Brooks Pfeiffer (New York: Rizzoli/The Frank Lloyd Wright Foundation, 1994), 147.

25. Frank Lloyd Wright, "At Florida Southern College," in *Frank Lloyd Wright: His Living Voice*, ed. Bruce Brooks Pfeiffer (Modesto, Calif.: The Press of the California State University, Modesto, 1987), 70.

26. Frank Lloyd Wright, "The Language of an Organic Architecture" (1953), in *Frank Lloyd Wright Collected Writings: Volume 5, 1949–1959*, ed. Bruce Brooks Pfeiffer (New York: Rizzoli/The Frank Lloyd Wright Foundation, 1995), 62.

27. Wright, "Autobiography, Book Three," 4:372.

28. Leif Inge, "Closer to Eternity: Stretching Beethoven's 9th: Norwegian Artist Creates 24-Hour Version of Famous Work," *All Things Considered*, National Public Radio, November 26, 2002.

29. Strange/Beautiful, http://www.strangebeautiful.net/2009/01/08/9-beet-stretch/.

30. Kevin Ferguson, "Ein Kleine Nacht Music," *District Weekly* (Long Beach, Calif.), May 7, 2008.

31. Sisario, "Beethoven's Ninth around the Clock."

32. Kyle Gann, "Norwegian Minimalist Raises Beethoven Molto Adagio Bar," *Village Voice*, February 10, 2004, http://www.villagevoice.com/2004-02-10/music/norwegian-minimalist-raises-beethoven-molto-adagio-bar/, accessed July 9, 2009.

33. Mark Swed, "Beethoven's Lasting N-n-i-i-i-n-n-t-h-h," *Los Angeles Times*, November 27, 2006, E1.

34. Greg Sandow, "*9 Beet Stretch*," *Greg Sandow on the Future of Classical Music*, April 9, 2004, http://www.artsjournal.com/sandow/2004/04/9_beet_stretch.html.

35. Marc Shulgold, "Beethoven Birthday Bash a Happy, if Puzzling Affair," *Rocky Mountain News*, December 9, 1992, Entertainment/Weekend, 83.

BIBLIOGRAPHY

Adler, Guido, and Theodore Baker. "Schubert and the Viennese Classical School." *Musical Quarterly* 14, no. 4 (October 1928), 473–85.

Adler, Jerry. "African Dream—Days of Empire." *Newsweek,* September 23, 1991, 42.

"African American Involvement in the Vietnam War, Speeches and Sounds." http://www.aavw.org/special_features/speeches_speech_carmichae101.html, accessed March 14, 2010.

Albrecht, Otto E. "America's Early Acquaintance with Beethoven." In *Music, Edition, Interpretation, Gedenkschrift Günter Henle*, 13–22. Munich: G. Henle Verlag, 1980.

Algernon, Austin. "Cultural Black Nationalism and the Meaning of Black Power." Paper presented at the annual meeting of the American Sociological Association, Atlanta, August 16, 2003. http://www.allacademic.com/meta/p107842_index.html.

Altman, Rick. *Silent Film Sound.* New York: Columbia University Press, 2004.

Andy Warhol's Marilyn Prints. Interview [probably with BBC], 1981. http://www.webexhibits.org/colorart/marilyns.html, accessed April 5, 2010

Armstrong, Louis. "The Jargon File, Version 4.2.2, 20 Aug 2000." Ed. Eric S. Raymond and Guy S. Steele. http://www.gutenberg.org/dirs/etext02/jarg422h.htm, accessed January 18, 2010.

Asante, Molefi. *The Afrocentric Idea.* Philadelphia: Temple University Press, 1987.

———. *Kemet, Afrocentricity, and Knowledge.* Trenton, N.J.: Africa World Press, 1990.

Babbitt, Milton. "Who Cares if You Listen." *High Fidelity,* February 1958, 38–40, 126–27.

Bagley, Christopher. "Tea and Symphonies." *Premiere,* January 1995, 69.

Barlow, D. H. "Music." *Godey's Lady's Book* 44, no. 5 (May 1852), 305.

Barrow, Arthur A. "Music and Films." *Views and Film Index,* 16 May 1908, 4.

Baskerville, John D. *The Impact of Black Nationalist Ideology on American Jazz Music of the 1960s and 1970s*. Lewiston, Maine: Edwin Mellen Press, 2003.

"Beethoven Services Today." *New York Times*, March 27, 1927, 23.

Benjamin, Park. "The True Rights of Women." *Godey's Lady's Book* 28, no. 6 (June 1844), 272.

Bergquist, James M. *Daily Life in Immigrant America, 1820–1870*. Santa Barbara, Calif.: Greenwood Press, 2008.

Bernstein, Leonard. *The Joy of Music*. New York: Simon & Schuster, 1957.

Berry, Chuck. *Chuck Berry: The Autobiography*. New York: Harmony Press, 1987.

Berry, Ira. *Sketch of the History of the Beethoven Musical Society of Portland, Maine, 1819–1825*. Portland, Maine: Stephen Berry, 1888.

Berwick Sayers, W. C. *Samuel Coleridge-Taylor, Musician: His Life and Letters*. London and New York: Cassell and Co., 1915.

Bilbeise, Yasim. "Not in Kansas Anymore." *Hi Fructose Magazine*, December 5, 2009. http://www.hifructose.com/index.php?option=com_content&task=view&id=442&Itemid=56, accessed April 15, 2010.

Blavatsky, Helena P. *The Secret Doctrine*. London: Theosophical Publishing Company, 1888.

———. *The Voice of the Silence*. London: Theosophical Publishing Company, 1889.

Boggs, Joseph M., and Dennis W. Petrie. *The Art of Watching Films*, 7th ed. New York: McGraw-Hill, 2008.

Boulez, Pierre. "Sonata, que me veux-tu." In *Orientations: Collected Writings of Pierre Boulez*, ed. Jean-Jacques Nattiez, 154. Trans. Martin Cooper. Cambridge, Mass.: Harvard University Press, 1968.

Bradshaw, David. "The Best of Companions: J. W. N. Sullivan, Aldous Huxley, and the New Physics." *Review of English Studies*, n.s. 47, no. 186 (May 1996), 189–90.

Brandenburg, Sieghard. "Viewpoint: On Beethoven Scholars and Beethoven's Sketches." *19th-Century Music* 2, no. 3 (March 1979), 270–74.

Britt, Bruce. "Isabella Rossellini Stands in for Her 'Immortal Beloved.'" *San Francisco Chronicle*, December 15, 1994. E3.

Brower, Harriette. "Leo Ornstein, An Ultra Modern Pianist and Composer." *Musical Observer*, August 1915, 467.

Brown, Earle. "The Notation and Performance of New Music." *Musical Quarterly* 76, no. 2 (1986), 181.

Broyles, Michael. *The Emergence and Evolution of Beethoven's Heroic Style*. New York: Excelsior Music Publishing Company, 1987.

———. *Mavericks and Other Traditions in American Music*. New Haven, Conn.: Yale University Press, 2004.

———. *"Music of the Highest Class": Elitism and Populism in Antebellum Boston*. New Haven, Conn.: Yale University Press, 1992.

Buch, Esteban. *Beethoven's Ninth: A Political History.* Trans. Richard Miller. Chicago: University Press, 2003.

Bukofzer, Manfred. "Caput: A Liturgico-Musical Study." In *Studies in Medieval and Renaissance Music,* 217–310. New York: Norton, 1950.

Burke, Edmund. *A Philosophical Enquiry into the Origin of our Ideas of the Sublime and Beautiful.* 1757. London: J. Dodsley, 1770.

Burnham, Scott. *Beethoven, Hero.* Princeton, N.J.: Princeton University Press, 1995.

Butler, Nicholas Michael. *Votaries of Apollo, The St. Cecilia Society and the Patronage of Concert Music in Charleston, South Carolina, 1766–1820.* Columbia: University of South Carolina Press, 2007.

Carden, Joy. *Music in Lexington before 1840.* Lexington, Ky.: Lexington Fayette County Historic Commission, 1980.

Carson, Clayborne. *In Struggle: SNCC and the Black Awakening of the 1960s.* Cambridge, Mass.: Harvard University Press, 1981.

Chávez, Charles. "The Music of Mexico." In *American Composers on American Music: A Symposium.* Ed. Henry Cowell. Palo Alto, Calif.: Stanford University Press, 1933.

Chen, Anne Hui-Hua. "Beethoven in America to 1865." Ph.D. diss., University of North Carolina, Chapel Hill, 1976.

Chevalier, Leila. "The Battle of the Music-Makers between the Ultra-Modernists and the Reactionaries Rages War to the Death." *Modernism* 17 (October 1922), 405.

Chevigny, Bell Gale. *The Woman and the Myth: Margaret Fuller's Life and Writings.* Boston: Northeastern University Press, 1994.

Cooke, George Willis. *John Sullivan Dwight, Brook-Farmer, Editor, and Critic of Music.* Boston: Small, Maynard, 1898.

"Copying Beethoven, Full Production Notes." http://www.vervepics.com/copyingbeethoven.shtml.

"Cubists and Futurists Are Making Insanity Pay." *New York Times,* March 16, 1913, SM1.

D'Albert, Eugen. "Ludwig van Beethoven." In *The International Library of Music for Home and Studio,* vol. 1, *Music Literature.* New York: The University Society, 1927, 103–18.

Dance, Charles. "Count Basie interview." *The World of Swing.* New York: Charles Scribner's Sons, 1974.

Deezen: Design Magazine. http://www.dezeen.com/2008/08/21/fiona-thomson-at-new-designers, accessed June 22, 2010.

de Lerma, Dominique-Rene. "Beethoven as a Black Composer." *Black Music Research Journal* 10, no. 1 (Spring, 1990), 118–22.

———. "Beethoven as a Black Composer." http://myrtlehart.org/content/view/182/174/, accessed June 17, 2008.

Delgado, Richard. "Are Hate-Speech Rules Constitutional Heresy? A Reply to Steven Gey." *University of Pennsylvania Law Review* 146, no. 3 (March 1998), 865–79.

———. "Campus Anti-Racism Rules: Constitutional Narratives in Collision, Or, Why There Are Always Two Ways of Looking at a Speech Controversy." In *Must We Defend Nazis? Hate Speech, Pornography and the New First Amendment*, ed. Jean Stefancic, 46–70. New York: New York University Press, 1997.

———. "Rodrigo's Thirteenth Chronicle: Legal Formalism and Law's Discontents." *Michigan Law Review* 95, no. 4 (February 1997), 1105–49.

Delgado, Richard, and Jean Stefancic. *Understanding Words That Wound*. Boulder, Colo.: Westview Press, 2004.

Dembosky, April. "Listening to Schroeder: 'Peanuts' Scholars Find Messages in Cartoon's Scores." *New York Times*, January 13, 2009. http://www.nytimes.com/2009/01/14/arts/design/14pean.html, accessed February 19, 2010.

DeMott, Benjamin. "Rock as Salvation." *New York Times*, August 25, 1968, SM30.

Dent, Edward J. "Beethoven and a Younger Generation." *Musical Quarterly* 13, no. 2 (April 1927), 317.

Dobrusky, Pavel, and Per-Olav Sørensen. *Beethoven 'N' Pierrot*. Switzerland/France: kfm Verlag, n.d.

Downes, Olin. "Regarding the Ring." *New York Times*, February 7, 1937, 167.

———. "The Workshop of Beethoven." *New York Times*, March 20, 1927, X8.

Drabkin, William. "New Beethoven Insights." *Musical Times* 120, no. 1634 (April 1979), 304.

———. "Viewpoint: On Beethoven Scholars and Beethoven's Sketches." *19th-Century Music* 2, no. 3 (March 1979), 274–76.

"Drama: Musical Biography and Musical Farce." *Life*, April 21, 1910, 55.

Dwight, John S. "Academy of Music—Beethoven's Symphonies." *The Pioneer*, January–February 1853, 26–28, 56–60.

———. "Address Delivered before the Harvard Musical Association, August 25, 1841." *Musical Magazine* 3 (August 28, 1841), 259, 263–64.

———. "Beethoven in Boston." *Dwight's Journal of Music* 34, no. 11 (September 5, 1874), 294.

———. "Concerts of the Past Winter." *The Dial* 1, no. 1 (July 1849), 124.

———. "The History of Music in Boston." In *The Memorial History of Boston*, vol. 4, ed. Justin Winsor, 426–27. Boston: James R. Osgood, 1881.

———. "Music." In *Aesthetic Papers*, ed. Elizabeth P. Peabody, 31–32, 36. Boston: The Editor; New York: G. P. Putnam, 1849.

———. "Music as a Means of Culture." *Atlantic Monthly* 26 (September 1870), 322.

———. "Music Review. Music in Boston During the Past Winter. No. IV." *Harbinger* 1, no. 12 (August 30, 1845), 188, 194.

———. "Musical Review." *Harbinger* 5, no. 21 (October 30, 1847), 327.

Early, Gerald. "Afrocentrism: From Sensationalism to Measured Deliberation." *Journal of Blacks in Higher Education,* no. 5 (Autumn 1994), 86.

Eberhart, Jonathan. "Commentary: The Day the Sky Was Opened." *Science News* 122, no. 14 (October 2, 1982), 220–21.

Ein Skizzenbuch von Beethoven aus dem Jahre 1803. Leipzig, 1880; reprint, New York, 1970.

Ellwood, Robert S. *Religious and Spiritual Groups in Modern America.* Englewood Cliffs, N.J.: Prentice-Hall, 1973.

Elson, William H. *Pre-Primer.* Chicago: Scott, Foresman, 1930.

Erskine, John. *The Philharmonic-Symphony Society of New York, Its First Hundred Years.* New York: Macmillan, 1943.

Everdell, William R. *The First Moderns: Profiles in the Origins of Twentieth-Century Thought.* Chicago: University of Chicago Press, 1997.

F. C. G. "Afrocentrism." *American Journal of Economics and Sociology* 52, no. 2 (April 1993), 192.

Ferguson, Kevin. "Ein Kleine Nacht Music." *District Weekly* (Long Beach, Calif.), May 7, 2008.

Fertig, Walter L. "John Sullivan Dwight: Transcendentalist and Literary Amateur of Music." Ph.D. diss., University of Maryland, 1952.

Fife, Austin E. "Research in Folklore under the National Defense Education Act." *Journal of American Folklore* 74, no. 292 (April–June 1961), 146.

Fifth Annual Report of the Boston Academy of Music. Boston: Perkins, Marvin, 1837.

"Final Report on Recent Incidents at Ujamaa House." Board of Trustees of the Leland Stanford Junior University, Stanford, Calif., 1989. Palo Alto, Calif.: Stanford University Archives.

Fink, Robert. "Beethoven Antihero." In *Beyond Structural Listening? Postmodern Modes of Hearing,* ed. Andrew Dell'Antonio, 109–53. Berkeley: University of California Press, 2004.

FitzGerald, Edward. "Rubaiyat of Omar Khayyam." http://www.therubaiyat.com/fitzindex.htm, accessed August 5, 2010.

Flemming, Arthur. "The Philosophy and Objectives of The National Defense Education Act." *Annals of the American Academy of Political and Social Science* 327 (January 1960), 132–37.

Forbes, Elliot, ed. *Thayer's Life of Beethoven.* Rev. ed. Princeton, N.J.: Princeton University Press, 1967.

Forbis, Wil. "An Interview With the Great Kat." *Acid Logic,* June 1, 2001. http://www.acidlogic.com/great_kat.htm, accessed February 8, 2010.

"14 Emmy Nods for 'Twin Peaks.'" *Detroit Free Press,* August 3, 1990, 1C.

Fox, Margalit. "Betty Friedan, Who Ignited Cause in 'Feminine Mystique,' Dies at 85." *New York Times,* February 5, 2006. http://www.nytimes.com/2006/02/05/national/05friedan.html, accessed November 13, 2007.

Fox, Robert Elliot. "Afrocentrism and the X Factor." *Transition,* no. 57 (1992), 19.

Freshman, Clark. "Were Patricia Williams and Richard Dworkin Separated at Birth?" *Columbia Law Review* 95, no. 6 (October 1995), 1568–1609.

Fryer, Paul H. "'Brown-Eyed Handsome Man': Chuck Berry and the Blues Tradition." *Phylon* 42, no. 1 (1st qtr., 1981), 64.

Fuller, Margaret. "Entertainments of the Past Winter." *The Dial* 3 no. 1 (July 1842), 61.

———. "Lives of the Great Composers." *The Dial* 2 no. 2 (October 1841), 150–51.

———. "Youth. Autobiography." In Margaret Fuller, William Henry Channing, Ralph Waldo Emerson, and James Freeman Clarke, *Memories of Margaret Fuller.* 3 vols. 1:9–58. Boston: Phillips, Sampson and Company, 1857.

Gabel, Peter, and Duncan Kennedy. "Roll Over Beethoven." *Stanford Law Review* 36, no. 1/2 (January 1984), 1–55.

Gagne, Cole, and Tracy Caras. *Soundpieces: Interviews with American Composers.* Metuchen, N.J.: Scarecrow Press, 1982.

Gann, Kyle. "Norwegian Minimalist Raises Beethoven Molto Adagio Bar." *Village Voice,* February 10, 2004, http://www.villagevoice.com/2004-02-10/music/norwegian-minimalist-raises-beethoven-molto-adagio-bar/. Accessed July 9, 2009.

Gatta, John. *Marking Nature Sacred: Literature, Religion, and Environment in America from the Puritans to the Present.* New York: Oxford University Press, 2004.

Gayle, Addison, ed. *The Black Aesthetic.* Garden City, N.Y.: Doubleday-Anchor, 1971.

Geiringer, Karl. "'The Structure of Beethoven's 'Diabelli Variations.'" *Musical Quarterly* 50, no. 4 (October 1964), 496–503.

Gerson, Robert A. *Music in Philadelphia.* Westport, Conn.: Greenwood Press, 1970.

Gey, Steven G. "The Case against Postmodern Censorship Theory." *University of Pennsylvania Law Review* 145, no. 2 (December 1996), 193–297.

———. "Postmodern Censorship Revisited: A Reply to Richard Delgado." *University of Pennsylvania Law Review* 146, no. 4 (April 1998), 1077–95.

Gilman, Lawrence. *Toscanini and Great Music.* New York: Farrar and Rinehart, 1938.

Glauert, Amanda. "The Double Perspective in Beethoven's Opus 131." *19th-Century Music* 4, no. 2 (Autumn 1980), 113–20.

Gossett, Philip. "Beethoven's Sixth Symphony: Sketches for the First Movement." *Journal of the American Musicological Society* 27, no. 2 (Summer 1974), 248–84.

Gould, Jonathan. *Can't Buy Me Love: The Beatles, Britain and America.* London: Piatkus. 2008.

"The Grand Musical Festival in Boston, Inauguration of Crawford's Statue of Beethoven." *New York Times,* March 3, 1856.

Griffes, Paul. *Modern Music and After: Directions Since 1945.* Oxford: Oxford University Press, 1995.

Haggerty, Sandra. "Beethoven and Negro History Week." *Los Angeles Times,* February 11, 1970.

———. "'Beethoven Was Black'—-???." *Los Angeles Times,* May 13, 1970.

Haley, Alex. "Playboy Interview: A Candid Conversation with the Militant Major-Domo of the Black Muslims." *Playboy,* May 1963, 53–63.

Harris, William J., ed. "Introduction." In *The LeRoi Jones (Amiri Baraka) Reader.* New York: Thunder's Mouth Press, 1991.

Haskell, Harry. *The Early Music Revival: A History.* London: Thames and Hudson, 1998.

Hatten, Robert S. *Musical Meaning in Beethoven.* Bloomington: Indiana University Press, 1994.

Heline, Corrine. *Beethoven's Nine Symphonies Correlated to the Nine Spiritual Mysteries.* Santa Barbara, Calif.: J. F. Rowny Press, 1963.

Henahan, Donal. "Do You Speak Classical or Pop?" *New York Times,* August 9, 1981, D1.

Henderson, W. J. "Beethoven After a Hundred Years." *Musical Quarterly* 13, no. 2 (April 1927), 164.

———. "Concert Ends in Uproar." *New York Herald,* March 5, 1923. In Carl Ruggles folder, Irving S. Gilmore Music Library, Yale University, New Haven, Conn.

Hennessee, Judith. *Betty Friedan: Her Life.* New York: Random House, 1999.

Herz, Frederick. *Rasse und Kulter.* Leipzig: A. Kröner, 1925.

Higgins, Paula. "Women in Music, Feminist Criticism, and Guerrilla Musicology: Reflections on Recent Polemics." *19th-Century Music* 17, no.2 (Autumn 1993) 185.

Higginson, Thomas Wentworth. *Cheerful Yesterdays.* Boston and New York: Houghton, Mifflin and Company, 1898.

Hitchcock, H. Wiley. "Tin Pan Alley." *Grove Music Online,* Oxford University Press, http://www.oxfordmusiconline.com.proxy.lib.fsu.edu/subscriber/article/grove/music/27995?q=Tin+Pan+Alley&search=quick&pos=1&_start=1#firsthit, accessed January 13, 2010.

Hoard, Christian. "Album Reviews." *Rolling Stone* online, posted December 30, 2002. http://www.rollingstone.com/artists/nas/albums/album/99319/review/6067946/gods_son, accessed February 24, 2010.

Hoffmann, E. T. A. "Review of Beethoven's Fifth Symphony." In *Beethoven, Symphony No. 5 in C minor,* ed. Elliot Forbes, 150–63. New York: Norton, 1971,

Hudspeth, Robert N., ed. *The Letters of Margaret Fuller.* 6 vols. Ithaca, N.Y.: Cornell University Press, 1983.

Inge, Leif. "Closer to Eternity: Stretching Beethoven's 9th: Norwegian Artist Creates 24-Hour Version of Famous Work." *All Things Considered,* National Public Radio, November 26, 2002.

James, George. *Stolen Legacy*. New York: Philosophical Library, 1954.

Jeffries, Judson L. *Huey P. Newton: The Radical Theorist*. Jackson: University Press of Mississippi, 2002.

Jennison, Samuel. "Reminisces of an Ex-Pierian." In Scrapbook at Harvard Musical Association, Boston.

Jérôme-Joseph. *Cours complet d'harmonie et de composition*. 3 vols. Paris: chez l'auteur, 1806.

Johnson, Allen et al. *Dictionary of American Biography*. New York: American Council of Learned Societies, 1928–1937.

Johnson, Douglas. "Beethoven Scholars and Beethoven Sketches." *19th-Century Music* 2, no. 1 (July 1978), 3–17.

Johnson, Douglas, Alan Tyson, and Robert Winter. *The Beethoven Sketchbooks: History, Reconstruction, Inventory*. Berkeley: University of California Press, 1985.

Jonas, Oswald. "An Unknown Sketch by Beethoven." *Musical Quarterly* 26, no. 2 (April 1940), 186–91.

Jones, LeRoi (Amiri Baraka). *Black Music*. New York: William Morrow & Company, 1970.

Kalamu ya Salaam. "Historical Background of the Black Arts Movement (BAM)." In *The Magic of Juju: An Appreciation of the Black Arts Movement (BAM)*. Chicago: Third World Press, forthcoming. http://www.black-collegian.com/african/bam1_200.shtml, accessed October 17, 2008.

Kant, Immanuel. *Observations on the Feeling of the Beautiful and Sublime*. 1764. Trans. John T. Goldthwait. Berkeley: University of California Press, 1960.

Kennedy, Adrienne. "A MELUS Interview: Adrienne Kennedy, Wolfgang Binder, Adrienne Kennedy." *MELUS* 12, no. 3 (Autumn 1985), 99–108.

———. *People Who Led to My Plays*. New York: Knopf, 1986.

Kerman, Joseph. *The Beethoven Quartets*. New York: Alfred A. Knopf, 1967.

———. "Beethoven Sketchbooks in the British Museum." *Proceedings of the Royal Musical Association*, 93rd sess. (1966–1967), 77–96.

———. "Beethoven's Early Sketches." *Musical Quarterly* 56, no. 4 (October 1970), 515–38.

———. "How We Got into Analysis, and How to Get Out." *Critical Inquiry* 7, no. 2 (Winter 1980), 311–31.

———, ed. *Ludwig van Beethoven, Autograph Miscellany from Circa 1786 to 1799*. 2 vols. London: Trustees of the British Museum, 1970.

———. "Sketch Studies." *19th-Century Music* 6, no. 2 (Autumn 1982), 175.

Kerman, Joseph, and Alan Tyson. "Beethoven." *New Grove Dictionary of Music and Musicians* 3:382. Oxford: Oxford University Press, 1930.

Kinderman, William. *Beethoven*. Berkeley: University of California Press, 1995.

Kinsky, Georg, and Hans Halm. *Das Work Beethovens: Thematisch-Bibliographisches Verzeichnis Seiner Sämtlichen Vollendenten Kompositionen*. Munich: G Henle Verlag, 1955.

Kirby, F. E. "Beethoven's Pastoral Symphony as a *Sinfonia caracteristica.*" *Musical Quarterly* 56, no. 4 (October 1970), 605–23.

Kivy, Peter. "Communications." *Journal of the American Musicological Society* 28, no. 2 (Summer 1975), 397–98.

Koehleer, Robert. "Grandiose 'Beethovens' Twists the Myth." *Los Angeles Times,* January 24, 1992, 22.

Korsyn, Kevin. "J.W.N. Sullivan and the Heiliger Dankgesang: Questions of Meaning in Late Beethoven." *Beethoven Forum* 2 (1993), 133–74.

Kraft, Siv Ellen. "To Mix or Not to Mix: Syncretism/Anti-Syncretism in the History of Theosophy." *Numen* 49, no. 2 (2002), 142–77.

Kramer, Lawrence. "The Harem Threshold: Turkish Music and Greek Love in Beethoven's 'Ode to Joy.'" *19th-Century Music* 22, no. 1 (Summer 1998), 78–90.

Krehbiel, Henry Edward. *The Philharmonic Society of New York.* New York and London: Novello, Ewer & Co., 1892.

Kretzschmar, Herman. "Anregungen zur Förderung musikalischer Hermeneutik." *Jahrbuch der Musikbibliothek Peters 1902,* 45–66. Reprinted in *Gesammelte Aufsätze über Musik und Anderes* 1 (Leipzig, 1911), 168–92.

Kuksi, Kris. "Biography." http://kuksi.com/biography/, accessed June 24, 2010.

Kunz, Mary. "Ludwig in Love." *Buffalo News,* January 9, 1995, D1.

LaSalle, Mick. "Well-Composed 'Beloved' Looks at Ludwig's Loves." *San Francisco Chronicle,* December 16, 1994, C3.

Lawrence, Charles R. "If He Hollers Let Him Go: Regulating Racist Speech on Campus." *Duke L. J.* 1990, no. 3 (June 1990), 431–83.

Lawrence, Vera Brodsky. *Strong on Music: The New York Music Scene in the Days of George Templeton Strong, 1836–1875.* Vol. 1, *Resonances, 1836–1850.* New York: Oxford University Press, 1988.

Lazerow, Jama, and Yonhuru Williams, eds. *In Search of the Black Panther Party: New Perspectives on a Revolutionary Movement.* Durham, N.C.: Duke University Press, 2006.

Lefkowitz, Mary. *Not Out of Egypt: How "Afrocentrism" Became an Excuse to Teach Myth as History.* New York: Basic Books, 1996.

Lenz, Wilhelm von. *Beethoven et ses trios styles.* Paris: G Legouix, 1909.

Lockwood, Lewis. *Beethoven: The Music and the Life.* New York: W. W. Norton, 2003.

———. "Beethoven, Florestan, and the Varieties of Heroism." In *Beethoven and His World,* ed. Scott Burnham and Michael Steinberg, 27–47. Princeton, N.J.: Princeton University Press, 2000.

———. "Eroica Perspectives: Strategy and Design in the First Movement." *Beethoven Studies 3,* ed. Alan Tyson, 85–105. Cambridge: Cambridge University Press, 1982.

———. "Film Biography as Travesty." *Musical Quarterly* 81, no. 2 (Summer 1997), 190.

———. "On Beethoven's Sketches and Autographs: Some Problems of Definition and Interpretation." *Acta Musicologica* 42, fasc. 1/2 (January 1970), 32–47.

Loesser, Arthur. *Men, Women and Pianos*. New York: Simon and Schuster, 1945.

Longyear, Rey M. "Beethoven and Romantic Irony." *Musical Quarterly* 56, no. 4 (October 1970), 647–64.

Lowell, Edward J. *The Hessians and the Other German Auxiliaries of Great Britain in the Revolutionary War*. New York: Harper and Brothers, 1884. http://www .americanrevolution.org/hessians/hess4.html, accessed June 22, 2009.

Ludwig, Emil. *Beethoven, Life of a Conqueror*. Trans. George Stewart McManus. New York: G. P. Putnam's Sons, 1943.

Marable, Manning. *Race, Reform and Rebellion: The Second Reconstruction in Black American, 1945–1982*. Jackson: University Press of Mississippi, 1984.

Marks, Martin Miller. *Music in the Silent Film: Contexts and Case Studies, 1895–1924*. New York: Oxford University Press, 1997.

Maslin, Janet. "The Music Almost Tells the Tale." *New York Times*, December 16, 1994, C4.

Mason, Daniel Gregory. *Beethoven and His Forerunners*. New York: Macmillan, 1930.

———. *The Quartets of Beethoven*. New York: Oxford University Press, 1947.

Mason, Lowell. *Address on Church Music: Delivered by Request, on the Evening of Saturday, October 7, 1826*. Boston: Hilliard, Gray, Little, and Wilkins, 1827.

McAlpin, Colin. "Musical Modernism: Some Random Reflections." *Musical Quarterly* 16, no. 1 (January 1930), 4–5.

McClary, Susan. *Feminine Endings: Music, Gender and Sexuality*. Minneapolis: University of Minnesota Press, 1991.

———. "Getting Down Off the Beanstalk." *Minnesota Composer's Forum Newsletter*, January 1987, 7.

Mcculloh, T. H. "All in Ludwig's Family, 'The Beethovens.'" *Los Angeles Times*, Valley ed., January 12, 1992, 87.

McLellan, Dennis. "Carole Eastman, at 69; Wrote 1970 Classic 'Five Easy Pieces.'" *Los Angeles Times*, February 28, 2004.

McLeod, Ken. "'A Fifth of Beethoven': Disco, Classical Music, and the Politics of Inclusion." *American Music* 24, no. 3 (Autumn 2006), 347–63.

Mellor, Anne K. *Romanticism and Gender*. New York: Routledge, 1993

Meredith, William. "Fate, Joy, and Propaganda: Beethoven from 1938 to 1945." Lecture delivered at "Joy's Legacy: Beethoven's Ninth," a Beethoven Festival and Symposium, Wake Forest University, Winston-Salem, N.C., March 1, 1997.

Meyer, Leonard. "Forgery and the Anthropology of Art." In *Music, the Arts, and Ideas: Patterns and Predictions in Twentieth-Century Culture*. Chicago: University of Chicago Press, 1967, 54–67.

———. "Some Remarks on Value and Greatness in Music." In *Music, the Arts, and Ideas: Patterns and Predictions in Twentieth-Century Culture*, 22–41. Chicago: University of Chicago Press, 1967.

Middleton, Richard. *Studying Popular Music*. Philadelphia: Open University, Press, 1990.

"Minor Topics." *Magazine of History* 8 (January–June 1908), 249.

"Modern Music." *Euterpeiad* 1, no. 4 (March 22, 1820), 14.

Morris, Edmund. *Beethoven: The Universal Composer.* New York: HarperCollins, 2005.

Moseley, Deborah D. "Beethoven, the Black Spaniard." *ChickenBones: A Journal for Literary & Artistic African-American Themes.* http://www.nathanielturner.com/beethoventheblackspaniard.htm, posted February 15, 2007, updated October 2, 2007, accessed March 3, 2008.

Moses, Wilson Jeremiah. *Afrotopia: The Roots of American Popular History.* Cambridge: Cambridge University Press, 1998.

Moving Picture World 25, nos. 4–6 (July 24, 1915), 627.

Mueller, Kate Hevner. *Twenty-Seven Major American Symphony Orchestras: A History and Analysis of Their Repertoires, Seasons 1842–43 through 1969–70.* Bloomington: Indiana University Press, 1973.

Neal, Larry. "The Black Arts Movement." *Drama Review: TDR* 12, no. 4 (Summer 1968), 28–39.

Newman, William S. *The Sonata Since Beethoven.* New York: W. W. Norton, 1972.

Nightingale, Benedict. "Stage View; It Should be Called 'Ustinov's Twentieth.'" *New York Times,* April 29, 1984, H5.

Nohl, Ludwig. *Beethoven Depicted by His Contemporaries.* London: W. Reeves, 1880.

Nottebohm, Gustav. *Ein Skizzenbuch von Beethoven aus dem Jahre 1803.* Leipzig: Peters, 1880.

Novak, Barbara. *Nature and Culture: American Landscape and Painting, 1825–1875.* New York: Oxford University Press, 1995.

Nugent, Frank S. "The Screen." *New York Times,* November 22, 1937, 15.

Nystrum, Derek. "Hard Hats and Movie Brats: Auteurism and the Class Politics of the New Hollywood." *Cinema Journal* 43, no. 3 (Spring 2004), 31.

Ogbar, Jeffrey O.G. *Black Power: Radical Politics and African American Identity.* Baltimore, Md.: Johns Hopkins University Press, 2004.

Okerlund, Arlene Naylor. "Beethoven at San José State University." *Manuscript* 57, no. 4 (Fall 2005), 281–91.

Paine, J. K. "The New German School of Music." *North American Review* 116 (April 1873), 217–45.

Parrington, Vernon L. *The Colonial Mind, 1620–1800.* Vol. 1 of *Main Currents in American Thought.* New York: Harvest Books, 1954.

Partch, Harry. *Bitter Music: Collected Journals, Essays, Introductions, and Librettos.* Ed. Thomas McGeary. Urbana: University of Illinois Press, 1991.

Person-Lynn, Kwaku. "Thanks to Filmmakers, Composer's Life Still a Mystery: Beethoven's Racial Ties Misrepresented Again." *Los Angeles Times,* February 13, 1995, 3.

Petteys, Leslie. "Theodore Thomas's 'March to the Sea.'" *American Music* 10, no. 2 (Summer 1992), 170–82.

Peyser, Joan. *Boulez*. New York: Schirmer, 1976.

Posner, Richard. *Overcoming Law*. Cambridge, Mass.: Harvard University Press.

"Programs of Concerts in Boston, 1817–1863." Manuscript collection in Boston Public Library, Boston.

Prothero, Stephen. "From Spiritualism to Theosophy: 'Uplifting' a Democratic Tradition." *Religion and American Culture* 3, no. 2 (Summer 1993), 215.

Rapeé, Erno. *Encyclopedia for Motion Pictures*. New York: Belwin, 1925.

"Records." *High Fidelity* 3, no. 6 (Jan.-Feb. 1954), 52.

"Records of the Arionic Sodality, Cambridge: N. E. 1813." Manuscript book, Harvard Musical Association Library, Boston. September 12, 1830.

Rich, Adrienne. *Diving into the Wreck, Poems of 1971 and 1972*. New York: W. W. Norton, 1972.

Rich, Frank. "Theater: 'Beethoven's Tenth' With Peter Ustinov." *New York Times*, April 23, 1984, C11.

Ringer, Alexander L. "The Art of the Third Guess: Beethoven to Becker to Bartók." *Musical Quarterly* 52, no. 3 (July 1966), 304–12.

Rivele, Stephen. "An Introduction to the Film 'Copying Beethoven.'" http://www.lvbeethoven.com/Fictions/FictionFilmsCopyingBeethoven.html, accessed November 28, 2007.

Roberts, Gene. "Why the Cry Over 'Black Power.'" *New York Times*, July 30, 1966, 89.

Rocks, David. "Beethoven Movie Has Mystery Role." *San Francisco Chronicle*, August 5, 1994, C13.

Rockwell, John. "Music: In-Depth Beethoven Experience." *New York Times*, February 10, 1987, C18.

———. "Old Instruments May Herald the Future." *New York Times*, February 22, 1987, H1.

Rogers, Joel A. *Sex and Race*. Vol. 1, *Negro-Caucasian Mixing in All Ages and Lands*. New York: Helga M. Rogers, 1942. Vol. 2, *The New World*. New York: Helga M. Rogers, 1942. Vol. 3, *Why White and Black Mix in Spite of Opposition*. New York: Helga M. Rogers, 1944.

Rosen, Charles. *The Classical Style*. New York: W. W. Norton, 1971.

Rosenfeld, Paul. *Discoveries of a Music Critic*. New York: Harcourt, Brace & Co., 1936.

———. *An Hour with American Music*. Philadelphia: J. P. Lippincott Company, 1929.

Rothstein, Edward. "How Can a Movie So Right Be So Wrong?" *New York Times*, January 1, 1995, H31.

———. "Music: Debuts in Review." *New York Times*, November 21, 1982, 70.

Saloman, Ora Frishberg. *Beethoven's Symphonies and J. S. Dwight*. Boston: Northeastern University Press, 1995.

Sanders, Ernest. "Form and Content in the Finale of Beethoven's Ninth Symphony." *Musical Quarterly* 50, no. 1 (January 1964), 59–76.

———. "The Sonata-Form Finale of Beethoven's Ninth Symphony." *19th-Century Music* 22, no. 1 (Summer 1998), 54–60.

Sandow, Greg. "The Concise Beethoven." *New York Times,* November 6, 2005. http://www.nytimes.com/2005/11/06/books/review/06sandow.html?pagewanted=print, accessed May 11, 2009

———. *"9 Beet Stretch": Greg Sandow on the Future of Classical Music,* April 9, 2004. http://www.artsjournal.com/sandow/2004/04/9_beet_stretch.html.

Schauffler, Robert Haven. *Beethoven, the Man Who Freed Music.* New York: Doubleday, Doran & Company, 1935.

Schering, Arnold. *Beethoven und die Dichtung.* Berlin: Junker & Dünnhaupt, 1936.

Schindler, Anton. *Beethoven as I Knew Him.* Trans. Donald MacArdle. Chapel Hill: University of North Carolina Press, 1960.

Schonberg, Harold C. *The Lives of Great Composers.* New York: W. W. Norton, 1981.

Seeger, Charles. "Carl Ruggles." In *American Composers on American Music: A Symposium,* ed. Henry Cowell, 14–35. New York: Frederick Ungar Publishing, 1933.

Shulgold, Marc. "Beethoven Birthday Bash a Happy, if Puzzling Affair." *Rocky Mountain News,* Wednesday, December 9, 1992.

Simmons, Nancy Craig. "Margaret Fuller's Boston Conversations: The 1839–1840 Series." In *Studies in the American Renaissance,* 195–226. Charlottesville: University Press of Virginia, 1994.

Sisario, Ben. "Beethoven's Ninth Around the Clock." *New York Times,* April 11, 2004.

Slater, Abby. *In Search of Margaret Fuller.* New York: Delacorte Press, 1978.

Slobodin, Carol Schulz. "Sputnik and Its Aftermath: A Critical Look at the Form and Substance of American Educational Practice Since 1957." *Elementary School Journal* 77, no. 4 (March 1977), 259–64.

Smethurst, James Edward. *The Black Arts Movement: Literary Nationalism in the 1960s and 1970s.* Chapel Hill: University of North Carolina Press, 2005.

Solomon, Maynard. *Beethoven.* 1977. Rev. ed. New York: Schirmer Books, 1998.

Sonneck, Oscar. *Beethoven: Impressions of His Contemporaries.* New York: G. Schirmer, 1926.

Squires, Paul C. "Beethoven's Concept of the Whole." *American Journal of Psychology* 48, no. 4 (October 1936), 684–88.

Stewart, James T. "The Development of the Black Revolutionary Artist." In *Black Fire: An Anthology of Afro-American Writings,* ed. LeRoi Jones and L. Neal, 3–10. New York: William Morrow, 1968.

Stilwell, Robynn J. "'I Just Put a Drone under Him . . .': Collage and Subversion in the Score of 'Die Hard.'" *Music and Letters* 78, no. 4 (November 1997), 561–80.

Stix, John. "Yngwie Malmsteen and Billy Sheehan: Summit Meeting At Chop City." *Guitar for the Practicing Musician,* March 1986, 56–59, 64, 76.

Story, William W. *An Address Delivered before the Harvard Musical Association in the Chapel of the University at Cambridge, August 24, 1842.* Boston: S. N. Dickinson, 1842.

Stowell, Robin. *Beethoven, Violin Concerto.* New York: Cambridge University Press, 1998.

Sullivan, J. W. N. *Beethoven, His Spiritual Development.* 1927. New York: Vintage Books, 1960.

———. "Beethoven the Man." *John O'London Weekly* 6 (February 11, 1922), 611.

Swed, Mark. "Beethoven's Lasting N-n-i-i-i-n-n-t-h-h." *Los Angeles Times,* November 27, 2006, E1.

Szigeti, Joseph. Liner notes for *Early Recordings of Fritz Kreisler.* Berkeley, Calif.: Music and Arts Programs of America, 1988. CD-290(2).

Tame, David. *Beethoven and the Spiritual Path.* Wheaton, Ill.: Theosophical Publishing House, 1994.

Taruskin, Richard. "The Authenticity Movement Can Become a Positivistic Purgatory, Literalistic and Dehumanizing." *Early Music* 12, no. 1 (February 1984), 3–12.

———. "The Spin Doctors of Early Music." *New York Times,* July 29, 1990, H1.

Teeter, Lawrence. "Thanks to Filmmakers, Composer's Life Still a Mystery." *Los Angeles Times,* February 13, 1995, F3.

Temperley, Nicholas. "The Movement Puts a Stronger Premium on Novelty than on Accuracy, and Fosters Misrepresentation." *Early Music* 12, no. 1 (February 1984), 17.

Thomas, Theodore. *A Musical Autobiography.* Ed. George P. Upton, with a new introduction by Leon Stein. New York: DaCapo Press, 1964.

Tommasini, Anthony. "Composers Mining the Music of Their Youth." *New York Times,* April 18, 1999.

"Toscanini-Beethoven." *Time,* February 14, 1927. http://www.time.com/time/magazine/article/0,9171,730012,00.html, accessed August 17, 2010.

Tovey, Donald Francis. *Essays in Musical Analysis,* vol. 2. London: Oxford University Press, 1935.

"Transatlantic Jet Flight Celebrates Fifty Years." *London Telegraph,* October 6, 2008. http://www.telegraph.co.uk/travel/3146988/Transatlantic-jet-flight-celebrates-50-years.html, accessed February 15, 2010.

Tusa, Michael C. "Noch einmal: Form and Content in the Finale of Beethoven's Ninth Symphony." *Beethoven Forum* 7 (1999), 113–37.

Tuveson, Ernest Lee. *The Avatars of Thrice Great Hermes.* Lewisburg, Pa.: Bucknell University Press, 1982.

Tyson, Alan. "Stages in the Composition of Beethoven's Piano Trio Op. 70, No. 1." *Proceedings of the Royal Musical Association* 97 (1970–1971), 1–19.

Upton, George P., ed. *Theodore Thomas, A Music Autobiography,* vol. 1. Chicago: A.C. McClurg, 1905.

Upton, William Treat. *Anthony Philip Heinrich, a Nineteenth-Century Composer in America.* New York: Columbia University Press, 1939.

Van Deburg, William J. *New Day in Babylon: The Black Power Movement and American Culture, 1965–1975.* Chicago: University of Chicago Press, 1992.

Van den Toorn, Peter. "Politics, Feminism, and Contemporary Music Theory." *Journal of Musicology* 9, no. 3 (Summer 1991), 1–37.

Von Glahn, Denise. *The Sounds of Place: Music and the American Cultural Landscape.* Boston: Northeastern University Press, 2003.

Von Glahn, Denise, and Michael Broyles. "Musical Modernism before It Began: Leo Ornstein and a Case for Revisionist History." *Journal of the Society for American Music* 1, no. 1 (February 2007), 29–56.

Walser, Robert. "Eruptions: Heavy Metal Appropriations of Classical Music." *Popular Music* 11, no. 2 (October 1992), 263–308.

———. *Running with the Devil: Power, Gender and Madness in Heavy Metal Music.* Hanover, N.H.: University Press of New England, 1993.

Weales, Gerald. "What Were the Blacks Doing in the Balcony?" *New York Times,* May 4, 1969, SM38.

Weber, Elisa. *9 Beet Stretch.* Unpublished paper, Florida State University.

Webster, James. "The Form of the Finale of Beethoven's Ninth Symphony." *Beethoven Forum* 1 (1991), 25–62.

Weigand, Elizabeth. "'The Rugmaker's Daughter', Maud Allan's 1915 Silent Film." *Dance Chronicle* 9, no. 2 (1986), 241–42.

Whitesitt, Linda. *The Life and Music of George Antheil, 1900–1959.* Ann Arbor, Mich.: UMI Research Press, 1983.

Wiebe, Robert H. *The Opening of American Society.* New York: Alfred A. Knopf, 1984.

Wierzbicki, James. "Banality Triumphant: Iconographic Use of Beethoven's Ninth Symphony in Recent Films." *Beethoven Forum* 10, no. 3 (Fall 2003), 113–38.

Wilding-White, Ray. "Remembering Ruth Crawford Seeger: An Interview with Charles and Peggy Seeger." *American Music* 6, no. 4 (Winter 1988), 443.

Williams, Patricia J. *The Alchemy of Race and Rights.* Cambridge, Mass.: Harvard University Press, 1991.

Winter, Elise. Interview with Moises Kaufman, April 9, 2009. http://gothamist .com/2009/03/09/moises_kaufman_playwright_and_direc.php, accessed December 29, 2009.

Wood, Ralph. "The Meaning of Beethoven." *Music and Letters* 15, no. 3 (July 1934), 209–21.

Woodard, Komozi. *A Nation within a Nation: Amiri Baraka (LeRoi Jones) and Black Power Politics.* Chapel Hill: University of North Carolina Press, 1999.

Woodley, Edith. "Aunt Tabitha's Fireside. No. II. -Paul's Impromptu." *Godey's Lady's Book* 43, no. 2 (August 1851), 106.

Wright, Richard. *Black Power: A Record of Reactions in a Land of Pathos.* New York: Harper, 1954.

Yang, Mina. "Für Elise, circa 2000: Postmodern Readings of Beethoven in Popular Contexts." *Popular Music and Society* 29, no. 1 (February 2006), 2.

Zimmer, Mark. "Copying Beethoven" (review). http://www.digitallyobsessed .com/showreview.php3?ID=9329, accessed February 18, 2009.

INDEX

Page numbers in italics refer to illustrations.

MICHAEL BROYLES is Professor of Music at The Florida State University and was previously Distinguished Professor of Music and Professor of American History at The Pennsylvania State University. He has published one previous book on Beethoven, and his most recent book, *Leo Ornstein: Modernist Dilemmas, Personal Choices* (IUP, 2007), written with Denise Von Glahn, won the Irving Lowens Prize from the Society for American Music as the best book on American music in 2007.